Charles Gates Dawes

Charles Gates Dawes

A Life

Ⅹ

ANNETTE B. DUNLAP

NORTHWESTERN UNIVERSITY PRESS AND THE EVANSTON HISTORY CENTER

EVANSTON, ILLINOIS

Northwestern University Press
www.nupress.northwestern.edu

This book was made possible through a generous grant from the Tawani Foundation.

Printed in the United States of America

10 9 8 7 6 5 4 3 2 1

Library of Congress Cataloging-in-Publication Data

Names: Dunlap, Annette, 1955– author.
Title: Charles Gates Dawes : a life / Annette B. Dunlap.
Description: Evanston, Illinois : Northwestern University Press and the Evanston History Center, 2016. | Includes bibliographical references and index.
Identifiers: LCCN 2016017267 | ISBN 9780810134195 (pbk. : alk. paper) | ISBN 9780810134201 (e-book) | ISBN 9780810134218 (cloth : alk. paper)
Subjects: LCSH: Dawes, Charles Gates, 1865–1951. | Vice-Presidents—United States—Biography. | Statesmen—United States—Biography. | Bankers—Illinois—Chicago—Biography.
Classification: LCC E748.D22 D86 2016 | DDC 321.8/042092 [B] —dc23
LC record available at https://lccn.loc.gov/2016017267

CONTENTS

Gallery follows page 162.

Charles Gates Dawes

INTRODUCTION

☒

Applauded on Exit

Boston's Old North Church stands at 193 Salem Street, just a few blocks from Boston Harbor. The traditionally styled structure boasts a high and visible steeple, an architectural feature that was useful in 1775, when no exterior electric lights would have dimmed a beacon shining from that spire.

The church and Paul Revere were immortalized by Henry Wadsworth Longfellow in his poem "Paul Revere's Ride," with its famous line "One if by land, and two if by sea." The poem is a lyric recounting of Revere's midnight ride to warn the colonists of a pending British attack. Revere's name is engraved on a plaque commemorating that ride, but it omits the name of his companion, who had a longer ride than Revere and was more successful in getting out the word of the enemy's approach. The British caught Revere but not his compatriot.

Revere's coconspirator was William R. Dawes Jr., and on April 18, 1925, the sesquicentennial anniversary of that famous night, Dawes's great-great-grandson, U.S. Vice President Charles Gates Dawes, helped to commemorate the events.

In the eight years before he became vice president, Dawes oversaw procurement for the American Expeditionary Forces in World War I, served as the nation's first director of the Bureau of the Budget, and gave his name to the commission that restructured Germany's reparations payments. The vice presidency represented the sixty-year-old Dawes's sixth or seventh career, depending on who was counting. At the end

3

of his vice presidential term, Dawes went on to become ambassador to the United Kingdom and to participate in the 1930 disarmament talks. He returned to the United States in 1932 to head up the newly created Reconstruction Finance Corporation (RFC), a government agency that gave emergency loans to railroads, financial institutions, and businesses hit by the Great Depression.

When Dawes resigned from the RFC in June 1932, he had been on the national stage for over a decade, enjoyed widespread public support, and was occasionally urged by well-wishers to run for president. But if you were to ask someone today about Charles Gates Dawes, the response you would likely get would be: "Who?"

I certainly had never heard of Charles Dawes when the Evanston History Center contacted me about writing his biography. A short outline of the key milestones in his life was included in the initial information provided by the center's director, Eden Juron Pearlman. A cursory glance, read with a twenty-first-century mind-set, led me to believe that Charley was a long-forgotten favorite of several of our less-celebrated presidents. His life was framed by the various positions that he held under four presidents over the course of nearly five decades. Once I got into Dawes's voluminous archives, I quickly realized that I could not have been more wrong. The more I learned about him, the more I came to understand that he defied easy categorization.

To properly describe the nature and character of Charley Dawes, one must pull out a list of superlatives. He was simultaneously a brilliant intellect and a down-to-earth realist. He cultivated an aura of irascibility as a foil to his enemies, but in the midst of a war, he was described as having the heart of a woman in the body of a man. He appeared to have abandoned any formal practice of the Presbyterian faith in which he was reared, but he demonstrated generosity and charitableness toward others, particularly the less fortunate, that were exemplary models of faith in action. He moved between the realms of government, business, and the arts with enviable ease, in an era when such versatility raised no eyebrows and violated no conflict-of-interest laws. But if you asked Dawes how he viewed himself, he would reply that he was first and foremost a businessman.

As a young man, Charley quickly discovered that he had a sixth sense for the art of the deal and for homing in on the next lucrative business opportunity. Born a few months after the end of the American Civil War, Charley came of age as the United States experienced booming growth. That economic explosion passed by his hometown of Marietta, Ohio, and Charley's father encouraged his eldest son to make a life for himself elsewhere. In 1887, Dawes followed others from Marietta to the state of Nebraska, where the railroads were offering cheap land to encourage settlement. The railroads' offers did not draw Dawes; family did. A cousin, James W. Dawes, was then serving as the state's governor and encouraged young Dawes to come west. Charley moved to Lincoln, was admitted to the bar, and sought to build a law practice.

It wasn't long before Dawes recognized that he had more potential as a real estate investor than as an attorney. He was fortunate to have two mentors who provided his initial sources of capital. One was his law professor, Jacob D. Cox, who trusted his former law student to invest money on his behalf in Nebraska. The other was Charley's uncle by marriage, William W. Mills, president of the First National Bank of Marietta, an institution founded by Dawes's maternal grandfather, Beman Gates. Mills financed Charley's early business ventures and did his best to rein in his impulsive nephew's sometimes reckless pursuit of wealth.

Over the next decade, Dawes began to build his business empire through a series of corporate acquisitions and land purchases. When he outgrew Mills's capacity to finance his ventures, Dawes established a relationship with Chicago banks. He decided there was more of a future for him on the shores of Lake Michigan than on the prairies of Nebraska, and he moved to Chicago in 1895.

Dawes helped raise money and build an organization for William McKinley's 1896 presidential campaign, a role that put the neophyte on the national political map. Charley proved an able and competent financial manager. He also demonstrated the same cockiness in the political arena that had driven his business decisions. Dawes repeatedly pressed for a cabinet appointment. To appease his young protégé, McKinley named Dawes comptroller of the currency.

Dawes served as comptroller from 1898 until 1901, and in those few years he developed a permanent love-hate relationship with the politics of governing. He was impatient with bureaucracy and nursed a strong distaste for "go along to get along" compromise. Charley was a thorn in the flesh of his enemies, who became the target of his brashness. He was also a devoted loyalist, regularly turning a blind eye to the faults or peccadilloes of his friends.

Dawes's ego overrode his ambivalence toward politics, and he took on the powerful Yates-Lorimer machine of Illinois politics to run for the U.S. Senate in 1902. His prospects for success were questionable from the outset. The Republicans, the party of Lincoln, held a tight grip on Illinois's electoral politics, and the Republican Party machine, headed by Governor Richard Yates Jr. and Congressman William Lorimer, held a tight grip on the party. Charley's chances were slim, but he had a plan. If he lost the election, he intended to open a bank. And in 1902 that is exactly what he did.

From 1902 until America's entry into World War I in 1917, Charley Dawes built a strong financial institution in Chicago, the Central Trust Bank, and became the financier for the multiple business ventures that made up the portfolio of the family business, Dawes Brothers, Inc. Dawes Brothers served as a holding company for the nationwide network of utilities and oil companies that he and his brothers, Rufus, Henry, and Beman, either purchased or created during the first decade and a half of the twentieth century. Rufus headed up the municipal utilities, which included manufactured gas and, eventually, electric power. Henry and Beman led the oil businesses. As the corporation's profitability grew, Charley offered shares in Dawes Brothers to close and trusted friends who could be counted on not to challenge any of the investment or divestiture decisions made by the brothers. These investors included Illinois Senator Lawrence Y. Sherman, General John Pershing, General James Harbord, Illinois Senator Shelby Cullom, and, at one point, Albert, the king of Belgium.

Charley was fifty-one years old when the United States declared war on Germany in March 1917. He pulled strings with his business associates and appealed to Pershing to receive a commission in the army.

From the standpoint of war preparedness, Wilson's declaration of war on Germany was precipitous. The United States had few weapons, little ammunition, not enough vehicles, scant building materials, insufficient uniforms, and meager food with which to arm, transport, house, clothe, and feed a military engaged in war. Pershing appointed Dawes as head of procurement, and, before long, Dawes had organized and coordinated purchasing for all of the American Expeditionary Forces.

Dawes's impressive organizational skills, further enhanced by the Allied victory in the war, gained him national attention. Warren Harding wanted Dawes as his secretary of the treasury, a position Dawes turned down in exchange for becoming the nation's first director of the newly formed Bureau of the Budget. There, Dawes's waspish attitude toward bureaucracies stood him in good stead. He used the authority of his office to impose spending controls on a recalcitrant executive branch and to put into place standards of accountability that have provided the groundwork for all subsequent federal budgetary processes.

Dawes committed to serving as budget director for only one year. He returned to his home in the Chicago suburb of Evanston in June 1922 with the expectation that he would resume his position as chief executive officer (CEO) of his bank and as a leader in the greater Chicago business community. However, Dawes's expertise during the war, combined with his availability, made him the perfect candidate to lead a commission to renegotiate the war reparations agreement between Germany and the Allies. The commission, which became known as the Dawes Commission, was perceived as so successful that it earned him the Nobel Peace Prize, which he shared with Sir Austen Chamberlain.

Dawes returned to the United States from his reparations work just as the 1924 election season was heating up. He was the man of the hour, and there was strong interest in having him fill the number-two slot on the Republican presidential ticket as Calvin Coolidge's running mate. Coolidge was characteristically silent about his preference, and Dawes was nominated as a compromise candidate.

Accepting the vice presidency might not have been a good move for an outspoken activist like Charley Dawes. From the start of the campaign through the end of his term, Charley often clashed with Coolidge. The two men maintained a polite, if frosty, relationship, and neither would ever publicly acknowledge the tension between them. However, Charley still had many friends in the administration, especially the men who had served with him in the Bureau of the Budget. They included Andrew Mellon and Herbert Hoover, both of whom, like Dawes, were self-made millionaires who had made a commitment to public service.

When Hoover was elected president in November 1928, he named Dawes as ambassador to the United Kingdom. It was an important posting, because the deadlines set by the Dawes Commission for war reparations had come and gone, and new negotiations had begun as Germany struggled to make its payments to the Allies. The United States was also actively negotiating for further international disarmament. Charley's experience and his firsthand knowledge of the inner workings of the agreements made him a natural choice as ambassador.

The years as ambassador were frantic ones. Dawes virtually commuted between the United States and the United Kingdom to help his brother Rufus raise money for the upcoming Century of Progress International Exposition, a world's fair to be held in Chicago in 1933. When the U.S. stock market crashed at the end of October 1929, Charley monitored the nation's economic decline from London, exchanging lengthy, analytical letters with his brother Henry about their, and the nation's, financial future. President Hoover struggled with a recalcitrant Congress for passage of relief measures. When that body approved the creation of the Reconstruction Finance Corporation (RFC), a government agency that would bail out banks, Hoover tapped Dawes to head it.

Dawes's tenure as the head of the RFC was short-lived. He resigned in June 1932 to rescue his own bank, Central Trust, which faced the danger of going under. Dawes returned to Chicago to engineer its successful rescue. He never held public office again but maintained a strong position of leadership in the Chicago business community until his death in 1951 at the age of eighty-five.

Dawes's prominence in the Chicago business community and his numerous, valuable contributions to American government raise the question: why isn't Charles Gates Dawes better known? The answer needs to be broken down into two parts. The first is how he structured his business life, and the second is whom he served in his political life.

In terms of measurable riches, Charles Dawes was as wealthy as any of the powerful Chicago industrialists of his day, including railroad car magnate George Pullman; department store creator Marshall Field; International Harvester scion Charles Deering; philanthropist and Sears founder Julius Rosenwald; and meatpacker Gustavus Swift. (It is interesting to note that one website omits Dawes from its list of prominent

Chicago industrialists and financiers, even though he financed the operations of some who are listed.) Perhaps the key difference is that Dawes kept the accumulation of his assets closely held—none of his corporations, with the exception of common stock for the bank, were ever publicly traded. In the days before *Forbes* magazine could ascertain the value of the assets of prominent businesspeople, especially those with privately held wealth, Dawes's net worth stayed off the radar screen.

Dawes's wealth was shared. As each of his brothers came of age, he created the financing for the businesses each brother would lead. Except for some of the oil companies, Dawes Brothers, Inc. served as the umbrella, or holding, corporation for the brothers' various enterprises.

The four brothers, Charles, Rufus, Henry, and Beman, remained close and supportive of one another throughout their lives. Despite their fraternal jealousies and occasional animosities, the brothers never doubted one another's loyalty. They exchanged constructive criticism of their business judgment and engaged in good-natured brotherly teasing. For all of his bluster and angry outbursts, Charley was at heart a humble man who recognized the skills of his brothers, sought their input, and shared in the decision-making. American history likes to celebrate iconoclasts and ignore team players. When it came to business, Charles Dawes was a consummate team player.

Dawes also served under chief executives whom history treats as lesser lights in the pantheon of American presidents. William McKinley is far eclipsed in the national narrative by his successor, Theodore Roosevelt, even though McKinley laid the groundwork that made the United States a nation to be reckoned with internationally. Harding is tainted with fathering a child out of wedlock while in the White House, among other sexual escapades, not to mention the Teapot Dome scandal, in which Harding's secretary of the interior went to prison for taking bribes. Harding is rarely recognized for selecting some brilliant men for his cabinet, among them Andrew Mellon, Charles Evans Hughes, and Herbert Hoover. Neither is Harding recognized for shifting the power of the government in the direction of the executive branch.

As vice president, Dawes sometimes took a stand against his own president, Calvin Coolidge, and he also had the temerity to try to change the Senate's rules. But, as is the case with most vice presidents, Dawes made little difference in the governing of the United States, and his name even appears on some lists of the "worst vice presidents."

Herbert Hoover's presidential record is overshadowed by his handling of the Great Depression. Dawes's disarmament work as ambassador to the United Kingdom is long forgotten in the aftermath of World War II.

As the Depression deepened and Franklin D. Roosevelt's administration strengthened its power and influence, history turned away from the Republican men who had successfully brought the nation through an industrial revolution and economic growth. Roosevelt's accomplishments, and the resulting changes to American society, have dominated our national narrative for seventy years. FDR's unprecedented three completed presidential terms and his four elections to the presidency mark him as unique in the annals of American government. His "brain trust," the group of experts he assembled to advise him; his optimism; and the contributions of his wife, Eleanor, make it easy to focus on the world created by his leadership. Historian Doris Kearns Goodwin rightly describes the FDR era as "no ordinary time."

However, a more balanced historical accounting reveals that many policies and institutions that we take for granted as part of our twenty-first-century life were created by Republicans in the first three decades of the twentieth century, and Dawes had a hand in their formation. The mind-set that governed the treaty decisions made when Germany was defeated once again in World War II was framed by the work of the 1919 Treaty of Versailles, the Dawes Commission, and the 1930 Geneva Disarmament Conference. Dawes was one of the few bankers of his day to support the establishment of a federal reserve system, a central banking system that could influence the supply of money and credit. The Dawes brothers' utility investments brought electrification to small and medium-sized cities, and their oil exploration contributed to the development of an independent oil sector.

Charles Dawes used profanity liberally, and, at one point, he became known as "Hell and Maria" Dawes for employing that epithet in a congressional hearing. His profane speech and irrepressible behavior belied a man whose idea of an enjoyable evening was to sit quietly in his library reading philosophy or history, while he smoked his cigar or pipe and chatted occasionally with his beloved wife.

Dawes was fond of quoting the seventeenth-century Spanish philosopher Baltasar Gracián: "Devote more attention to a successful exit than to a highly applauded entrance." Charles Gates Dawes is long overdue for an accounting of his extraordinary life and his many successful exits from his varied careers: he deserves our applause.

CHAPTER 1

✕

Heir to a Legacy

Worshippers at Marietta, Ohio's First Presbyterian Church knew why Rufus Dawes had slipped into the sanctuary during the Sunday morning service on August 27, 1865. His wife, Mary, was in labor, and the baby wasn't going to wait until church dismissed. Mary Dawes never quite forgot her embarrassment at having to summon the doctor so publicly, but she cherished her firstborn son, who shared her birthday.

Charles Gates Dawes—Charley, as he would be known throughout his life—was the namesake of Mary's beloved brother, Charles Gates. Only two years apart in age, Mary and her brother (Mary was the older) were inseparable growing up in Marietta. Charles Gates died when he was caught between two train cars on his way to the front during the Civil War, and his tragic death left her grief-stricken. The new baby boy filled a void in Mary's heart. She wrote her father, Beman Gates: "I want to bring him [the baby] up to fill our poor lost Charley's place to you and Mother just as much as possible, to show the same thoughtfulness and loving attentions to you that <u>he</u> did."[1]

Mary Gates Dawes was the daughter of Beman Gates and Betsy Shipman Gates. By the time Mary was born, in 1842, her father was well on his way to becoming one of the most politically powerful and wealthiest men in Marietta. He descended from a line of Gateses who had emigrated from England and were one of the earliest families to arrive in New England, a well-respected clan that was "conspicuous for representatives of strong character and moral worth, which elements were transmitted to many of the descendants."[2]

Beman was the son of a Congregational minister and part of a large family. With few opportunities in the Connecticut town where he lived, he set out with a friend for Tennessee in 1838, at the age of twenty, in search of a teaching position. The two men ran out of money when they reached Marietta, Ohio.

Nestled in the foothills of the Allegheny Plateau at the confluence of the Muskingum and the Ohio Rivers, Marietta was founded by a group of Massachusetts residents on April 7, 1788. It was the first settlement in the Northwest Territory, a huge area covering Ohio, Indiana, Illinois, Michigan, Wisconsin, and part of Minnesota. When Beman Gates arrived fifty years later, Marietta was a growing, prosperous town with a strong interest in national politics and a deep commitment to education. It was the perfect place for an ambitious and energetic young man.

Gates quickly made friends and impressed people with his sincerity and earnestness. A year after his arrival, several young Marietta businessmen offered Beman the editor's position on their newly established weekly newspaper, the *Marietta Intelligencer*. Established to compete with the existing *Marietta Gazette*, the *Intelligencer*'s owners expected the paper to represent their energy and interests.

Gates quickly disabused his new employers of the idea that he could be controlled. In his first piece as editor, Gates wrote:

> The subscriber, in commencing his duties as editor, wishes it to be distinctly understood that he has no prejudices to foster, no partialities to indulge, and no invidious feelings to gratify. He will not suffer himself to be influenced by the opinions of others in any way incompatible with perfect freedom of thought and action. He speaks particularly on this point because he has been charged with being under the control of influential men in this town. He will be equally ready to bestow praise upon his political enemies when merited, or censure upon his friends when necessary.[3]

Gates eventually became the owner of the *Intelligencer*, and he made politics a central focus of its reporting throughout his tenure. He was committed to the Whig Party, founded by Henry Clay and established in response to Jacksonian democracy. The Whigs were alternately viewed as favoring the wealthy and big business, as championing humanitarian reform and states' rights, and as supporting labor and fuller suffrage.

The party's success in electing presidents William Henry Harrison and Zachary Taylor in the 1840s gave it life for a few decades, and, during the years of Whig ascendancy, the *Intelligencer* had a strong voice in the community. Gates also adopted new technologies that increased the scope of his reporting. He installed a telegraph machine in the paper's offices and announced that he would print Zachary Taylor's inaugural address on March 5, 1849, the day on which the new president delivered it. The telegraph gave Gates better access to news from his correspondents in Columbus, the state capital; in Washington, D.C.; and in New York City. He even extended his reach internationally, reporting on events in Spain, Portugal, Austria, and the United Kingdom.

As a civic leader, Gates advocated for improvements in infrastructure in southeastern Ohio. He became a partner in the building of the Marietta and Cincinnati Railroad, and, in 1855, he became the railway's vice president and superintendent. With the demise of the Whig Party and the rise of the Republican Party, in 1856, Gates lost interest in politics. He had a growing family, and his integrity and reputation had opened new business opportunities. Gates had married Betsy S. Shipman on October 20, 1841. Their daughter Mary was born in 1842; their son, Charles, who would be killed in the Civil War, was born in 1844; and their youngest, Betsy, came along in 1853.

Beman Gates became a successful investor in the newly developing oil and gas industries. He is said to have organized the largest sale of oil to Europe during the 1850s, after the lubricant and its uses were first discovered in southeastern Ohio. He was an incorporator of the Marietta Gas Company in 1867. In 1863, he established the First National Bank of Marietta, and he continued as its president until 1887, when his son-in-law William W. (W. W.) Mills assumed the presidency. Gates also served as a trustee of Marietta College for a number of years. Beman Gates was characterized as a man of prudence, economy, and practical good sense.[4] Charley inherited these traits, along with Gates's insatiable love of books, his boundless energy, his unabashed outspokenness, and his formidable business acumen.

From the Dawes side, Charley was heir to a long and proud history that was intertwined with the founding of the nation and the establishment of the Northwest Territory. It was Charley's great-great-grandfather William R. Dawes Jr. who joined Paul Revere to alert Bostonians of the imminent arrival of the British army. Samuel Adams's cousin John Adams told him that they had seen "four noble families rise up in Boston—the Craftses, the Gores, the Daweses and Austins." The Daweses were known as "honest, industrious God-fearing men, from the first to the last; men who owned land, and went to the polls as they went to church. They never hesitated to draw their swords in the cause of right."[5]

Another of Charley's paternal great-great-grandfathers, Manasseh Cutler, helped to organize the Ohio Company, which settled the region that makes up present-day Ohio. Cutler was directly responsible for the insertion of the clause prohibiting slavery in the Northwest Ordinance, which established a government for the Northwest Territory, and he established Ohio University in Athens. His son Ephraim was one of the original founders of Marietta. Ephraim provided a room in his home for one of the first schools in the town and helped to establish Marietta College. Education was important to the Daweses and Cutlers, as were religion, politics, and success in business.

Charley's father, Rufus Robinson Dawes, was a graduate of Marietta College who fought in the Civil War and was brevetted as a brigadier general following completion of four years of service. Mary Gates Dawes attended the Female Seminary at Ipswich, Massachusetts, the closest thing to a girls' college available in the early 1860s. The couple imparted a love of learning and an appreciation for the written word to all their children. Mary kept a small daily journal, and she passed that habit to her eldest son. Charley was an avid and sophisticated reader who studied philosophers and historians for pleasure, as well as a gifted and prolific writer.

Charley eventually became the eldest of six children, all of whom lived to adulthood. The second child, Rufus Cutler Dawes, was born in 1867, followed by another boy, Beman Gates, in 1870. A girl, Mary

Frances, was born in 1872, and a fourth boy, Henry May, in 1877. The youngest, Betsey Gates, came along in 1880.

The family home, at 508 Fourth Street in Marietta, was filled with love, praise, and encouragement. Charley inherited his mother's sunny disposition and enthusiastic energy. Rufus instilled a sense of service and the courage to stand up for one's principles in the face of critics. "When I see the pitfalls, snares and failures into which young men become entangled because of lack of courage to act according to their own conscientious convictions, I think of you with great hope," Rufus wrote his son in 1881, when Charley was sixteen years old. He continued:

> I have seen you withstand temptation and insist prevailing some
> times to which you felt you ought to—Do you know that the
> power to withstand the drift of general opinion when it is wrong is
> what marks a man more than anything else? But this must not be
> mistaken for a habit that some have of criticism and objection . . .
> Don't habituate yourself to taking the opposite side. Always agree
> with the prevailing sentiment unless it is wrong, then be <u>right</u> and
> be quietly patient.[6]

Music was vital to the Dawes family. The family held regular songfests, as their grandfather Beman Gates had done. Charley loved and enjoyed music, but he never learned to read it. He often composed tunes in his head and would come flying in the door of his home and rush to the piano to pick out the music by ear before he lost the tune running through his head. Music offered Charley a creative outlet for his highly analytical mind.

Rufus Dawes was elected as a Republican to the U.S. Congress in 1880, where he joined another newly elected Ohio congressman, William McKinley. Charley accompanied his father to attend the inauguration of President James A. Garfield and to see his father sworn in. It was Charley's introduction to Washington politics.

From his seat in the members' gallery, Charley identified some of the most powerful members of the Republican-dominated Congress: Senator Joseph Hawley of Connecticut, a former Union general and wartime colleague of Rufus Dawes; future House Speaker Thomas Brackett Reed of Maine; and a distant relative, Senator Henry L. Dawes of Massachusetts. "The House looks very disorderly," Charley wrote of his first impressions of Congress. "All the desks are covered with paper. The members are all either clapping for pages or talking with each other. . . . [Hiester] Clymer of Penn[sylvania] is in the Speaker's Chair. He pounds with his gavel all the time to keep order, but he does not succeed very well."[7] Charley's observations hint at an early distaste for the trivialities and inefficiencies of the legislative process—a process he would try to amend, without success, when he became vice president of the United States.

Charley Dawes graduated from Marietta Academy in June 1880 at the age of fifteen and enrolled at Marietta College, class of 1884. His sense of humor and ability to poke fun at himself were evident in his answers to the questions for the class statistics page:

Eyes: Two
Hair: Straight
Temperament: Nervous
Nose: Large
Profession: Undecided
Politics: Republican
Choice for Next President: Dawes of Ohio
Matrimonial Intentions: A little
Matrimonial Prospects: None

He listed soda water as his favorite dish, the romanticist Sir Walter Scott as his favorite author, and Edgar Allan Poe as his favorite poet.[8]

Marietta College was a classic liberal arts school that drew young men from the nation's midwestern elite. They were the sons and grandsons of the founders and the first-generation risk takers who had developed the industries and infrastructure that formed the economy of the states stretching from the Allegheny Mountains to the Rockies. Although Dawes was a hometown boy, his college classmates exposed him to a wider world.

Upon graduation, Charley enrolled at Cincinnati Law School (now the University of Cincinnati College of Law). He was one of the two youngest students in his class. The school's dean was Jacob D. (J. D.) Cox, a Civil War veteran, former governor of Ohio, and secretary of the interior in the early years of the Ulysses S. Grant administration. Cox was noted for his efforts at civil service reform in the Interior Department, at a time when the Grant administration was under attack for excessive use of the spoils system, accused of giving too many civil service appointments to its friends and supporters.

From 1873 until 1878, Cox was president of the Toledo and Wabash Railroad, and he would have been acquainted with Beman Gates and Rufus Dawes. Those connections boded well for Charley. Cox took a liking to young Dawes, and the dean became one of Dawes's early business investors as well as a mentor after Dawes graduated from law school.

The law appealed to Dawes's logical mind and was a good fit for his prodigious verbal skills. He was a strong student, graduating in the top ten of his class in a year when tenths of decimal points separated the highest-ranked students. Charley was active in the Blackstone Club and the Mansfield Society, two organizations that encouraged debate and public speaking—neither of which Dawes ever shied away from throughout his career.[9]

Dawes formed close friendships with several of his law school classmates that lasted throughout his lifetime. Two in particular were Clayton Delamatre, a native Nebraskan who returned home to practice law and encouraged Charley's move to that state; and Atlee Pomerene, who served Ohio as a U.S. senator and succeeded Dawes as chair of the Reconstruction Finance Corporation, at Dawes's recommendation, after Dawes resigned to return to Chicago.

Dawes graduated from law school two months shy of his twenty-first birthday, and, by law, he could not be sworn in as an attorney until he reached his majority on August 27, 1886. Not one to be idle, Charley spent the intervening months working at his father's lumberyard. For a young man on the cusp of beginning his career, and particularly for someone with Dawes's intellect and energy, the wait seemed interminable. Even after Dawes became eligible to practice law, he was restless. His family's influence and power could open doors, but opportunities in Marietta were limited by the region's lackluster economic development.

A few adventurous nineteenth-century Marietta residents set their eye on Lincoln, Nebraska. For Dawes, an interest in Lincoln was bolstered by support from his father's cousin James W. Dawes, who had been elected Nebraska's governor in 1883 and was still in office in 1886. The governor promoted Lincoln to his cousin as a city of great prospects for a young man just starting out. Letters from Clayton Delamatre also helped generate interest in Nebraska as a land of opportunity for an ambitious and hard-working individual. Rufus, who agreed that there were limited opportunities for his son at home, encouraged Charley to go.

Cox provided a letter of introduction for Dawes to U.S. Senator Charles F. Manderson. "Permit me to introduce my young friend C.G. Dawes, Esq.," Cox wrote the senator, "who expects to make his home in Nebraska. He is a son of Gen. Rufus Dawes of Marietta, late M[ember of] C[ongress] from that district, and of the oldest of our New England-Ohio stock. He is also a graduate of our Law School, a student of brilliancy and fine promise, and a gentleman of excellent principles and character."[10]

Repeating what his Grandfather Gates had done fifty years earlier, Charley sought opportunities in a new place. He gathered up his belongings and boarded a train for Lincoln. He left Marietta with a few dollars in his pocket, his letters of introduction, and the optimism of youth.

CHAPTER 2

X

The Entrepreneur

When Charley arrived in Lincoln on the chilly evening of April 25, 1887, he found a neatly gridded city on the flat and dusty plains of southeastern Nebraska. Multistory office buildings dominated the center of Lincoln, and residential developments radiated out from downtown and bordered the cultivated fields that early settlers had painstakingly cleared from the native grasslands. Networks of railroad tracks and roads for horse-drawn conveyances wound through and around the city. The terrain was a marked contrast to the trees, rolling hills, and rivers of Dawes's native Marietta.

Lincoln had been founded in 1856 as the village of Lancaster. Omaha was the original capital of the Nebraska Territory, but when Nebraska gained statehood in 1867, the capital was moved and Lancaster's name changed to honor Abraham Lincoln, the recently slain president. Lincoln's civic and government leaders banded together to encourage manufacturing firms to locate there. Lincoln's lack of natural resources and its small population could not compete with larger cities for potential employees, but its location between Omaha and Kansas City made it an ideal railroad hub. Ten railroads crisscrossed through the city. The Burlington and Missouri River Railroad (B&MR) was the town's largest employer.

For most of Lincoln's short history, the town leaders had been unified in their efforts to boost the city economically. But by the time Charley arrived, factions had arisen, each with an opposing idea of what

Lincoln needed to grow. The growing Populist influence abhorred the saloons, gambling halls, and brothels that dominated Lincoln's Tenderloin district. Traditional boosters had a live-and-let-live philosophy; business was business. Within a few short months of his arrival, Charley would be forced to choose sides.

Charley's connection to former Governor Dawes and his letters of introduction from J. D. Cox rapidly opened doors. The leading men of the city befriended him, including John Fitzgerald, who was president of the First National Bank and a real estate developer. Fitzgerald connected Charley with key leaders on the Lincoln Board of Trade and introduced the new arrival to the Irish National League, an influential social and political group founded by Fitzgerald.

Charley was admitted to the Nebraska bar in June 1887. Three weeks later, he became the attorney for the Lincoln Board of Trade. Dawes wrote to Clayton Delamatre: "I have got a pretty good thing here for a beginner. . . . All the replevin suits that are managed by them will be entrusted to me. The letter that I wrote on the state by-law was what gave me the chance, and I am glad now that I had the gall to write it. I am in constant communication with the best business men of the city."[1]

The Board of Trade filed a suit against the Atchison and Nebraska Railroad (A&N) for unlawfully consolidating with the B&MR. The legal action was one of several that Lincoln's reform-minded business leaders had launched against the railroads. In their minds, the railroads' dominance over Lincoln's economy contributed to the city's failure to thrive as a manufacturing hub. They blamed the railroads' high rates for Lincoln's economic troubles.

The existing rate structure grew out of a settlement among the railroads in response to their rate wars of the 1870s, when fierce competition forced railroads to cut their rates so much they operated at a loss. The rates did not differentiate between intrastate and interstate transport. Consequently, shippers typically paid higher charges for freight shipped within the state of Nebraska than they paid for goods sent across the country.

Charley's decision to accept the Board of Trade case aligned him squarely with a group of reform boosters who wanted to break the railroads' hold on the city and clean up the Tenderloin district. It was the only time in his career when he was squarely aligned with the Populists, but ideology did not drive him. As he had noted to Delamatre, working for the Board of Trade offered him the connections he needed to get ahead. As the board's legal representative, he was squarely against general public opinion. Too many people in Lincoln depended on the B&MR for employment.

Dawes worked on his brief for several months and filed it with Nebraska Attorney General William Leese in mid-November. Charley's argument reflected his mastery of the nuances of the law and his skill at developing a well-reasoned case using narrow parameters. The brief charged that, as a result of the consolidation between the A&N and the B&MR, the railroad now had exclusive control over rates, which discriminated against the communities that it served and violated the state's Constitution. "This road, by entering into a combination to stifle competition, against the express words of the [state] constitution, has broken faith with the state to such an extent as to render it liable to a forfeiture of its corporate franchise," Charley argued.[2]

Leese responded cautiously to Dawes's brief. "Your letter makes a strong prima facie case against the companies," the attorney general wrote to Dawes. "And while I do not wish that any act of mine would do an injury to any person or corporation, I recognize the fact that the law is no respecter of persons." Leese promised to study the matter and provide Dawes with a more detailed response.[3]

After five weeks of review, Leese found in favor of Dawes's argument and filed a petition with the Nebraska Supreme Court at the end of December 1887. Leese asked the court to declare the B&MR's franchise forfeited and to appoint three trustees to seize the railroad, sell it, and give the proceeds to the school fund after deducting the total of the railroad's liabilities.[4] Leese signed the petition with both his and Dawes's names.

Leese built his case against the railroads on the arguments that Dawes had established in the brief: the Nebraska Constitution prohibited the consolidation of competing rail lines in the state. Turner M. Marquette, the attorney for the B&MR, argued that the railroads had a lease, not a consolidation. Marquette maintained that such a lawsuit was an exercise in "kingly power" that should be used only when there is no other remedy.[5]

Nebraska Supreme Court Justice Samuel Maxwell handed down his opinion on April 27, 1888, in favor of the plaintiffs. The decision, noted the *Omaha Daily Bee*, "is the most important in the history of the struggle against corporations in the annals of the state."[6] Charley joined the reformers in celebration and basked in approbation from his father and J. D. Cox. "Congratulations from all the friends. To you belongs the honor of a great victory," Rufus wired his son.[7] "Dear Friend Dawes," Cox wrote to Charley, "I have been very busy or I should have made haste to congratulate you on your very distinguished victory. . . . Your friends hereabouts are elated at your success."[8]

The victory was indeed a heady one, but Charley soon discovered that one win in the State Supreme Court did not translate into a lucrative law practice. He needed a steady stream of routine business, such as real estate transactions, wills, and business contracts, to make a living. The work only trickled in, and he struggled to make ends meet.

Dawes's early months in Lincoln were uncanny parallels of his Grandfather Gates's experiences in Marietta. Charley instilled confidence in people and quickly gained their trust. "There is more business and hustle in Dawes, and more results from him than any attorneys we have ever had any experience with in your town," Francis Beidler, a Chicago client of Charley's, wrote a Lincoln business associate.[9] Key businessmen introduced him into the right circles and welcomed him wholeheartedly into Lincoln society. He was admitted into the Mt. Pleasant Garden Club, described as the oldest social club in the state, whose members were Lincoln's respected social leaders. He frequented the opera and the theater, and donated to support their operations.

Through the Irish National League, he met William Jennings Bryan, an attorney from Illinois, who had arrived in Lincoln shortly after Charley began his work for the Board of Trade. Bryan initiated a group called the Round Table, a club where members read and held lively discussions on politics, philosophy, religion, literature, and science. Originally completely Democratic in membership, Bryan opened the doors to Republicans under the influence of his friend and law school classmate Adolph Talbot, a Republican, who introduced Charley to the group.[10]

Dawes and Bryan had their Presbyterian faith in common, and in the late 1880s their law offices and their homes were near one another. The two men enjoyed the intellectual repartee of the Round Table, but the difference in their party affiliations was only the tip of the iceberg when it came to their outlooks on life. Bryan's populism made him an outspoken champion for the free silver movement, which called for unlimited coinage of silver to increase the money supply. Bryan was also a strong proponent of Prohibition and an advocate for women's suffrage. As editor of his weekly magazine, *The Commoner*, which he founded in 1899, Bryan followed Dawes's career in the first decade of the twentieth century and regularly criticized his views and speeches.

Unlike Bryan, Charley was not a social crusader. But, as Rufus Dawes had remarked to his son years earlier, Charley was unafraid to take on the status quo if he believed he was right. He had inherited his grandfather's and father's distaste for the control political machines had over party politics. His native impatience made him a natural enemy of inefficiency in government, and his analytical mind sought solutions to seemingly intractable problems. When the nation suffered through the Panic of 1893, he wrote a treatise on banking reform and advocated for the gold standard. The purpose of the standard was to set a value for currency and silver against the internationally recognized value of gold. Supporters of a gold standard believed that its establishment would ease credit and give banks confidence to lend money. Charley saw decisions made under the Sherman Antitrust Act that stymied the growth of businesses and jobs, and he argued for its repeal. However, Charley did not take up some of the pressing social issues of the day. He remained silent on women's suffrage, and while he did not drink alcohol, he never spoke out in favor of the Volstead Act that banned the manufacture, sale, and distribution of alcoholic beverages.

Dawes and Bryan had political orbits that crossed throughout their lives. Bryan was William McKinley's opponent for the presidency in both the 1896 and the 1900 elections. Charley established his political bona fides as a lieutenant for the McKinley organization and then as the president's comptroller of the currency. In 1924, Bryan's brother, Charles, was the Democrats' vice presidential candidate; Charles Dawes was the candidate for the Republicans. Charles Dawes and William Jennings Bryan maintained a respectful and mutually appreciative friendship, but they were never especially close.

On the other hand, Charley developed a close relationship with another Lincoln newcomer who arrived in 1891. The relationship would eventually have profound consequences for the nation and for both men.

The United States Army detailed Second Lieutenant John J. Pershing to the University of Nebraska in August 1891 to teach military science. Lincoln society quickly embraced the bachelor soldier, and he met Charley through mutual acquaintances. The two often ate together at Don Cameron's diner, a local eatery with a fifteen-cent lunch counter.

Pershing was five years older than Dawes. He was born in the north-central Missouri town of Laclede, where his father ran a general store and served as the town's postmaster. Pershing's father had also borrowed heavily to purchase farmland in the surrounding area. The Panic of 1873 ruined the family's finances, and the elder Pershing became a traveling salesman to earn money for his family. Thirteen-year-old John was left in charge of the family and the farm.

John eventually became a teacher in the neighboring county and enrolled in the normal school in Kirksville (now Truman State University) to earn his teaching certificate. Following his graduation, Pershing returned to Chariton County to continue teaching, with the hope of returning to college to study law.

An advertisement for the entrance examination to West Point caught Pershing's attention. Lured by the offer of a free education, Pershing decided to take the test. Only one person from his congressional district would be granted entrance to the Military Academy. Pershing had the highest test score, and he entered West Point in 1882.

Prior to arriving in Lincoln, Pershing had served in the cavalry in Arizona, New Mexico, and the Dakota Territory. He had learned some of the culture and language of the Native American populations in the West, which gained him respect among the tribes. He developed a habit of studying his adversaries—a skill that would help him in later years.

Pershing had never lost his desire to study law, and he enrolled in the University of Nebraska School of Law in 1893, with the intention of eventually leaving the military and setting up a law practice. By then, Dawes had seen the handwriting on the wall. He discouraged Pershing from abandoning his military career. "Better lawyers than either you or I could ever hope to be are starving in Nebraska," Dawes counseled his friend. "I'd try the Army for awhile yet. Your pay may be small, but it comes very regularly."[11] Pershing did complete law school, but he stayed in the army.

A tongue-in-cheek article in the *Nebraska State Journal* included Charley in its list of 1888 "leap year catches," referring to an old tradition that it was acceptable for women to propose marriage on February 29 in a leap year. He was described as an "attorney-at-law and anti-monopoly agitator, age twenty-four [he was actually only twenty-two], weight 135, height medium, dark hair and the neatest moustache in Lincoln; is rapidly rising in his profession; seems to have a disposition to go back to see somebody in Ohio occasionally but is worth trying anyway. Call at board of trade office at regular hours."[12]

Charley's mustache was impressive. It was black and full, neatly parted in the middle, and it spanned the entire length of his upper lip. The mustache intensified his dark eyes that, even in a black-and-white photograph, conveyed a glint of humor and suggested a keenly observant young man. His straight hair was parted just to one side of the center of his forehead. Dawes's most prominent feature was his nose. Long, straight, and fleshy, it dominated his face. His nose, combined with his slightly cleft chin and large ears, gave Dawes a distinctive appearance, but he was not a head turner.

The "somebody" whom Dawes was seeing in Ohio was Caro Dana Blymyer, the youngest child of William Henry (W. H.) Blymyer and Caroline Lucy Fearing. Caro had a pedigree of her own. She was a descendant of Miles Standish, a passenger on the *Mayflower* and a key leader in the Plymouth Colony, and of Paul Fearing, the first delegate from the Northwest Territory to the Continental Congress and a colleague of Manasseh Cutler's. Caro was also descended from the Revolutionary War leader Israel Putnam, who distinguished himself at the Battle of Bunker Hill, and Michael Hillegas, the first treasurer of the United States.[13]

W. H. Blymyer owned Blymyer Iron Works, a successful foundry in Cincinnati. Following the end of the Civil War, Blymyer had sold his business in Mansfield, Ohio, and relocated to Cincinnati to take advantage of renewed trade between the North and the South. Cincinnati offered an excellent commercial gateway to the Mississippi River via the Ohio River. Blymyer's foundry made steam engines for agricultural use and cast-iron bells that were used in churches, fire stations, schools, and factories.

Caro stood just above five feet tall, wore size-two shoes, and weighed less than one hundred pounds at her wedding. She was dark-haired and had large, expressive dark eyes. Her nose, in contrast to Charlie's, was upturned. She had high cheekbones and a round chin, and early photographs convey an air of serenity. Caro had been a debutante, but she was also an independent-minded young woman. She scandalized her peers by riding astride her horse in the countryside at a time when it was considered more ladylike for a woman to ride sidesaddle.[14]

Charley and Caro likely met through some of Caro's family's ties in Marietta. The courtship flourished while Charley was in law school in Cincinnati, and it was strong enough to survive his year in Lincoln before the two married on January 24, 1889.

The couple settled into a modest home in Lincoln, all that Charley could afford on the meager earnings from his law practice. On the occasion of the couple's fortieth wedding anniversary, he recalled: "The phrase in the wedding service: 'With all my worldly goods I thee endow' was a hollow mockery in my case, for after the ceremony at Cincinnati the railroad fare to Lincoln consumed the bulk of my 'worldly goods.'"[15]

Caro quickly fit in with Charley's active social life in Lincoln. They attended plays, concerts, and social events, and went camping with other couples in the summer. Their first child, a son named Rufus Fearing, was born on December 14, 1890. A daughter, Carolyn, was born on July 12, 1892.

Charley was devoted and loyal to Caro throughout their lives. As Charley's income increased over time, the couple adopted the lifestyle typical of well-to-do families of the era. They employed caregivers—such as nannies or governesses—to look after their children, and Caro regularly accompanied Charley on his many business and political trips. As the years went by, their marriage reflected the values of upper-middle-class families. Charley built his network of business and political contacts. Caro managed their home. When Charley's earnings from his investments became stable, he assigned the income from his first company, Dawes Business Block Company, to Caro so that she would have her own funds. She used them to care for sick and orphaned children—charitable work in which she demonstrated her own impressive set of administrative skills.

Charley Dawes's ever-active mind was not content simply to build a reputable law practice. He was determined to become rich. Real estate offered an excellent business opportunity in a young, midwestern city such as Lincoln. Charley formed the Dawes Business Block Company (DBB Co.) in late 1887, with the initial plan to manage commercial properties. J. D. Cox was one of Charley's early investors, as were his brother Rufus, his uncle W. W. Mills, and his cousin William R. Dawes, who was the property manager.

The first few years of DBB Co. proved profitable, and on January 1, 1891, Charley and William incorporated the firm. W. W. Mills, J. D. Cox, and Rufus Dawes were the other officers. The nature of the business, according to their incorporation papers, was the "buying, selling, renting, owning, and managing of real estate, the investing of funds upon commission, and issuing mortgages or mortgage bonds."[16]

From 1891 through mid-1893, Charley went on a buying spree. Mills functioned as his nephew's financier, and he cautioned Charley on his recklessness. "There is no necessity of your hurrying to get rich," Mills counseled. He added, "You think this property a great bargain. It may be, but the fact that is has been on the market for years, with no takers, would indicate that [other] capitalists did not share your virus."[17] In spite of his scolding, Mills provided the money.

Charley had been working on a deal throughout 1892 to put together an investment team to purchase the Lincoln Packing Company, a slaughterhouse and pork-processing enterprise that had ceased operation. The team consisted primarily of the officers of the American Exchange National Bank, of which Charley was now a director. They were Isaac M. (I. M.) Raymond, bank president; S. H. Burnham, vice president; and Daniel Wing, cashier (a position equivalent to treasurer). Rufus Dawes and W. W. Mills had also agreed to invest. The business had two packinghouses, sheds, yards, pens, waterworks, and about four hundred acres of land near West Lincoln. The idle equipment was still in good shape. Lincoln's business community was abuzz with excitement as rumors began to circulate that Lincoln Packing would get back into operation.[18]

As he seemed to do with increasing frequency, Mills once again urged his nephew to be circumspect. "As far as the Stock Yards matter is concerned you of course realize the importance of going slow as far as your own and my interests are concerned. It is not a good plan to push too far out from shore. There is too much uncertainty in the future," Mills warned, little realizing how soon his warnings would become reality.[19]

A few weeks later, Mills again urged prudence, citing his concerns about the future of the financial markets. Money had already begun to tighten in the eastern financial centers, and Mills's sources advised him to expect even worse. He was also watching the hog market and advised Charley that he thought Raymond's cash projections a little too optimistic. Based on Mills's own calculations, he expected the profit margins at the proposed packinghouse to be narrow. Nevertheless, Mills was still willing to underwrite the stock issue on the packinghouse deal.[20]

At the start of 1893, Charley was hard-charging as ever. "Dear Millionaire of Lincoln, Respected Superior," Rufus wrote his brother in April 1893. "Your humble servant has received the pamphlet in praise of Lincoln and has noticed where you seem to stand in financial circles. He takes the opportunity to renew his expressions of submission which were begun under circumstances which you will recall."[21]

Mills, too, remained optimistic, even though he had repeatedly advised Charley that the nation's financial markets were tightening. "You need not be afraid, my dear boy, of my failure to take care of you so far as I have ability," his uncle assured him. "I can help you out in this emergency and it will not take my 'hair off' either. I have perfect confidence in you or I would never have done what I already have. I know as well as I know anything that my confidence will never be betrayed and so you need have no scruples on that score."[22]

By May 1893, the nation had plunged into the worst depression since the founding of the Republic. When Grover Cleveland entered his second, nonconsecutive presidential term in March, he found the U.S. Treasury depleted by nearly $10 million worth of gold. In August, he called Congress into special session to repeal the Sherman Silver Purchase Act, passed in 1890, which required the Treasury to purchase a set amount of silver at the market price. Preferred payment for the silver purchases was in gold, as opposed to greenbacks. In the wake of the national gold deficit, business ground to a standstill. Farm commodity prices tumbled, and bank failures (long before the days of deposit insurance) became rampant, especially in farming communities and small towns.

Lincoln was hard-hit. "Want and misery exist on all sides," Charley observed. In one of his first admissions of the overwhelming generosity with which he would later be noted, he acknowledged that he was trying to help a few families who lived near the packing plant.[23]

By summer, Charley had begun to feel the effects of the downturn. He did his best to stall creditors or to negotiate smaller payments. He sought new creditors from whom he could borrow to pay off existing creditors. Mills could no longer help him. He sent Charley a terse telegram in October: "Recent heavy shrinkage makes absolutely necessary postponement payment your check two weeks."[24]

All of Mills's predictions had come true: Charley had gotten in over his head. It is a mark of both his ability to elicit trust from others and his innate integrity that he survived the panic without massive losses. In 1919, when he was upset with a business decision made by his brother Beman, Charley wrote: "Before the panic of 1893 I used to sign a large flourish after the last letter of my name as you do. After the panic of 1893 I noticed to my surprise that the flourish on the tail of my signature had vanished."[25] Dawes did not learn the lesson well enough in 1893. Within two years, he would make the same mistake and over-extend himself again.

Charley not only managed his own struggling accounts through the Panic of 1893 but also worried about his parents' financial situation. His father's Marietta railroad lumber and cross-tie business had come to a standstill. Rufus had gone to Chicago and was promised orders by the Pullman Company for passenger cars when the economy rebounded, but, as he wrote Charley, there was no demand for freight cars, and the "tie trade is dead and buried."[26]

Of greater concern to both brothers was their father's health. Rufus Sr. had never fully recovered from a stroke he suffered in 1889, and he remained partially paralyzed. He got around in a wheelchair, but his mobility was so limited that the Marietta College Board of Trustees met in the Dawes home so that the general could continue to serve.

"Father is feeling pretty well now," Rufus confided in a letter to Charley, "and yet I am discouraged that he does not get his strength faster."[27] Carrying the weight of his responsibilities to his parents and a new wife,

Rufus resigned his position as vice president of DBB Co. in December 1893. He suggested that Beman, whom Charley had helped to set up in business in Lincoln in 1892, replace him. "He can be of greater service to the business than I have been," Rufus wrote Charley.[28]

On the home front, Charley and Caro's son, Rufus Fearing, had suffered from a series of unnamed illnesses through the year. The family doctor recommended that they take their son to a warmer climate for the winter, so Charley, Caro, and Rufus spent the winter of 1893–1894 in Galveston, Texas, while Mary Dawes came to Lincoln to care for baby Carolyn.

Galveston gave Charley time to reflect. Lincoln had changed since 1887. Although he had a strong network of social and business connections, Dawes had not established himself as one of the city's leading attorneys. Income from his law practice was sporadic. By contrast, the challenges of business excited Charley's fertile imagination and energetic mind much more than the mundane work of estate administration and will preparations.

A sensational trial known as the great Sheedy murder trial had adversely affected his law practice. Mary Sheedy and her African American lover, Monday McFarland, were accused of murdering Mary's husband, John Sheedy. Sheedy had been a saloon and hotel owner and part of Lincoln's traditional business booster group. His businesses operated in Lincoln's rough Tenderloin district, the section of the city that reformers had tried to shut down for over a decade. Charley had a minor role in the trial as a consultant to one of the defense attorneys, for whom he researched and appraised the value of Sheedy's real estate holdings. Mary Sheedy and Monday McFarland were acquitted, to the shock of much of Lincoln.

Within the city's business community, divided sentiments deepened into a permanent schism between the two booster groups. Businesses did little to attract new investment. The economic downturn that began in 1892 and continued through 1893 further weakened opportunities for Charley to build a successful law practice. "I struck Lincoln right at the top of the boom, and then it started sliding," Charley observed.[29] It was time to move on.

CHAPTER 3

X

A Budding Politician

Over the next several years, Charles Dawes laid the foundation for the remainder of his long and productive life. He abandoned his plans to practice law and instead searched for what he called a "natural monopoly" from which to develop a business empire.[1] The monopoly he chose was manufactured gas, a by-product of coal and petroleum, which was used to provide gaslight to homes and street lamps and lighting and fuel to industries. He found companies for sale in three cities: Akron, Ohio; La Crosse, Wisconsin; and Chicago.

The choice of companies was not random. Charley's paternal grandfather and uncle had business interests not far from La Crosse. Akron was one hundred thirty miles from Marietta, and Charley and Caro had already made the decision to move from Lincoln to Chicago. After returning home from Galveston in the spring of 1894, the couple left their children in Lincoln and took to the road so that Charley could meet with the companies' owners and work out the terms of each deal.

Manufactured gas plants were the first utilities to operate from a centralized location and provide lighting to homes and businesses through a network of pipelines. In 1890 there were an estimated seven hundred plants in operation in the United States. By 1900 that number had increased to nine hundred, and there were over one thousand plants by 1905.[2]

Because of the high cost of infrastructure, municipalities granted exclusive territories to individual gaslight companies. Rates were set to guarantee the company sufficient revenue to be profitable and stay in business. For a businessperson who understood how to operate a plant, control costs, and provide customer service, a manufactured gas plant offered a potentially lucrative opportunity. At the time Charley was finalizing his deals, however, the industry stood on the edge of a major transformation as electric power began to replace gas as a lighting source.

Local communities gave no indication that they saw change on the horizon. In October 1895, the Village Board of Wilmette, Illinois, representing the community just to the north of Evanston, granted Northwestern Gas Light Company (the Chicago company Charley was considering) a ninety-nine-year franchise to service the Wilmette community, including a contract to provide street lighting. "I am accused by my friends of being a little optimistic in my predictions of the future of the N.W. Gas Co.," Dawes noted in his journal after securing the Wilmette agreement. "If we hold the territory (and we will) in less than ten years this property will be one of the finest gas properties in the country."[3]

From 1894 through 1900, Charlie expanded his holdings on Chicago's North Shore, acquiring the companies that serviced the communities of Kenilworth and Gross Point (now part of Wilmette). In 1900, he consolidated the North Shore gas franchises into the North Shore Gas Company, based in Waukegan, Illinois.[4]

At the same time that Dawes was looking to purchase Northwestern Gas Light, another energetic entrepreneurial visionary also arrived in Chicago. His name was Samuel Insull. Insull was an English immigrant who had served as Thomas Edison's personal assistant, and he quickly proved himself an able and astute businessman. Insull rose rapidly through the ranks of Edison's General Electric Company (GE), becoming GE's second vice president. When internal politics pushed Insull out of the company in 1892, he moved to Chicago to take charge of the Chicago Edison Company (now part of Commonwealth Edison). Insull's arrival was providential for the electric company. It coincided with the 1893 World's Columbian Exposition, also known as the Chicago World's Fair. One hundred thousand incandescent bulbs, twenty thousand decorative "glow lights," and five thousand arc lamps illuminated the fairgrounds, lighting the fair so brightly it was called the

"White City." The fair's generators produced more than twice the electric lighting Chicago Edison furnished its customers.

The brightly lit fair showed people what electric power could do. Insull exploited those expectations and built a market for electric consumption. His dream of bringing electric power to every home coincided with Dawes's plans to take over gas plants that were then furnishing lighting to households.[5] While Insull promoted electric lights for homes, Dawes wanted to convince those same householders that they should use gas as a home heating fuel and for cooking. Both men built their utility empires on the shores of Lake Michigan.

Over time, ownership of manufactured gas plants proved to be a sound business decision. By 1910, Charley, his three brothers, their cousins William Dawes and Knowlton Ames, and their uncle Will Mills owned a string of manufactured gas plants across the United States, stretching from Louisiana to Seattle, Washington. Their portfolio of plants became the foundation for the privately held Dawes Brothers, Inc., the holding company that Charley created and through which he built his financial empire.

At the end of November 1894, Dawes published his first book, *The Banking System of the United States and Its Relationship to the Money and Business of the Country*. It was a small volume that he wrote as a response to the bank panic of the previous year.

More than a hundred years after its founding as a nation, the United States still had a banking system that was a mélange of federally and state-chartered institutions. The National Bank Act of 1863 had established a system of national banks and moved the nation one step closer to a national currency backed by U.S. government securities. It did not, however, eliminate state-chartered banks or ban those banks' practice of issuing their own currency that was redeemable in gold, silver, or other metals.[6] The state banks' custom of circulating banknotes, together with the provisions of the Sherman Silver Purchase Act, had generated a run on the U.S. Treasury's gold reserves in 1892 and led to the subsequent panic.

In his small volume, Dawes discussed the causes, and potential cures, for bank panics. He demonstrated a keen insight into the economics of banking and an appreciation for the nuances of monetary policy. A bank was a community institution, Dawes explained, not a "private corporation organized for profit." It is a "public corporation serving the business community, its depositors, whose funds are loaned by these officers to the community, as demand creditors of the community, and its borrowers as debtors of the depositors."[7]

Banks functioned as clearinghouses for transactions between individuals and businesses. Since over 90 percent of all banking transactions took place using either checks or drafts, a type of check drawn on the bank's funds rather than on an individual account, banks needed something stronger than the regional clearinghouses that facilitated the transfer of funds among banks. Sounding like a latter-day Alexander Hamilton, Dawes called for a board with national oversight of banks and the creation of a national monetary policy:

> The crying need of the day is for a currency so flexible in the hands of the Government that, when bank credit is diminished by widespread withdrawal of deposits, and life-blood is being drawn from business, it can be increased by the Government under some such plan as exists in England today, or under some other proper restrictions, and in some way used to lessen the awful process of such a liquidation as that of 1873 and 1893.[8]

Banking circles discussed the issues that Dawes raised in his book at the time of its publication. Some of his opinions ran contrary to the views expressed by many of the nation's established bankers, including his own uncle. Dawes was in favor of a British-style tax, paid by the banks, that would function as a form of insurance. He suggested that the tax be based on the amount of a bank's deposits and argued that such a fund would have prevented the bank runs and the Panic of 1893.[9]

Then U.S. Treasury Secretary John G. Carlisle released his own plan to avoid future bank panics shortly after Dawes's book was published. Carlisle favored "caveat emptor"—"let the buyer beware"—and he argued that bank customers would be savvy enough to know which banks were safe and would choose the banks to which they took their business accordingly. The fallacy of Carlisle's argument, as critics pointed out, was that it ignored the vast number of communities that had only one bank with which to do business.

Dawes continued to revise his views over time. When Congress began to look seriously at a bank insurance scheme, following the Panic of 1907, Dawes, by then a bank founder and president himself, had reversed his opinion from his 1894 book. He publicly opposed an insurance plan that levied an equal tax across all banks, arguing that insurance was a risk-based tool. From Dawes's point of view, the insurance tax should be a function of the risk faced by a bank. So, a smaller bank that had a higher probability of failure because of the community it served should pay a higher rate than a bank that served a more diverse economy. However, the larger problem, in Dawes's mind, was that a variable tax was unconstitutional. So, he ultimately concluded that, for the time being, there was no viable bank insurance scheme. It would be forty years after the publication of Charley's book before a Democratic president and Congress would create a bank insurance plan. The Federal Deposit Insurance Corporation (FDIC) was formed in 1933 in response to the massive bank failures triggered by the Great Depression.

However, Dawes's idea of a centralized bank clearinghouse did eventually find its way into the creation in 1913 of the Federal Reserve System. The Fed, as it is now known, was set up in response to the Panic of 1907 and charged with overseeing national monetary policy in such a way as to reduce the chances of future panics. Dawes's Chicago bank would be the first in the city to become a member of the Federal Reserve.

Charley's family and friends were his harshest critics. Rufus, in reviewing the prepublication manuscript, told him: "Your argument stands on its own feet, but, in my opinion, it will gain no strength when it seeks illustration in the late panic and present depression."[10]

Will Mills took exception to his nephew's argument for the gold standard. "I am a believer in the gold standard," he wrote, "but I have been compelled reluctantly to modify my views somewhat during the last year." After considering the events that led to the Panic of 1893, Mills determined that bimetallism (the use of both gold and silver as a monetary standard), as accepted by other countries, was the appropriate monetary policy to pursue.[11]

J. D. Cox provided such a detailed critique of Dawes's discussion about prices and their relationship to the medium of exchange—that is, currency—that Charley reprinted it in the appendix of the book.

Nationally, the book made little impact. A tiny handful of newspapers reviewed the book, albeit favorably. The *Los Angeles Herald* observed: "If this little manual of eighty pages were placed in the hands of Populists and free silverites it would tend to disabuse their minds of many monetary delusions."[12]

Advocates and critics aside, Charley wanted one person in particular to read *The Banking System of the United States*. That person was an old family friend from his father's days in Congress and the current governor of Ohio—William McKinley. "Dear Sir: Many thanks for yours of the 7th," McKinley wrote Charley in response to receipt of the book. "I will, at the earliest opportunity, look over the book which you so courteously sent me. Please accept my thanks for your kindly interest in matters political."[13]

A native of Canton, Ohio, McKinley attained the rank of major in the Civil War and had served in the U.S. House of Representatives. He was first elected to Congress in 1876 and served there alongside General Rufus R. Dawes from 1881 to 1883. McKinley lost the 1882 election, but the voters returned him to the House in the following election cycle. He was again defeated in the 1890 election—the result of voter anger at the tariff he sponsored, which bore his name. By putting taxes on foreign goods, the McKinley Tariff raised the prices that Americans had to pay for many things. In 1891, McKinley was elected governor of Ohio and began to consider a run for the presidency after the defeat of Republican Benjamin Harrison in 1892.

Dawes had met McKinley in 1894 both in Columbus, Ohio, and in Lincoln, and became one of McKinley's earliest supporters. During 1894, when he was not working on business deals and wrapping up his affairs in Lincoln, Dawes gathered support from influential politicians in Nebraska, Wyoming, and North Dakota on McKinley's behalf.

Mills did not see McKinley as presidential material. "Mr. McKinley has not been brave enough yet to announce himself [on the gold standard]," Mills wrote Charley. "He is the most magnificent illustration of [Saint] Paul's motto, 'This one thing I do,' of any of our public men, but he is not broad enough or big enough for the presidency of the United States."[14] Charley, on the other hand, believed that McKinley was the "coming man."

Dawes's work on the McKinley campaign was the beginning of a curious love-hate relationship that Dawes had with both politics and politicians. "Politics as a profession I cannot admire," he wrote in his journal in early 1893. "The men who are in our legislatures are many of them honest, and a very few of them, fearless; but the majority seem to be cringing sycophants, trimmers, and cappers—men who are mere puppets operated by strong but unseen hands."[15]

Dawes's attitude about politics was one of the curious contradictions in his life. He was deeply loyal to McKinley, as he would later be to Warren Harding. Both McKinley and Harding had gained national ascendancy through the "unseen hands" of the Ohio Gang—a group of Ohio businessmen and kingmakers who deftly managed both men's campaigns. Dawes avidly supported the political career of his friend Lawrence Y. Sherman. Sherman's support came from a group of bankers and businessmen who expected to receive tangible benefits in exchange for their financial backing. Yet Dawes took on the Illinois political machine of millionaire Charles Yerkes, Congressman William Lorimer, and Governor Richard Yates Jr., which he considered to be corrupt, with an indignation that bordered on religious zealotry.

Charley's Grandfather Gates died on December 17, 1894, bringing what had otherwise been a fruitful year to a somber close. Both Rufus and Mills had kept Charley apprised of his grandfather's steady decline. Gates suffered a form of dementia as he neared the end of his life. He had days of perfect lucidity and others when he became violent and did not recognize his wife or family members. It was a bittersweet passing. Gates was released from his suffering, but the Dawes brothers had lost a mentor and encourager.

In early January 1895, Charley wrote Caro from his rooms at the Union League Club in Chicago that he was sick with a bad cold and that she should pack up the house and come to Illinois. They purchased a house at 1632 Sheridan Road in Evanston.

On the shores of Lake Michigan, Evanston, Illinois, grew up around Northwestern University. The school was founded in 1851 and opened its doors to students four years later. The Methodist Church also established Garrett Theological Seminary adjacent to the university. As a university and seminary town, Evanston attracted an educated and socially active population. The city became the headquarters of the

Woman's Christian Temperance Union (WCTU), which was built into a formidable international force by Frances Willard, an Evanston resident, who served as the first dean of women at Northwestern University. The influence of the church and the WCTU could be seen in an ordinance banning the sale of alcohol within four miles of Northwestern's campus.

Evanston's population in 1890 was just under 16,000. It was a progressive community that once boasted of having more brains per capita than any other community in the region and successfully maintained an identity separate from that of Chicago. By the time Charley and Caro moved into their home on Sheridan Road, Evanston provided telephone service, free mail delivery, and a choice between two newspapers. Several philanthropic and cultural organizations had already been established, including the Woman's Club of Evanston.[16] Although Charley had a long commute into Chicago, Evanston offered him and Caro many of the intellectual and cultural pastimes that they had come to enjoy in Lincoln. Before long, the community became their home.

Charley Dawes was as focused on getting William McKinley elected president as he was on getting his business deals solidified, and he traveled in January 1895 to meet for the first time with Cleveland businessman Marcus A. Hanna, often called Mark, McKinley's campaign manager. Dawes presented a plan to organize rallies in the western states with McKinley supporters as speakers. Dawes impressed Hanna with his commitment and aggressiveness, and Hanna assigned him the responsibility for building a McKinley organization in Illinois. "We are depending upon your organization for your state and will be glad to cooperate with you in any adjoining territory you may find missionary work to do," Hanna wrote his enthusiastic operative.[17]

In early 1896, the Illinois Republican Party backed U.S. Senator Shelby Moore Cullom as its favorite-son candidate for the Republican presidential nomination. Cullom had been a member of the U.S. House, served as Illinois governor for six years, and then was elected to the Senate in 1883. His home was the state capital, Springfield, and his influence extended throughout Illinois. Ideologically, Dawes and Cullom shared common cause regarding regulation of the railroads. As a freshman senator, Cullom had been audacious enough to buck

Senate seniority rules and introduce legislation establishing an Interstate Commerce Commission that would regulate the railroads and rail and water routes. His bill finally passed in 1887, the year Dawes headed to Nebraska. Cullom became chair of the new Senate Committee on Interstate Commerce.[18]

The state Republican Party—the party of Abraham Lincoln—had held a monopoly on Illinois politics since Lincoln's election in 1860. By the 1890s, a powerful group of politicians led by John R. Tanner and Richard Yates, whose father had previously been a governor and political powerhouse, controlled all nominations for offices at the state and federal levels. Tanner, from southern Illinois, ran his half of the state and could either deliver or withhold votes for statewide candidates.

Instead of working with Tanner and Yates to secure a commitment to McKinley after a token show of support for Cullom, Dawes set himself up as the anti-machine outsider. It was a similar approach to the one he had taken in Lincoln. The difference was that Dawes had a political and business safety net under him in Lincoln in the form of John Fitzgerald of the Irish National League and the city's reform boosters. In Illinois, Dawes was a newcomer taking instruction from Hanna, based in Ohio, and dependent on his own political instincts.

The Illinois nominating convention, held in May 1896, ultimately voted a pro-McKinley delegation to the Republican National Convention. Dawes deserved much of the credit for the McKinley victory. However, Charley's approach to securing that support branded him as an interloper and a troublemaker. His decision to buck the powerful Tanner organization would deny him a chance to run for the U.S. Senate and permanently establish him as an outsider to the national Republican Party for the remainder of his public service career.

As far as Hanna and McKinley were concerned, Charley proved an able lieutenant. McKinley's nomination as the Republican presidential candidate was far from a sure thing. He faced two strong opponents. Thomas B. Reed, known as Czar Reed, was the formidable Speaker of the House. Reed had been a U.S. representative from Maine since 1877 and had acquired the moniker because he controlled the House with an iron fist. "Reed's Rules" directed business on the House floor. If Reed wanted a bill brought to a vote, it came up, and if he did not want legislation voted on, it never emerged from committee.

McKinley's other opponent was Iowa Senator William B. Allison. Like Reed in the House, Allison was a powerful legislator in the Senate. He chaired the Senate Appropriations Committee and was considered one of the Senate Four, a quartet of senators who controlled legislation in the Senate Chamber.

The economy, still not fully rebounded since the 1893 depression, was the key issue in the 1896 election. With William Jennings Bryan as the Democrat and Populist front-runner, the free coinage of silver versus the establishment of a gold standard became one of the hot-button issues of the campaign. Allison was a committed bimetallist. McKinley, as Mills had accurately assessed, refused to take a definitive stand on the issue. Reed, likewise, was coy.

Allison's candidacy forced the McKinley camp to pay careful attention to its organization in the western states, where there was strong support for the free coinage of silver. "I had a pleasant letter from Senator Warren of Wyoming today. He is, as I had hoped, and so is [Wyoming Representative Frank W.] Mondell, quietly for McKinley, but they report that the Allison men are making some inroads in the State. Can you not get someone in Chicago to take matters up out there and push them vigorously?" Hanna requested of Dawes in February 1896.[19]

Hanna also asked Dawes to see what he could do to build up the McKinley forces in Montana, Idaho, Nevada, and New Mexico. The states' Republican conventions for the selection of delegates to the National Convention were to be held soon, and Hanna felt the pressure. "Time is slipping away so rapidly that what is done, should, of course, be immediately undertaken," he urged Dawes.[20]

McKinley developed a fondness for his young organizer. He told Mills and Charley's brother, Rufus, when they met in Chicago at a Lincoln Day dinner, that Charley was "a genius" and "the greatest boy I ever knew."[21] McKinley wrote to Charley after he had won Illinois's support: "I cannot find words to express my admiration for your high qualities of leadership. You have won exceptional honor. You had long ago won my heart."[22]

It was a heady time for the thirty-one-year-old Dawes. "This is the most important winter in my career this far," he wrote Caro, who was in the South with the children and had asked him to join them. "I am making more progress among men and securing greater prestige than at any time in my life. Apart from my business to leave at such a critical time might lessen my hold on the political situation."[23]

Charley's attitude toward the Tanner machine had not damaged his business associations. He had an impressive network of contacts, and he was not shy about asking them to donate to McKinley's campaign. By mid-March, he managed a $25,000 subscription effort, had commitments for the funds, and promised to fill any gaps with his own money if one of the donors failed to come through.[24] As the campaign progressed through the spring, Hanna looked to him to find funding to support the McKinley organization that Dawes was developing in the western states.

Other McKinley supporters recognized Dawes's value to the campaign. General John McNulta, who had served in the Illinois State Senate and as a one-term member of Congress, praised Dawes to McKinley. "I cannot commend too highly the work done by Mr. Dawes. He has a natural aptitude for organization and is a good judge of men. His freedom of affiliation with any faction is a great help to him. I have never known better work done in this state considering the circumstances."[25]

At the Republican National Convention in early June, McNulta attempted to twist Tanner's arm to support Dawes as Illinois's representative on the Republican National Committee. Tanner would have none of it. McNulta need not have worried; a higher honor awaited Dawes. Hanna named Charley to the Republican Executive Committee, charged with running the McKinley campaign. In its announcement of Dawes's selection, the *Chicago Daily Tribune* mistakenly referred to him as "Charles T. Dawes."[26]

The Republicans established dual headquarters for the 1896 campaign—an office in New York City and one in Chicago—in recognition of the importance of the western states to McKinley's chances for election. Charley headed up the Chicago office and served as the national campaign's de facto treasurer. His assistant was Francis J. Kilkenny, an Irish immigrant who had moved to Chicago after graduating from the University of Notre Dame in South Bend, Indiana. The two men were close in age, but Kilkenny, facing discrimination as an Irish immigrant, had struggled to find a job. He was working as a cloakroom attendant at the Union League Club and was a McKinley supporter. No doubt, Charley saw something of himself in the earnest young man, and he offered Kilkenny a position as his personal assistant. Kilkenny jumped at the chance. It was a serendipitous decision. Kilkenny would serve in a variety of capacities as Charley's personal assistant for the balance of his career and would benefit from Charley's generosity and financial wizardry.

As head of McKinley's Chicago headquarters, Charley oversaw the printing and dissemination of campaign literature, a task he described as onerous. He monitored the incoming funds and insisted on control of expenditures. He used a bid process before letting any contracts for work on behalf of the campaign. At the end of July, he informed both McKinley and Hanna that "the system of expenditures has been perfected" but went on to add, "The system of collecting funds, in view of demands upon us here, becomes of vital importance. The prevailing impression that money will be easily raised leads each individual to evade or lessen his just subscription." Dawes urged Hanna to impress this situation on the "eastern men," so that the campaign contributions would not taper off. Dawes told McKinley that the money must be on hand in the campaign accounts before Dawes would spend it.[27]

Demands for literature poured into the Chicago office during the fall, and it was difficult to keep sufficient fliers and other publications in stock. A typical complaint was that supporters could not get materials from their state central committees. In Illinois alone, nearly ten thousand pieces of literature and campaign buttons were requested in one month's time.[28]

Charley prepared regular monthly statements for Hanna on the financial condition of the McKinley campaign. On October 13, 1896, the campaign showed total receipts of $940,000. The printing expense alone was nearly $250,000. Just under $375,000 was disbursed to the various state committees. By Election Day, the campaign had raised the unprecedented amount of nearly $2 million.[29] The McKinley campaign was the single most expensive campaign in the history of the Republic up to that time, and its expenditures became the subject of a congressional investigation following the election.

McKinley was elected on November 3, 1896, with just over 51 percent of the popular vote and 271 electoral votes.[30] Dawes sent a congratulatory telegram to the president-elect, who replied: "Thanks for your message. You must now take a rest. Since my election, I have often thought of you, for my heart is full of gratitude for all you have done."[31]

Charley and Caro traveled to Canton the week after the election to congratulate the president-elect personally. Dawes's friends pressed for a cabinet appointment on his behalf. At Hanna's direction, Charley urged his friends not to approach McKinley. "If he proffers this honor, it will be unsolicited," Dawes told them.[32]

Behind the scenes, Dawes sought an appointment. Hanna was noncommittal. He told Charley that McKinley needed to be free to nominate those with whom he felt most comfortable.[33] Hanna's reply was disingenuous and unfair, considering the enormous energy Dawes had poured into creating and financing McKinley's western organization. Although he never said so, Charley had overseen the McKinley campaign at great risk to his own financial well-being. Dawes's newly acquired manufactured gas plants were underperforming, and Charley had several notes due that he could not cover. He spent much of 1896 as he had 1893, looking for new sources of loans to pay off old debts.

While Hanna advised Dawes to restrain his own ambition, Hanna was pulling strings to get McKinley to name the aging Ohio senator John Sherman to a cabinet post, thus leaving the Senate seat vacant for Hanna to grab. This is exactly what he did when McKinley nominated Sherman to be secretary of state.

McKinley, too, dangled the possibility of a cabinet post before Charley. The president-elect flattered his young protégé, encouraged his visits to Canton, and suggested the possibility of a cabinet appointment on several occasions. The newspapers mentioned that Dawes was a possible cabinet selection. His family rooted for him. "We are watching the papers very closely now as to news of your political prospects," Henry wrote. "The family is divided in their predictions. Aunt Lucy, Rufe and I are backing you for the cabinet and are gradually winning the rest of the family over to our side."[34]

The first signs that a cabinet post was not likely came during a visit to Canton in mid-December. McKinley asked Charley if a failure to appoint him to the cabinet would alter the friendship that had grown between them. Charley believed that McKinley was sincere. Dawes assured the president-elect that their friendship was not dependent on an appointment.[35]

With that assurance, McKinley proceeded to discuss prospects for the various cabinet offices with Dawes. He asked Dawes to contact Allison to determine the Iowa senator's interest in the secretary of state position. Hanna's name was mentioned for postmaster general, the usual appointment for a president's campaign manager.

Dawes got behind the selection of fellow Chicagoan Lyman J. Gage for the position of secretary of the treasury, the position that Dawes himself had desired. He lobbied McKinley to appoint Gage, even as Senators Sherman and Allison and Vermont Republican Senator Redfield Proctor pushed to have Shelby Cullom nominated. McKinley assigned Dawes the task of meeting with Gage to sound him out on his interest.

Charley and Caro traveled regularly from November until the inauguration in March to meet with the McKinleys in Ohio. Charley was enamored with McKinley, and the older man treated Dawes as a surrogate son. Caro and Ida McKinley had, likewise, formed a close friendship. Whether that affection blinded Charley to how the "unseen hands" were at work in McKinley's cabinet selections, or whether Dawes was flattered simply to have access to power, Dawes's journal and letters offer no insights.

At a visit with McKinley in Cleveland on January 9, McKinley once again hinted that he might have no cabinet position for Dawes, and if that proved to be the case, then McKinley wanted to offer Dawes the position of comptroller of the currency. Dawes replied that he would accept the position and consider it a "crowning honor."[36] It was a gracious response, considering that the job was not even McKinley's to offer at the time.

The Office of the Comptroller of the Currency (OCC) originated as part of the 1863 National Currency Act (later called the National Bank Act) and was amended slightly when the National Bank Act passed in 1864. The initial purpose of the act was to establish a mechanism to sell bonds to generate cash to fund the Civil War and to back a national currency. Under the act, the OCC was authorized to write the rules that national banks would follow. Banks that applied for national charters were required to meet specific capital requirements and submit to federal oversight. The comptroller appointed bank examiners to oversee the national banks' compliance with the rules.

There was one little wrinkle in the banking law: the comptroller was appointed for a five-year term and reported directly to Congress. The law was written that way to prevent the comptroller's arbitrary removal from the position.[37] The term of the current comptroller, James H. Eckels, did not expire until April 1898, and he made it clear that he would not resign before the end of his tenure. One Washington paper declared that Dawes's appointment as comptroller "bears the mark of a canard on its face from the fact that the term of Comptroller Eckels will not expire until April 1898, more than a year and a month after Major McKinley's inauguration."[38] At the official announcement of Dawes's appointment, McKinley stated that neither he nor Dawes was pressuring Eckels to resign.

The offer of the comptroller's position was a disappointment, and the fact that the position would not be open for another fourteen months had to rankle. Nevertheless, Dawes responded to the appointment with his characteristic optimism and played the role of the good political soldier to McKinley.

Shortly before the election, J. D. Cox had written to Charley: "I wish I could sit down in a corner with you and discuss the political situation philosophically. . . . I hope we shall elect McKinley and that you will have had enough of politics this year to last you a lifetime."[39]

Charley's political appetite, however, had just been whetted. He and Caro packed their bags and boarded a train at the end of February 1897. They were headed to Washington to see William McKinley inaugurated.

CHAPTER 4

※

Comptroller of the Currency

William McKinley took the oath of office on a sunny Thursday, March 4, 1897. "Happy Consummation of the Great Quadrennial Event," read the headline in the Washington *Morning Times*, which estimated that nearly 250,000 people saw the inauguration.[1] Charley was no longer a lanky fifteen-year-old tagging along with his father. Dawes was an invited guest and an intimate of the new president, and he enjoyed his access to the White House. That evening, with seventeen people in tow, including his siblings Rufus, Henry, and Betsey, Charley attended the inaugural ball. He, Caro, and the rest of his family stayed out until 3:00 A.M.[2]

The year 1897 was peripatetic for Charley. Rail travel made it easier than ever for the president to be publicly accessible, and McKinley liked to spend time away from the White House. Charley met McKinley at a variety of cities during the president's first year in office, including New York City and Nashville, Tennessee, as well as making frequent trips to Washington. Many of Dawes's visits were social, but given McKinley's sometimes informal style of conducting business, social access equated to political access. Dawes served McKinley as a combination political aide and the son the president never had. Charley contacted potential appointees to ambassadorial and consular positions on McKinley's behalf. He recommended nominees for federal positions in Illinois, such as postmaster and the internal revenue collector for the state's Southern District. He also served as a sounding board for McKinley on matters of banking and currency reform.

Caro often accompanied Charley on the trips to Washington to spend time with the First Lady. Ida McKinley was a warm-hearted and highly intelligent woman who had managed her father's bank prior to her marriage. She had given birth to two daughters, both of whom died in childhood. Katherine was born in 1871. Ida was born in April 1873 and lived until August of that year. Mrs. McKinley developed a form of epilepsy following the birth of baby Ida, and her health further declined after Katherine succumbed to typhoid fever in 1875. In the early years of the McKinley administration, the First Lady was a socially engaged woman who enjoyed small dinner parties, played euchre (a game similar to bridge), and took afternoon carriage rides. The deep and abiding mutual affection between Caro and Ida lasted until Mrs. McKinley's death in 1907.

Charley neglected his business as he built a political base for himself. His cash position was as bad as it had ever been, and the letters from his creditors were harsh. His efforts to extend his due dates met with unusually strong resistance. The seller of the Lincoln Packing Company, Luther Allen, who was financing the purchase, responded scathingly to Charley's request for an extension: "Your letter of the 18th [September] inst. was duly received and I am compelled to say the subject matter was not only a surprise, but a disagreeable one. I have been several times assured by Mr. Mills and yourself that there would be no question as to the payment of the notes at their maturity and had banked upon that assurance in all my own transactions." Allen had covered for Mills and Dawes with his own bank, believing they would pay on time. Having placed his own creditworthiness on the line, Allen wanted his money.[3]

Edwin Brown, a foundry owner and another of Charley's creditors, wrote on September 16, 1897: "I am 'dead busted' and could use to good advantage some interest. You paid me up to June 1st, 1897."[4]

Will Dawes, who managed the Dawes Business Block properties in Lincoln, sent Charley a plea for funds to pay notes and property taxes coming due. Will had attempted to raise cash by selling some DBB Co. stock, but he could not find any buyers. "Just now you are obliged to advance a good deal of money to keep things going here and I feel very keenly any call that comes on account of personal matters," Will wrote his cousin and business partner.[5]

In the meantime, Charley's family looked to him for financial assistance. "I find father very much worried—and not without reason," wrote Rufus. "They are hard up for cash and have several bills to pay." Rufus had dissuaded his father from taking out a $1,000 mortgage secured by the company's sideyard by offering to write and see how Charley could help. "I know this will trouble you," Rufus acknowledged, "but they are really in a pinch."[6] Charley sent his father bonds from Northwestern Gas, which his father sold for less than face value at the bank to acquire cash.[7]

On November 3, 1897, the Commercial National Bank of Chicago elected James H. Eckels its president. He announced his intention to resign as comptroller of the currency on December 31, clearing the way for Charley to assume the position.

Commercial National elected John C. McKeon as its vice president. At the time, McKeon was the examiner for the National Bank of Illinois, which was in serious financial trouble and on the brink of closing its doors. As one of the strongest financial institutions in the Midwest, the bank had clearinghouse connections with New York banks, and its default affected those banks as well as the depositors and creditors in and around Chicago. The situation with the National Bank was further complicated by the suicide of its top two officers. To assure a smooth transition, Eckels named Huntington W. Jackson as McKeon's replacement.

As a courtesy to a fellow Chicagoan, Jackson informed Dawes of the pending appointment. Charley responded in what would become a trademark when he disagreed with a decision. He lost his temper and angrily declared that Eckels had no right to make an appointment so close to his resignation without first consulting him. Dawes told Jackson that if he took the examiner's post, Dawes would replace him with his friend General John McNulta after January 1.

Eckels was understandably upset. Secretary of the Treasury Lyman Gage, another Chicagoan, expressed his displeasure. Word of the meeting between Dawes and Jackson reached the White House, and McKinley summoned Charley to Washington. Gage and Eckels expected the president to tell Charley to back down. They were mistaken. McKinley disliked interpersonal conflict, and he held a tolerant, paternal esteem for the brilliant, if irascible, younger man. To the surprise of many, McKinley supported Dawes. The president's failure to reprimand Dawes and his refusal to insist that Dawes honor Eckels's appointment rewarded Charley for his behavior. A tantrum had allowed him to control the situation and disarm his opponents. Dawes repeatedly used that tactic throughout his professional career because it often produced the desired results. He treated the public outrage and controversies generated by his outbursts with insouciance, typically dismissing calls for retractions with a curt, "I stated my position without apology for it needed none."[8]

The dustup over the Jackson appointment did not affect Charley's confirmation by the Senate. His nomination as comptroller of the currency sailed through the chamber in two hours, shepherded through the Finance Committee and onto the Senate floor by Marcus (Mark) Hanna, now a senator from Ohio, and Illinois Senators Shelby Cullom and William Mason. Dawes was sworn in on December 31, 1897. Had the intense scrutiny faced today by presidential nominees occurred in December 1897, Dawes might not have been confirmed. His financial situation and business dealings alone would have raised questions about his fitness to serve in the comptroller's position. He had borrowed $15,000 from McKinley to pay off his note on a block of commercial real estate in Lincoln, which would certainly have come to light.[9]

Dawes compartmentalized his activities. He saw no conflict of interest between his regulatory role as a comptroller and his dependence upon the goodwill of his personal bankers, from whom he sought the extension of payment deadlines and additional credit with which to pursue his business deals. Since he was not personally examining the banks' books, Dawes reasoned, he was doing nothing wrong.

As comptroller, Dawes assumed a public persona of utmost propriety. He declined an invitation to speak to a group of New York bankers because he believed he would appear too close to the people he was charged with regulating. Within three weeks of taking office, he set a policy that prohibited bank examiners from working as examiners-for-hire for the banks they were assigned to regulate. He believed that the examiners were less likely to be impartial when they conducted their reviews for the government if they also carried out private internal reviews paid for by the banks.

Dawes brought his reformer's mind-set to the Office of the Comptroller. Confidence in the safety of banks was still shaky in the aftermath of the

Panic of 1893. Throughout his tenure, he sought to improve the office's efficiency and its effectiveness in preventing bank failures. He implemented a system of uniform, semiannual bank examinations nationwide. Previously, national banks in Boston, New York City, Philadelphia, and Baltimore had only been examined once a year.[10] Underlying Dawes's policies was his strong belief, first discussed in his book on banking, that a bank had a responsibility to its community, its depositors, and its creditors. His views were put to the test as soon as he took office.

Philadelphia's Chestnut Street National Bank did not open its doors on December 24, 1897. Eckels had monitored the bank for some time, and on Christmas Eve, the bank's examiner, William M. Hardt, declared the bank insolvent. Like the Illinois National, the Chestnut Street Bank was considered a strong regional bank, with clearinghouse connections in New York and large business depositors.

In the remaining days of Eckels's tenure, the bank's president, William M. Singerly, offered a plan whereby he would provide the stock of another of his companies, the newspaper the *Philadelphia Record*, as collateral to satisfy the bank's creditors. Upon taking office, Dawes appointed two receivers to manage the bank's liquidation—George H. Earle Jr. and Richard F. Cook. Without sufficient time to examine all of Singerly's holdings, Earle and Cook accepted the bank president's proposal and recommended it to Dawes. By January 10, 70 percent of the bank's depositors had accepted the plan, and Dawes issued a memorandum giving the remaining 30 percent of the depositors until January 20 to indicate their willingness to go along with the proposal.[11] He ignored recommendations that he reevaluate Singerly's proposal before approving it.

In late February, Earle and Cook determined that the *Record*'s assets were overvalued. Singerly died of a heart attack on February 27, 1898, and the plan initially approved by the majority of stockholders needed to be reconsidered. In his first major ruling as comptroller, Dawes acted on his belief that banks were public institutions with responsibilities to their communities. He ordered the Chestnut Street's directors and stockholders to assume 100 percent of the liability to their depositors, and he declared a 10 percent dividend to the creditors.[12]

Dawes's ruling was new policy. From the beginning of banking, shareholders of an insolvent bank were assessed for the difference between its debts and losses and the estimated proceeds from liquidation of its assets, which could take months, if not years. A shortfall between the proceeds and the estimated liability was not unusual. Dawes broke with previous comptrollers' practices and assessed the shareholders a second time to pay the balance.[13]

Dawes's policy eventually led to a Supreme Court ruling. In the case of *Studebaker v. Perry*, Clement Studebaker, a shareholder in the insolvent National Bank of Kansas City, Missouri, refused to pay a second assessment levied by Dawes to cover the bank's debts after the first assessment on the shareholders proved insufficient. The receiver for the Kansas City bank, John Perry, filed the case against Studebaker on November 9, 1899. The lower court upheld Dawes's practice, and Studebaker appealed the decision. The case ultimately reached the Supreme Court, which heard arguments on January 17 and 20, 1902 (after Dawes had resigned as comptroller), and found sufficient legal precedent to uphold the practice.[14] Subsequently, it became routine for shareholders to be assessed for the differences between a bank's assets and its liabilities as part of the liquidation of an insolvent bank.

In one of life's ironic twists, Dawes would find himself, as a shareholder in the Central Trust Bank that he founded in 1902, held liable on two separate occasions for insolvencies. The first time was in the Lorimer bank scandal, when William Lorimer was indicted for misappropriation of funds that led to the failure of his La Salle Street Trust and Savings Bank in 1914. The second time was when Dawes reorganized the Central Trust in 1932 to save it from bankruptcy. In both instances, Dawes and his fellow shareholders went to court to avoid paying their assessments.

The explosion on February 15, 1898, on the battleship USS *Maine*, berthed at Havana, Cuba, permanently changed the complexion of the McKinley presidency. Dawes had a front row seat. "Great excitement is occasioned by the disaster, but in view of the immediate disclaimer and other acts of the Spanish authorities, it will hardly lead to anything like war," Dawes recorded in his diary in the early days of the crisis.[15]

Dawes's initial assessment of the events led him to believe that war was unnecessary, and he was convinced that McKinley would stand firm against considerable pressure to initiate hostilities with Spain. One of those urging war was Theodore Roosevelt (TR), serving as acting secretary of the navy. His immediate response to the explosion had been to put the navy on full alert. "Theodore Roosevelt came in urging war and emphasizing the dangers of delay, having learned of the sailing of the Spanish torpedo flotilla," Charley noted in his journal.[16] McKinley was not easily persuaded. "Impatience is not patriotism," the president told his young protégé, adding, "Those who were so impatient at the first have not yet gone to the front."[17]

From February until the declaration of war in late April, Dawes observed the transformation in McKinley's handling of the intelligence regarding the explosion and conditions in Cuba. Newspaper reports of atrocities on the island lent credence to the argument for war. Gradually, the rationale for hostilities moved away from retaliation for the presumed attack on the *Maine* to providing assistance to the rebels in Cuba fighting for their independence and relief to those starving in the Cuban *reconcentrados* (concentration camps).

Finally, McKinley was persuaded to declare war on Spain, and he sent his message to Congress on April 11, 1898. Congress issued the declaration on April 25 and authorized a $200 million bond issue to fund the war. As comptroller, Dawes authorized the printing of bank currency for any bank that advised him of its plans to purchase the new bond issue.[18]

Dawes's open access to the White House allowed him to follow closely the prosecution of the Spanish-American War. He served as a sounding board for the president, a role Charley would reprise with John J. Pershing in World War I. McKinley frequently invited Dawes to lunch or for an afternoon carriage ride to discuss war matters. Dawes was with McKinley when the president learned of the American victory in Manila, the Philippines. McKinley shared his plan to make George Dewey an admiral once the victory was confirmed. Dawes read the incoming telegrams on war progress and listened as the president described his problems with Secretary of War Russell Alger, who had proved an ineffectual leader and circumvented McKinley's authority. On a carriage ride, McKinley discussed his intention to call for 75,000 troops to prosecute the war.[19]

McKinley laid out what would become the foundation for U.S. expansionism: the annexation of the Philippines, acquisition of the island of Puerto Rico, and establishment of Cuban independence.

Dawes had a front row seat as the president transformed the United States into an international power.

The Washington years gave Dawes an opportunity to build up political capital that he could use in the future. He and Caro hosted a steady stream of old Marietta friends and new political acquaintances. Dawes maintained regular contact with Mark Hanna; Iowa Senator Albert B. Cummins, who had been an early McKinley supporter; and Dawes's friend John McNulta. Dawes developed a close relationship with Frank O. Lowden, a Chicago attorney and law professor at Northwestern University, who had political aspirations and would eventually become an Illinois governor. Dawes became good friends with Judge William R. Day, an Ohioan who was another adviser to McKinley. Day became secretary of state in the middle of the war and would go on to become a Supreme Court justice.

Lowden and Albert Beveridge became two of Dawes's closest long-term friends. Beveridge was a highly intelligent, ambitious politician who had his sights set on the White House. When the two met, Beveridge was in Washington working to build his own political connections. He was elected to the U.S. Senate from Indiana in 1899 and told Dawes that he planned to run for president in 1904. As the relationship between the two men deepened, Dawes became increasingly impressed with Beveridge's intelligence and insights.

Beveridge advocated free trade between the United States and its newly acquired protectorate, Puerto Rico. It was a courageous stance for a Republican legislator. Although the economic record proved that the McKinley Tariff had been disastrous for American trade, the Republican Party still advocated protectionism to shield American industries from foreign competition. Beveridge was one of the first legislators to speak in favor of American expansionism. He became political allies with Theodore Roosevelt and helped to organize the Progressive Party in 1912. Beveridge's support of Roosevelt did not lessen the close friendship he shared with Dawes, although Dawes and Roosevelt never became close. Beveridge wrote a biography of Abraham Lincoln and a four-volume biography of Chief Justice John Marshall, which won the Pulitzer Prize. Dawes deeply admired his friend for his scholarship, and the two maintained a correspondence until Beveridge's death in 1927.

Charley was less successful in building a good relationship with his fellow Chicagoan, Secretary of the Treasury Lyman Gage. Gage and Dawes shared a conservative approach to finance, and they both agreed on the need for a gold standard and a stronger currency. However, they did not see eye-to-eye on how to bring about those changes. As comptroller, Dawes shared his reports with Gage as a professional courtesy, but not for the purposes of collaboration, and Dawes openly disagreed with Gage on various policy matters. One can only guess what Gage thought of the brash young comptroller. Although the two men served together for four years, Gage mentions Dawes only one time in his memoir—when Dawes introduced Gage before he made a speech.

Dawes first publicly challenged Gage's views over the issue of asset currency in his annual comptroller's report for 1898. Gage favored a policy that allowed banks to issue their own banknotes, called asset currency because they were backed by a percentage of the assets that the bank owned. Dawes saw serious dangers in this approach.

Reiterating his arguments from *The Banking System of the United States*, Dawes maintained that a bank's most important function was as a middleman between the depositor and the borrower. Under the then-current practice, a bank's noteholder (creditor) would have pre-eminence over a depositor if the bank was declared insolvent. Dawes argued that the issuing of asset currency was "inherently wrong and unjustified by any grounds of public policy." He argued that the creation of asset currency would harm small, rural banks and be "so revolutionary as to bring about the most injurious conditions in the general business of the country."[20]

In 1896, delegates from boards of trade of twelve midwestern cities had gathered in Indianapolis and called for a large monetary convention of businessmen to examine banking practices and recommend ways to avoid another economic downturn such as the one in 1893. The convention first met in Indianapolis in 1897. A second, larger convention met in 1898, bringing together nearly five hundred of America's top corporate leaders. The conclusions of the 1898 Indianapolis Monetary Convention supported Gage's views. Dawes's alternate position found support among some Chicago bankers and bankers in smaller communities around the nation. It was a courageous stance to take. Dawes's opinion directly challenged Gage and the more established eastern

55

banks, which would have benefited from the ability to issue asset currency. Ultimately, Dawes's view favoring the depositor over a noteholder was the one that gained preeminence in national banking policy.

In 1899, Dawes tackled the elasticity of money held in banks and available for loans. It was another banking issue that he had addressed in his book on the U.S. banking system. In his annual report to Congress, Dawes wrote that banks needed a method by which they could lend money even when the economy was not performing well. He believed that economic depressions could be avoided if banks could still make short-term loans and keep money in circulation. He also saw his proposal as a way to protect the depositors of banks that were struggling due to tight money. Dawes referred to his approach as emergency banknote circulation.

To cover the emergency banknotes, Dawes advised a tax on bank loans to create a fund sufficient to redeem the emergency banknotes in full. The fund would be financed by monies from the solvent issuing bank and a pro rata share of the assets of the insolvent banks. The key to Dawes's recommendation was to avoid the need to give preferential treatment to noteholders over depositors of the insolvent banks. The tax was to be large enough to force the retirement of the emergency notes as soon as the monetary crisis had passed.[21]

In today's language, we would refer to Dawes's idea as creating a stimulus package. In 1899, it was a radical proposal, although Gage, likewise, had struggled with a means to establish elasticity in the money supply. Dawes was anxious to see an amendment in support of his proposal added to the currency reform bill that would be introduced in the opening session of Congress in December. It was the bill in which McKinley requested Congress to adopt a gold standard.

Had the events in Cuba not transpired, it is generally believed that McKinley would have introduced gold standard legislation in 1898. With the swift and victorious conclusion to the war and McKinley's reelection campaign on the horizon in fall 1900, the fall and winter session of Congress in 1899 and 1900 was the time to secure legislative approval for a controversial subject.

The Republican majorities in both houses of Congress did not guarantee McKinley every vote. There were silver Republicans, including his opponent for the Republican presidential nomination, Senator

William B. Allison. In the House, McKinley faced another former opponent for the nomination, Speaker Thomas B. Reed, on whose word the legislation would either make it to the House floor or die ignominiously in committee.

In his December 1898 address to Congress, McKinley referred to the need for currency reform legislation. This was his euphemism for the establishment of a gold standard. Over the course of the spring and summer of 1899, the Senate Four (Allison, Nelson Aldrich of Rhode Island, Orville Platt of Connecticut, and John Spooner of Wisconsin) and House leaders met to craft a bill that would quickly win approval in both chambers when Congress reconvened at the end of the year. McKinley's efforts were further aided when Reed decided to resign from Congress in June 1899. Reed was replaced by David B. Henderson from Iowa, who was much more malleable than his predecessor.

Dawes was excluded from the inner circle working on the gold standard legislation. It is one of the few times during the McKinley years when he was denied direct access to the president to discuss pending legislation or current events. The exclusion may have been a decision of Gage's, who likely felt that Dawes lacked the temperament to handle the sometimes delicate negotiations.

Dawes failed to read his lack of involvement as a subtle warning to lie low. Blithely oblivious to the delicacy of the negotiations between the White House and Congress, Charley doggedly pursued the Senate Four to get his amendment for his emergency banknote legislation added to the currency reform bill. Dawes met with Speaker Henderson shortly before Congress was set to reconvene at the beginning of December and found him hesitant to address the proposal. "He seemed favorably impressed with the amendment," Dawes recorded in his journal, "but said that it must be added in conference committee between Senate and House, if at all: for he did not dare risk re-opening the form of report with the caucus committee which is already agreed upon."[22]

Allison, whose support for any financial legislation was essential, was blunter. "I called on Senator Allison and talked over the finance bill [gold standard legislation] of the Senate, also the chances for the adoption of my plan, which are none too flattering."[23]

Dawes was present at the White House when the bill was signed into law on March 14, 1900, but all he could think about was that his amendment was not part of the new law. "My recommendation for a bond secured elastic circulation fell by the wayside," he recorded in his journal by way of noting his attendance at the signing ceremony.[24]

On August 2, 1899, General Rufus R. Dawes passed away. Charley had last seen his father alive a month earlier, when he had traveled to Marietta after receiving word that the general was rapidly failing. July 4, 1899, had been Rufus Dawes's sixty-first birthday. He could still recognize his eldest son but was barely able to speak with him.

Charley was en route by train from Washington to Marietta when he received the telegram telling of his father's death. "For us the light had gone from the day, and all was darkness, save memory and faith," Charley mourned.[25]

Following the funeral, the brothers discussed their parents' financial situation. It was a given that Charley would return to Washington. Rufus Cutler Dawes had moved to Evanston the previous year to assume management responsibilities for the gas companies. Beman, still in Lincoln at the time, was eying opportunities in Newark, Ohio. Henry, the youngest of the four boys, remained in Marietta and took charge of what was left of the railroad tie and lumber business.

By early 1900, it was evident that the November election would be a repeat of 1896, with McKinley running as the Republican incumbent and William Jennings Bryan running as both a Democrat and a Populist. This time around, however, McKinley was sure to have enough delegates to get on the ballot. His popularity had soared with the United States victory over Spain, and the passage of the Gold Standard Act of 1900 had secured the loyalty of eastern bankers. Delegate selection at each of the state conventions would be, for the most part, perfunctory.

Charley attended the Illinois Republican State Convention, which convened on May 7, 1900, in Peoria. McKinley had sent Dawes to the convention to ensure support for the renomination of Shelby Cullom to the U.S. Senate. In the ensuing three years since McKinley had taken office, Cullom had separated himself from the Lorimer-Tanner faction. He had become a loyal lieutenant in the Senate for McKinley and moved the president's legislative agenda through the committees where Cullom had influence. He and Charley had developed a close friendship.

John R. Tanner was the state's sitting governor and the de facto head of the Illinois Republican Party. Together with Billy Lorimer, the two men exerted strong control over state politics. Lorimer's influence dominated Cook County and environs, while Tanner's strength lay in southern Illinois.

At the start of the convention, the Lorimer-Tanner machine controlled the members of the State Central Committee. If the machine maintained its control, it would influence the selection of every Illinois Republican candidate from the U.S. Senate to the delegates to the Republican National Convention. Although there appeared to be no obstacle to Cullom's selection by the machine, Charley was determined to dislodge its control. Going against McKinley's express wishes to avoid alienating any Republican group, Charley challenged Lorimer and Tanner's power.

William (Billy) Lorimer, known as the "Blond Boss" of Chicago's West Side because of his fair hair, had gained political control of the Cook County machine through skillful coalition building. Lorimer was an English immigrant who had been elected to the U.S. House in 1898. His father was a Presbyterian minister, but Lorimer married an Irish Catholic woman, fathered a large family, and identified strongly with the large Roman Catholic population in Chicago. Understanding that his political strength would come from meeting the needs of the diverse immigrant groups in Chicago, Lorimer found ways to identify with each of the largest nationalities—German, Irish, Polish, and Russian-Jewish. His ability to deliver Chicago's West Side made him a key player in Illinois machine politics.

The Lorimer-Tanner candidate for the Republican gubernatorial nomination was Judge Elbridge Hanecy, who served on the Illinois Circuit Court. Hanecy, who had ruled in 1891 that the state's antitrust law was unconstitutional, had strong support from Chicago's business community. Dawes, who would eventually speak against the federal Sherman Antitrust Act, had no known personal animosities against Hanecy, other than that he was Lorimer and Tanner's man.

Dawes's first challenge against the machine's forces took place with a meeting of the credentials committee, where he prevented several Tanner-backed delegates from being seated at the convention. With that victory in hand, Dawes next challenged the selection of a temporary chair of the convention. If Tanner prevailed, his choice, John J. Brown, would be named temporary chair. If Dawes triumphed, Dawes himself would become the convention's temporary chair. The announcement of Dawes's candidacy for the temporary chairmanship was "the first cloud that has come over the skies of the Hanecy candidacy since Peoria was invaded," observed the *Chicago Daily Tribune*. "Politicians generally regarded it as a master stroke, and a glance at its effect will show the wisdom of Mr. Dawes's candidacy."[26]

The eighty-one-year-old Tanner refused to go down without a fight. He arrived at the convention against the advice of his physicians and visited county delegations to solicit support for Brown as the convention chair and for Hanecy as the Republican gubernatorial candidate.

When it was announced that Dawes was the candidate for the temporary chair from the Cullom camp, Lorimer threatened to bring a debate on the Puerto Rican tariff to the State Convention floor to sidetrack proceedings. Unlike Cullom in the Senate, Lorimer, a congressman from Cook County, had not been a loyal foot soldier to McKinley in the House. McKinley had issued an executive order following the United States acquisition of Puerto Rico as a protectorate that placed the island's imports and exports on the same tariff schedule as if the goods had been shipped to or from the United States. Some members of Congress, including Lorimer, questioned the constitutionality of the president's action. Unfortunately for Lorimer, the majority of the Illinois convention delegates considered his threat to debate the tariff at the state convention a bluff.[27]

Lorimer's tactics backfired, and Dawes was elected temporary chair of the convention. It was the first time in the history of the state's Republican Party that the convention had not carried out the recommendations of the State Central Committee. Richard Yates Jr., whose father had been Illinois governor during the Civil War years, received the nomination for governor. He was selected after Lorimer, Hanecy, and Tanner abandoned their own candidates and pushed for convention support for Yates. Cullom was easily renominated for the Senate. The convention's final resolutions confirmed the state Republican Party's support for McKinley's policies.

Dawes returned to Washington to face McKinley's paternalistic disappointment in Charley's actions. He acknowledged to McKinley that he should not have dragged the administration into a state political situation, especially since the president had the support of all the state's factions. However, as Dawes so often did when his behavior was called into question, he justified his actions. Dawes told the president he was convinced that if he had not led the charge against the machine, it would remain "invincible." Once again, McKinley was tolerant of Dawes's overzealousness. "While the President wisely never takes an unnecessary risk, no one accepts with greater pleasure one necessary to a proper end, and in the Peoria matter he had evidently decided that the necessity existed."[28]

Dawes arrived in Philadelphia for the Republican National Convention on June 16, three days before its official start. The great unknown was the selection of McKinley's vice presidential candidate. Vice President Garret Hobart had died in office on November 21, 1899, at the age of fifty-five. Because there was then no constitutional provision for replacing a deceased vice president, the field was open.

The prevailing sentiment going into the convention was that U.S. Representative Jonathan Dolliver of Iowa was the leading contender. Secretary of the Navy John D. Long was also making a bid. The governor of New York, Theodore Roosevelt, was considered the dark horse candidate.

Mark Hanna adamantly opposed Roosevelt's selection and threatened not to accept the chairmanship of the Republican National Committee if Roosevelt was nominated. Hanna had good reasons for discomfort with Roosevelt as McKinley's running mate. As a member of the U.S. Civil Service Commission and president of the New York City Police Board, Roosevelt had demonstrated a strong moral streak that fought against corruption and immorality in government. Roosevelt's candidacy was the result of pressure from Thomas C. Platt, New York state's Republican boss, who wanted to get the fiercely independent Roosevelt out of the governor's mansion. Platt pressured Roosevelt to seek the Republican vice presidential nomination, convincing him it would be a stepping-stone to the presidency in 1904.

In response to Hanna's threat, Dawes contacted McKinley's personal secretary, George B. Cortelyou. Charley arranged the call so that when he was talking to Cortelyou, McKinley was also on the line, listening to the conversation. The setup gave McKinley cover. He was not directly involved in the conversation, but he could advise Cortelyou what to say. Hanna received word to keep "hands off" the selection of the vice presidential candidate.[29]

Dawes spent most of the summer solidifying his influence in Illinois politics and building a political base of his own. He began to lay the groundwork for a Senate run in 1902. Charley had successfully maneuvered the state Republican Caucus to select his friend Graeme Stewart as the national committeeman from Illinois. Dawes secured appointments for eighty assistant sergeants-at-arms, and together with the tickets given him by McKinley and Charley's own wrangling for seats, Dawes brought two hundred of his own people to the convention.[30]

Following the convention, he met with officers of the Illinois state Republican Executive Committee and Senator Cullom. In Chicago, he dined with Joy Morton, founder of the Morton Salt Company; Judge R. C. Kerens; and vice presidential nominee Theodore Roosevelt. Dawes worked throughout the summer, commuting between Washington and Chicago by train, to ensure McKinley's victory in Illinois and Cullom's reelection.

McKinley won easily, and the Republicans carried the Illinois state legislature. Since direct election of U.S. senators would not begin until 1913, following the ratification of the Seventeenth Amendment to the Constitution, Cullom's reelection to the Senate was not a certainty. Although many legislators were pledged to Cullom, they did not have to vote for him. Governor-elect Yates and several legislators mentioned to Dawes that they would support him against Cullom for the Senate seat. Dawes declined the offer, saying that it would be a breach of honor. His closing journal entry for December 31, 1900, read: "The selfish politician destroys himself."[31]

On June 23, 1901, Dawes submitted his resignation as comptroller of the currency, effective at an unspecified date in the future. He did not believe he could effectively discharge his duties as comptroller while campaigning for office. McKinley asked Dawes to keep the resignation confidential for the time being. On July 3, Dawes informed the president that his resignation was effective October 1.

Two days after he tendered his resignation, Charley read an article in the *Century Magazine* by an obscure Princeton University professor,

Woodrow Wilson. The article, "When a Man Comes to Himself," traced the spiritual and emotional journey that a man makes through adulthood as he learns to harness his energies and interests and use them for unselfish service. "Christianity gave us, in the fullness of time, the perfect image of right living, the secret of social and of individual well-being; for the two are not separable," Wilson wrote in his conclusion. "The man who receives and verifies that secret in his own living has discovered not only the best and only way to serve the world, but also the one happy way to satisfy himself."[32]

Wilson's conclusion was an echo of Dawes's own thoughts at the end of 1900. He placed a copy of the article inside the leaves of his journal with the hope that his children would one day read both the journal and the article, and thereby gain an understanding of their father.

Dawes was also moved by another one of Wilson's observations: "It is the discovery of what [men] can *not* do, and ought not to attempt, that transforms reformers into statesmen."[33] Dawes had spent his last several years attempting to implement reforms as comptroller. His challenges to Illinois machine politics were another effort to change the status quo. He had begun to understand the limits of his own influence and power, and as he prepared to run for the Senate, Dawes saw that he needed to change his tactics. His brother Rufus had given him a piece of valuable advice: "Think radically but speak conservatively to command influence."[34]

Dawes first mentioned threats to McKinley's life in his journal in August 1899. Prior threats had reached the president, but Dawes reported having received information from Hanna with a high degree of credibility. A group of anarchists based in Paterson, New Jersey, had plans to assassinate the empress of Austria; the king of Italy; the czar of Russia; the Prince of Wales or his mother, Queen Victoria; the president of the United States; and the emperor of Germany. At the time of Hanna's letter, the king of Italy had already been assassinated, and that assassin had confirmed ties to the Paterson group. Hanna asked Dawes to communicate the danger to McKinley. McKinley brushed off the concern.[35]

Dawes was at work at his office at the Treasury Building on September 6, 1901, when Sam Small Jr., a newspaper correspondent, rushed in to report that the president had been shot at the Pan-American

Exposition, a world's fair in Buffalo, New York. Rumors circulated that an attempt would be made on McKinley's life, and he had been urged to add more security. The president brushed off the concerns, expressing doubt that anyone would want to kill him. His assassin, Leon Czolgosz, was a self-described anarchist.

After confirming the news of the attack on McKinley, Dawes purchased train tickets to travel to Buffalo. His and Caro's last visit with the McKinleys had been on August 14. Charley had walked with the president, and then McKinley had taken Caro and Ida McKinley for a drive.[36]

Upon his arrival in Buffalo on September 7, Dawes met Cortelyou and several other of the president's aides, as well as Mark Hanna and the president's sisters. Ida McKinley was there, but she stayed in a room by herself. The initial prognosis for McKinley appeared hopeful, so much so that Dawes returned to Washington on September 11.

On September 13, he was awakened early in the morning with the news that the president had taken a turn for the worse. Once again, Dawes set off for Buffalo, arriving there at eight in the evening. He, along with the physician, the president's sisters and brother, and other friends, sat a vigil with the dying president, who breathed his last early Saturday morning, September 14.

Charley's Chicago friend, newspaperman H. H. Kohlsaat, arrived in Buffalo on Sunday morning. He found Charley in the small library of the Milburn House, where McKinley had been taken following the assassination. Dawes's grief, Kohlsaat said, "could not have been greater had his own father been in the coffin."[37] Kohlsaat had neatly summed up the relationship Dawes had had with the president. McKinley had been a friend, mentor, and surrogate father to Charley, and, as Dawes wrote in his diary, "The chief was gone."[38] He and Caro rode the presidential train that took McKinley's remains home to Canton.

With McKinley's death, Charley became even more anxious to leave Washington. Roosevelt had already named William Barret Ridgely, another Illinois man, to succeed Dawes as comptroller. Dawes worked with Ridgely during the last few weeks of September to help him get acclimated to his position.

The morning of September 30, Charley put Caro and their children on the train for Marietta. He went to his office at the Treasury

Building, where well-wishers who had worked with him over the last three-and-a-half years surrounded him. They included the examiners from the Chestnut Street National Bank, Earle and Cook, as well as his friend Dan Wing and another associate from Lincoln, Gus Hanna. As the day ended and Dawes left the comptroller's office for the final time, he recorded an uncharacteristically somber thought: "I felt a sense of relief rather than of regret. The death of President McKinley, who was so much to me, changed Washington for me, and I am glad to go."[39]

CHAPTER 5

X

The Empire Builder

When Charley first decided to run for the U.S. Senate from Illinois, he fully expected McKinley's backing to assure his victory. McKinley's death did not change Charley's plans, but the absence of presidential support changed the dynamic of his campaign.

With John Tanner's death in May 1901, the Yates-Lorimer machine replaced the Tanner-Lorimer coalition. The other half of the machine, Governor Richard Yates Jr., controlled much of southern Illinois, as Tanner had done. But Charley believed that Yates lacked the level of influence Tanner had possessed. "Advices from Illinois indicate that Yates is aggressively opposing my senatorial aspirations," Dawes recorded in his journal on September 2, 1901. "He seems to be a man of small caliber, however, and to have few qualities of effective leadership."[1]

Meanwhile, Lorimer, the "Blond Boss," had further solidified his hold over Cook County. Chicago Congressman Joseph G. Cannon, who would serve as Speaker of the House from 1903 to 1911, joined forces with Lorimer to control delegates to the State Convention. The two threw their support behind eight-term Congressman Albert J. Hopkins for the Senate seat. Charley expected Theodore Roosevelt to visit Illinois on his behalf. Confident of victory, Dawes observed: "The fight will be clean-cut and either Lorimer or I must be counted out when it is over. Unless my opponents buy it [the election], I think I will certainly win."[2]

Like McKinley, Roosevelt determined that it was foolhardy to take sides in internal state squabbles. He also had another reason to avoid any show of favoritism in the Illinois senatorial race. TR lacked a national political base of his own, and he needed to build one across all factions of the Republican Party to secure the presidential nomination in his own right in 1904. He could not afford to alienate a machine as powerful as Yates and Lorimer's.

Undaunted, Dawes actively campaigned in search of delegates. He spent entire days talking with people in towns throughout Illinois. He enjoyed life on the campaign trail. Dawes had a campaigner's natural gift for pressing the flesh, and the daily rounds of meetings energized him. But the political lines were clearly drawn.

The Republican State Convention endorsed Hopkins when it met on May 8. Dawes graciously conceded: "Recognizing that a convention of 1,500 delegates must be considered as fairly representative of the will of a majority of the party, with feelings of deepest gratitude to the friends who have so loyally supported me, and with only the kindest feelings toward my opponents, I hereby announce my withdrawal as a candidate for the United States Senate."[3] Privately, he placed much of the blame for his failure on Roosevelt. "President Roosevelt, while endeavoring to be impartial, created the contrary impression and greatly injured me," he observed in his diary.[4]

Charley claimed to be relieved to be out of politics, but he never truly quit. He enjoyed the game, and, with his defeat, Dawes changed roles and became a behind-the-scenes kingmaker. He proved himself an able fund-raiser, and candidates frequently sought his financial support and his business acumen. Charley's role as a Republican power broker made him a natural go-to person for individuals seeking national committee assignments and judgeships, and he happily interceded on behalf of friends and colleagues to secure positions for them. Over time, Charley developed a reputation as a strong anti-machine Republican, a man of serious business, and one who strived to remain above reproach.

In 1904, Dawes set aside his strong distaste for Roosevelt and worked for the president's election. Marcus Hanna shared Charley's views on TR, and a year before the election, Hanna talked with Dawes about challenging Roosevelt's nomination on the floor of the National Convention. Reprising the role he had played when TR had been selected vice president at the 1900 Republican convention, Dawes advised Hanna that such a move would embarrass Roosevelt and help the Democratic ticket. Dawes's recommendation prevailed.[5] When Hanna died unexpectedly on February 15, 1904, Roosevelt had an unencumbered path to the Republican presidential nomination.

Charley's work to break the power of the Yates-Lorimer machine began to bear fruit. The Republican State Convention nominated his good friend Lawrence Sherman as lieutenant governor and Sherman's political ally Charles Deneen for governor. Their nominations were more than just a defeat for the Blond Boss and his supporters. The Deneen-Sherman ticket benefited state civil service employees. Tanner and Yates had required them to pay an assessment to the Republican Party in exchange for keeping their jobs. The requirement was abolished with the machine's defeat. "And thus endeth for the present a fight in which for a time, I strenuously engaged," Dawes noted as comment to the Deneen-Sherman triumph.[6]

Charley had two plans in mind when he left his comptroller's post in 1901. Plan A was to run for the Senate. Plan B was to start a bank. A week after his political fate was decided in May 1902, Charley formed the Central Trust Company of Illinois, a state-chartered bank. His incorporators were part of the "Who's Who" of the Chicago business community: Graeme Stewart, a prominent businessman and community leader; Charles Deering, founder of the International Harvester Company; A. J. Earling, president of the Chicago, Milwaukee, and St. Paul Railway; attorney Max Pam, who would serve as general counsel for the bank; B. A. Eckhart, whose B. A. Eckhart Milling Company would eventually become the Archer Daniels Midland Company; and Dawes's friend and political ally Frank O. Lowden.[7]

Dawes's natural optimism overrode any sense of defeat in the Senate race. He wrote in his journal:

> I turn again to active business life, grateful for the fortune which took me into politics and now takes me out. All we can do is to do our best, and with gratitude to Providence accept that which happens was the wisest for us. All that has heretofore happened to me has been for the best—and I know that defeat must be now

for the best. I turn to business with the keen joy of a man entering from a political atmosphere one where promises are redeemed, and faith is kept.[8]

Of all of the multiple enterprises and positions that Charles Dawes held throughout his life, banking was his true calling. At its core, banking is about people—reading them, understanding their motivations, and assessing their ability to manage money. Dawes had a gift for explaining finances to the least educated person, and he had a heart for making banking services available to people of all economic strata. Dawes's intention was to make Central Trust "a big bank for small people financially as well as for the larger ones. . . . A depositor line made up of a multitude of small accounts is more stable and valuable than one made up of a few large accounts."[9]

Dawes quickly realized his dream. Between its impressive board of directors and Charley's growing stature in the community, Central Trust attracted individual savers, larger depositors, and businesses. Deposits topped $8 million before the bank was fully three years old. Its success reflected Dawes's business and political connections, his conservative business philosophy, and the high level of customer service the bank provided regardless of the size of the depositor. *Banker's Magazine* observed: "The Central is destined, Chicago bankers believe, to become a bank of the very first rank in both size and influence at this important center."[10]

Dawes bolstered his position in both the Chicago and the national business community through numerous speeches and articles that he wrote for the *Saturday Evening Post* and the *North American Review*. His opinions served as a counterpoint to the muckraking reporting by reform-minded writers such as Ida Tarbell and Lincoln Steffens, whose exposés of the Standard Oil Company and urban corruption eventually captured President Roosevelt's attention and inspired an anticorporate movement.

Dawes was unabashedly pro-business. He challenged the reformers' ideas in an article in the January 28, 1905, issue of the *Saturday Evening Post*. "The world gives quick applause to the reckless critic," he observed. "The long, hard road to general public respect may commence in criticism, but it must be honest criticism designed to destroy evils, not simply individuals, except as necessarily involved in the destruction of evils; and then this road must lead to constructive efforts." He challenged the critics' view of corporations and the call for reform of the Sherman Antitrust Act that would amend how corporate stock is valued. The critique, argued Dawes, comes "from the refusal . . . to consider what portion of present abuses are due to the business device called a corporation . . . and what are due to perverted human nature and therefore will exist as long as human nature does—corporations or no corporations."[11]

Dawes's former friend and adversary William Jennings Bryan often commented on Dawes's speeches in his newspaper, *The Commoner*, which was published in Lincoln and read nationwide among the Populists. The movement saw Bryan as its standard-bearer, and Tarbell and Steffens championed its causes. Commenting on a speech that Dawes made in November 1905 to the Nebraska Bankers Association, Bryan noted that Dawes spoke against the competitive, or antitrust, system and that he referred to trusts as the "cooperative system." Dawes used the example of three boys fighting for the same apple in a tree. One boy would emerge as the victor under the competitive system, but all would get a share under the cooperative system. "Mr. Dawes might have carried his figure to its conclusion," Bryan commented, "by explaining that while under this 'cooperative system' the three boys would divide the apple, the owner of the orchard would be entirely deprived of the fruits of his toil."[12]

Dawes's pro-business stance, when viewed through the lens of Populism, suggests that he was more aligned with eastern interests. That was not how he saw himself. Not until the start of World War I did he build friendly relationships with eastern banks. He did not forget the humiliation he had suffered when he sought loans from them during the Panic of 1896. Dawes's support of the gold standard, viewed by the Populists as a tool that the large eastern banks would use to control the smaller midwestern and western banks, came from his belief that a standard would help prevent severe depressions, not because he saw it as a way for banks to control the money supply.

As comptroller, Dawes had issued a ruling that prevented the establishment of branch banks in a city, a move sought by the larger, eastern banks. Even after he founded Central Trust, Dawes continued to oppose the establishment of branches. He argued that branch banking would remove decision-making from local lenders and ultimately lead to a consolidation of banks, thereby reducing competition and concentrating banking power in just a handful of national banks. Dawes never saw a contradiction between his support for corporate trusts and his opposition to branch banks.

Dawes experienced the divide between eastern and western banking interests firsthand during the Panic of 1907. During the height of the panic, he observed currency from the subtreasury building in Chicago being loaded onto trucks for shipment to New York. He contacted a few of his fellow Chicago bankers to let them know what he had seen. He learned that James B. Forgan, president of First National Bank of Chicago, had requested $1 million from the U.S. Treasury the previous day and had his request denied.

The lack of cash was felt keenly in Chicago. Payment to the railroads for mail transportation was due, and banks in southern Illinois had too little cash on hand for companies to make their payrolls. The money needed to stay in the Midwest.

Dawes called his friend Secretary of the Treasury George B. Cortelyou to complain. Cortelyou's initial response was that New York's needs were direr, but Charley's call made an impact. Within a few days of their conversation, Cortelyou returned $3 million in cash to Chicago. The funds were insufficient to meet all the cash needs of the banks in Illinois, but they were enough to forestall a widespread panic.[13]

The Panic of 1907 triggered another round of congressional hearings on banking reform. As had occurred in 1893, the nation's gold reserves had declined, depositors lined up to withdraw their money, and the gross national product decreased. Senator Nelson Aldrich, who chaired the Senate Committee on Finance, sponsored legislation in 1908 that included a call for the issuance of emergency currency, among other provisions, and that included the insurance tax that Dawes had once advocated but now opposed. Dawes traveled to Washington to testify in support of the emergency currency portion of the bill. "If remedial legislation is not had at this time," he told the committee, "this country will go through another panic unprotected, and we will be face to face with what we have been through in the past."[14] To Dawes's satisfaction, the Aldrich-Vreeland Act became law in May 1908, without deposit insurance, but with provisions to issue emergency currency.

Aldrich-Vreeland established a study group called the National Monetary Commission, chaired by Aldrich, whose recommendations ultimately led to the Federal Reserve System. The commission's original suggestion—a centralized bank to help control the nation's money supply—met with overwhelmingly negative public reaction amid fears that the end result would be nationalization of the banks. The bill died in Congress in 1912.

The Republicans lost the presidency and control of Congress in the 1912 election. The new Congress once again picked up the Monetary Commission's recommendations. Carter Glass, a Virginia Democrat, now chaired the Banking and Currency Committee. Glass crafted legislation that called for a system of regional banks that reflected the differences across the United States. President Woodrow Wilson sought an oversight board to supervise the banks. Following vigorous debate in both the House and Senate, the final legislation established between eight and twelve regional banks; a Federal Reserve Board made up of presidential appointees and selected government officials, including the comptroller of the currency; and a Board of Governors composed of bankers.[15]

The fundamental purpose of the Federal Reserve—to control the nation's money supply and prevent bank panics—resembled the recommendations Dawes had outlined in his 1894 book on the U.S. banking system. When Wilson signed the Federal Reserve Act on December 23, 1913, Dawes, with approval from his shareholders, became the first state-chartered bank in the nation to join the newly established system. He defended the Federal Reserve, noting that it would put his state-chartered bank on a more even par with national banks, improve Central Trust's exchange facilities, and provide the bank with closer supervision and examination.[16] The Federal Reserve System did not eliminate bank runs or economic depressions, as Dawes would discover firsthand in 1932, but its creation was a crucial step in standardizing banking practices nationwide.

On December 18, 1905, the Illinois newspapers announced the failure of three Chicago banks, the Chicago National Bank, the Home Savings Bank, and the Equitable Trust Company. Reported losses ran to $26 million. Dawes's friend and banker John R. Walsh controlled all three institutions.[17]

Dawes and Walsh's relationship had grown since the latter first lent money to help Dawes keep the American Exchange National Bank in Lincoln afloat and to enable Charley to buy the Lincoln Packing Company. The two had been partners in several business deals, including, together with Samuel Insull, the purchase of gas and electric companies that served the communities of Harvey, Blue Island, and Chicago Heights in southern Cook County.[18]

Walsh's bad temper did not endear him to the majority of the Chicago banking community, and rumors had circulated for years that he made risky investments that other bankers avoided. That is likely one reason that he assisted Dawes during the Lincoln years when others would not. Now, it was discovered that Walsh's investments were not only risky but also unethical.

The bankers who reviewed Walsh's financial condition included Dawes; his predecessor as comptroller, James Eckels; and Edward Lacey, another former comptroller. James B. Forgan and John J. Mitchell, president of Illinois Trust and Savings Bank, were also named to the committee. William Barret Ridgely, Dawes's successor and still the current comptroller, led the review. The men uncovered a trail of loans Walsh had made to his own enterprises and his directors, and the forged notes and misinformation he used to hide the true condition of his institutions from the national bank examiners.[19]

Ridgely determined that the best way to avoid a bank panic in Chicago was to have several other national banks guarantee the failed banks' deposits—a move not wholly supported by the other members of the review committee. Several members wanted to make an example of Walsh to deter other banks from similar practices. Dawes demanded that Walsh and his directors give up their private assets, valued at $4.6 million, as guarantees against their bond with the clearinghouse. These assets included the Chicago Southern and Indiana Southern Railways. Forgan supported Dawes's demand and withheld his support for Ridgely's proposal until the committee concurred. In the end, the most important consideration was to avoid a bank panic, and the committee assented to Ridgely's proposal and Dawes's requirement.[20]

On March 2, 1906, Walsh was arrested for making false statements to the bank examiners. He did not come to trial until November 18, 1907, and the trial dragged on until March 13, 1908—more than two years following Walsh's arrest. The sensational case included an assassination attempt on Walsh's attorney and the evidence of an assistant comptroller who testified on behalf of the defense that banks frequently broke the rules. Walsh was convicted and sentenced to five years in prison.[21]

Dawes was assigned as a receiver for the railroad properties, and he worked throughout 1906 and 1907 on their reorganization so that they could be sold and a cash distribution made to the depositors of Walsh's banks. It was a measure of Dawes's loyalty to his friend that he undertook the work while many others in the Chicago business community had turned their backs. In August 1907, Walsh wrote to Charley: "This is written to thank you again for the help you have given me in getting my affairs into shape—your kindness will not be forgotten by me while I live and after I am gone there will be left some fellows who will remember it. Meantime one of these days I hope to have an opportunity to do something for you."[22]

Walsh would never have that chance. He died from a heart attack nine days after he had been released on parole. Walsh had served twenty-one months of his sentence at the United States Penitentiary at Leavenworth, Kansas.

When one reads Charles Dawes's journals and letters, one is immediately struck by how immersed Dawes was in a number of business ventures apart from his banking responsibilities. His son Dana remembers his father as always working on a column of figures. Even during his years in Europe as purchasing agent for the American Expeditionary Forces, when Charley spent his days negotiating for food, fuel, and transportation for the troops, he took the time to correspond with his brothers about the conditions of their mutual enterprises.

Charley's portfolio of manufactured gas facilities had grown significantly since his initial purchases in 1894 and 1895. Some of the businesses he acquired had added electric service under his ownership. The group of companies was rapidly turning into a small conglomerate. By the end of 1902, the brothers owned a string of utilities that were housed under a holding company called Union Gas and Electric Company. These utilities included the West Hammond (Indiana) Gas and Electric Company, which gave them control of the franchises serving

East Chicago, Whiting, and Indiana Harbor. The brothers also owned companies in Shreveport, Louisiana, and East St. Louis, Illinois. The feather in their cap was the addition of Seattle Gas and Electric Light Company in Washington state in early June 1904—a deal Charley personally negotiated. The brothers purchased the utility for $1.7 million and arranged a bond issue to finance the deal. Rufus became president of the company.[23]

Charley was almost never named an officer (his brothers generally filled the officers' roles), but he invariably held the position of majority shareholder. As majority shareholder, Charley stood either to gain the greatest amount of income or to suffer the largest loss. However, as time went on, and the businesses proved their value, Charley sold off blocks of his shares to close and trusted friends. The early beneficiaries of Charley's generosity and financial acumen included three men who had been with Charley since the Lincoln days: S. H. Burnham, Charles A. Hanna, and R. I. Speer; and his friends and political colleagues Lawrence Y. Sherman, George B. Cortelyou, and Shelby Cullom.[24]

Oil proved the next logical step in the family's business ventures. Charley made his first venture into the oil world with his cousin Charles H. (C. H.) Bosworth in 1896. Bosworth expressed an interest in a wildcat oil venture, and he wanted to manage the enterprise. He and Charley each contributed $1,500. They had other unidentified investors who contributed lesser amounts. The venture must have been successful enough to encourage Charley to build a portfolio of oil interests.[25]

By 1901, oil was clearly the up and coming industry for anyone who had the money and was willing to take the risk. Spurred by the discovery of the Spindletop geyser in Texas, over 1,500 oil companies were chartered nationwide in that year alone.[26]

The Hastings Oil Company was one of those companies. Hastings Oil grew out of a partnership between Charley's brother Henry and W. T. Hastings, a Marietta businessman. After trying to keep his late father's business solvent for two years, Henry decided to strike out on his own. When Henry initially consulted Charley about the deal, Henry was frank. "Producing properties, like everything else in the oil business, are more or less uncertain investments, but so far as the safety of the investment is concerned, they are not to be classed by any means with wild catting."[27]

Charley did not commit immediately, but Henry persisted. "Oil is going down now and it is likely that we will have some good opportunities to buy from people who are alarmed at the turn of the market," Henry wrote his brother in a follow-up letter. "If you do not want to do this I would not like to urge you as I would regret it if our venture should not be successful."[28]

Charley finally agreed, and the papers were filed with the West Virginia Secretary of State on August 23, 1901, with $500 paid in capital. W. T. Hastings; Henry and Beman Dawes; their sister Betsey's husband, Harry Hoyt; and another associate, M. Burlingame, also of Marietta, were the incorporators.[29] The investors purchased a West Virginia company that had an annual production of thirty thousand barrels.

Serendipity brought another outstanding oil investment opportunity to Charley's attention. The Caddo Oil Fields, near Shreveport, Louisiana, struck oil in 1905. Charley and Rufus owned the Shreveport utility company, Southwestern Gas and Electric Company, giving them advance information about the field and its potential. Charley became a trustee in his own name of two oil wells, and he had an interest in three other wells as co-owner of the Broussard Oil Company, where he shared joint ownership with Samuel M. Felton, president of the Chicago Great Western Railway; Albert J. (A. J.) Earling; and Marshall M. (M. M.) Kirkman. Beman was Broussard's president.[30]

By 1907, it was clear that the brothers; their cousins and business partners Will Dawes, Knowlton Ames, and C. H. Bosworth; and their uncle W. W. Mills needed to restructure their holdings. They formed Dawes Brothers, Inc. (DBI), a privately held corporation that housed the stocks and other holding companies for the family businesses. The original holdings of Dawes Brothers included $300,000 worth of stock in Central Trust Company of Illinois; $177,000 worth of shares in Union Gas & Electric Company; $110,000 worth of stock in a syndicate of gas companies; and $13,000 in cash, for a total of $400,000 in cash and assets.[31] That amount is equivalent to $9.8 million in 2015 dollars.[32]

Rufus, Beman, and Henry were officers. Charley and W. W. Mills were members of the board. DBI benefited from the complementary strengths each man brought to the enterprise, but Charley always thought of it as *his* company.

Beman's aggressiveness at finding deals contributed significantly to the net worth of DBI. Much as Charley had done when he first started to build his empire, Beman actively sought businesses that were undervalued but showed promise to turn a profit and remain money makers. "As a schemer he is second only to yourself," Rufus had once written Charley about their younger brother.[33]

Beman had proved his ability as an effective executive when he kept a Lincoln coal company afloat during the 1893 depression, a business venture for which Charley had arranged the financing. In 1896, Beman moved from Lincoln to Newark, Ohio, where he became the president of the Newark Gas Light Company. Charley, who had set up the financial structure, was vice president. Newark would become Beman's base of operations for the remainder of his life.

Rufus was not as aggressive as either Beman or Charley in identifying deals, but he had an excellent understanding of financial relationships and served as an effective troubleshooter when problems arose at one of DBI's companies. Henry demonstrated much of the same business acumen as Charley, and, over time, Charley turned to his youngest brother as his own financial adviser and account manager. The oldest and the youngest of the Dawes brothers had a closeness borne of mutual respect and appreciation.

Charley's days of borrowing from one lender to pay off another were gone. His philosophy was that a bank president should not depend upon borrowed money for his personal businesses, a philosophy underscored by the Walsh debacle that he had helped to untangle. As DBI's financier, Charley required stock or other collateral in exchange for any loans he arranged for his brothers. He expected payment to be made on time or a letter of explanation for the delay and an anticipated payment date. Among the four, the brothers treated small amounts of money, even as little as one or two dollars, with the same importance as they did hundreds of thousands of dollars. Regardless of the amount of the check, each brother asked for a receipt.

By 1914, the brothers had truly struck oil. On April 9, 1914, Beman, with Charley's connections in the financial community providing access to loan funds and capital, reorganized the Columbus Oil and Fuel Company and several other oil company holdings into the Ohio Cities Gas Company. Charley was the largest personal shareholder in the newly formed corporation, and he also subscribed to a large block of stock, which he sold to the growing list of nonfamily shareholders in Dawes Brothers, Inc.

Ohio Cities was an umbrella corporation for seven different companies. It controlled the entire gas distributing business in Columbus and Springfield, Ohio, with a base of 64,864 customers. Net earnings for the fiscal year ending March 31, 1915, were over $1 million, with a reported net profit of $250,834.[34]

Meanwhile, the Progressives' influence on municipal government affected the management and potential profitability of Seattle Gas and Electric Light, which came under intense scrutiny. The city conducted hearings to determine whether the utility should be converted to municipal ownership. Rufus, who was Seattle Gas and Electric Light's president, wrote Charley that "the public sentiment [for municipal ownership] has been noticeable here as well as in other parts of the country." The Washington State Public Utilities Commission carefully investigated the company and commended Seattle Gas and Electric Light's service "to the highest degree," Rufus wrote, which "endorses our engineering judgment, and speaks in flattering terms of the abilities of our manager." At the time of the hearings, the city of Seattle was facing a fiscal crisis—a situation that worked in favor of keeping utility ownership private. Nevertheless, as gas and electric service became increasingly commonplace in homes at all income levels, there was a growing sense that the utilities should not pay dividends to shareholders or make what were perceived as excessive profits.[35] As public sentiment about power utilities changed, the brothers began to reduce their investments in the industry.

In 1915, Charley made an unusual investment in the restaurant chain Horn & Hardart (H & H). It had begun in Philadelphia in 1902 and expanded to Manhattan in 1912. H & H introduced the idea of fast food to the United States with its coin-operated machines set in cafeteria-style restaurants called "automats." Over time, H & H became the largest restaurant chain in the United States and reportedly served as many as 800,000 people daily.[36]

George P. Earle, the examiner who had handled the Chestnut Street National Bank failure, introduced Charley to the restaurant's owners. Dawes's investment in H & H reflected his innovative thinking when it came to business. By 1915, H & H was growing steadily, although, as one of its board members noted in a letter to Dawes: "If we could only get these gentlemen to move faster and develop their business by opening new places, we could get an enormous return on our stock." But the shareholders were already experiencing unprecedented returns for any business, and most especially a restaurant chain. The company regularly showed a 50 percent gain in sales and profits.[37]

In the summer of 1909, Charley and Caro purchased a large château-style home at 225 Greenwood Street, at the corner of Greenwood and Sheridan Road, in Evanston. The home gave them a magnificent view of Lake Michigan.

The Greenwood Street home had been built for Robert and Virginia Sheppard, leaders of Northwestern University, who had commissioned construction of the house in 1893. The New York–based firm Henry Edwards-Ficken designed it, one of only a half dozen houses in the city designed by architects based outside of Chicago. Other eastern architects who had designed Evanston homes included the prestigious H. H. Richardson of Boston, and Richard Morris Hunt and McKim, Mead, and White, both New York firms.

The new Dawes home featured an unusual combination of Romanesque and Gothic styles, with rounded towers at the ends of the house and a Gothic-style hallway, accented with arches and detailed woodworking, traversing the length of the ground floor.[38] For a house with its grandeur and size, it had a sense of coziness still evident today.

Caro furnished the home with comfortable furniture, Tiffany lamps, and Oriental rugs. She maintained a greenhouse, which gave her great pleasure. Charley spent much of his free time in the library, which would eventually amass some 3,500 volumes. The Daweses lived in the Greenwood Street home for the rest of their lives, and the Dawes House, as it is now known, witnessed the triumphs and tragedies that the family experienced over the coming decades.

CHAPTER 6

X

Banker and Philanthropist

The Republican presidential nominee in 1908 was William Howard Taft, and Dawes readily supported his fellow Ohioan. The two men shared a similar political outlook. They viewed "good government" as one in which honest men—defined as men who did not take bribes—held office and where appointees fulfilled their duties in a businesslike and efficient manner. They favored limited government and supported the growth of businesses. The two men also shared a love of music. Taft's wife, Helen Herron "Nellie" Taft, had studied music in college, and, like Charley, she was a strong supporter of the musical arts.

The Taft men urged Charley to become their campaign treasurer, but he declined the position, citing his responsibilities to his bank. Nevertheless, after considerable pressure from the Taft organization, Dawes consented to serve as treasurer of the National Republican Congressional Committee. He traveled extensively around the country to raise money for various candidates. The Republicans kept their majorities in both houses of Congress. Charley used the political capital he had accumulated and his network of contacts in Congress to influence votes on legislation that affected his bank and his businesses and to secure appointments for various friends.

The Republicans had won in Illinois, and when the state legislature met on January 20, 1909, to formally choose their senator, it was a foregone conclusion that they would reelect Albert J. Hopkins. Hopkins had been the Yates-Lorimer candidate selected over Charley in the

1902 Senate race. To everyone's surprise, the legislature deadlocked, and no candidate received a majority. Support for Hopkins declined with each subsequent ballot. The legislature met over a total of 125 days, from January 20 to May 26, before it finally selected Congressman William Lorimer as Illinois's next senator. His name surfaced as a possible compromise candidate after he met with Governor Deneen in mid-May. Lorimer returned to Washington on June 8, 1909, to await being sworn in as senator.

On April 30, 1910, the *Chicago Tribune* published a story alleging that Lorimer's campaign manager, Lee O. Brown, had bribed an Illinois state legislator to vote for Lorimer. Three other legislators came forward with similar stories. Lorimer asked the U.S. Senate to look into the charges. The investigation was assigned to the Senate Committee on Privileges and Elections.

The committee's Republican majority found no evidence of bribery. Indiana Senator Albert Beveridge, a member of the committee who had become aligned with the Progressive wing of the Republican Party, refused to support the findings. Beveridge argued that the legislators accused of taking the bribes had been found to have "unusual sums of money in bills of large denominations" right after they were approached to vote for Lorimer. Beveridge discounted Lorimer's claims of ignorance of the bribes, noting that Lorimer had carefully managed his congressional campaign.[1]

The full Senate opened debate on the committee's report on January 18, 1911. After six weeks of contentious arguments, the final vote, taken on March 1, 1911, was 40 yeas and 46 nays to void Lorimer's election.[2] The vote should have ended the matter, but it did not.

Albert Beveridge's Senate term ended on March 3, 1911, and Senator Robert La Follette, a Wisconsin Republican and leader of the Progressive wing, urged the Senate to reopen the investigation. La Follette based his request on new reports in the Chicago newspapers, which asserted that $100,000 had been spent on bribes to secure Lorimer's election to the Senate. The Illinois State Senate buttressed La Follette's position with a report tying Lorimer and high-ranking Illinois executives to campaign corruption.[3]

The Lorimer hearings became a national cause célèbre. His exposure took on the characteristics of a crusade among the Republicans in the

Progressive camp. The Senate Committee on Privileges and Elections reopened the investigation in the summer of 1911. Over a year's time, the members heard 180 witnesses and compiled eight volumes of testimony. The majority report concluded that there was no support for the allegation that Lorimer was directly linked to the wheeling and dealing that had bribed legislators for their votes. The minority report concluded that there was substantial new evidence to prove that Lorimer had been directly involved. Lorimer maintained he was innocent. The Senate voted on July 13, 1912, and voided his election.[4]

The Lorimer trial mirrored the split within the national Republican Party. Progressives had lost patience with President Taft's ideas of good government and his support of big business. They were anxious for deeper and more far-reaching reforms, including direct election of senators; more direct access to policy making through referendum and initiative, which would allow citizens to place issues on the ballot; and a reining in of what they saw as unbridled capitalism. Roosevelt, who was unhappy with Taft, agreed to run as the presidential candidate on the Progressive, or Bull Moose, ticket. Beveridge helped to organize TR's campaign.

The split among the Republicans in 1912 handed the White House and both houses of Congress to the Democrats. Charley had managed the senatorial campaign of his friend Lawrence Y. Sherman. Sherman had been philosophical about his chances when he first entered the race, but he had become embittered during the campaign and did not expect to be chosen by the legislators. "It seems to be my last fight," Sherman wrote Dawes in January 1913, as the state legislature prepared to choose two senators—one to replace Cullom, and the other to replace Lorimer. "So many faithful friends have borne my burdens, I want them to win next time with a new man."[5] In the last Senate election to be decided by state legislators, Sherman was surprised to be chosen to fill the unexpired portion of Lorimer's term. Democrat J. Hamilton Lewis took over Shelby Cullom's seat.

Lorimer returned to Chicago in the summer of 1912, where his supporters heralded him as a victim of "trial by press." He took up day-to-day management of the La Salle Street National Bank and the La Salle Street Trust Company, which he had founded in May 1910. Lorimer served as the bank president, and his son, William Lorimer Jr., was the bank's secretary. Charles B. Munday, owner of a milling company and an officer in a network of banks throughout Illinois, was vice president. Munday had a reputation of questionable integrity in the Chicago banking community and would spend much of his career in prison, where he served time for financially related crimes, including conspiracy to commit fraud and embezzlement.

In 1911, Lorimer asked Charley to clear—that is, to settle pending transactions—for the La Salle banks through the Chicago clearinghouse. Lorimer furnished Dawes with a report attesting to the banks' solvency, but Dawes declined to clear for them. The political attacks on Lorimer, Dawes explained, extended to attacks on the banks. At some point, Dawes expected that the La Salle banks would need to borrow money to meet an emergency, and he was unwilling to be in a position where he would be asked to furnish those funds. Dawes offered to accompany Lorimer to meet with Forgan, head of the Chicago clearinghouse. However, Lorimer had already met with Forgan, who apparently had more detailed inside information on the La Salle banks' condition than what was in the auditor's report and had advised Lorimer to close the banks. Dawes, after hearing Forgan's recommendation, agreed. At the least, Dawes advised Lorimer, he needed to end his association with Munday. Lorimer promised to do so.

Lorimer did not liquidate, and Munday remained an officer of the La Salle banks. Upon his expulsion from the Senate, Lorimer reorganized the La Salle Street National Bank and the La Salle Street Trust Company into the La Salle Street Trust and Savings Bank, a state-chartered bank with a reported capitalization of $1 million and a $250,000 surplus.[6] To meet the cash-on-hand requirements of the state bank examiner, Lorimer asked Dawes if he would provide the $1.25 million in cash, backed by a cashier's check drawn on the Central Trust Company. Dawes agreed. The money was placed in La Salle Street Trust and Savings Bank's vault long enough to be counted by the examiner. After the examiner declared the bank solvent and fit to be granted a charter, the cash was returned to Central Trust's vault.[7]

Lorimer's request came six weeks after tragedy struck the Dawes family. Rufus Fearing Dawes died suddenly on September 5, 1912, while vacationing at Lake Geneva, Wisconsin. He had been with friends on a raft in the middle of the lake and was swimming to shore when he suddenly cried out and sank from view.[8]

Two hours elapsed before Charley and Caro heard of the drowning. They immediately secured a train and rushed to the scene. Dawes brought with him a Pulmotor—a new invention that forced air into the lungs of a drowned or asphyxiated person. In the meantime, doctors had worked on young Rufus without resuscitating him.[9]

The story made page one of the *Chicago Daily Tribune*. But, as Dawes recorded in his journal, the papers "could not tell of our unspeakable anguish of soul as we came to our splendid boy lying prostrate upon the bank of the lake, surrounded by the men who were still working to revive him."[10]

Rufus Fearing Dawes was "the pride and hope of his [father's] life"—the primary reason Dawes had faithfully kept a journal for nearly ten years and the motivation for many of his business endeavors. The young man had shown every indication that he had the same drive and determination as his father; so much so, that Dawes insisted on telling everyone what a hard worker his son was, and that the two weeks that he was in Wisconsin were his only two weeks of vacation for the year.[11]

The doctors ruled that the young man suffered heart failure as he was swimming. There is every reason to believe that he had a damaged heart. In February 1906, he had been quarantined with diphtheria.[12] Rufus also contracted typhoid fever in 1908 while working with an engineering corps in South Dakota.[13] A letter from Dawes's friend Lawrence Sherman mentions Rufus being seriously ill. "Your letter came this morning," Sherman wrote on October 4, 1909. "I am so glad you have been spared the affliction that came so near you. I knew Rufus was ill. I did not write or call you up when in Chicago but I made inquiries about how Rufus was. . . . at times, I was afraid to inquire. . . . I know how much better and brighter the world is when the fear of bereavement is removed."[14] Both diphtheria and untreated typhoid fever can cause heart damage.

A year and a half after his son's death, Dawes shared the young man's personal journal with some of his closest friends. Sherman, who was well acquainted with grief, wrote Charley a heartfelt and encouraging letter. The senator had been widowed twice; his second wife had died after only two years of marriage and left Sherman with an infant daughter. In his note to Dawes, Sherman wrote:

I believe in a continuance of life hereafter in some form, I cannot believe death ends all for a human being. . . . Some seem destined to a few years but are given early insight and deep understanding beyond their years. Rufus Fearing was one of those. . . . So, I like to think such as our loved departed ones are by an all wise God's purpose still watching us and continuing their way as part of the eternal plan. Their years with us were short, but they survive in a fitter place.[15]

The loss of a child, at any age, can lead to estrangement between a married couple, and sometimes a divorce. It is a testimony to the innate character of both Charley and Caro, and to the strength of their devotion to each other, that they dealt with their pain creatively and philanthropically. They adopted a son, Dana McCutcheon Dawes, in December 1912. He was named for Caro's family and Charley's close friend John T. McCutcheon, a *Chicago Tribune* political cartoonist. Helen Dawes, Rufus's wife, wrote of the family Christmas celebration that year: "We went before dinner to Charley's where we saw the beautiful baby sitting up in his carriage and looking rosy and well."[16] Two years later, on Thanksgiving Day, 1914, Helen wrote about another new addition to the Charles and Caro Dawes household—baby Virginia, possibly Helen's namesake, because Helen's middle name was Virginia.[17]

In honor of his son, Charley, with his brother Henry, founded the Rufus Fearing Dawes Memorial Hotel. Dawes announced that he and Rufus Fearing had been working on the hotel project. It was an outgrowth of Rufus Fearing Dawes's work at the Young Men's Christian Association (YMCA) in New York City's Bowery district, where he became interested in providing accommodations for homeless men. It was also an extension of Charley Dawes's compassion for the homeless.

Charley had long offered assistance to people whom he knew to be in need, and one of his first efforts on behalf of the homeless came during a 1903 trip to New York when he noticed men sleeping on park benches in the rain as he returned to his hotel. Unable to shake the scene from his mind even after he retired to his room at the Waldorf, Charley dressed, went back downstairs, and secured the assistance of a police officer. By the time the two returned to the park, Dawes found about thirty men there. He arranged for meals and lodging for them for the night.[18] The experience stuck with him. In Chicago he routinely emptied his pockets of loose change (to the point that, when he was older, Caro made him empty his pockets before he left home because she was afraid he might be harmed by someone he had stopped to help). He often paid for lodgings for homeless men he encountered on the streets.

The Rufus Fearing Dawes Hotel stood at the corner of Madison and Peoria Streets in Chicago. Constructed at an estimated cost of $100,000, the hotel was designed to accommodate three hundred men and provide emergency shelter for another two hundred. A single room could be rented for ten cents a night. Beds in a shared room cost five cents a night, and meals ran from two to five cents each.[19]

The hotel opened on January 1, 1914, and was filled to capacity in an hour. The *Tribune* called it a "Flop De Luxe"—that is, a fine cheap lodging. Henry assuaged fears that the hotel would encourage laziness. He announced plans to establish a free labor bureau by asking local businesses to notify him when they needed workers. "We will not provide permanent lodgings to any man," Henry explained. "The professional idler will not be welcome."[20]

"May the New Year that you have made more tolerable for three hundred unemployed men be full of happiness for you," Sherman wrote upon the hotel's opening. "Full of the very best sort of happiness, that won by doing good to others."[21]

Charley and Henry eventually opened another Rufus Dawes Hotel in Boston in 1916, and in 1917, they established a hotel for women in Chicago that they named for their mother, the Mary Gates Dawes Hotel. The Dawes Hotel Corporation, led by Charley and Henry, operated the facilities until 1939, when the Chicago hotels were leased to the Chicago Christian Industrial League, a nonprofit social service agency that helps the homeless.[22] The balance sheets reveal that the hotels frequently operated at a loss, and the brothers made up the difference out of their personal funds. The hotels were the most visible of Charley's many and diverse philanthropic activities.

Charley supported Caro in her work with abandoned children, which she began when she moved to Evanston in 1895. Caro was one of the founders of the Illinois Children's Home and Aid Society, an organization that helped find homes for abandoned children. She served as second vice president in 1907 and then assistant treasurer from 1909 to 1929.[23] Caro frequently brought home babies and hired a trained nurse to help sickly infants regain their health so they could be adopted. She became famous for her "orphan parties," held on the grounds of the Daweses' Greenwood Street home, where Caro served cake and ice cream and used her best silver. Funding for her work came from the income she received from the Dawes Business Block Company. Charley could not bring himself to sell his first successful business, even after he relocated to Chicago, but he signed over the revenue from DBB Co. to Caro so that she would have an income of her own.

In 1910, Charley became one of the guarantors and a vice president of the newly created Chicago Grand Opera Company. Harold McCormick, chairman of the board of International Harvester, was president of the opera company, and the other vice president was Otto H. Kahn, an international financier with the investment banking firm Kuhn, Loeb, & Co. The troupe's artistic director, Cleofonte Campanini, staged innovative performances that attracted a wide audience. In an effort to reach a broader audience, the company performed on Saturday afternoons, when ticket prices were half those of an evening performance.[24]

Campanini staged an impressive repertoire, and the company attracted world-renowned artists. The group performed ten different operas per season, including such favorites as *Aida*, *The Girl of the Golden West*, *Samson et Dalila*, and *Don Quixote*. Average receipts ranged from $400,000 to just over $500,000 annually. Even with such impressive revenues, the organization failed to turn a profit.[25] Nevertheless, the opera's backers, including Dawes, continued to support it with personal donations.

Charley generously aided promising musical talent by becoming a patron for a number of musicians. The most successful recipient of Charley's largesse was the violinist Francis MacMillen, who came from Charley's hometown of Marietta. MacMillen gained world renown and performed throughout the United States and Europe, including special audiences with members of the royal families throughout the Continent. In 1905, Dawes had given MacMillen $1,000 to travel to Europe to study.[26]

To thank Dawes for his support, MacMillen secretly arranged for the publication of a composition for violin and piano that Dawes had written in 1907 called "Improvisation." Dawes first learned of its publication when he saw it in a music store window. Dawes wrote a second composition, "Melody in A Major," in 1911. The composition achieved modestly successful sales and was periodically performed by the violinist Fritz Kreisler. During Dawes's years as vice president and ambassador to the United Kingdom, the piece was usually played when Dawes entered a room at a formal event. By then, he privately commented, he was sick of hearing it.[27]

Charley and Caro were approaching their fiftieth birthdays when they each were hospitalized with unidentified health problems. Charley was in the hospital in December 1914 for surgery. His friend George B. Cortelyou learned of it through his son Bruce, who had connections with Dawes through the Chicago Opera. "I was very sorry to hear from Bruce that you had been under the weather and was [sic] to be in the hospital for several days," Cortelyou wrote his friend. "I hope you got along all right there and will be on the road to your usual health by the time this reaches you. I have always thought of you having such a sound constitution and enjoying what is curiously called 'good health' that it came as a shock to me to know you were having any kind of trouble physically."[28]

In February 1915, Caro underwent major surgery. There are no known accounts of the surgery in the Dawes papers, and only one letter from Rufus's wife, Helen, to Mary Beman Dawes alludes to Caro's successful operation. Dana, in an oral history that he recorded later in life, suggests that the surgery was a double mastectomy for cancer.[29]

Rena Decker, or Deedee, nursed Caro through her recovery. Caro had originally hired Deedee as a nurse and nanny at the time of Virginia Dawes's adoption. Deedee had been a registered nurse at Evanston Hospital and had served with the American Expeditionary Forces (AEF), the military force the United States sent to Europe during World War I. Prior to becoming a nurse, Decker had taught school near present-day Mundelein, Illinois. She became an integral part of the Dawes family and a companion to Caro.[30]

Carolyn Dawes married Melvin B. Ericson on June 5, 1915. Ericson, who joined his father-in-law in banking, had been long known to the family and had been a close friend of Rufus Fearing Dawes's. Charley's gift to his daughter was a home that he purchased for her and her new husband at 210 Davis Street in Evanston.[31]

One of the highlights of the wedding was the presence of Mary Gates Dawes, who was approaching her seventy-third birthday and whose health had become uncertain. Six weeks before Carolyn's wedding, Mary had written Charley: "I want to go up to Carolyn's wedding, but have felt for some time that it was doubtful if I should be able to do so. However, I will not decide till I get my wedding dress home, and if it is very beautiful, I may decide to go!"[32]

Mary did attend, much to the joy of the entire family, but the next month, she suffered a stroke at her home. Henry's wife, who, like Rufus's wife, was also named Helen, helped to nurse Mary and provided regular updates from Marietta. It was touch-and-go for several weeks, but Mary finally rallied.

By September, Mary Dawes had resumed her routine activities, including attending church. Her spark and optimism was reflected in a note she wrote Charley on September 9, informing him of her efforts to raise money to help some of their relatives serving as missionaries in Persia (now Iran). She requested each of her children to send one dollar for themselves and their spouses, and each of her grandchildren to send twenty-five cents. "I should do myself proud," Mary wrote her son. "Where is the family that could raise so large a sum by this method?" she asked in a postscript.[33]

After she received Charley's check, which was apparently for more than the requested $2.50, Mary sent him a note. "Thank you for your very generous response to my request for $2.50! It is really quite exciting as my letters come in. I planned to raise in my family, to the exclusion of myself, $18 or $20, and now I am going to make our contribution up to $100—and I expect that will be more than all of the church will give!"[34]

In June 1914, Lorimer's La Salle Street Trust and Savings Bank was declared insolvent and ceased operations. The bank had reported growing deposits throughout 1913 and into 1914. Its 1914 report to the state auditor showed deposits at $5.4 million. The board declared a quarterly dividend of 1.4 percent on its stock.[35] In April 1914, La Salle had relocated to a new building at La Salle and Quincy Streets, purchased

at a cost of $500,000. By all outward appearances, La Salle was a grow-
ing, thriving financial institution. When the bank examiners began
to investigate La Salle's finances to determine the cause of the insol-
vency, they uncovered a pattern of unsecured loans to the members of
the board and to Lorimer himself. The examiners also discovered that
Dawes had lent Lorimer $1.25 million so that the bank could receive
its state charter.

A grand jury investigated Lorimer and Munday for criminal conspiracy. Dawes was called to testify regarding the loan. Sounding much like
the assistant comptroller who had testified on behalf of the defense in
the John R. Walsh trial and said that banking rules are often broken,
Dawes defended the loan as a common practice among Chicago banks.
"Some of the grand jurors took a keen interest in the jugglery," the
Day Book, a Chicago newspaper, commented about Dawes's testimony.
"After Dawes told them the ins and outs of the deal jurors told Dawes
any kind of a crook in Christendom can start a bank without a cent
of cash or collateral if he can only find some banker willing to be as
kind-hearted as Charlie [sic] Dawes was to Billie [sic] Lorimer's La Salle
Street Trust & Savings Bank."[36]

Why, having been a comptroller and well aware of the importance
of sufficient cash on hand, would Dawes engage in this "common practice" and make the loan to Lorimer? For years, Dawes had traveled the
country and spoken about the importance of sound banking practices
and the need to protect depositors over investors. Dawes's bank was
a member of the Chicago clearinghouse; he served on its committee.
Dawes was frequently called upon to act as a receiver in bank and corporate bankruptcies. His decision to provide the cash to allow La Salle
to receive its state charter flew in the face of everything Dawes had ever
advocated. The loan was so out of character and such an error in judgment that the best explanation may be that Dawes was so grief-stricken
after his son's death that his decision-making was impaired.

The grand jury determined that, under the statutes of the state of
Illinois, the Central Trust officers had not violated the law. However,
W. C. Niblack, the receiver for La Salle, filed charges against the Central Trust Company on September 24, 1915, and sought to recover
$1,487,854.16 from Central Trust and an amount equal to the par value
of the shares held by the bank's stockholders.[37]

Central Trust fought to have the suit dismissed. In February 1916, Judge Thomas G. Windes declared that the bank "had a hand in a case of fraud. . . . I think from the facts alleged in the bill as to transactions between the Central Trust company and the La Salle Street bank and its officers that it is clearly a case of fraud, if those allegations can be supported by proof."[38] The case went to trial at the same time as arguments were being heard in Lorimer's and Munday's criminal trials.

Lorimer was tried separately from Munday. The "bank wreck" trial, as some papers termed the proceedings, dragged on from fall 1915 into spring 1916. Both Forgan and Dawes testified on behalf of the prosecution against Lorimer. Niblack, the receiver, gave evidence on behalf of the defense. He placed the blame for the bank's failure on Munday, whom he accused of having stolen from the bank. Munday was convicted; Lorimer was acquitted.

The ruling on Central Trust's case was handed down on July 7, 1916. Circuit Court Judge Frederick A. Smith ordered Central Trust to pay La Salle Street National Bank's depositors the $1.25 million it had lent plus 5 percent interest from October 21, 1912.[39] Central Trust appealed the decision. The appeal worked its way through the court system, ultimately accumulating 13,571 pages of testimony. The final verdict was handed down as Dawes returned from his work on the Reparations Commission and was being considered as a possible vice presidential candidate in April 1924. The verdict held Central Trust liable for $108,055.75, with interest at 5 percent from September 24, 1915, the date the suit was filed, until June 12, 1924, along with the costs of court. It was a fraction of the original amount that Niblack had attempted to collect, but the verdict became ammunition for Dawes's enemies in his many years as a political candidate and appointee.[40]

As the Lorimer case dragged through both the courts of law and the courts of public opinion, Dawes showed little concern for the impact on his bank's business. He faced a much larger threat to his bank: his decision to participate in the Anglo-French loan that the New York banks, led by J. P. Morgan, had agreed to underwrite as World War I dragged into its second year.

Austria-Hungary had declared war on Serbia on July 28, 1914. Gavrilo Princip, a Serbian extremist, had assassinated the empire's Archduke

Franz Ferdinand and his wife, Sophie. The assassination triggered cross-border hostilities. Russia warned Austria-Hungary that it would not permit Austria-Hungary to embarrass Serbia, which depended on Russia for political and military support. Russia mobilized its units on its common border with Austria-Hungary in a defensive move. When Russia ignored Austria-Hungary's demand to pull back, Germany, in support of its ally Austria-Hungary, declared war on Russia. Russia's ally France then ordered a mobilization, and France and Germany declared war on each other. Germany immediately invaded the neutral country of Belgium, and the United Kingdom declared war on Germany to honor its treaty obligations with France and Belgium.

The United States, under the leadership of President Woodrow Wilson, took an officially neutral stance and refused to sever diplomatic ties with Germany and Austria-Hungary, but Wilson's policies were anything but neutral. He allowed the United States to furnish arms, food, and equipment to the British and French, and he honored the Allies' blockade of ships containing supplies for Germany and the other Central Powers—Austria-Hungary, the Ottoman Empire, and Bulgaria.

In the early twentieth century roughly half of Chicago's population was of either German or Irish descent, and those two groups sympathized with the Central Powers. Those who were not overt sympathizers favored American neutrality. The owner of the *Chicago Tribune*, Robert R. McCormick, was vocally isolationist in his newspaper. Throughout the Midwest the prevailing attitudes were either pro-German or a desire for the United States to stay out of the war.

On September 30, 1915, six days after Niblack filed his suit on behalf of La Salle's depositors against Central Trust, Dawes received a telegram from J. P. Morgan & Co., often referred to as the "House of Morgan." The three-page communiqué invited him to join a syndicate of bankers that was forming to administer the Anglo-French loan that Washington had approved two weeks earlier. "We invite you to become associated as syndicate managers with us and with these other [banking] houses and institutions . . . and to make such participation in this syndicate as you may desire," read a portion of the telegram that was signed simply "J. P. Morgan & Co."[41]

The face behind the "J. P. Morgan" signature belonged to Thomas W. Lamont, a financier with a résumé similar to Charles Dawes's. Lamont had demonstrated his astute financial acumen shortly after he graduated from Harvard University by successfully reorganizing a food importing and exporting firm, Cushman Brothers Company. From Cushman Brothers, Lamont and his brother-in-law formed a company that specialized in what would today be considered corporate turn-arounds. Lamont came to the attention of a Morgan partner, Henry P. Davison, who asked Lamont to join the banking firm. Lamont became the youngest person to be made a partner at Morgan.

Lamont had initially asked John Forgan for his assistance in organiz-ing the subscriptions for the Anglo-French loan among Chicago banks, and Forgan had informed Lamont that his chances for success in Chi-cago were slim. Lamont visited Chicago between September 25 and September 27 in an effort to garner the bankers' support. However, the recent substantial withdrawal of funds by foreign depositors from one of the area banks had made the region's bankers wary of participating in the unsecured loan. Lamont's telegram to Charley was a follow-up to several days of intensive lobbying to get Dawes on board.

The total value of the Anglo-French loan was $500 million. Banks would purchase the bonds at 96 percent of their value at a 5 percent interest rate and offer them to investors at 98 percent with an interest rate of 5.5 percent. The British and French governments guaranteed the bonds.[42]

The House of Morgan, which had offices in both the United King-dom and France, agreed to negotiate the terms of the loan. The loan was popular among the eastern banks, especially those based in New York City and Boston, but, among midwestern and western banks, sup-port was tepid. The midwestern and western banks' customers, many of whom were farmers and small businessmen, would not benefit from the sales of munitions and war matériel that the loan proceeds would pur-chase. These banks viewed the loan as a tool of Wall Street to control their smaller institutions.

Dawes was anxious about making the commitment. He and his board expected to suffer severely for their decision to participate in the loan. A telegram from Lamont revealed how quickly he had been able to size up Central Trust's founder and president. "For your private information," Lamont wired Dawes, "one of Chicago's leading bankers, hearing of your proposed independent action in case united action fails, declared this morning that you would never have the nerve to do it. I never saw a greater opportunity for independent action."[43]

Dawes did have the nerve. In a statement prepared for the *Chicago Tribune*, he explained that his support of the loan was to help American exports and the American economy. "Our own bank . . . is neither pro-Ally nor pro-German in its sympathies or affiliation," Dawes explained. "I also believe in the real patriotism and neutrality of our American citizens, and I do not for one minute think that in any large numbers they will resent any action taken upon a sound business basis and unquestionably in the interest of our own nation, to which we all owe our first allegiance and devotion."[44]

That night, Dawes's friends insisted that two guards be posted at his Evanston home. They learned that he had received death threats as a result of his decision to support the Anglo-French loan.[45]

Letters requesting accounts to be closed began arriving within days of Dawes's announcement that he would become part of the syndicate. One of the more polite letters explained the customer's reasoning:

> Gentlemen:
>
> In response to your letter of October 6, addressed to my wife, permit me to advise you that her savings account, as well as the account of her mother and my own, were withdrawn from your bank for two reasons.
>
> First, as a matter of principle. We do not believe in praying for peace and permitting our money to be used to continue the war.
>
> Second, while we admit the knowledge and banking experience of the officers of the bank, we do not concur in or approve of any war loans that involve our personal funds.[46]

Shareholders also sent letters to board members requesting that the bank not offer the loan bonds. "Our bank has been built up on conservative lines and we should not endanger the safety of it by investing in doubtful loans. One of our bankers considers this loan not worth seventy-five cents on a dollar and why should the bank take chances? Mr. Charles Dawes . . . certainly used poor judgment."[47]

The bank prepared a daily report on the total number of accounts withdrawn, the average activity on the account over the previous four months, the dollar value of the business lost, and any other banking activity the customer may have had, such as loans or the purchase of securities. In many cases, the accounts represented multiple thousands of dollars in lost deposits. While Dawes believed that his decision was patriotic, it initially proved to be bad business.

The eastern bankers and Dawes talked up the loan as an excellent investment opportunity, but they seriously misread public support. An intensive advertising campaign, instigated at Dawes's suggestion, failed to attract investors. On December 15, sixty days after the bonds were offered and the deadline for the syndicate, only $320 million worth of bonds were sold. The syndicate, to comply with the terms it had agreed to with the British and the French, would have to absorb the $180 million balance among its members. The New York Times reasoned that the sixty-day sales period was too short a time to offer the bonds and the reason for the failure to sell the entire issue. Other papers believed the poor subscriptions reflected an underlying skepticism among the American public about the soundness of the loan.[48]

As the time to subscribe to the offering drew to a close, an angry customer mailed a copy of the prospectus to Dawes with the word "Disgrace" scrawled across it in thick black ink and underlined twice. At the bottom of the page, the sender wrote: "Out comes my account and hundreds of others. Hope you lose every dollar."[49]

At $900,000, Central Trust's sales were a relatively small amount compared to the subscriptions secured by the New York banks. Customer anger ran deep and lingered long after the subscription period closed. When the value of the bonds dropped to 94¾ in early 1916, a former customer clipped a copy of a Central Trust advertisement from the newspaper that read: "The fear of want will haunt you just so long as you don't make it your business to provide against it—by *saving*." The customer wrote below this line on the ad: "Does not the thought of having invested part of your depositors' money in Anglo-French's haunt you? (94 now)."[50]

Time, however, vindicated Dawes's decision. By April 1916, Central Trust had recovered from the lost business, and total deposits had increased from $42 million when it first offered the loan to $44.5

million by March 1916. An unnamed bank officer told *Bonds and Mortgages*: "That was the best thing our bank ever did. . . . By the middle of December [1915] we had lost $300,000 of our accounts and taken on $3 million more. . . . About one-half our possible increase has been due to our subscription [to the Anglo-French loan]."[51]

CHAPTER 7

✕

Military Man

"There is one choice we cannot make, we are incapable of making," President Woodrow Wilson asserted in an impassioned speech before a joint session of Congress on April 2, 1917, when he asked Congress to declare war on Germany. "We will not choose the path of submission and suffer the most sacred rights of our nation and our people to be ignored and violated. . . . The world must be made safe for democracy."[1] The request for a war declaration was an about-face for a president who had campaigned for reelection with the slogan "He kept us out of war."

As recently as January 22, 1917, Wilson made a speech expressing his hope for a "peace without victory," where all nations would be treated equally in the conflict, rather than some being declared winners and others losers.[2] Wilson had continued his theme of peace in the world in his second inaugural address on March 4.

Events at the start of 1917 ultimately changed Wilson's mind. In January, Germany rescinded the *Sussex* pledge. Named for an unarmed French passenger liner the Germans had torpedoed on May 4, 1916, the pledge was Germany's promise not to attack unarmed vessels in exchange for Wilson maintaining U.S. diplomatic ties with Germany. Germany never held to its commitment, in large part because its military leaders argued that America's Anglo-French loan and its sales of supplies to the Allies proved that the United States was not neutral. When Wilson threatened to break diplomatic relations, the military convinced the kaiser that the president was bluffing. They discovered how they had misread Wilson when he broke ties with Germany on February 3, 1917. Germany responded with stepped-up attacks on American merchant and passenger ships, sinking several vessels and killing hundreds of civilians.

At the end of February, the British government shared with Washington the decrypted Zimmermann telegram, a message the British had intercepted on January 19, 1917. Authored by German Foreign Minister Arthur Zimmermann, the encoded message requested Mexico's support in the war in exchange for German assistance in helping Mexico reclaim the lands it had ceded to the United States. The British government had withheld the contents of the telegram to prevent the Germans from discovering that their codes had been broken.[3]

This chain of events led to the United States formally declaring war against Germany on April 6. Wilson chose Dawes's longtime friend General John J. Pershing to command the American Expeditionary Forces (AEF).

Pershing was called to Washington once the declaration of war was official to meet with Wilson and his secretary of war, Newton Baker. At the conclusion of the meeting, Pershing had the understanding that he would lead American troops as a division commander. A few days later, Baker informed the general that his role had changed: Wilson had named Pershing commander in chief of the American forces in Europe. He was ordered to begin selecting his staff.[4] Mobilization of American troops began immediately.

At the age of fifty-one, Dawes sought a commission in the army. He is unusually silent in his *Journal of the Great War* about his motivations. Charley and Caro were rearing Dana and Virginia, now ages five and three, respectively. Dawes's bank was flourishing, and Dawes Brothers, Inc. continued to expand as the oil business grew.

Coming from a line of military patriots, Dawes may have felt a need to participate directly in the war. His decision to enlist may have been his response to the realization that he had passed the half-century mark. Whatever his motivation, Dawes contacted his friend and sometime business partner Samuel M. Felton, who, as president of the Chicago Great Western Railway, was assisting the military in raising a regiment of engineers. Citing his railroading experience—as a young man, he had earned money to pay for law school by working with railroad surveying crews—Dawes pressed his argument for a commission with the regiment.

In mid-April, Dawes traveled to Washington to lunch with Pershing at the Metropolitan Club there. He asked for help getting an appointment. "I was not much impressed with his pretensions as an engineer or as a prospective military possibility," Pershing wrote in his memoir of the meeting with Dawes, "but I did have knowledge of his business ability and experience and knew that he would be valuable in some position requiring his qualifications, so I spoke to the secretary of war on his behalf."[5]

Dawes received his commission as a major and was assigned to the 17th Engineer Regiment. He traveled to his training post in Atlanta by private railcar on May 27, 1917, accompanied by his commanding officer, Colonel John S. Sewell, a West Point graduate.

Charley was immediately drawn to Sewell. "Col. Sewell is a wonderful man and one of the most congenial to me I have ever met," Charley wrote to Caro. He then added the key qualities he found in Sewell: "He is a man of action—a natural leader, and an original thinker."[6] Caro, Carolyn, and Sewell's wife followed shortly afterward, and they remained in Atlanta during the few weeks it took to assemble the regiment.

In the days before his departure for Atlanta, Dawes sent letters to his closest friends informing them of his decision. Illinois Governor Frank Lowden responded to the news of Dawes's enlistment with dismay. "Dear Charley," Lowden wrote,

> I am a good deal thunderstruck by your letter of May 17. Of course I commend your patriotism in wishing to go to France, but I cannot help but believe you will be needed at home during the next two or three years as you have never been in the past. Personally, I shall need your advice from time to time as I never did before. Men of far vision are not any too numerous, and Illinois and the United States would be better served with you within their borders at this critical moment.[7]

As if to drive his point home, Lowden wired Dawes the next day: "Expressing firm conviction that you are needed at home in this crisis. Fear you did not get letter. . . . Hope you will not decide to go without fullest consideration."[8]

Herbert Hoover attempted to draw Dawes into another type of war service. Wilson had named Hoover food administrator and assigned him the task of ensuring that there was enough food to feed the troops without creating shortages for the civilians at home. Dawes had met with Hoover during his April visit to Washington, and Hoover had asked Dawes then to join him in the food administrator's office. Learning of Dawes's enlistment, Hoover wired: "I am still fixed in my ideas about your greater usefulness in food control and would like to know if your resentment would be implacable if I ask the president to assign you to this department."[9] Dawes wired back: "Under no circumstances do such a thing. It would be unfair and cruel, and I know you would not consider it." To Dawes's great relief, Hoover did not pursue the matter.[10]

Charley immediately took to the military life. "I get up early and work all day," he wrote to Caro on June 1. "I work at least two hours a day getting into physical [shape]. . . . It is already having an effect on my health. I feel better than I have [for months]."[11]

As he had in civilian life, Charley watched out for members of his extended family. He spoke to Sewell about enlistment for Will Dawes's son, and he wrote Caro that Sewell offered to take their son-in-law, Melvin Ericson, into the regiment if he did not go into ordinance. Ericson ended up serving in the Aviation Section of the Signal Officers' Corps.

Dawes also looked after Francis Kilkenny, who had enlisted in the army and had the rank of private. Dawes tapped Kilkenny as his personal aide, and he served Charley in that role throughout the war.

Upon completion of their training, the 17th Engineers left Atlanta for New York on July 26, where they joined with the 12th Engineers on the HMS *Carmania*, bound for Liverpool, England. Both the *Carmania* and its captain had an interesting history. The *Carmania* had engaged an armed German passenger liner, the SMS *Cap Trafalgar*, off the coast of Ilha da Trinidade, South America, on September 14, 1914. The *Carmania*'s captain, J. T. W. Charles, had once been the captain of the ill-fated ocean liner *Lusitania*, although not when a German U-boat torpedoed it in 1915.

The reality of going off to war was evident in Charley's letter to Caro, written aboard the train as the regiment headed from Atlanta to its ship in New York. "You were a great help to me in Atlanta, and I shall always remember our visit there. There is little to say at such a time as this except to tell you how much I shall miss you and the children. . . . Keep occupied, and try to be with other people the same thoughtful and helpful woman you were at Atlanta." His final line betrayed the level of emotion he had tried to conceal behind his advice. "I am going to do my best; and it is all in a day's work whatever comes. I love you all, and know you all love me."[12]

Caro wasted no time contributing to the war effort. The precipitous entry of the United States into the war meant that it lacked sufficient clothing to send off with the soldiers. All across America, men, women, and children organized to knit socks, sweaters, and hats for the soldiers. Caro organized a knitting group in Evanston, furnished the yarn, and made sweaters for the men. Even though the ship crossed the Atlantic Ocean in August, the weather was still cold. "Your sweaters are doing wonders for us all as it is quite cold. Many tell me of their appreciation," Charley wrote Caro while still en route to Europe.[13]

Charley's mother also took up knitting. The war grieved Mary Gates Dawes. Her eldest son and three of her grandsons, William, Gates, and Charles, had all enlisted. A year after Charley's departure, she wrote in her Line-A-Day diary: "Fifty-three years today since my only brother died. War then—war now. Oh, why is it permitted?"[14]

Knowing that he would be based in France, Charley struggled to learn French. He soon learned that he was not as gifted as Caro, who had become fluent after years of study with a group in Evanston. So Dawes decided that it would be best to learn a few key words. Tobacco (*tabac*) was one of them.

Charley smoked an estimated twenty cigars a day. It was rare to see an impromptu photo of him without a cigar in his hand. He switched to pipe smoking during the war, after a British officer gave him a pipe. Dawes's trademark pipe was an unusual shape, evoking iconic images of Sherlock Holmes, with most of the pipe's bowl sitting below the stem.

Dawes's transatlantic crossing was perilous. Two other troopships, the *New York* and the *Belgic*, left New York at about the same time as the *Carmania* and were attacked by German U-boats as they crossed the Atlantic. The *Carmania* was one of the first ships to make the crossing in a convoy system set up by U.S. Navy Admiral William S. Sims. Naval destroyers accompanied the ship on its voyage and gave chase to submarines that approached.

Dawes was in charge of boat drills, when the men practiced getting on deck and into their assigned boats and rafts as quickly as possible in the event of a submarine attack. With his usual attention to efficiency, Dawes quickly determined that, under current practices, it was impossible for an entire crew to assemble and climb into life rafts if the ship came under attack. He kept a record of the time it took for regiments to arrive on deck from the hold when given the order and rewrote the boat drill manual based on his findings. He sent the report up to Pershing, who adopted Dawes's recommendations and implemented them as the new boat drill procedure.

In the midst of learning French and organizing boat drills, Charley managed to find time for music. He discovered that a number of the men had brought musical instruments with them, and he organized a band and held regular practice. "Our band is steadily improving," he wrote Caro from aboard ship. "We keep up our routine work aboard ship in addition to our 'boat drill.'"[15] He proudly reported that the musical ensemble led the regiment as it disembarked in France.

The first few months of military experience invigorated and transformed Dawes:

> For myself I find everything new and interesting—the few hardships and all. . . . I have found among these new friends and associates and in this new environment a new interest in life, a new career, however humble, to make, and in thinking back the only experience in my life with which I can compare it in its excitement are the early days of college life with its new friends and duties and competitions.[16]

At heart, though, he was still a banker.

From the moment he set foot on European soil, Dawes began to connect with financiers in the United Kingdom, France, and Belgium. When his regiment arrived in London, Dawes took a day to lunch with the two principals of J. P. Morgan's British affiliate, Morgan, Grenfell & Co., Edward "Teddy" Grenfell and Charles F. Whigham. Morgan, Grenfell administered the British portion of the Anglo-French loan proceeds, and it coordinated British purchases of armaments and food with United States firms. Charley held similar consultations with

Morgan's French affiliate, Morgan Hartjes, when he arrived in Paris. Like its British counterpart, the French bank handled transactions between the French military and American suppliers.[17]

The House of Morgan played a key role throughout the war. When hostilities began in 1914, then-Chancellor of the Exchequer David Lloyd George (who was the British prime minister in 1917) asked Grenfell, through his American contacts, to approach the American rifle manufacturers Remington U.M.C. and Winchester Repeating Arms Company with a request to increase production. Seeing an additional opportunity for his bank, beyond underwriting the Anglo-French loan, Morgan's CEO, Henry P. (Harry) Davison, offered to function as a centralized purchasing agent for the Allies. His stated objective was to eliminate competition for matériel for the war. It also allowed J. P. Morgan to earn a commission on every sale it transacted.[18]

Charley's meetings were more than courtesy calls. The entry of the United States into the war meant that its military would compete for the same weapons and supplies that the British and French had been purchasing for the previous three years. The Morgan affiliates had in-depth knowledge of the finances and stockpiles of their respective nations. Dawes's connections with these international bankers, and his understandings of the inner workings of their institutions, put him in a key position to assist the U.S. effort.

Dawes reconnected with the Belgian minister of finance, Aloys Van de Vyvere, who was in Le Havre, France, when Charley and his regiment arrived. The two men had met during the latter's trip to Chicago prior to the war, where they found they had much in common, including a love of opera. In his typical eschewing of conventionality, Dawes had taken to calling Van de Vyvere "Boss," as opposed to "Your Excellency," explaining to the Belgian that the term was a way of conveying companionability and good fellowship, while still acknowledging authority. Instead of staying with his regiment on his first night in Le Havre, Dawes was a guest of the Belgian government at Van de Vyvere's lodgings.[19]

The final destination of the 17th Engineers was Saint-Nazaire, France. Pershing had designated this port city, on a Loire River estuary in Brittany, along with Brest, La Pallice, and Bassens, for American use. The first U.S. troops had arrived in Saint-Nazaire on June 26, 1917, and there had been a slow, steady stream of arrivals since. Although the troops numbered only in the hundreds, the steady influx of men and war supplies strained the small town and its port. The French used Saint-Nazaire as a prison camp for German soldiers, and then the Americans arrived and looked for billets in private homes and warehouses to store their supplies. The 17th had barely gotten settled in Saint-Nazaire before its officers identified several shortcomings with the facilities. After a meeting to outline their needs, the men designated Dawes to travel to Paris to report to Pershing personally.[20]

In the twenty-first century, with a multibillion-dollar defense budget and a well-equipped standing military, it is difficult to comprehend how utterly unprepared America was to enter World War I. Pershing inventoried his available equipment before he sailed for Europe. The United States had 285,000 Springfield rifles, 400 light field guns, and 150 heavy field guns. There were fewer than 1,500 machine guns of four different types, and the parts were not interchangeable. World War I was the first war to use airplanes as part of its attack tactics. The army had only thirty-five qualified aviators, and the fifty-five available training aircraft were not equipped to engage in combat.[21]

The United States was not industrially prepared, either. Textile plants were not tooled to mass-produce uniforms. It would take nearly a year to retool automotive plants to manufacture trucks, ambulances, and tanks that could be shipped to Europe. The same was true for the U.S. shipbuilding program, which was moribund.

Pershing described America's lack of readiness to enter the war: "When the acting Chief of Staff went to look in the secret files where the plans to meet the situation that confronted us should have been, the pigeonhole was empty. In other words, the War Department was face to face with the question of sending an army to Europe and found that the General Staff had never considered such a thing."[22]

General Johnson Hagood served as chief of staff to the section that would ultimately become known as the Services of Supply (SOS). Hagood echoed Pershing's assessment:

> The fourteen years, 1903 to 1917, during which the General Staff
> has been in existence, had not been spent in making plans for war,

the purpose for which it was created, but in squabbling over the control of the routine peace-time administration and supply of the Regular Army and in attempts to place the blame for unpreparedness upon Congress. . . . But our unpreparedness did not come from lack of money, lack of soldiers, or lack of supplies. It came from lack of brains, or perhaps it would be fairer to say lack of genius.[23]

The British and French wanted American troops to replace their exhausted soldiers on the battlefield. They requested arms, tanks, ships, and planes. Pershing dared not admit that the United States had none. In his initial meetings with his European allies, Pershing learned for the first time since the onset of hostilities how devastated they were. The Allied nations had suffered massive shipping losses. They feared food shortages and a lack of coal as the winter of 1917–1918 approached. After a few short weeks in Europe, Pershing summed up his assessment in his diary: "Basically the Allied situation appears to be worse than reported."[24]

Within the U.S. Army, the rivalries that Hagood had observed in Washington had followed Pershing to Europe. The Quartermaster Corps and the Corps of Engineers bid against each other in attempting to secure supplies from the French and the British. This was particularly true with regard to lumber, which both corps needed for wharves, docks, barracks, and hospitals. Traditionally, each section negotiated its own purchases, but Pershing quickly recognized that practice would not work with the exigencies he faced. He assembled a group of officers to make recommendations on ways to eliminate the competition and suggested a consolidated approach to purchasing. Pershing's officers told him that a purchasing board was illegal. Pershing overruled their objections with a curt objection of his own: "An emergency confronted us and it was no time to discuss technicalities."[25]

On August 20, Pershing created a General Purchasing Board. Expectations were that he would name a general as purchasing agent, but Pershing decided that a competent banker of lesser rank would do. "Have detailed Lieutenant Colonel Dawes as Chief of Purchasing Board," Pershing recorded in his diary on August 29. "He tried to beg off, but when its importance was explained he gracefully accepted."[26] General Order

No. 28, issued on August 13, 1917, officially appointed Charley as general purchasing agent and charged him with organizing the board.[27]

Charley wrote to Caro:

> The greatest task of my life lies before me, for the orders have issued placing under me all the purchasing done in Europe for the American Expeditionary Force in France. For this enormous undertaking General Pershing feels that I am the man, and I have gladly accepted . . . It will mean a few more gray hairs by the time I get back, but it means also the opportunity to be of service in a large thing to my country in its time of greatest trial.[28]

Nevertheless, he regretted leaving the 17th.

Dawes coordinated all purchasing for the U.S. Army, the Red Cross, and the Army Young Men's Christian Association (YMCA) in France. He was given "practically unlimited discretion and authority to go ahead and devise a system of coordination of purchases; to organize the board; to arrange the liaison connections between the French and English army boards and our own; to use any method which may seem wise to me to secure supplies for the army in Europe which to that extent will relieve our American transports in their enormous burden."[29]

Dawes worked directly under General James G. Harbord, a Kansas native whose military career differed dramatically from Pershing's. Harbord had walked the seventy miles from his home to matriculate at Kansas State Agricultural College (now Kansas State University) in Manhattan, Kansas, with the intention of becoming a telegraph operator. As a land-grant college, partially supported by the sale of federal land, Kansas State required its students to participate in the Reserve Officers' Training Corps (ROTC) to prepare for future military service. Harbord quickly discovered that the disciplined military life appealed to him. At the urging of his ROTC instructor, Harbord took the test for West Point. But he learned, four days later, that another candidate with the same score, who was one year younger, was chosen for the single available slot. Abandoning thoughts of the military, Harbord became an assistant principal at a local Kansas school system upon graduation. The following year, Harbord's alma mater hired him as its telegraphy instructor and assistant librarian.

However, the military continued to draw Harbord. The army had a policy of giving enlisted men eligibility for consideration for a commission if they performed exemplary service for at least two years. The process was highly selective, but Harbord took his chances and enlisted in January 1889. Three years later, he was awarded with a commission for his ability to stay cool under pressure, his abstinence from alcohol, and his ability to use a typewriter—a skill learned as a result of his interest in telegraphy.

Harbord came to the attention of Pershing at the end of the Spanish-American War. Harbord had spent the few months of the conflict suffering from malaria at one of the mosquito-infested army camps in Jacksonville, Florida. He and Pershing connected in Huntsville, Alabama, where Pershing was returning from serving in Cuba, and where Harbord was reassigned after recovering from his illness.

In the confusion of redeploying Pershing's unit, the 10th Cavalry Regiment, from Cuba to the United States, Pershing lost track of eight hundred horses. Harbord, with his trademark cool-headedness, located the missing animals. When it came time for Pershing to identify someone as chief of staff for the European theater, Harbord was his man.[30]

Harbord recalled meeting Dawes initially in 1901 while the latter was still comptroller of the currency and Harbord was assistant chief of the Bureau of Insular Affairs at the War Department. Harbord had also been with Pershing when he met with Dawes in April after Congress passed its declaration of war on Germany. Harbord observed in his memoir, "From their [Pershing and Dawes's] conversation it rather struck me at the time that we should see him [Dawes] over here fairly soon."[31]

Harbord shared Pershing's views about Dawes's abilities to coordinate purchasing. "He [Pershing] has confidence in Dawes' business ability, for in the years since he first knew him Dawes has become a great banker and amassed a fortune, and [Pershing] has implicit faith in his integrity and patriotism. From what I have seen of his friend, I share the Chief's feeling."[32]

The general purchasing agent had extensive responsibilities. He oversaw supply forecasting and the maintenance of statistical information. Representatives from the Red Cross, the Army YMCA, the Navy, the Signal Corps, and the Air Service all reported to Dawes. Pershing determined that all foreign countries that were part of the Allied effort would also answer to the purchasing agent.[33] "It is a man's work," Dawes recorded regarding his new assignment, "but I am thankful beyond words that, now that I have come here instead of remaining in America, it is work which will count for my country in its time of greatest trial."[34]

In Dawes, Pershing had a devoted and trusted friend, and a highly competent and dependable one, who would dedicate himself to getting the job done. "Dear fellow, and loyal friend," Dawes recorded in his diary about the general. "I hope I do not fail him."

Ever-present between the two men was their shared loss of loved ones. Dawes wrote in his *Journal of the Great War*:

> As we rode up together [from Paris to Chaumont, France] there occurred an instance of telepathy which was too much for either of us. Neither of us was saying anything, but I was thinking of my lost boy and of John's loss and looking out of the window, and he was doing the same thing on the other side of the automobile. We both turned at the same time and each was in tears. All John said was, "Even this war can't keep it out of my mind."[35]

Pershing's personal tragedy was even more poignant than Dawes's. On August 27, 1915, Pershing lost his wife and three young daughters to a fire in their home in the Presidio, in San Francisco. Only his son, Warren, age 7, survived.[36] Pershing had left his family in California while he was on duty in Texas because he believed they would be safer. For the remainder of his life, guilt plagued Pershing over his decision.

Dawes relocated to Paris and set up office at the Hôtel Ritz. All of France's railroads and telegraph lines ran through the city like spokes of a wheel, and the French agencies with which Dawes would interact had headquarters in Paris. A telephone line gave him direct access to Pershing in Chaumont, and the two men had a standing appointment to lunch together on Friday. Charley was shocked by the conditions he found in Paris. "The hand of death seems laid on this city. Can hardly realize it is the same Paris I visited twenty years ago this year."[37]

Dawes arranged for some of his trusted business colleagues to be commissioned as captains and join him in Europe as part of the Purchasing

Board. They included Central Trust's vice president, W. T. Abbott, and fellow financiers Nelson Dean Jay, president of Guaranty Trust Company, and Clarence Dillon, founder of the investment firm Dillon, Read & Co. "I am gradually gathering around me men who are equal to the emergencies which constantly arise. One of the most useful of the officers in my office is Major Hartjes, the senior member of Morgan Hartjes and Company," Dawes confided to his brother Henry.[38]

H. Herman Hartjes was detailed to Dawes to assist him in negotiations with the French military and French government. Hartjes had personal relationships with most of France's political leaders. Dawes selected several men from the 17th Engineers, as well as men recommended by Pershing and Harbord, to serve as purchasing agents in the surrounding neutral countries of Spain, Portugal, Switzerland, and Denmark. He also positioned liaisons in the United Kingdom, France, and Italy. These on-the-ground eyes and ears would prove vital to Dawes's ability to locate essential supplies.

One of Dawes's earliest negotiations involved an arrangement between Belgium and the United States for use of Belgian locomotives. He met with Van de Vyvere, and the two men traveled through Dunkirk, France, which the Germans bombarded almost nightly. It was Dawes's first time coming under attack as he traveled. "The first raid had but a comparatively mild interest for us, since the bombs struck at a very considerable distance," he wrote matter-of-factly to his mother. "We had not proceeded, however, more than half an hour when we suddenly found ourselves surrounded by great shafts of white light directed toward a spot above us in the sky, which, of course, we could not see through the top of our limousine. . . . Around us on all sides the anti-aircraft guns were firing at the airplanes. It seemed to us even then that we had a center seat for an interesting performance." The Germans were aiming for a munitions factory nearby. On the group's return trip to Paris, they found a crater a mere one hundred and forty yards from the road they had recently traveled.[39]

Shipping capacity had become a problem at the start of the war and would remain a challenge until its end. The United Kingdom and France had a combined shipping capacity of twenty-one million tons when the two nations declared war on Germany. Until early 1917, when Germany declared open warfare on all vessels, British shipbuilding had kept pace with losses. Now, it could barely replace what it was losing on a monthly basis. British shipping losses in March 1917 were 500,000 tons, and April losses were estimated to surpass 800,000 tons.[40] The Germans had sunk fifteen ships in British waters during the eleven days Pershing crossed the Atlantic, departing New York on May 28 and arriving in Liverpool, England, on June 8.[41] The magnitude of the loss had not been revealed to the United States in advance of its declaration of war on Germany.

The convoy system that U.S. Admiral Sims, together with British Vice Admiral Lewis Bayly, had developed immediately began to reverse the losses in transatlantic crossings, but the danger of transoceanic travel would not be wholly eliminated until late spring 1918, and replacement tonnage could not keep pace with losses.

As the winter of 1917–1918 loomed, Dawes scrambled to find ships to transport British coal to France. Germany had control of France's coal region, so England had become the source of most of France's coal since the winter of 1914–1915. France's coal needs for the forthcoming winter increased with the arrival of American troops. Dawes estimated that the immediate need, in September 1917 alone, was shipping to handle 50,000 tons of coal and 10,000 tons of supplies a month. By February 1918, 150,000 tons of coal would need to be shipped monthly. Coal was required both for heating and as fuel to operate the furnaces where French munitions were manufactured.[42]

Dawes met with Sims to ask him to release some of the boats he used as part of his convoy system. The admiral wanted to help, but he had his own concerns. He had requested additional destroyers to join the transport convoys, but Washington had denied his repeated appeals. Existing U.S. destroyers were needed to patrol the East Coast. Washington feared that deploying those ships to Europe would encourage German submarines to attack the mainland. Appeals to Pershing had brought no change in policy. Sims was unwilling to make any naval vessels available for transporting coal to service the Army.[43]

Dawes unleashed his trademark bluntness when Sims refused to help:

> The minute I said "coal" he [Sims] started on a strong complaint
> that the situation needed someone to handle it who knew it, that it
> was being handled piecemeal, that "this and that" was the way to do

it. What I came for was to borrow a ship, not to get a statement of what I knew to be the fact up to the time I took hold of the coal matter about a week ago. I got (apparently only) angry and proceeded to give him a good imitation of a man who knew what he was talking about, descending, I regret to say, to extreme statement.[44]

Dawes soon learned that his habit of losing his temper would not work with either the U.S. military or the Europeans. Charley nearly caused a diplomatic incident when he became angry at the way that British Quartermaster-General Sir John Cowans stalled on making a decision. "No, by God, you won't put this over for a month," Dawes burst out when Cowans asked for more time to make a decision regarding procurement. "You've been fighting this war for three years. Where have you got? Now we're here and we're going to tell you how to run this war. It's time for you British to learn that, if you're going to win, you've got to give up the methods of an effete monarchy." Cowans refused to continue the discussion, and he jumped up and left the room.[45] Months passed before he would agree to meet again with Dawes.

Pershing worked to solve the matter of coal transport. Whereas Sims was unattuned to the army's needs, U.S. Admiral Henry T. Mayo was more sympathetic. He offered the use of two colliers and suggested that coal be used as ballast in ships. Mayo's recommendations solved the coal supply problem for the winter, and Pershing issued orders demanding the strictest economy in use of the fuel. As Charley would soon discover, the logistics of transporting coal were just the beginning of the challenges he would face as the American Expeditionary Forces general purchasing agent.

Unlike the Spanish-American War, where the United States entered foreign territory with the intention of conquering the local population, the AEF were guests of the French in World War I. This added another layer of decision-making to every aspect of conducting the war, from ordering supplies to troop placements and housing. The French government established its own bureau within the American General Purchasing Board, with headquarters at the Hôtel Méditerranée in Paris. The French had a say in everything the AEF purchased for use in France, and, to save shipping, Pershing had ordered that as much as possible be bought in Europe.

Pershing found dealing with the French maddening. They did not seem to understand the imperative of close and timely cooperation with the Americans. Some of this could be attributed to a lack of understanding of how ill-prepared the Americans actually were, and some of it was simply the French way of doing business. Pershing was well-experienced with bureaucratic red tape, but in his opinion, "The art of tying things up in official routine was in swaddling clothes in America as compared to its development in France. After a few contacts with their system one marveled that the French had managed to get along so well in supplying their armies during three years of war."[46]

Charley became a scrounger extraordinaire. Before the Allies formed the joint Military Board of Allied Supply (MBAS) in June 1918, he and his staff scoured the Continent and looked for assistance to overcome blockades and embargoes on trade with neighboring nations. In 1915, they discovered that the bordering neutral countries—Denmark, the Netherlands, Sweden, Norway, and Switzerland—sold food and other goods to the Central Powers, and then imported what they needed for their own consumption. They evaded the Allied blockade on trade because the imports were for use in a declared neutral country. In many cases, these countries feared a German attack more than an Allied embargo, so they continued to supply the Central Powers.[47]

Two of France's closest neutral neighbors, Spain and Switzerland, were excellent sources of everything from mules to wristwatches, but both the French and the Americans had blocked trade with these two supposedly neutral nations. Dawes sought to lift the restrictions so that he could supply the AEF. Here, Hartjes's contacts proved helpful. He arranged a meeting with the French minister of blockade, together with American ambassador William Sharp, and the two men promised to find a way to permit trade between France and the neutral countries of Switzerland and Spain. It was a small, victorious step for Dawes's efforts.[48]

Rivalries among the Allies affected Dawes's work. He successfully located 600 Belgian-owned locomotives lying idle along the tracks. Belgium had refused to give them to England or France because it had already provided 1,100 trains and wanted to have an inventory on hand at the close of the war to start its own recovery. England and France were both angry with Belgium for not turning over the engines to them. Dawes, on the other hand, through his close friendship with Van de Vyvere, acquired the use of the locomotives for the United States. However, having the trains and running them on tracks were two different things. The French still controlled use of the tracks. In a rare show of frustration, Dawes wrote of the negotiation: "Am sick and tired tonight—but 'got there' as the official records will show."[49]

The Americans had their own inefficiencies. Officials in Washington determined ship loading and routing without input from Pershing's staff. Ships arrived in Europe loaded with matériel for both Saint-Nazaire and Bordeaux. Due to improper loading, the matériel had to be off-loaded twice, resulting in double handling of the freight. Items were shipped that were not needed, but supplies desperately needed, such as sawmills and axes to get wood for the upcoming winter, were not on board.[50]

In spite of the challenges and setbacks, Dawes established a track record of success. He was so resourceful at finding needed materials in Europe that he sometimes was criticized. "They say now we have found too many machine tools. Of course we do not have to take them if this is the case." Four hundred thousand railroad ties had been requisitioned from the United States, a fraction of the estimated 2.4 million ties that were needed. Dawes located 145,000 ties in Portugal and 50,000 in Spain to help the army get started. He wrote that the "Engineering Department seemed dazed when I got them the offer." Dawes took it all in stride, saying, "It is a gratification unspeakable to feel that if you make criticism, it is by doing work well instead of poorly."[51]

Dawes took an occasional few hours to enjoy what he could of Paris, usually with a friend or family member in tow. One afternoon at the end of November, Harbord and Dawes had lunch together and then strolled among the shops. Both men loved books, and they spent considerable time in the used book section of Brentano's. Dawes, Harbord wrote, "tossed into a pile book values that would have been the earnest subject of prayerful deliberation with me for a half a year, left a hundred dollars with Brentano's for the afternoon's work, and gave me about half the books he bought."[52]

Dawes's recall of that afternoon was considerably more modest: "Took him [Harbord], Major [Harvey] Cushing, Wade Dyar, and Dean Jay to lunch at Frédéric's. Then Harbord and I dug into second-hand books at Brentano's for an hour; then we went to my hotel room after a walk to read them."[53]

The brief respites were a good tonic, because the work challenged him. In mid-December, Dawes was fighting a cold and struggling to preserve his equanimity. "I stay in my room in the evenings, and outside of my business endeavor in every way to save my nerves. They have got to last through the war—and then, if we win, I guess they will remain in my possession."[54]

The arrival of Caro's Christmas presents in mid-December was a sharp reminder of Charley's separation from his family. "Your Xmas presents arrived today," he wrote his wife. "Was much touched by them—especially by what my dear little children had done with their own little fingers. You were right to send me something made by your own dear hands. It is appreciated more than anything you could buy."[55]

Still, he could not help but feel keenly his separation from his family. "This will be my Christmas letter to you," he wrote Caro on December 23. "And my expression of my devotion to you for all that you have been and are to me. . . . Kiss my dear Carolyn for me, whom I love so dearly—and my two dear little children who have done so much for us both." William and Gates joined him for dinner on Christmas Day.[56]

The winter of 1917 to 1918 was especially cold in Illinois, and the war had reduced the coal supply. "Caro has been living practically hand to mouth in her coal supply," Rufus wrote Charley in February, "and we are practically in the same condition." Rufus mentioned the possibility of sending the children elsewhere if coal could not be found.[57] The war impacted everyone on both sides of the Atlantic.

Caro had embarked on her own war effort. By December 1917, she had organized a group of women and supplied them with enough yarn to knit 1,800 sweaters for the troops.[58] Charley praised her for her work:

> The Headquarters building is insufficiently heated, and I am dictating this letter sitting over an oil lamp to keep my hands warm. This will indicate to you how necessary your sweaters are, for if one needs them in a building you can imagine how necessary they are out doors. We have hardly any clear weather. Rufus, Henry and Bertie, in letters just received, all spoke of your work. It is a wonderful accomplishment to have fitted out two regiments with sweaters.[59]

Charley's original regiment, the 17th, published a tribute to her in their newspaper, saying they owed more to her than "to any woman in the United States." "It is no small compliment," Charley proudly wrote Caro.[60]

Charley had left Henry in charge of his financial affairs, but Henry continued to solicit his brother's advice. Charley offered guidance, but he repeatedly reassured his brother that he was doing a good job. "Very greatly appreciate the able way in which you are looking after my matters," he praised Henry. "Your judgment has been sound in every regard . . . Business matters entirely secondary to me in these times."[61]

The details of his businesses may have been secondary to him in Europe, but Dawes was a born financier, and he was generous with his friends. He offered stock to Harbord, suggested that Pershing take a stake in the Ohio Cities Gas Company (advice Pershing followed), and invested money for Albert, the king of Belgium. "Until I think of writing you, it does not occur to me that such things would ordinarily be considered unusual," Charley confided in Caro when he told her about his service to the king and his contacts with lesser royalty.[62] Charley never discussed offering Hagood investment opportunities, an indication that he may not have had the same level of rapport with the general as he had with his other superiors.

Dawes was promoted to colonel in January 1918, and Pershing told him not to buy his eagles. "As a matter of sentiment," Pershing wanted to give them to his friend. At a dinner at Pershing's house on Sunday afternoon, January 16, Pershing pinned the eagles on Dawes's uniform. Van de Vyvere and Hartjes, who had accompanied Dawes from Paris to Chaumont, were also present.[63]

The need for nonmilitary labor to handle cargo at the ports, build rail lines, and construct buildings had been pressing from the first arrival of soldiers in Europe. Pershing had repeatedly requested Washington to provide stevedores to assist at the docks and other laborers to construct rail lines and warehouses so that soldiers could train for war. In early fall, Pershing asked Dawes to take responsibility for the acquisition of labor, and Dawes declined, claiming that he had ten men's work as it was. Pershing persisted, even after Dawes recommended another person for the position. In early February, Dawes acquiesced, and a labor bureau was created under the aegis of the Purchasing Board. "It is my duty—for an emergency exists—but I am heavily laden already. Still, 'between us girls,' I am glad of the opportunity," Dawes confided in his diary.[64]

John Price Jackson, who had been Pennsylvania's labor commissioner, headed the labor bureau. Its establishment relieved Pershing of responsibility for the daily administration of labor needs, but it did not ease the problems of dealing with the French bureaucracy. Pershing sought a total of 50,000 laborers. They were being hired from noncombatant European countries—Spain, Italy, and Norway—but they could not enter France without its approval. The French did not have the same sense of urgency that the United States did and dragged their feet. The labor issue was further complicated by the United States having to negotiate different wage rates for every group of laborers, based on their country of origin.

"I am glad to say that I am making good progress in my labor," Dawes wrote to Rufus on March 9, 1918, after detailing exactly who in the family was allowed to see the letter. He continued:

> Beside the General Purchasing Board and the French Mission I have now thirty-seven officers on my staff. Our total purchases now aggregate over three million tons and our agreements for replacement on this are only about two hundred and twenty-three tons, so that we have effected a saving in shipping space to date of about two million seven hundred thousand tons, an amount very much larger than that which our army has received from America owing to the scarcity of shipping space.[65]

It was a prodigious accomplishment and essential to the U.S. war effort.

Part of Dawes's progress with labor was the establishment, with Jackson's assistance, of a bureau for female labor, led by Elsie Gunther, who had come to Europe under the auspices of the Red Cross. Her office was set up in Tours, France, and she eventually oversaw approximately 12,000 women who took over a variety of clerical and other light duties.

At Hagood's request, Dawes submitted a daily memorandum. His report for March 12, 1918, gives a good sense of the range of activities that filled his days:

1. Conference with General [W. C.] Langfitt.
2. Discussion with all officers now in Paris connected with the Labor Bureau as to method of procedure.
3. Conference with representative of War Trade Board relative to export permits from Switzerland and cooperation of War Trade Board in securing supplies.
4. Conference with Commander-in-Chief on matter of securing an allotment of labor from B.E.F. [British Expeditionary Force].
5. Conference with the Commander-in-Chief and Major [James H.] Perkins, head of the Red Cross, resulting in orders asked by wire detailing Captain F.W.M. Cutcheon to present request for thirty thousand militarized laborers for A.E.F. to Italian Government.
6. Started investigation of merits of powdered milk, a substitute for milk, which can be obtained from Switzerland.
7. Another boatload of ties shipped from Spain.[66]

It was a typical day.

In an effort to improve efficiency with the services and supply lines needed to support the troops at the front, known, initially, as the "services of the rear," Pershing issued an order to consolidate all related services. At one of the first meetings of the newly reorganized body, now christened Services of Supply (SOS), William W. (W. W.) Atterbury, who had been head of the Pennsylvania Railroad and now served as chief of transportation, strongly protested the inclusion of his unit in the SOS. Citing the British example, where transportation worked independently of the other service branches, Atterbury argued that his operations should not be subject to the arbitrary wishes of local military leaders. Dawes, on the other hand, made an impassioned plea for the value of the SOS.

In a small room, with only a few present, Dawes delivered an oration, walking up and down the room and swinging his arms for emphasis. Dawes likened the military to a large corporation, a view that Pershing also shared. However, Dawes observed, unlike a typical corporation that operates for profit, the military corporation functions for one purpose, and one purpose only: to get a certain thing at a certain place at a certain time. In a statement that took aim at Atterbury's business experience (and possibly the fact that he had retained his civilian status instead of joining the military), Dawes added that it was the function of big business to offer its services to the military and to give advice, but to abide by the decisions of the military in case its advice was not taken.[67]

The meeting was Hagood's first impression of Dawes, and he liked what he saw. "Dawes practiced what he preached," Hagood observed. "In the course of time he became one of the biggest factors of the American effort in France, but he always maintained the attitude that the military knew what it wanted and how, when, and where; that his function was to help—not direct."[68]

Charles Dawes would never be a military man. By his own admission, Dawes had an undeniable indifference to various military conventions, which could be an embarrassment to Pershing, who was a stickler for military protocol. After attending a conference with Pershing, Harbord, and French Marshal Ferdinand Foch, Pershing stood with Harbord waiting for Foch to depart. "I saw him looking at me," Dawes recalled several days after the incident, "notwithstanding the sound of the cannon, and the general surroundings, with the look of mingled friendliness, admonition, and concern which characterizes his expression during some of my interviews with his better-disciplined military associates."[69]

Dawes thought perhaps he had spoken during the meeting in a manner that had bothered Pershing. While he reflected on his behavior, Dawes saw Pershing say something to Harbord. Harbord walked across the road and "carefully buttoned up my overcoat, which was opened, including the hooks at the top." Harbord murmured in Dawes's ear: "This is a hell of a job for the Chief of Staff—but the general told me to do it."[70]

Dawes later heard that there was a picture floating around of Pershing in England with one breast pocket unbuttoned. "For the picture I am going to search that country—to use it for justifiable defensive personal purposes," Dawes promised himself.[71]

From almost the moment that Pershing landed in Europe, he was besieged by requests from both the British and the French to incorporate American troops into their respective units and under their commands. In the early months, Pershing simply lacked the manpower to comply with the requests. However, as increasing numbers of U.S. troops arrived in France, the pleas came more frequently. Both British Prime Minister David Lloyd George and French Premier Georges Clemenceau went behind Pershing's back and pressed President Wilson and Secretary of State Newton Baker to order Pershing to combine his men with theirs. Pershing held his ground. He believed that Americans would fight better under their own flag than under the flag of a foreign country. It became clear, however, that a joint military command was needed. On March 26, 1918, British General Douglas Haig and French Marshal Ferdinand Foch came to an agreement by which Foch would be recognized as the supreme allied commander. Pershing had not attended the meeting, but when he learned of the decision, he agreed.

Dawes saw the establishment of an Allied Command as an opportunity to press for an inter-Allied commitment on matters of supply. In a lengthy letter to Pershing that was at times obsequious in its flattery, Dawes made a cogent argument for closer coordination of purchasing among the three major allies.

Some of Dawes's recommendations were born out of the months of unending frustration that he experienced as he attempted to gain commitments from the French regarding needed animals, forage, food, and railway access—not to mention getting the French to follow through once the commitment had been made. As Dawes noted in his April 13, 1918, letter to Pershing:

> The United States is at this time using an immense amount of tonnage for the purpose of building enormous warehouses and dockage facilities. It is doing this notwithstanding the warehouses of France and England are being emptied and will continue to grow emptier. . . . Owing to the steadily lessening amount of supplies there is a large amount of French warehouse capacity now idle, and at the same time we are proceeding, at the heavy expense of current tonnage, on plans to immensely increase our warehouse facilities.

Dawes went on to argue that if a single designated authority determined the disposition of supplies, ship tonnage, and warehouses, then waste and duplication could be greatly reduced.[72]

119

Pershing and Dawes met almost daily from April 14 until April 18 to discuss Dawes's proposal. Dawes pressed his case for military unification of the rear. He believed it was essential if the soldiers were to fight at their best. Late in the evening on Thursday, April 18, Pershing summoned Dawes. The general had agreed to Dawes's proposal and had already presented it to Clemenceau, who immediately accepted it. The French prime minister wondered why no one had thought of the idea before. The only question that remained was whether the English would agree.[73]

Harbord had once observed of Dawes:

> Advocating something in which he is very much interested, he needs scarcely more encouragement than faint acquiescence to begin talking about "your plan." He sinks his pride of authorship in his zeal for furthering his cause. . . . Just now he is sounding the trumpet over General Pershing's plans for coordinating Allied Supply matters in much the same way that tactical and strategical unity is had through the Foch command. Actually, the idea is his own. At least the first I ever knew of such a policy it was outlined by him in a letter to the C. in C. [commander in chief] last April before I left G.H.Q. [general headquarters].[74]

There was still the matter of convincing the British, who were not as quick to agree as the French had been. Pershing dispatched Dawes to London. Dawes met with Paul D. Cravath, an American attorney who had committed to facilitating relations between the United Kingdom and the United States during the war. Cravath had presented Dawes's views to Alfred Milner, Viscount Milner, an influential member of Lloyd George's war cabinet, and Milner had responded favorably. The man "who was blocking things up" was Dawes's old nemesis, Quartermaster-General Sir John Cowans.[75]

A planned meeting of the war council had been canceled because Milner could not return from France in time. Dawes, however, was anxious to see things move forward. He arranged to meet Cowans; General Cyril Crofton-Atkins, who was British director of general transportation; and Cravath and Dwight Morrow, head of the American Shipping Board, who had accompanied Dawes from Paris. With Lloyd George and Milner already in agreement, Cowans gave his assent. Milner followed up with a letter to Pershing, and the Military Board of Allied Supply (MBAS) was officially formed. Pershing designated Dawes as the AEF representative on the board.

Dawes moved rapidly toward consolidation of the rear, even in the absence of his British and French counterparts, who had yet to be appointed. With the danger of submarine attack during transatlantic crossing reduced, American troops were arriving at a rate of approximately 250,000 men per month. The bottleneck now was the difficulty of finding enough vessels to get them to Europe.

Supply needs jumped in conjunction with the increase in troop arrivals. In early June, Dawes needed 80,000 horses immediately and a total of 100,000 over a sixty-day period. With the new board in place, the French quickly agreed to furnish the 80,000. The other challenge was to find adequate forage. The ease of communication created by the MBAS was not lost on Dawes. "Why on earth someone was not doing this on a comprehensive scale three years ago, between the French and the English, I do not know. But their present acquiescence in any plan for improvement is indicative of a useful future for our effort."[76]

At the end of May, German General Erich Ludendorff launched his third offensive along Chemin des Dames, a ridge along the Aisne River. Long-range bombs pounded Paris, and a German invasion seemed imminent. The French government began to make plans to evacuate the city. AEF officers contacted Dawes to see if he could find out where the French intended to flee. He could not get an answer.[77]

Both the French and the British were exhausted from fighting throughout the spring. Foch asked Pershing for assistance, and, for the first time since America entered the war, the general believed the Allies had sufficient troop strength and know-how to engage the Germans head-on. In their initial battle, the Americans routed the Germans at Cantigny, France, but not without considerable loss: 200 officers and troops were killed or missing, and 669 were wounded.[78] The psychological victory, however, was considerable. Americans had proved themselves on the field of battle, and the Germans had suffered an unexpected defeat.

Over the next month, the Americans began to replace the exhausted French and British in battles. Pershing activated the Second Infantry Division. Harbord was given command of its Fourth Brigade, which was composed of marines. Over the next month, Americans fought to defend French territory along the Marne River. Casualties were high—the result of the Americans' inexperience and poor intelligence provided by the French. At one point, reports came in that Harbord had been killed at the Battle of Belleau Wood in France. Dawes denied it. "I just had a note from him and it wasn't postmarked *Hell*," Dawes said in defiance of the rumors.[79] By the end of July, the Allies had halted Ludendorff's third major offensive, and the scene was set for the final offensive that would end the war.

The activity at the front kept Dawes busy in the rear. "The great counter-attack of the French and our army keeps bringing almost hourly emergencies to be dealt with," Dawes wrote in his diary on July 21. Ammunition and transportation were vital to the offensive. "If we can get the men and supplies to keep up the present counter-attack, the German salient toward Chateau-Thierry can be pinched off."[80]

In early August, Dawes met with Herbert Hoover, who had arrived in Europe to get a sense of the food situation. The French continued to suffer severe shortages of food, in large measure because there was no one to cultivate the fields and much of the country's farmland had become battlegrounds. The English, on the other hand, had a food surplus. Dawes worked with Hoover to arrange for British concessions to provide food for France.

Adequate forage also continued to be a serious problem. To ensure sufficient feed for the animals, Pershing ordered that the Americans reduce their forage ration to that of the English.[81] Even with the ration adjustment, Dawes struggled to find hay at Is-sur-Tille, in France's Burgundy region, which served as a depot for American supplies.

By the end of August 1918, the same internal jockeying for power that had beleaguered Pershing as he built the AEF began to affect the MBAS. Foch requested increased power over the rear in supply and transportation. Having finally established his own independent divisions, Pershing could not risk losing control of his lines of communication. He reminded Foch that the existing structure of the MBAS allowed central control over the Allied rear without harming functions that were essential to AEF operations.

In a masterful endgame, Dawes drafted a lengthy memorandum to Pershing outlining the accomplishments of the MBAS since its

creation three months earlier. These included consolidation of ammunition, coordination of transport, identifying sufficient supplies of
wood, and adjustment of the forage ration. Dawes then went on to note
that his French and British counterparts were both higher ranked in
their respective armies, and he offered to resign and be replaced by the
chief of staff. After completing his memo, Dawes discussed it with General Charles Payot of France, whom, Dawes knew, had been attempting
to gain control over all decision-making:

> Upon telling Payot of my intention [to resign] . . . he so strenuously
> objected to my leaving the Board that I had to promise him I would
> not do so of my own volition. . . . He stated that it was through my
> relation to the Board that he could secure the cooperation of the
> departments of the French rear under civil control, which they would
> not accord to him as a member of the Board unless associated with
> myself who have conducted in the past a large part of the negotia-
> tions of the AEF with the French civil government. . . . I don't think
> any one was ever more surprised than I was to hear this from Payot.[82]

In early September, the Americans won a decisive victory at the
Saint-Mihiel salient. The AEF was now nearly one million in strength.
The joint Allied command was beginning to pay off. For the first time
since the start of the war, the Allies could coordinate their attacks
all along the front with what became the last offensive—the Meuse-
Argonne Offensive. The unified attack prevented the Germans from
bringing in reserves, and it eventually defeated the Germans.

The string of Allied victories put more pressure on supply issues in
the rear. The Americans needed motor transport, rolling stock for the
railways, and construction materials. The AEF had requested 1,300
automobiles and thousands of trucks. They had asked the French to
lend them trucks, and the French had asked the same of the Americans.
There was an increasing need for ambulances, and twenty base hospitals had arrived without equipment. There were shortages of machine
guns and trench mortar ammunition, and inadequate ordnance. Dawes
did everything he could to fill these needs.

At the same time, Dawes still struggled to find enough laborers.
Hagood had requested that three combat divisions be detailed to SOS

to handle the labor shortage. Pershing had denied the request. On September 15, Dawes received a telegram informing him that Portugal had approved his request to recruit 5,000 workers. Reflecting the optimism that had begun to creep into the Allies' minds, Dawes wrote, " 'To him who hath shall be given.' Victory is making our great task easier—though it is hard enough yet."[83]

Dawes was cautiously optimistic. The summer had been one of unending challenges, and the rapid advance of Allied troops into long-held German positions increased the demands on his office. In late August, Dawes had met with Hagood and given him an uncharacteristically pessimistic assessment of his outlook. "Dawes told me that unless there was some relief within the next ninety days, the SOS, he thought, would collapse. Up to this time the most critical point in our problem was the question of ships—the race between the shipbuilders at home and the German submarine campaign. But this crisis had passed. . . . Dawes and I agreed that the real neck of the bottle at this point in time was rail and motor transportation in France."[84]

On September 23, 1918, at 12:30 A.M., Dawes wrote in his diary:

> I have not written anything before about our new offensive, which starts tomorrow [the beginning of the Battle of the Argonne, which actually began on September 26], because I did not dare trust it even to a paper which would remain on my person. . . . We shall have twenty-five divisions on hand under General Pershing available for the drive. Instead of striking at Metz—which we hope the Germans expect—our left flank, as I understand, will be in the neighborhood of Varennes, west of Verdun. We are bombarding Metz, but the General's eyes are elsewhere. St. Mihiel was but a preliminary effort. The next is our *great* movement.

Dawes's role in the offensive was to find supplies. He spent most of the morning of September 22 working out details on transportation and attempting to acquire 60,000 horses from Spain.[85]

The need for animals became imperative as the AEF advanced. On September 25, Pershing sent Dawes a coded message asking him to make a personal appeal to the French for more horses. Dawes found his friend 30,000 additional horses from the French army. "As I have always maintained, emergency is after all the greatest coordinator," Dawes observed in his diary.[86]

As the Allies advanced, Dawes's days were filled with incessant conferences as he did his best to meet Pershing's requests on a continent that had been at war for over four years.

In early October, Dawes alerted Harbord that the French and English were still attempting to take over Pershing's management of the rear. Secretary of State Newton Baker had arrived in Europe, and Dawes was concerned that, without someone to represent Pershing's opinions to the secretary of war, the other nations' views would hold sway. Pershing had successfully dissuaded Baker from naming General George Goethals, of Panama Canal fame, as a co-commander with responsibility for the rear. However, the possibility that Baker would change his mind remained until the day the Armistice went into effect. Three weeks before the Armistice, Dawes observed in his diary: "This I know: that John Pershing is being attacked in the rear while fighting at the front by those who would like so to divide the American army as to destroy largely its entity—something inconceivably unjust considering its great accomplishments and apparently without the excuse of military necessity."[87]

In the entire army, John J. Pershing probably had no one as loyal to him as Charles G. Dawes. Throughout the duration of the war, and well after it, Dawes looked after Pershing and his interests. Sometimes that concern bordered on the maternal—worry over the severity of Pershing's cold, fear that he had contracted pneumonia, or anxiety that Pershing was not getting enough rest. Always, Dawes was the close friend who served as a combination confidant and cheerleader, repeatedly encouraging Pershing to hold fast in his insistence that the AEF fight under its own flag. "The C. in C. and our country have no more devoted servant than he," Harbord wrote of Dawes, "in the performance of a duty that in my judgment could not have been so well performed by any other man."[88]

There are, of course, no crystal balls in war. Even as the Allies began to tally up significant victories throughout September, many people believed the war would rage on well into 1919. However, on October 3, the day before Dawes alerted Harbord to his concerns about a pending supply shortage, the German imperial chancellor notified Wilson, through the Swiss government, of its interest in opening negotiations for a cease-fire.[89]

In the waning weeks of the war, Dawes was still trying to secure upward of 13,000 horses to meet the needs of the artillery. Foch advised the board to acquire sufficient trucks in case the Germans made a massive retreat east when the Armistice went into effect. Dawes thought he could find 12,000 vehicles but believed the Allies really needed double that figure. It was during these final weeks that Dawes received his promotion to brigadier general. Dawes's modesty was such that one could easily miss any reference to the new rank in reading his journal: "[Hugh A.] Drum [chief of staff of the First Army] like myself is wearing his stars for the first time. Am much impressed with his ability."[90]

Pershing arrived in Paris on November 3, and Dawes met with him to provide updates on the supply situation as well as be apprised of the peace talks. Even with the tremendous successes of the American army, criticism of the organization of the rear continued. At Dawes's recommendation, Pershing made a statement to a *New York Times* reporter to address the naysayers, but it seems never to have been printed. Later that evening, after taking Pershing to his train so the general could return to the front, Dawes had a car accident. "Smashed up in the automobile . . . and bumped my head, but not enough to prevent it working as usual."[91]

At 8:00 A.M., Paris time, on November 11, 1918, Colonel Robert Bacon telephoned Dawes to tell him that the Armistice had been signed. "For the first time since being over here I did not anticipate an emergency," Dawes recorded in his diary later that night.[92]

Dawes described his day to his mother: "Under his [Pershing's] direction my day was given to reversing suddenly the tremendous business engine of the American Expeditionary Force. . . . I only noticed casually the singing and cheering crowds on the streets."[93]

Dawes did experience the cheering fully later in the evening. He secured a box at the Folies Bergères and took Harbord with him to see the show *Zig-Zag*, which, according to Harbord, Dawes had already seen five times. The house was packed, and the last act brought in a chorus in sets of eight, grouped by each of the Allied nations. The flags they carried bore the names of the victories of their respective countries. When the U.S. flag appeared, "The Americans, until then fairly quiet during the evening, raised the roof with their cheers." The following night, Dawes hosted Harbord and Pershing at the show again.[94]

Three days after the Armistice, Dawes accompanied Pershing on a trip to decorate British General Douglas Haig with the Distinguished Service Medal. Before going, Dawes wrote his mother, Pershing promised that if Charley "landed smoking at Marshal Haig's he would not only invoke upon my head the combined maximum military penalties for capital offenses but in addition would endeavor to apply personal chastisement on the spot."[95] As Pershing had observed nearly a year and a half earlier, Dawes was not much of a military man, but he had proved to be a formidable purchasing agent. Dawes was anxious to go home, but Pershing was not ready to send Charley back to civilian life.

CHAPTER 8

✕

Hell and Maria Dawes

The work of the MBAS skidded to an abrupt halt with the signing of the Armistice, and Dawes and his staff now looked at how they could make an operational U-turn and manage an entirely new set of challenges. The immediate need was to continue feeding people and livestock. The Italian government notified Dawes that it had a total of two hundred thousand horses and one million Austrian prisoners, and no food for either the animals or the men. The MBAS had surplus food, and, with Pershing's approval, Dawes authorized the sale of flour to Italy. He sold $3 million worth of food to Belgium, a country the Germans had attempted to starve since invading it at the start of the war.[1]

In the meantime, the AEF continued to requisition supplies. Two million American soldiers, thousands more civilians in support and charitable positions, barracks, hospitals, warehouses, vehicles, and weaponry lay scattered across western Europe, most of them in France.[2] Since the United States fought as an invited guest, operating on foreign soil, and with no intention of remaining an occupying force, no precedents existed. The United States needed to create new policies to handle troop demobilization and the transfer of property purchased or constructed on foreign soil.

Immediately after Dawes arranged the sale of food to Belgium, Washington cabled that Herbert Hoover would handle the sale of foodstuffs in the army's possession. In addition to his role as food administrator, Hoover had added to his portfolio the leadership of the U.S. Grain Corporation and the U.S. Sugar Equalization Board, two subsidiaries of the Food Administration that bought and sold grain and sugar, respectively; and the Inter-Allied Food Council, consisting of the food administrators of France, Italy, the United Kingdom, and the United States. He continued to head the privately funded Commission for Relief in Belgium, which he had established to address wartime famine in Belgium, and he was in charge of a fledgling American program looking at how to restore Europe's economy and feed its population.

Hoover arrived in London on November 25, 1919, with the intention of bypassing Europe's military leaders and using his team of civilians to take charge of policy decisions. The Europeans thought otherwise. The Supreme War Council, a panel created in 1917 to improve military cooperation between France, Italy, and the United Kingdom, retained its power in postwar decision-making and insisted that Hoover secure its support for his food relief work.

Hoover encountered the same conflicts among nations with his food relief program that Dawes had experienced as general purchasing agent. Chief among the disagreements was France's unwillingness to permit food shipments to Germany. Hoover, whose humanitarian views reflected his Quaker upbringing, tacitly acknowledged the council's authority, but he insisted that the United States oversee food distribution to avoid such disagreements. He decided that Dawes was the man who could help him achieve his goals of feeding all the European nations involved in the war.

Hoover arrived in Paris on November 27 and met with Dawes. The two men shared a modest lunch, and Hoover outlined his plans for food relief for war-torn Europe. He indicated his desire to have Dawes go to Berlin to oversee the effort there and proposed the plan to Pershing. Pershing, however, was noncommittal. After a meeting with Dawes, Pershing, Harbord, and Army Chief of Staff General James McAndrew, Pershing decided that Dawes needed to remain in Paris to wrap up MBAS matters and assist with the liquidation of equipment. As he had at the beginning of the war, when Hoover wanted Dawes to work with him in the U.S. Food Administration, Charley asked his friend to drop the matter.

In truth, Dawes wanted neither to go to Berlin nor to stay in Paris. He wanted to go home. His businessman's personality, which had been so welcomed by the military during the war, was now forced to take a backseat to the bureaucracy that began to assert itself with the signing of the Armistice. From Charley's perspective, now that his assigned tasks were completed, it was time to move on.

He was also homesick, and he could finally give in to the exhaustion he had managed to keep at bay for fifteen months. The war had taken its toll. "I must have <u>peace</u>. My nerves are not what they used to be," he wrote Caro at the time he was meeting with Hoover. "If I have not had enough of <u>conflict</u> in life, nobody has."[3] When Melvin Ericson brought Dawes pictures of his grandson and namesake, Charley wrote wistfully, "[Mellie] brought me some pictures of my new grandson whom I would much like to see in person."[4]

The shooting war was over, but a new enemy was afoot. An influenza pandemic, the deadliest in modern history, swept around the world and claimed more soldiers' lives than war injuries.[5] In Europe, barracks and close living quarters made American soldiers especially susceptible. Rank was no protection, and the flu was particularly virulent among the young. Dawes watched, helplessly, as men who had survived the battlefield died from disease. The casualties included one of Pershing's aides, Colonel Carl Boyd. "His loss is a heavy one to General Pershing who relied upon him greatly," Dawes eulogized Boyd in his journal. "He was a noble character. He leaves a wife and daughter with whom we all mourn."[6]

When Henry wrote from home to ask if Charley would allow the Daweses' hotels to be used as infirmaries to house those who had contracted the flu, Charley readily gave his approval. It was the least he could do to help the situation in Chicago and Boston while the postwar bureaucracy kept him in Paris.

In the midst of his despondency, Charley rallied his trademark optimism to encourage his friend Lawrence Sherman to run for reelection in 1920. After being elected to the Senate to fill Lorimer's unexpired term in the last election decided by state legislators, Sherman had been reelected by popular vote to a full term in 1914. Seven years later, he was ready to go home to his cornfields and let the younger generation take over. The Democrats controlled the Senate, and Sherman felt ineffective. He told Dawes that his only options were to vote "no" and to criticize. "The waste and maladministration here are frightful," Sherman confided to his friend. "While we have been making the world safe for democracy, the present style of democracy is unsafe for this country."[7]

Sherman also had personal reasons for not running again. He had turned sixty in 1918, was his daughter's only surviving parent, and was determined to spend more time with her. He had gradually lost his hearing, and he had difficulty following conversations and debates. None of the medical specialists whom Sherman had seen could help him, and it had become difficult for him to participate in social functions and large meetings.

Dawes did his best to encourage Sherman to rethink his decision. "So far as your deafness is concerned it is an annoyance to you rather than an impairment to your usefulness. . . . The brilliancy of your intellect, your vast experience and high purpose cannot be affected by ear drums." As far as the younger generation taking over, Dawes predicted: "During the next ten years in the United States, in my judgment, we will be governed by our best minds."[8] Sherman appreciated his friend's advice, but he knew his own heart, and he retired from the Senate, much to Charley's disappointment.

In the weeks and months following the Armistice, both France and the United States recognized the magnitude of Dawes's contributions to the war effort. France named Dawes a commander of the Legion of Honor, the premier honor of the French Republic. "[General Dawes] has always had at heart to ensure the most intimate liaison and the most complete cooperation between the French and American services," read part of his commendation. "[He] always endeavored to smooth out all difficulties and to assure the most cordial understanding between the two armies."[9] The medal was delivered to General Headquarters in late January, and Harbord wrote Dawes of its arrival: "I am looking forward to seeing the ribbon on your manly chest the next time we meet."[10]

In January, Dawes received the U.S. Army's Distinguished Service Medal (DSM) in recognition of "his rare abilities, sound business judgment, and aggressive energy [which] were invaluable in securing needed supplies for the American Armies in Europe."[11] Pershing commended

Dawes for having "unswerving zeal" and for picking "assistants who possessed the highest degree of specialized ability" in a variety of areas.[12]

"My dear Charley," Caro wrote him after he received the DSM. "You certainly are being decorated these days. I am glad that they realize what you have done."[13]

However, the accolades did nothing to lessen Charley's boredom or homesickness, and his discontent deepened when he learned that Secretary of State Baker had named him as the military member of the U.S. Liquidation Commission. The commission was assigned to dispose of the surplus stocks and to settle claims and accounts between the Allies and their agents and the United States.

Dawes saw the commission's task as thankless and fraught with political peril. He was convinced that Congress would look over the commission's shoulder and question its every move. In this, time proved him right. Dawes had been motivated as general purchasing agent because he believed he was saving lives. He saw no expression of patriotism in the proposed work of the commission, but he also recognized that he was qualified to do the job and that he needed to accept it.

The United States had approximately $1.3 billion worth of both movable and immovable property in France at the end of the war.[14] Shipping the movable property back to the United States would have delayed the return of the two million American troops in Europe. Existing ship capacity could accommodate the return of 250,000 troops monthly, and the final transport of troops would not take place until the latter part of 1919.[15] From a political standpoint, the return of the movable property was undesirable amid fears that the surplus would flood the market and reduce domestic manufacturing output.

The immovable property consisted of U.S.-constructed hospitals, barracks, docks, and warehouses—all permanent structures. In light of the new threat of Bolshevism coming from Russia, the Americans urged their Allies to purchase the surplus and use it for defense against a potential threat from the East. The question was how the Allied nations would pay, because their currencies were unstable and the exchange rates fluctuated wildly with the U.S. dollar.[16]

Baker announced the formation of the U.S. Liquidation Commission on February 11, 1919, and it held its first organizational meeting in Paris on March 17. The other three members of the four-man commission were Judge Edwin B. Parker, former priorities commissioner of the War Industries Board, a government agency that coordinated the purchase of military supplies; retired U.S. Senator Henry F. Hollis, a New Hampshire Democrat; and Homer H. Johnson, the former president of the Cleveland, Ohio, Chamber of Commerce.[17] The commission arrived at its terms of sale in mid-July. The United States settled over $873 million in claims against it among the Allies, including the United Kingdom, France, Belgium, Italy, and nongovernmental entities. France agreed to pay $400 million for American property valued at close to $1 billion in what was termed a bulk sale. Other properties not included in the bulk sale were valued at approximately $423 million. The United States financed the purchase by the sale of ten-year, 5 percent bonds.[18] Dawes considered the negotiations to be one of the "big business trades of all time."[19]

With the bulk sale to France nearly completed, Dawes resigned from the commission on July 26, 1919. He would leave Paris the next day. Dawes's pending resignation finally allowed him to travel to England for the christening of his godson and namesake, Charles William Ambrose Dawes, an event that had been postponed several times due to Dawes's work on the Liquidation Commission. He arrived in Britain in late June, with Pershing in tow.

The ceremony had a profound effect on Dawes emotionally. Charley saw in his young godson the reconnecting of the British and American sides of the Dawes family. He outlined the ties in a letter to his mother. William Dawes of Boston, who rode with Paul Revere, was the fourth William Dawes, and he fought against the British. Charley's nephew, William, was the eleventh Dawes, and he commanded a tank manned by Englishmen on the Hindenburg Line, Germany's defensive position on the Western Front in World War I, and they fought a common enemy. The infant Charles was named for his father, William; Ambrose, who was a common Dawes ancestor; and Charles, the eldest son of Rufus and Mary Dawes. This would "indicate a reunion of fine old stock in common purpose hereafter," Charley proudly wrote his mother.[20]

In his final weeks abroad, Dawes embarked on a round of visits to the men who had become not only colleagues but also close friends over the last two years. He dined twice with Payot, who awarded Dawes the Croix de Guerre. With his typical generosity, Dawes arranged for the artist Jo Davidson, who had sculpted busts of Dawes and Pershing, to make one of Payot.

Charley traveled to Belgium to say farewell to his friend Aloys Van de Vyvere. The king of Belgium had conferred upon Dawes the Order of Leopold, and Charley went to the king's country estate to receive the honor in person.

Dawes spent the morning of July 27th with Pershing. Later in the afternoon, in the company of Harbord and Frank McCoy, Charley went to the Louvre to look once again at the Winged Victory of Samothrace and at the Roman statues.

Charley departed for Brest on Monday, July 28, accompanied by Kilkenny and two other aides who had been with him through the war, J. C. Roop and Dalton Mulloney. They boarded the USS *Leviathan* and sailed west, almost exactly two years since Dawes had departed New York on the *Carmania* for the unknowns of war.

Aboard the *Leviathan*, Dawes conferred with the lieutenant in charge of the boat drill and compared the new version with the drill Dawes had developed. He noted one oversight in the current drill book: "No provision had been made for oil lamps or lanterns to be strung along the boat-drill routes to be used if the torpedo explosion should put the ship's dynamos out of commission." The new drill would leave them in darkness. "Well, it is all over now, anyway," Charley concluded.[21]

The poignancy of Dawes's return to the United States was felt on both sides of the ocean. Harbord wrote him: "Your departure from Paris has made a good deal of difference for me. I do not care to wax sentimental over a homely, somewhat irresponsible, theater-frequenting, Ritz-residing, moral wreck like yourself, but I swear to you I never missed any man as much in my life as I have missed you."[22]

Charley returned to a hero's welcome in Evanston and Chicago, but he eschewed the accolades. His contentment came from holding his grandson Charles Dawes Ericson, who was now one year old. He found the peace and quiet he had sought for so long at home with Caro, sitting and reading in his library. Dawes returned to his position as president of Central Trust, happy and content to once again be in charge and on his own turf. "[I] assure you there is nothing more certain to bring one verbal expressions of appreciation like the loaning of money upon good collateral," he wrote Harbord.[23]

With his return to Chicago, Dawes resumed his charitable and cultural activities. He and Caro regularly attended the opera. Charley once again acted as a patron to promising young musicians. He rejoined Henry in the oversight of the operations of the Rufus and Mary Dawes Hotels.

Herbert Hoover also finally succeeded in drafting Charley for his food relief efforts. Dawes held the post of treasurer for the Illinois committee of the European Relief Council, which Hoover had created. The council served as a fund-raising entity to collect money to buy food for the approximately 3.5 million destitute and sick orphans who faced starvation in 1920 and 1921. The council sought to raise $33 million between fall 1920 and fall 1921 to pay for medical supplies, food, and clothing for those children. It distributed the supplies throughout Europe, regardless of national politics, through a variety of agencies, including the American Friends Service Committee, several Rockefeller family funds, and the Young Women's Christian Association.[24]

Dawes set up the account for the Relief Council at the bank, and the committee launched a special campaign for contributions at Christmastime. The campaign pulled in donations from people from all walks of life. It received gifts ranging from as little as $1 to $50,000. The Illinois committee, under Charley's leadership, raised over $935,000.[25]

Throughout his business career, Charley was a man who would discard precedent and look to do what commonly was not done. He demonstrated his lack of respect for convention in his investments in utility companies, in his willingness to take a chance on oil exploration, and in the way he grew his bank. Today, when organizational management and systems analysis are routinely taught in business programs, it is impossible to remember that there was a time when such principles were considered novel and experimental. Such was Dawes's approach to centralized purchasing, and, although he had no way of knowing it at the time, his role as the AEF's general purchasing agent was the start of a revolution in how the United States government and the United States military would eventually manage their budgets and procurement.

Herbert Mayhew (H. M.) Lord was named an assistant to General George Goethals, then chief of the army's Purchase, Storage and

Traffic Division, in October 1918. Although the war was nearly over when Lord assumed his new responsibilities, with the title of finance director, Lord quickly became aware of the efficiencies that Charley's centralized purchasing system had created for the military. Building on Dawes's approach, Lord created a central Finance Division in the army. The new division eliminated a fragmented system of military procurement, checked for duplication, and placed the payment of the army's bills in one single department. The simplified accounting procedures allowed the director of finance—in this case, Lord—to take an unbiased approach to making purchasing decisions.

While Dawes was still wrapping up his work with the Liquidation Commission, Congress began its hearings into the purchasing conducted during the war. Its initial inquiry focused on Lord's decision to centralize the purchasing function and whether businesses had profited during the war. Lord, sounding much like Dawes, defended his decision. "The new system was absolutely necessary to the protection of the government," he explained. "Without an independent finance division an independent audit of disbursements is impossible."[26]

The committee proceeded to question the use of dollar-a-year businessmen—men who volunteered to serve as purchasing agents for the government for a token one-dollar annual salary. Dawes had recruited some of these men to assist him. They represented, Lord explained, "the best business ability in the nation." The army's inspector general had found only twenty cases of dishonesty in the thousands of transactions that were made.[27]

The committee's probe was the beginning of a lengthy congressional investigation by the Joint Committee on the Conduct of the War. In Dawes's opinion, it was an exercise in second-guessing. Lord traveled to Chicago to meet with Dawes in early October, as the hearings got under way. He advised Dawes that members of the committee planned to call him to testify regarding his work as general purchasing agent. Dawes had hoped to avoid being called, but he assured Pershing that he would appear when summoned.[28]

Dawes appeared before the Senate Subcommittee on Military Affairs on November 4. The atmosphere in the hearing room was friendly. The committee conducted its hearings on a range of topics, which included questions about the advisability of a centralized purchasing function.

Dawes echoed the contents of letters of support he had written on Lord's behalf and addressed to the chairs of the Joint Committee. Army purchasing and finance would function better as bureaus separated from the work of the Army General Staff. He explained to the senators that, prior to his military service, he had assumed that an organization as large as the U.S. Army would operate along general business principles, which presupposed a centralized purchasing and centralized payment structure. However, the army spent millions of dollars needlessly in the purchase of supplies because of competition between the various departments.

Dawes used a series of maps and charts that he had maintained during the war to explain his monthly purchases. He impressed and fascinated the senators with the details. Senator Howard Sutherland, the subcommittee chair, asked Dawes if he would submit his report for the record. Dawes was surprised at the request. "This report is mine—I did not suppose anybody was ever going to read it. I have never yet been able to get anybody to read it, even my mother, but it is a good thing, gentleman."[29] The hearing had failed to be the ordeal Dawes had dreaded, but it would not be his last appearance before a congressional committee.

John Pershing returned from Europe on September 8, 1919, to massive celebratory parades. Enormous crowds greeted Pershing as he made stops in New York City, Philadelphia, and Washington, D.C. He used these speaking opportunities to share the tremendous accomplishments of the AEF. Wilson awarded him the title of general of the armies of the United States, the highest possible military rank.

Pershing's name immediately surfaced as a potential presidential candidate. He gave the idea little credence when it was first mentioned in Europe shortly after the Armistice was signed, but now the general seriously considered a run and confided in Dawes. The two discussed a victory parade in Chicago, but Charley demurred. He advised his friend to go slow in scheduling his public appearances and to go home and get some rest. By the end of September, Pershing disappeared from public view.

Although Pershing was a close and dear friend, Dawes was uncertain about helping him put together a campaign. At the time of Pershing's return, the country was experiencing massive labor unrest. In September alone, three hundred fifty thousand steelworkers walked off the job in the largest strike in U.S. history, and Boston's police force went on strike.[30] Massachusetts Governor Calvin Coolidge fired the entire police force when it refused to return to work. Labor's anger at employers fueled the strikes. Business owners rescinded their recognition of labor unions, laid off workers, and pulled back benefits they had given during the war years. Rampant inflation wiped out the wage gains workers had received in the previous two years. By the end of 1919, one out of every five workers had walked off the job in industries as far-ranging as textile factories and steel mills.

Pundits and critics called the unrest "radicalism," a term fueled by the belief that both the American Federation of Labor (AFL) and the International Workers of the World (IWW) were strongly influenced by the Bolsheviks and their Communist ideology. Dawes, as a conservative businessman, had little sympathy for the unions. Acknowledging the labor unrest, he wrote Pershing: "The hope of the country, in my judgment, lies now in the fact that the business element is willing and is preparing to fight radicalism to the last ditch."[31]

The early favorites for the Republican presidential nomination were Illinois governor and Charley's friend Frank O. Lowden, General Leonard Wood, and Pershing. When a group of supporters approached Dawes about getting behind Wood's candidacy, Dawes gave his usual reply that he was out of politics—but not so "out" that he had no preferences. He informed Wood's backers that his choices were Pershing first, Lowden second, and then the field.

Pershing resumed his public tour in December, scheduling stops in Chicago and St. Louis. Chicago organized a parade, a reception at the Art Institute, and a banquet in the Gold Room of the Congress Hotel. Charley gave an address at the banquet in advance of Pershing's speech. Pershing was gracious, charming, and studiously apolitical. His talk repeated the theme of his speeches in the fall and focused on the Allies' victory.

The final Chicago event, a public meeting at the Auditorium Theatre, recognized Pershing alongside Chicago men who had served under him. There were cries of "the next president," but Pershing did not respond with any indication that he was considering a run.[32] A quotation from an unnamed man, described as being as close to Pershing as any man in the United States—and sounding much like Dawes—sought to quell rumors about presidential ambitions: "Of course, men have talked of General Pershing as a presidential possibility. It is only natural. But General Pershing is not a candidate in any sense of the term."[33] Dawes reported to Harbord on the Chicago visit: "The General's trip was a great success. . . . His speeches could not have been better, especially the one at the great Auditorium meeting where he received the most inspiring reception I have ever seen."[34]

In late January, J. G. Quekemeyer, Pershing's aide-de-camp, wrote Dawes a confidential letter. Quekemeyer saw the Republican Party as lukewarm to Pershing's candidacy, and he believed that Wood was a more appealing candidate to the Republican machine because he could more easily be controlled. Pershing lacked a base of support in the Republican Party even though his father-in-law, Francis E. Warren, was a well-respected Republican senator from Wyoming and could have organized support for Pershing. Quekemeyer also thought that if the Republicans, who would hold their nominating convention first, did not choose Pershing as their candidate, then the Democrats would pick him.[35] Quekemeyer's analysis was astute, and Dawes concurred.

Dawes and Pershing continued to correspond throughout the spring of 1920 regarding the likelihood of the general receiving the Republican nomination. Dawes held back from giving his friend unqualified support. Drawing large crowds and public accolades was not the same as building a campaign organization. Dawes encouraged Pershing to find supporters in Nebraska, the state where the general had established residency, who would help him put together a grassroots movement. If he could get support at home, Charley advised his friend, there was potential to build a national campaign.

In the meantime, Wood had put together a strong organization and attracted a lot of money. He won committed delegate support in a number of states; was said to have significant backing from women, who would be voting for president for the first time; and received encouragement from the business community.

Hiram Johnson of California was also a well-supported contender for the nomination. As Theodore Roosevelt's vice presidential running mate on the 1912 Progressive Party ticket, Johnson still commanded a sizeable following, particularly among the Progressive wing of the Republican Party. He had won several primaries but had not secured sufficient funds to mount an effective campaign. Johnson lacked emphatic support from party regulars, who saw him as a defector from the party ranks when he ran with Roosevelt in 1912.

The third leading candidate was Dawes's longtime friend Frank Lowden. Lowden had gained delegate support in several states, although his home state of Illinois, heavily controlled by the anti-Lowden faction in Cook County, did not give him its unqualified support.

By the end of May, Wood's nomination looked all but certain. Then, just before the Republicans were to convene their convention in mid-June, questions surfaced regarding agreements Wood presumably entered into in exchange for $1 million in campaign funds. Supporters urged him to request an accounting of funds from his campaign manager, John T. King, and Wood did so. When King refused to respond, support for Wood's candidacy weakened.

Dawes had long doubted Pershing's chance of political success, and Wood's faltering campaign did not change his mind. Charley decided to back his long-term political ally Lowden. He wrote Pershing about what he had decided, and the general, ever gracious, understood Dawes's decision. Pershing assured Charley he would have done the same thing if he were in Dawes's shoes.[36] Pershing presciently predicted how he thought the convention would go: the Republicans would nominate a dark horse candidate. That is exactly what happened.[37] The candidate was Warren G. Harding of Ohio. Calvin Coolidge, now nationally recognized for his hard stance against the Boston police, was the vice presidential candidate.

Harding was a former newspaperman and a first-term U.S. senator with a reputation of "going along to get along." He had no real interest in the presidency, but his wife, Florence Kling Harding, and his political associate and campaign manager, Harry Daugherty, maneuvered him into it. There is no evidence that Dawes ever met Harding or personally knew Daugherty. However, in the close circles of the banking and oil worlds in which Dawes and his brothers circulated, they likely got word that Harding would be friendly to business interests. Daugherty had served as a lobbyist for several major corporations and had experience in crafting legislation.

Pershing and Dawes expressed their pleasure at Harding's selection as the Republican nominee with an exchange of telegrams. To Harbord,

Dawes wrote: "I believe that he [Harding] can be elected and if he is elected we will return governmentally to a condition of sanity."[38]

Labor unrest was not the only issue that confronted American business. The introduction of the income tax in 1913 had reduced people's disposable incomes and placed an additional administrative burden on business owners. The potential payment of taxes influenced Dawes's decisions about taking salary as income or receiving dividends from stock as income (which were not taxed at the time). An excess profits tax was levied against corporations and reduced businesses' total net income.

Dawes published an article in the October 2, 1920, issue of the *Saturday Evening Post* titled "The Next President of the United States and the High Cost of Living." He had written the piece after both the Republicans and the Democrats had held their nominating conventions (James M. Cox, another Ohioan, and future President Franklin Delano Roosevelt of New York were the Democratic nominees for president and vice president, respectively). Dawes had written his article after Wilson vetoed a bill to provide for a national budget system that would have required the president to submit an annual budget to Congress covering the full range of federal activities and would have mandated an independent auditing of accounts. At that time, government agencies individually submitted their budget requests to Congress.

Dawes argued that while the American public was interested in the outcome of the November election, its real concern was a desire to see a "reduction of the high cost of living and the restoration of normal conditions of life." Ignoring the inflationary conditions of the economy and aftereffects of the war, Dawes wrote that the high cost of living was the result of high taxation. He identified the excess profits tax as the primary culprit because it was repeatedly collected in the prices consumers paid. "Mister Average Consumer" initially favored the tax, thinking it was levied against "the rich manufacturer." But, Dawes maintained, the consumer, "who is generally looking out for Number One, began to realize that he . . . was the one who was paying it."[39]

Dawes reiterated his now familiar phrases about reducing governmental spending by treating government as a business. The best way to achieve this was to view the president of the United States as the chief executive of a large concern who had power over his appointed officials. In the wake of Wilson's veto of the national budget system legislation, Dawes called for Congress to give the chief executive power over the spending of appointed officials. The law's effectiveness would lie in the president's determination "to exercise his full power to compel the spirit as well as the letter of departmental coordination. He must become the personal sponsor before his departments, before Congress and before the people, of a plan of government-business unification."[40]

The article caught Harding's attention, and, shortly after he won the election, he invited Dawes to his home in Marion, Ohio, for a visit. Dawes told Harbord that the trip was merely a get-acquainted session, although Dawes privately speculated that he was being considered for either secretary of war or secretary of the treasury. It was déjà vu. Charley was once again traveling to Ohio to meet with a president-elect, and he was again considering a cabinet position.

In late December, Harding offered Dawes the position of secretary of the treasury—the post he had once coveted under McKinley. But Charley Dawes was a different man, with a higher degree of self-awareness and more attuned to his gifts. He knew that he had no patience for managing government bureaucracies. His skill lay in creating new organizations. The *Chicago Tribune* reported that Dawes was the president-elect's choice for secretary of the treasury, but following a report on Dawes's meeting in Marion, it referred to him as being chosen "to clean out the Washington stable" as part of Harding's plan to reorganize the government.[41]

Dawes turned down the cabinet post, and Harding offered it to another Wall Street outsider who could command respect among New York financiers—Pittsburgh banker Andrew Mellon. Mellon accepted the job.

Dawes testified before Congress's Subcommittee No. 3 of the Select Committee on Expenditures in the War Department on February 2 and 3, 1921, the same committee that had called him as a witness in October. The three members of the subcommittee were Oscar Bland, an Indiana Republican; Henry Flood, a Democrat from Virginia; and Royal Johnson, a South Dakota Republican. The subcommittee delved into reports of waste, fraud, and overspending during the war and following the Armistice.

Dawes testified all day on February 2. The members led him through an explanation of how he had entered the army and attained his rank. They asked how he had come to be selected as the AEF's general purchasing agent. There were questions regarding his purchasing authority and how prices were determined. They wanted to know if he had encountered war profiteers who were intent on defrauding the government.

Throughout the day, Charley maintained an air of respect and decorum toward the three men as he explained his enlistment in the 17th Engineers and Pershing's selection of him to be the purchasing agent. He gave full credit to Pershing for coming up with the idea of a centralized purchasing function, and he explained to the congressmen the French government's requirement that the Americans buy the majority of their supplies through France and the French control over pricing. And, yes, Dawes said, some people attempted to sell things to the government at outrageous prices, and the ones he knew about had been deported.

Charley's replies went beyond answering the committee's questions. At every opportunity, he argued for the importance of running the federal government like a business. He had a sympathetic listener in Royal Johnson, who agreed with Dawes. It was, for the most part, an amicable day.

Charley returned the following morning, February 3. The committee opened the hearing by repeating questions it had asked the previous day, particularly inquiries related to Charley's investigation of reports of waste and destruction of American property. Again, Charley explained that he had heard of the reports. Yes, he told the committee, he had investigated them. And, as he had the day before, he explained that some property had been destroyed because it was too damaged to be sold or returned to the United States, and it would have also required 40,000 soldiers to guard it.[42]

Within the first hour of testimony on the second day, it was clear that Dawes had lost patience with the repetitive questioning. In his answers, he took every opportunity to question the motives of the committee. Charley accused it of politicizing the war effort. At one point, he became so excited that he roamed about the hearing room, infused his language with "damns," and repeated his theme of reducing waste and fraud in the federal government. "If you men would spend just one quarter of the time trying to see the waste that goes on by hundreds of millions right here under your noses, instead of trying to put fly specks on our war record, you would be doing a much bigger public service and we would have a hell of a lot better government," he told the committee. He insisted that not one dollar was wasted in France and "damn it all, the business of an army is to win a war, not to quibble around with a lot of cheap buying."[43]

Then, in the phrase that would be identified with him until well into his old age, Dawes raised his voice and thumped the table so hard the inkstands jumped: "For every mistake made in the AEF, you have been making the same mistake here in Washington for a hundred years. Hell Maria, we weren't trying to keep a set of books. We were trying to win a war."[44]

Members of Congress were aghast at Dawes's behavior and his language. Over the next several days, they debated a resolution to censure him for his use of profanity in a hearing. Newspapers had a field day with his performance. The *Washington Times* printed a column, "Dawg-on-It-Dawes," with humorous digs at his behavior. In the meantime, Johnson, Bland, and Flood met on February 4 to decide whether to suspend hearings until the new Congress came into session. They made no mention of Dawes's testimony. Their final witness before they adjourned was Judge Edwin B. Parker, the chair of the Liquidation Commission.

Prevailing public sentiment embraced Charley's "bad boy" tactics. Dawes's friends in the military applauded him. "All of Washington is agog over your splendid testimony and they approve of it in every detail, even to the cuss words," Pershing wrote him. "There were two editorials in the New York Herald about it regretting that there was not somebody to cuss out a few other people in the country."[45] Labor had been having its say against business practices with their strikes, but Dawes tapped into the resentment against government held by the business community.

A few months earlier, Dawes had written Lawrence Sherman about his propensity to engender a strong response to his own vehemence:

> You are right about my once in a while getting on a head of steam which has to blow itself off. I do not seek opportunities for this, but being in the state of mind I am, when I am called into mild

occasions for an ordinary appearance, I generally precipitate an armed conflict. . . . But in these days, no self-respecting man, when the opportunity comes, can fail to stand up and be counted on the side of sanity and reason.[46]

Dawes wanted to be a part of returning the government to his definition of sanity.

CHAPTER 9

✕

The Ax Wielder

*H*istorians typically do not remember Warren G. Harding as a man who made a profound impact on the power of the presidency, but, by the end of his first three months in office, he had transformed the executive branch into the entity with which we are familiar today. The man primarily responsible for that change was Charles G. Dawes.

In the final months of the Wilson administration, the American Legion released a report detailing the problems wounded veterans faced in obtaining needed services. When Harding took office, he immediately formed a committee to investigate and named Dawes as its chair. Other members included the president of the American Legion; Theodore Roosevelt's sister Corinne Robinson; TR's son Theodore Roosevelt Jr., an assistant secretary of the navy; plus several other private citizens.

Dawes submitted his report to Harding at the end of April. The Dawes Committee identified many of the same issues as the American Legion report had. In 1919, Congress passed legislation moving the medical care of veterans from military hospitals to the Public Health Service. The legislation included funds for the building of new hospitals, but the new facilities were insufficient to meet the demand, and veterans complained of bureaucratic insensitivity. The committee cited inefficiencies in the administration of vocational rehabilitation programs that were designed to help wounded veterans earn a living. The Bureau of War Risk Insurance, charged with screening disabled soldiers for eligibility for special veterans programs, was too centralized. It required veterans to travel to Washington to be assessed.

The report called for the establishment of an office of veterans affairs, under which the Bureau of War Risk Insurance, the Federal Board for Vocational Education, and other agencies would be housed. The committee recommended that the Bureau of War Risk Insurance establish offices around the country to make it easier for the veterans. The objective was to reduce duplication and inefficiencies in meeting veterans' needs.[1]

Congress acted on the recommendations and established the Veterans' Bureau on August 9, 1921. Its head reported directly to the president, making the Veterans' Bureau the second civilian agency created in the executive branch, after the Bureau of the Budget. The recommendation was Dawes's initial footprint on the changing landscape of presidential power.[2]

When Harding signed the Budget and Accounting Act into law on June 10, 1921, oversight of federal expenditures shifted from Congress to the president. The act created the Bureau of the Budget and charged it with formulating fiscal programs, clearing legislative proposals from federal agencies, and preparing an annual budget. The act also created the General Accounting Office (GAO), now the Government Accountability Office, the congressional budget arm established to operate independently of the bureau.[3] Barely had the ink of Harding's signature dried when he announced that Charles G. Dawes would be the bureau's first director.

Public reaction to Harding's choice was overwhelmingly favorable. The controversy over Dawes's congressional testimony had long since been forgotten, and reporters even used the "forbidden" phrase to describe Dawes's appointment in glowing terms. "The injection of a considerable portion of 'Hell and Maria' into the financial affairs of the administration of this government exactly meets the popular belief of what is needed," the *Washington Herald* wrote approvingly. Dawes's banking and organizational experience was viewed as a big plus, as were his blunt personality and ability to "brush aside all nonessentials and the rubbish of technical details."[4] "The selection of Mr. Dawes is the President's assurance to the American people that the experiment in budgetary reform is to be carried out under the direction of one of the ablest bankers in the country, and a man peculiarly fitted for the work by his recent experience in France," columnist George Rothwell Brown wrote in the *Washington Post*.[5] "The country was fortunate that Harding had chosen Dawes," former president William Howard Taft observed in a *Post* op-ed. "No man is better fitted for this important place than he. His life's work has been the study of effective economy in the production of results."[6]

Taft tried, unsuccessfully, to implement budgetary reforms during his term as president. He submitted two budgets to Congress, which ignored both of them. In 1911, he formed the Commission on Economy and Efficiency. The commission made the argument that the president's role had become one of chief manager and administrator in chief, the very phrases Dawes had repeatedly used in his arguments for a federal budget.[7]

Much of Dawes's language about the president as head of a large business came from a document Taft submitted to Congress in June 1912. The six-hundred-page document, *The Need for a National Budget*, outlined overlapping and duplicative programs in the executive branch. It documented poor accounting techniques within the departments and made the case for centralized budgeting. When Wilson took office in 1913, he did not renew the commission's charter, and he did not submit a proposal for centralized budgeting until 1919.[8]

Wilson's reason for vetoing the budget act in 1920 was that one of its provisions was unconstitutional. As written, the bill would have taken away the president's right to terminate his appointees to the positions of comptroller general and assistant comptroller general. The House amended the bill to address Wilson's concerns and overrode his veto, but a filibuster in the Senate in the waning hours before adjournment prevented the bill from coming to a vote in that chamber.

The version of the legislation that Harding signed into law called for a presidential agency that was "in but not of the Department of the Treasury." The director and his deputy were directly answerable to the president and not subject to Senate confirmation. Congress retained the language regarding its ability to remove the comptroller general that Wilson had found objectionable. Harding was determined to have a budget office, and he did not veto the bill.[9]

Dawes's methodical mind and resolute personality were a perfect fit for the newly created position. He accepted Harding's offer on Tuesday,

June 21, and departed Chicago for Washington the following day. He jumped into action immediately upon his arrival in Washington on Thursday, June 23, even though the budget director's position did not officially start until July 1.

On June 29, Dawes issued his Circular No. 1. He outlined the four principles by which he planned to establish and operate the new bureau. The first principle was that the bureau was to be "impartial, impersonal, and nonpolitical." Second, the purpose of the director was to serve as an adviser to the president solely on matters of business administration. Third, the budget director acted as the representative of the president, and the director's sole purpose was to gather information for the president. This function gave the budget director precedence over any cabinet head or head of any other independent agency. Finally, each cabinet secretary was to appoint a representative from his own department. That individual would represent the secretary's views to the budget director, and the budget director had priority over the cabinet head in soliciting the departmental representative's advice.[10]

It was, and still is, an amazing appropriation of organizational power. With those four principles, Dawes established the culture of the Bureau of the Budget and the relationship of its head to the chief executive and other officials in the executive branch, including the secretary of the treasury. What is even more astounding is that, when Harding published the circular in his report to Congress, Dawes's principles went unchallenged by the legislators.

The first budget submitted was for fiscal year 1923, which would begin on July 1, 1923. Dawes, however, convinced Harding that a budget for fiscal year 1922 should be drawn up, even though the year began on Dawes's official first day in office. Dawes received support for his proposal from Secretary of the Treasury Andrew W. Mellon, who wanted to see cuts in federal spending so that he could gain support for a cut in taxes. Harding agreed.

Dawes held a first-of-its-kind mass meeting of six hundred bureau chiefs and members of the cabinet, with President Harding and Vice President Coolidge in attendance, on June 29. No one had ever before called together all the bureau heads and directors in one room. Dawes used the assembly as a combination pep rally, call to arms, and cudgel.

The collective personality of Harding's cabinet could best be described as schizophrenic. Several of the president's appointees were men of high integrity with a strong commitment to public service. In addition to Mellon, Harding had named Hoover secretary of commerce, and Charles Evans Hughes, who would succeed Taft as chief justice of the United States in 1930, as secretary of state.

Dawes had known Secretary of War John W. Weeks, a wealthy Massachusetts financier who made his fortune in banking and brokerage, for over twenty years. Weeks served in the U.S. House from 1905 until 1913, when he won election to the Senate. He served one term and was defeated in his reelection bid in 1918. Dawes characterized Weeks in a letter to Pershing as "on the square."

On the other side of the personality divide were members of Harding's Ohio Gang—the men who had skillfully managed Harding's dark horse presidential campaign, who had arranged for the financing of the race, and who expected to reap the rewards of their success through various machinations from their positions in the executive branch. At the head of this group was Harry Daugherty, the attorney general. A protégé of Mark Hanna's, Daugherty was a close friend of Harding's and his political manager. Daugherty had been instrumental in getting three other presidents elected to office: McKinley, Roosevelt, and Taft. It was Daugherty who met with several oilmen as he laid out the strategy to win Harding the Republican nomination, taking millions of their dollars in exchange for his assurances that they would have access to coveted oil reserves in California and Wyoming. Congress unsuccessfully attempted to impeach Daugherty, and he was indicted twice for defrauding the government in the disposal of alien property confiscated from German nationals by his office. He managed to stay in office until Coolidge demanded his resignation in April 1924.[11]

Charles Forbes was one of Daugherty's lieutenants. Harding named Forbes the first head of the Veterans' Bureau, and Forbes used the position to enrich himself by taking kickbacks from contractors who were building the veterans' hospitals and selling alcohol and drugs intended for those hospitals to bootleggers and drug dealers.[12] Forbes would remain in his position for two years before his perfidy was discovered. He was sentenced to prison on charges of defrauding the government on contracts.

Although not officially a member of the Ohio Gang, Will Hays had helped protect Harding during the campaign. Hays served as postmaster general for one year before going on to Hollywood to become the first president of the Motion Picture Producers and Distributors of America (now the Motion Picture Association of America). He arranged for the financing of the hush money that sent Harding's former paramour, Carrie Phillips, and her husband on an around-the-world tour to prevent them from going public about her relationship with the Republican presidential nominee.[13]

Albert Bacon Fall, an international lawyer and senator from New Mexico, had wanted to be secretary of state but settled for the position of secretary of interior. He quickly befriended Daugherty. Before being indicted and convicted, Fall pocketed approximately $800,000 in bribes for leasing government-owned oil reserves in Elk Hills, California, and Teapot Dome, Wyoming, to private oil companies.[14]

Harding opened the meeting of bureau chiefs with a strong statement of support for the newly established Bureau of the Budget. "There is not a menace in the world today like that of growing public indebtedness and mounting public expenditures," the president told the group. "There has seemingly grown up an impression that the public treasuries are inexhaustible things, and with it a conviction that no efficiency and no economy are ever to be thought of in public expense. We want to reverse things."[15] After some additional remarks, Harding introduced Dawes.

Dawes welcomed the bureau chiefs as business associates charged with the task of running efficiently the corporation that was the United States of America. Harding was president of that corporation, and Dawes was there to see that the government ran as a financially sound enterprise. He articulated the principles he had laid out in his circular. "The Director of the Budget, in gathering information for the use of the President, acts for the President, and his calls upon the chiefs of bureaus and other administrative officers for purposes of consultation or information take precedence over the cabinet head of a department, or any head of an independent organization," Dawes informed his audience.[16]

Dawes spoke for an hour in the sweltering heat, delivering his message with his usual energy and picturesque language. To the disappointment of the newspapers, he did not use one swear word. "The director walked out of the auditorium a perspiring but happy figure," the *New York Times* reported. "His collar was soggy, his coat collar damp, as a result of his efforts, but he felt that he had driven his message home."[17]

Harding was not spouting political hyperbole when he called the nation's growing debt a menace. In 1921, the United States was in the middle of a deep recession that saw unemployment peak at 11.7 percent, double what it had been in 1920. The gross national product had declined in one year by 17 percent.[18] Mellon strongly advocated reducing tax rates to stimulate job growth and balance the budget.

From the outset, Dawes was zealous about establishing the president's power to request budget data from his cabinet secretaries and their subordinates, and about solidifying the director's authority. "If I am timid in demanding right of way over department heads for the information gatherers of the Chief Executive," he wrote in his diary, "and trust to diplomacy or personal persuasion or acquaintance as an alternative, I am laying the foundation for the failure of my successors in office whose rights I must establish now by the creation of custom and habit."[19] In other words, he, not the president, would "wield the meat ax over their damned heads."

Dawes was assigned to Room 372½ in the Treasury Building and given an appropriation of $225,000 for employees and expenses. "One might as well be handed a toothpick with which to tunnel Pike's Peak," he complained.[20] But, as he had during the war, Dawes made do. His staff quickly filled the adjacent corridors, sending clerks from other sections of the Treasury Department scurrying to find work space.

Dawes called on his network of business associates to serve as "dollar-a-year men," starting with his vice president at Central Trust, William T. Abbott, who would serve as assistant director of the budget. Dawes also requested his former postwar colleagues General George Van Horn Moseley and Colonel Henry C. Smither to be detailed to him. Dawes's close friend Lawrence Y. Sherman came on board to assist with developing the budget for the District of Columbia, a federal responsibility. Henry and Rufus offered guidance as well, as would nearly a dozen other businessmen and friends of Dawes's.

Lieutenant Colonel James C. Roop and Lieutenant Francis Kilkenny were assigned to his office from the army. General Herbert Lord also joined the work at the Budget Bureau. From the start of his tenure, Dawes identified Lord as his successor.

Caro and the children would not join Dawes in Washington until early fall, so he moved into Pershing's apartment. Pershing was often absent, and the arrangement allowed Dawes to work in the evenings in peace and quiet. During most of July, Charley spent his evenings studying issues and holding meetings with key members of the administration who would be instrumental in helping him further develop the bureau's policies. General Charles E. Sawyer was especially useful in pulling together key people, including Albert Lasker, chairman of the U.S. Shipping Board, and Walter F. Brown, who headed up the committee authorized by Congress to recommend a reorganization of the executive branch. Dawes also dined frequently with the Harbords when Pershing was out of town.

The bureaucratic resistance to Dawes's efforts began to materialize in midsummer. He found himself spending considerable time winning over members of the administration. "[I am] constantly impressing the heads of the departments and establishments with the idea that I am just as determined as they are not to let the effort for necessary economy interfere with the efficiency of government functioning," Dawes noted after his first five weeks in office.[21]

One cabinet secretary who was not impressed with Dawes's efforts was Fall. He complained in a letter to Harding. The interior secretary expressed concerns that, in an effort to achieve economies, positions within the Bureau of Pensions and the General Land Office, both in his department, would be eliminated. Fall was, in fact, adding staff as fast as he could, and he was lobbying to have the U.S. Forest Service, an agency of the Department of Agriculture, moved under the Department of the Interior umbrella. Control of the Forest Service would have given Fall jurisdiction over federal woodlands in the contiguous forty-eight states, as well as woodlands in Alaska, which he sought to harvest. This was in addition to the control Fall had recently obtained over the Elk Hills and Teapot Dome federal oil reserves. Secretary of the Navy Edwin Denby had transferred that authority on May 31 in a little-noticed executive order signed by Harding.

Harding forwarded Fall's letter to Dawes with a request for his review and comment. In his reply, Dawes assured the president that he would not seek to cut jobs that actually brought revenue into the government.

Dawes cited the example of protecting positions in the U.S. Railroad Administration and the Internal Revenue Service. If Dawes suspected that Fall had ulterior motives, he did not express his thoughts in writing.

A month after assuming the budget director's position, Dawes provided Harding with a recommended budget for fiscal year 1922. He triumphantly reported to Harding: "I have . . . the honor to report $112,512,628.32 as the estimated savings in expenditures reported to me by the heads of departments and independent organizations, in compliance with your directions to all concerned to secure a reduction in expenditures under appropriations and balances available during the current fiscal year."[22]

Dawes had done much more in his first month of work than look for savings for the fiscal year 1922. Smither was assigned to look at the government's purchasing practices, and Moseley reviewed the surplus supply situation. The army and navy were primary targets for Dawes's budget cuts, and he expected to encounter strong opposition. His plan was to investigate the service branches' practices without arousing either their apprehension or their latent opposition.[23]

In spite of his comments that he would need to eschew diplomacy, Dawes recognized that the key to his success would be the trait that Harbord had identified years earlier: Dawes's ability to make the other person believe that the idea originated with him. "I must get the heads of these departments immediately concerned themselves in the matter so that the recommendations for necessary executive orders may come from them," he acknowledged. In that regard, Dawes sought to find "wise precedents" in matters where budgets and expenditures were duplicated across departments.[24]

The absence of any notable congressional opposition to Circular No. 1 emboldened Dawes in the use of executive orders. He was mindful of Congress's prerogatives, but he quickly discerned that he could "go pretty far by use of executive orders toward improving the present disgraceful lack of coordination, both in the use of surplus supply as well as in supply procurement."[25] What Dawes deftly achieved was to establish a line between the professional input of the "budget men," while at the same time recognizing that political considerations required a certain amount of fluidity.

Dawes drafted the entire operational structure of the Budget Bureau by executive orders and submitted them to Harding for his signature. Through these orders, Dawes created the Federal Purchasing Board, designed to coordinate purchasing across all departments, including the military, and the Federal Liquidation Board, which handled the disposition of all federally owned surplus property. Their creation was "done quickly, quietly, and without an appropriation of money."[26]

Work on the 1923 fiscal year budget began in earnest in early August. Requests for estimated expenditures were sent to all department heads. September 1 was the due date for preliminary reports. Harding and Dawes worked closely together, and Dawes found the association with the president delightful. He described Harding's mind as lightning quick. "I have 'cut down' on my advice and put more steam into gathering facts," Dawes observed in his notes. "If I don't volunteer the advice before I present the facts, he 'beats me to it' every time. . . . I have ceased to try and 'instruct' the President as much as I did in my earlier memoranda." The reason Dawes changed his approach, he added, was that he realized his "instruction" was superfluous.[27] It was a different take on Harding, who had gained the support of wealthy business and oil men for his presidential candidacy because he was considered an intellectual lightweight and a malleable "empty suit."

In the months since Dawes had joined the administration, he had developed a personal friendship with Harding. Neither a drinker nor a womanizer, Dawes did not fit in with the booze-filled, poker-playing Ohio Gang with whom Harding relaxed. But Dawes was a regular on Harding's yacht the *Mayflower*, and he enjoyed his pipe and a good game of poker. He was one of the only people whom Florence Harding allowed to smoke in the White House. As he had with other friends, Dawes provided financial management services to Harding, which consisted primarily of purchasing registered bonds and other low-risk investments. Dawes would continue to invest on Harding's behalf until the president's untimely death on August 2, 1923.

After little more than two months in office, Dawes was recognized by the American public as being second in authority only to the president. "No cabinet member may successfully gainsay his word, no party councilor nor unofficial adviser successfully traverses his rulings," reported the *New York Times*. "Without a portfolio, quartered in an office so obscure that it is designated by a fractional number, his fiat goes forth unchallenged by the mighty. He is the Administration Pooh-Bah."[28] Pooh-Bah was a mocking title for someone important, derived from a comic character in the Gilbert and Sullivan operetta *The Mikado*.

On September 14, Mellon and Dawes appeared before the Senate Finance Committee to tell them that Dawes had cut a total of $350 million from the budget, a savings in excess of $188 million over his original estimate. Spending reductions in the War Department, Shipping Board, Veterans' Bureau, and Railroad Administration provided $305 million of the cuts.[29] Dawes called the day before his appearance "the hardest day's work I have put in since returning from France."[30]

War Department savings would come from reduced spending by the navy and a reduction in the size of the army. Infantry regiments were reduced by one-third, cavalry regiments were decreased by approximately one-fifth, and engineering regiments were cut in half, although the total number of soldiers in those regiments would remain the same.[31] In the Veterans' Bureau, the savings came from a decline in war risk claims and reduced spending for vocational programs.

A writer for the *New York Tribune* observed:

> Nelson W. Aldrich, who generally knew what he was talking about, told the Senate away back in the days of the Taft Administration that $300,000,000 could be cut off of the government's annual expenditures by good business management. Congress paid no heed to him because at that time it wasn't interested in economy and scoffed at the idea of a budget system. General Dawes holds to the Aldrich theory. Fortunately, as director of the budget, he has had the opportunity to put his belief into practice—without let or hindrance from anybody.[32]

Even though the nation's unemployed had increased to nearly six million people, the prevailing view was that Dawes's cuts were the medicine the country needed to get back to a healthy economic condition.[33]

The *New York Times* was equally effusive in its praise. "In the changed times the country follows the work of General Dawes with admiration and applause. Every time he rolls up his sleeves to take a fresh crack at the Federal estimates, the response of the country is instantaneous. When the land is filled with citizens compelled to save in a pinch, it is good tactics for the Government to go into the economizing business."[34]

The accolades took a backseat on October 28, when Dawes's mother, Mary Gates Dawes, died. Her funeral was a small family affair, and she was buried on October 30 in Marietta. Her health had been failing for a number of years. She had been a devoted and supportive mother to Charley throughout his life. Dawes had a special relationship with her thanks to their shared birthdays and because he was the namesake of her brother. As is always the case with a beloved parent, Dawes felt her loss keenly.

Harding issued a document that Dawes titled "Magna Charta of the New System of Routine Governmental Business" as an executive order on November 8, 1921. It expanded on Circular No. 1 and set up the framework by which the Budget Bureau has operated ever since. The document provided the methodology by which departments were to revise their budget estimates and submit the revisions to the president. It reiterated Dawes's central tenet that the budget director gathers information and acts on the president's behalf. Each department's designated budget officer was responsible for presenting the cabinet secretary's proposed budget, together with supporting documents. The "Magna Charta" emphasized that the coordinating agencies answered to the budget director, and that the chief coordinator for general supply oversaw all routine activities of the federal government, under the supervision of the budget director. Every bureau was to be organized in a way that facilitated collaboration across all agencies. Ultimately, however, the president made the final decisions on budget amounts.[35]

A poignant exchange of letters between Harding and Dawes at Thanksgiving reveals much about Dawes's ability to give credit to others for accomplishments that were actually his own. "My Dear General Dawes," Harding wrote from the White House:

> You are always very gracious in your expressions, but I want you to alter your attitude somewhat. Instead of being good to you I am

anxious to be helpful. . . . I apprehend that we are going to have some difficulty in getting the cordial support of the Congress for the work which you have already done. We are going to come to a test of the budget system when we see what action Congress takes in its first consideration of the budget. I look forward to that test with some anxiety.[36]

Dawes replied:

If there is anything in the world that you have not done to help me I do not know what it is. . . . You know perfectly well that when I have gotten into a pinch I have come to you, and you have pulled me through. Your wider knowledge and experience with conditions here, and your close attention to your every executive act in connection with the affairs of this office, have brought it through with a minimum of error. [House Appropriations Chairman Martin B.] Madden telephoned me this morning that at the opening of Congress he wants me to come and with him to address the full Committee on Appropriations before they take up the consideration of the budget. This I shall do with great pleasure and with much confidence that the friendly relations which we are commencing to establish with Congress will be forwarded thereby.[37]

An overwhelmingly conservative press nationwide and a bipartisan group calling itself the National Budget Committee (NBC) sought to build widespread public sentiment in favor of the budgeting process. The NBC exerted pressure on Congress to cut spending and operate the government in a businesslike manner. Stanley H. Howe, a Republican activist who had worked to improve the condition of the poor in New York City and who would eventually become an aide to New York Mayor Fiorello La Guardia, headed the organization. Other founding members of the committee included Taft, who was now chief justice of the United States; former Democratic presidential candidate Alton B. Parker; financier Paul M. Warburg; and diplomat Henry L. Stimson. The local chapters were known as "Budget Guards," and they met weekly to discuss ways to apply pressure on the government to hold down expenses and, ultimately, to reduce taxes.

The New York Guard included a representative from the Otis Elevator Company, the Franklin Automobile Company, and a variety of manufacturers of retail goods, including clothing, jewelry, and stationery. John T. Pratt, a New York banker and member of the chapter, undertook a cross-country tour in November to encourage the formation of budget guards in major cities that would work to prevent reversals in the savings that Dawes had achieved.

Representative William R. Wood, an Indiana Republican characterized as a "watchdog of the treasury," made it clear that the Republican-controlled Congress intended to hold the line. Martin B. Madden, the chair of the Appropriations Committee, was even more direct. If the heads of the departments did not keep within the congressional appropriations, he would invoke an old, but still operative, statute and send those guilty of overdrafts to jail.[38]

Harding submitted the first formal budget of the United States, for fiscal year 1923, to Congress on December 5, 1921. The budget called for estimated total expenditures of $3.505 billion, against estimated total receipts of $3.34 billion, showing a potential deficit of $167.5 million. To prevent an actual deficit, the budget recommended that $150 million of the difference come from a reduction in the navy's supply account, and the balance of the savings come from cuts across the board. Spending in 1922 was $1.5 billion less than actual ordinary spending in 1921, and the estimated spending for 1923 would be $448 million less than projected ordinary expenses for 1922.[39]

Public reaction was overwhelmingly positive. Charley was given much of the credit for the work. "The effect of this budget statement upon Congress and the country," The Outlook editorialized on its front page, "will, we believe, be favorably influenced by the work already done by the budget bureau under its energetic and efficient director, Charles G. Dawes."[40]

Dawes met in closed session with the House Appropriations Committee on December 9 to explain and defend the budget. Judging by his diary entry, he acted in his usual, feisty manner. "My arm is still lame twenty-four hours after, from my forcible gesticulations during my speech."[41]

On February 3, Dawes convened all the department heads again, this time holding the meeting in DAR (Daughters of the American

Revolution) Constitution Hall. He spoke for nearly an hour, reaching, as he put it, "into some rat holes of covert hostility among the minor bureau chiefs."[42] In spite of his efforts, there were still concerns that the government would end the year with a deficit. Dawes would have none of that.

The meeting opened with a review of what the department heads had accomplished since the establishment of the Budget Bureau in July. Dawes, as usual, gave the credit for the spending reductions to Harding's effective leadership in implementing a unified plan across all the executive-level departments and agencies.

Dawes then addressed the criticisms that had been leveled against his coordinators by members of other departments. "My coordinators and I take our hats in hand and go around to the departments and try to stop trouble, and plead for reasonable action, in order not to be justly charged with the misuse of the great authority which the president has given us," Dawes informed the group in his typically feisty style.[43] He was just warming up.

Turning toward an aide, Dawes demanded, "Where are those brooms?" On cue, the aide handed Dawes two brooms. "This may look like a stage play," he told his audience, as he strode up and down the stage, stamping his feet. "But it is not, because things like this have got to stop."

"There is your broom that meets navy specifications," he showed the audience, pounding it on the stage. "And here are brooms that don't meet those specifications but sweep just as well. The navy bought 18,000 of its specifications brooms when it could have had 350,000 army brooms for nothing."[44]

The *New York Times* called the meeting a religious revival with Dawes playing the role of then-popular evangelist Billy Sunday, railing against the sin of government extravagance. Officials' opposition to efficiency was like "rat poison in breakfast food," Dawes charged, adding that "a day of judgment was at hand for them at the end of the year when their efficiency records were examined."[45]

The Harding administration had its work cut out for it. This was Congress's first experience with working through a budget. Although there was strong public sentiment for the legislators to adopt the document as presented, some factions within Congress were intent on setting the amounts of the appropriations above the budgeted levels. The National Budget Committee held a second annual convention in April to sustain public pressure for a balanced budget. Madden, Wood, and their fellow budget watchers on the Appropriations Committee faced challenges among their own members. In late March, the committee voted to add an additional $15 million to the army's budget for rivers and harbors.[46] *The Nation*, a publication not generally known for its conservative outlook, editorialized: "[The administration's budget] proposed an expenditure of $27,600,000 on the improvement of rivers and harbors. The House of Representatives by a vote of 172 to 75 has raised the amount to $42,800,000. It is a reasonable assumption that the increase represents 'pork' for the folks back home. But even if that assumption were proved to be false the increase would be a serious blow at scientific budget-making."[47]

The combination of controlled spending and tax cuts gave rise to the prosperous decade now known as "The Roaring Twenties." The United States had a budget surplus in 1920 of $291 million, and, by 1923, that surplus had more than doubled to $736 million. The biggest surplus year was 1927, when receipts exceeded expenditures by $1.16 billion.[48] By that time, Dawes was in his final year as vice president of the United States and looking pessimistically at the economic situation. With his banker's acumen, he recognized that overextended credit and growing inflation spelled the potential for another serious depression. It was a prescient assessment.[49]

Adjustments have gradually been made to the budgeting process. Dawes's cautious approach of underestimating revenues and overestimating expenses created the perception that more money would be available than expected, and Congress took increasing leeway in its interpretation of the budget document. Harding's successor, Calvin Coolidge, repeatedly urged Congress not to appropriate more money than was budgeted. When the Great Depression of 1929 proved to be intractable and lasted well beyond any previous economic downturn experienced by the United States, the theories of the British economist John Maynard Keynes, who held that the government should use deficit spending to stimulate an economy in recession, overrode those who believed the government should spend only what it took in. As Dawes anticipated, the budget staff were the professionals and the president made the political decisions, overriding the recommendations of the experts.

Dawes retired on June 30, 1922, and Lord replaced him as budget director. He would stay in that position until May 31, 1929. In a final acknowledgment of Dawes's dedication to budget reduction, Harding announced that government expenditures for 1922 would be $1.75 billion less than expenditures for 1921. The president gave all the credit to Dawes.[50]

Dawes's friends feted him as he prepared to return to Evanston. "He was the only man who could smoke a pipe in the . . . White House and get away with it," noted one article lamenting Dawes's departure as budget director. "In the process of setting things aright for Uncle Sam's pocket book Dawes incurred the dislike of many whom he found it necessary to upset. But his enemies melted away with the course of the months, and today 'Charlie' Dawes ranks among the most popular figures in figure-mad Washington."[51]

Dawes often quoted Baltasar Gracián, who wrote in his *Art of Worldly Wisdom*: "It is not the applause which greets one on entrance but on exit that is important."[52] Dawes was well applauded on his exit as budget director.

Dawes left the capital with a solemn pledge never to come back to Washington—his days in the limelight over forever. Or so he thought.

Fate had other plans.

Charles Dawes's mother,
Mary Beman Gates, prior to
her marriage to Rufus R. Dawes.

Courtesy of the Evanston History Center.

Rufus R. Dawes in his Civil War uniform.

Courtesy of the Evanston History Center.

The Rufus Dawes family: Charles, Henry, Rufus, Beman,
Betsey, and Mary Frances Dawes (*clockwise from upper left*).
Parents Mary and Rufus Dawes seated in foreground.

Courtesy of the Evanston History Center.

The four Dawes brothers: Beman, Henry, Charles, and Rufus
(*clockwise from upper left*).

Mary Gates Dawes (*top, center*) surrounded by her six children:
Charles, Mary Frances, Henry (*lower step*), Beman, Betsey,
and Rufus (*clockwise from upper right*).

Courtesy of the Evanston History Center.

Charles and Caro Dawes shortly after their
wedding on January 24, 1889.

Courtesy of the Evanston History Center.

Charles Gates Dawes, the nation's youngest
comptroller of the currency.

Dawes during his early years in Chicago.
Courtesy of the Evanston History Center.

The Charles Gates Dawes home,
225 Greenwood Street, Evanston, Illinois.

Rufus Fearing Dawes died at the age of 21 in 1912. Dawes referred to his son as a "splendid and complete young Christian gentleman."

Courtesy of the Evanston History Center.

Dawes's elder daughter, Carolyn Dawes Ericson.

Courtesy of the Evanston History Center.

Dawes (*center*) in Europe during World War I.
Courtesy of the Evanston History Center.

General Dawes (*far left*) at a meeting of the
Military Board of Allied Supply.

Courtesy of the Evanston History Center.

General Dawes (*right*) with General John J. Pershing, on Greenwood Street in Evanston.

Courtesy of the Evanton History Center.

Charles Dawes (*third from right*) and Rufus Dawes
(*second from left*) aboard the SS *America* en route
to Europe to serve on the Reparations Commission.

Courtesy of the Evanston History Center.

Dawes accepts the Republican nomination for vice president
in a speech delivered from the east terrace of his home at
225 Greenwood Street on August 19, 1924.

Courtesy of the Evanston History Center.

Charles and Caro Dawes, with daughter Virginia and son Dana, arrive in Washington for Charles's inauguration as vice president, 1925.

Harris & Ewing, photographer.
Courtesy of the Library of Congress.

Dawes during the vice presidential years.
Courtesy of the Evanston History Center.

Vice President Dawes greets kindergartners
outside his Evanston home.
Courtesy of the Evanston History Center.

Dawes delivers a speech at the Tomb of the Unknown
Soldier, Arlington National Cemetery.

Courtesy of the Evanston History Center.

President Calvin Coolidge and Charles Dawes in 1924.

Courtesy of the Library of Congress.

CHAPTER 10

X

Reparations Expert

The Treaty of Versailles, signed by the Allies and the Central Powers on June 28, 1919, officially ended the war in Europe. Article 231 stipulated that Germany and its allies accepted responsibility for initiating the war, and the Germans agreed to reimburse France, Belgium, and England for the value of coal, horses, cattle, ships, and railcars lost during the conflict. France would receive additional payments of pensions and separation allowances for its military. Belgium, which had been overrun by Germany within two weeks of the start of the war and occupied throughout the war's duration, would be paid reparations for the cost of Germany's occupation. The overall capital cost to Germany was fixed at $15 billion. Over and above its share of that amount, Belgium would receive approximately another $482 million.[1]

One of the American negotiators, Bernard Baruch, observed, in his report on the Versailles Conference, that if there had been an effort to establish a truly ideal peace, then even the victorious countries would have acted in a sacrificial and unselfish manner. However, "given the political tenor of the times," Baruch wrote, "if the negotiators had been forgiving toward Germany in the peace negotiations, the governments of England, France, and Belgium would have been overthrown."[2]

A Reparations Commission, sometimes referred to in the singular as the Reparation Commission, created to handle payments from Germany to the Allies, held a series of meetings and established a payment schedule on May 5, 1921. When the commission met the following year, on June 6 and 7, 1922, it concluded that under current economic and financial conditions, Germany could not meet its obligations. Germany was suffering rampant hyperinflation. Its unstable currency, the German mark, had become worthless in international exchange. The Allied powers were also experiencing postwar economic turbulence. Like the United States, they struggled to adjust to a postwar economy and were plagued with high unemployment and inflationary pressures.

Sir John Bradbury, representing the United Kingdom on the Reparations Commission, broached the subject of the formation of a committee of experts that would be charged with carefully examining Germany's monetary and fiscal condition with an eye toward its ability to secure foreign credit. The French inserted language stating that the committee's purpose was to ascertain Germany's ability to obtain a loan to honor its commitments under the Treaty of Versailles and to make its reparations payments according to the 1921 schedule.[3]

France and the United Kingdom disagreed over Germany's obligations. France refused to allow Germany's payment schedule to be adjusted, whereas the United Kingdom had a more lenient attitude than either France or Belgium regarding Germany's debt. Part of France's recalcitrance was tied to its own loan obligations. Both France and the United Kingdom owed the United States for the Anglo-French loan and other loans, and American bankers refused to write down the loans' value. France and the United Kingdom had also borrowed from each other, and their respective bankers likewise demanded full repayment.

The British believed that the value of the German debt defined under the treaty was essentially a bad debt and not fully recoverable. The British also argued that demanding the established payments from Germany would harm that nation's social and economic fabric.[4]

At the end of December 1922, Secretary of State Charles Evans Hughes, in a speech to the American Historical Association in New Haven, Connecticut, echoed Sir John Bradbury's call for the establishment of a nonpolitical committee of experts in finance and economics who would study Germany's economy and recommend a program. It was not America's position, Hughes maintained, either to dictate to Germany how much it should pay in reparations or to tell the United

Kingdom, France, or Belgium how much they should be willing to accept.[5] The United States position was that a committee of experts could make recommendations regarding payments to the heads of their respective governments. Hughes's speech signaled a U.S. policy change, and it was just the catalyst needed to push for a reexamination of the reparations schedule.

The United States had economic self-interest in the reparations issue being resolved. The United Kingdom and France had deflated their currencies, making their products cheaper than American goods on world markets. The instability on the Continent also reduced the demand for American investment. Germany's economic situation needed to be rectified, not simply so that the Allies would receive their payments under the terms of the treaty, but so that there could be some restoration to normalcy of international trade.

The reparations crisis intensified when France and Belgium invaded Germany's Ruhr region, the heartland of its coal production, on January 10, 1923, as a punitive action following Germany's missed payment. The United States and the United Kingdom strongly protested France and Belgium's move. The two nations insisted their actions were not an "occupation," but they proceeded to set up a customs barrier between the Ruhr and the rest of Germany. It was clear they had no immediate plans to pull back to their own borders.

Berlin organized a massive passive resistance in response to the French and Belgian presence on German soil. Ruhr factories and mines ceased production. Railroad and telegraph lines stopped functioning. France eventually conscripted locals to work the mines and took control of the railroads to ship out coal. By mid-1923, it became apparent that France's invasion had done little to generate reparations payments and much to reignite long-simmering hostilities.

France's ill-advised actions brought to a halt economic progress in Germany. Germany used the occupation as an excuse for its rampant inflation and the devaluation of its currency, which destroyed its purchasing power abroad. France suffered, too. The shutdown of German coal production forced France to import coal and coke from England and the United States at additional expense to keep French industries in production. Of the 114 blast furnaces in operation in France at the time of the Ruhr invasion, only 74 could continue operating.[6]

The French-Belgian occupation made a reparations settlement all the more essential. Discussions took place in the United States, the United Kingdom, France, and Germany throughout 1923 regarding the establishment of a committee of experts. The United Kingdom, Belgium, Italy, and Germany had signed on to the idea early in the year, but France held out until the collapse of production in the Ruhr forced its concurrence with the proposal.

On October 12, 1923, the United Kingdom's negotiator, George Curzon, Marquess Curzon, cabled Secretary Hughes to ask for American assistance in forming the experts' committee. Hughes agreed to American participation, but he made clear that the United States agreed with France's view that reparations payments were not to be tied to the Allies' debt to the United States. Hughes acknowledged that the United States had an economic interest in Germany's reparations payments, but that the amount and timing of those payments could only be determined after Germany's ability to pay had been established.[7]

By December 1923, two committees of experts had been formed. With his recent experience as America's first national budget director, Dawes was tapped to chair the First Committee of Experts. This committee would study the means of balancing Germany's budget and stabilizing its currency. The Second Committee of Experts, chaired by Reginald McKenna, a British banker, was to determine the amount of capital that had been exported out of Germany and identify a means to return the funds.[8]

Two more Americans, Owen D. Young and Henry Robinson, were invited to serve on the committees, Young on the First Committee of Experts, Robinson on the Second Committee. Rufus Dawes accompanied his brother to Europe and was designated as the chief of the staff of the First Committee of Experts.

Young had created the Radio Corporation of America (RCA) in 1919 and served as chairman of its board until 1929. He became president of General Electric in 1922 and moved into the chairman of the board position the following year. (He held the chairmanships of the two corporations concurrently through the 1920s.) Young had not met Dawes previously, but the two had many friends in common, including Harbord, who assured Charley that he would quickly make friends with Young. Young's assistant was Stuart M. Crocker, who acted as secretary to the staff.[9] Young brought to the American committee strong experience in international negotiations and personal relationships with German industrialists. Robinson, a Los Angeles banker, had served as an adviser at the Versailles Peace Conference and was a member of the commission that had considered the disposition of German ships.

The team set sail from New York on the SS *America* on December 23, 1923. The three men paid their own expenses and received no compensation for their work. This allowed them to present themselves as independent businessmen, rather than as representatives of the U.S. government. Coolidge's only instructions to Dawes were: "Just remember you are Americans."[10]

The press surrounded the group as it prepared to embark on the *America* and peppered the men with questions. Charley responded with his usual irascibility. When asked if he was "in a hopeful frame of mind" regarding the potential for the reparations to be paid, Dawes responded that his frame of mind was "none of your damned business. It's no use of you fellows getting brain fag by thinking up conundrums to put to me before the ship sails, because I do not intend to answer them."[11]

Young also declined to provide the reporters with specifics, although his tone was considerably calmer. "I have the impartiality of ignorance. I regard the questions to be settled by our committee to be business questions only."[12]

Caro accompanied her husband, and Jean Dawes traveled with her father, Rufus. The group disembarked in Cherbourg, France, on January 8, 1924, and proceeded to Paris, where the initial meetings would be held.

The British representatives on the committee were Sir Robert Kindersley and Sir Josiah Stamp. Ever the Anglophile, Dawes immediately established a rapport with both men. The Italians were Alberto Pirelli and Federico Flora. Dawes especially liked Pirelli, whom he described as "keen as a briar—ingenious and most open and honest in his views."[13] Belgium was represented by Émile Francqui and Baron Maurice Houtart. Jean Parmentier and Edgard Allix were the French committee members. Dawes recognized that Parmentier had a close relationship with French Premier Raymond Poincaré and that, without Poincaré's backing, the committee would have limited, if any, success.

America came to the negotiations with two things in its favor. First, it had remained relatively aloof from the reparations controversy. Second, since the U.S. Senate had failed to ratify the Treaty of Versailles, the United States had negotiated its own treaty with Germany.

From the start, the Americans took the lead. At the initial meeting of the Reparations Commission and the Committee of Experts, on January 14, Dawes got straight to the heart of the matter. He bluntly referred to the "pride and selfish interest of Allied officials [who were] nationalistic demagogues, foul, and carrion loving vultures."[14]

Dawes reviewed the previous decisions of the Reparations Commission, reminded his listeners of the number of dead from the war, recounted his service to the Allies as chief of supply procurement, and discussed his recent role as the first director of the budget. Then Dawes concluded: "The first step which we should take, it seems to me, is to devise a system for stabilizing Germany's currency, so that we can get some water to run through the budget mill. Let us build the mill after we find the stream to turn its wheels."[15]

It was easier said than done.

The First Committee operated under a cloud of suspicion and hostility. France, and to only a slightly lesser degree Belgium, believed they had a right to occupy the Ruhr. England had decried the French-Belgian move and called it an annexation plan. France believed Germany was doing everything it could to evade its responsibilities under the Treaty of Versailles. Germany watched as its neighbors retooled for war while they forced Germany to demilitarize. It was an inhospitable environment in which to seek a workable solution to the problem of reparations.

While Young handled many of the day-to-day negotiations, Dawes functioned in the dual capacity of keeping the committee moving forward and feeding information to the press. By providing regular, public updates on the committee's progress, Dawes maintained pressure on the Europeans, especially the French, to stay dedicated to a resolution of the reparations issues.

At the time France invaded the Ruhr region, the value of the German mark had fallen in purchasing power to the point where it required four thousand paper marks to equal one gold mark. By April, it took six thousand paper marks to equal one gold mark. By August 1923, the ratio was 1,100,000 to one gold mark, and by December, the ratio was one trillion to one.[16]

German businessmen with international connections hoarded foreign currencies. German municipalities, large corporations, and private business organizations issued their own currencies. Some of these currencies were backed by securities; many others were not. The German government issued treasury bonds in small denominations, and the railroads also circulated money. The critical question was: exactly what was the value of the money held by Germans inside the borders of Germany? Inflation was so rampant that Rufus observed, "All the printing presses in the world could not have turned out enough paper money to have restored the value of the circulating currencies to that of the money in use in 1913."[17]

Dawes, with his usual optimism, had high hopes that the committee would be successful. His opinion regarding French occupation of the Ruhr had changed since the previous year, when he had declared: "In less than two years, it will be universally recognized that the reasonable settlement of the reparations problems, which by that time should have been reached, was made possible by the French invasion of the Ruhr."[18]

Now, Dawes saw France's presence on German soil as the single major stumbling block to the committee's success. He was hopeful that it would be removed and optimistic that the committee could wrap up its work by March 1. In an echo of what Bernard Baruch had observed at the signing of the Versailles Treaty, Dawes declared: "If our plan is well conceived, public sentiment will overthrow any Government opposing it."[19]

As was typical of him, Dawes took the opportunity to renew relationships with his friends and colleagues in Europe. General Payot arrived in Paris from Havre for a visit. John Pershing was in France, working on his memoirs. Dean Jay worked for Morgan Hartjes in France. The Élysée Palace Hôtel, once the home of Dawes's MBAS offices, had been converted, somewhat fittingly, into a bank. Dawes had a strong sense of déjà vu. "It certainly seems like the old times to be with the old friends and again to be lying awake nights thinking over difficult problems."[20]

Dawes and his committee left Paris for Berlin on January 31. Rufus noted how modern the factories were and how intact the German infrastructure was between Cologne and Berlin. Nevertheless, there was relatively little manufacturing activity, and he characterized the people he encountered as subdued.[21]

The committee met with Dr. Hjalmar Horace Greeley Schacht, the recently elected president of the German central bank, the Reichsbank. Parents who knew American history and loved the United States gave Schacht his two middle names, the first and last names of an American newspaper editor.

Schacht immediately sought to stabilize Germany's hyperinflation. He recommended to the German government the establishment of a reserve currency, the Rentenmark, German for "security mark." During the war, nations had temporarily abandoned the gold standard for their currencies so that they could print money to pay their bills. Shortly following the war's conclusion, the Allies had returned to the gold standard. Schacht knew that pegging his Rentenmark to gold would communicate his desire to stabilize Germany's currency. It would also protect the Rentenmark from being hoarded or manipulated in world exchanges.

The Rentenbank, established by the German Reichstag at Schacht's urging, controlled the Rentenmark's circulation. The bank was charged with taking over the government's debt, providing credit to the government, balancing the budget, and establishing a stable currency. In essence, the Rentenbank functioned as a federal reserve bank, and its formation indicated the government's commitment to strengthen and stabilize the nation's monetary system.

Schacht established the exchange value of the gold Rentenmark at 4.2 gold marks to 1 U.S. dollar. One trillion paper marks were worth one gold mark. The objective of the valuation was to set an exchange rate that would attract foreign investment in Germany.[22] France predictably balked at the idea of Germany establishing a gold banknote, but Young skillfully negotiated French acquiescence, with helpful support from the Italian representative on the banking subcommittee. Schacht's work demonstrated to the committee that he had the authority, and the desire, to make Germany a reliable partner in world commerce once again.

The second step toward establishing an acceptable reparations framework was to identify a credible method that established Germany's ability to pay. Previous attempts to settle the reparations issue had used an asset valuation method that was based on 1912 values of Germany's fixed assets, but the method had limitations because of Germany's unstable currency. The recommendation was made to use the German railway system, a fixed asset that could be fairly valued at market rates, as a basis for creating revenue-bearing bonds.

Princeton economist Edwin W. (E. W.) Kemmerer, an adviser to the group, suggested that, rather than connect payments to asset values, reparations payments should be pegged to a percentage tax on Germany's gross income. The idea made sense because it was tied to current German productivity. Young heartily supported the plan. When Dawes proposed Kemmerer's idea to the British representatives Kindersley and Stamp, they wanted time to think about the proposal. The United Kingdom's ambassador to Germany, Edgar Vincent, Viscount D'Abernon, agreed to the concept.

Using the same underlying premise of current productivity, Kemmerer submitted a plan to Dawes that called for Germany to pay the Allies an annual percentage of its total national and state revenues over a fixed period of years. The plan's appeal was that it gave the Allies a stake in Germany's prosperity—the higher Germany's net income, the higher the reparations payment. The plan was less susceptible to fluctuations in gold prices, and it gave Germany control over its own tax revenues. The Kemmerer plan introduced elasticity into the reparations schedule. The Germans were not burdened with a punitive tax rate in lean years, but they would have the means to accelerate payments in prosperous times. The plan presupposed that normal economic conditions and a balanced budget could be established in Germany. The approach was simple and easily understood by the average citizen.[23]

World financial markets kept close tabs on the progress of the Reparations Commission, and the rumor mill was as active as Dawes's regular, official reports. Speculators drove up the value of the dollar relative to the French franc, the Belgian franc, and the Italian lira. The German mark, which had been relatively stable on world markets, declined. When word incorrectly circulated that Dawes had resigned from the commission over petty grievances with the German and Austrian embassies for failure to lower their flags in respect after the death of Woodrow Wilson on February 3, 1924, exchange rates gyrated until the false reports were quelled.

Dawes began to outline his thoughts on the final report during the second week of February. He advocated Kemmerer's recommendation that an assessment should take the form of a tax on income and added that Germany's tax rate should be in the same range as the tax rates of other Allied nations.

The more challenging issue revolved around the establishment of an account within a designated bank of issue through which the reparations payments would be made. The goal was to have a savings account in which the payments would be accumulated in such a way as to not adversely affect Germany's business success. Dawes observed that the only way in which this part of the agreement could be successful was for the Allies to avoid accepting German goods at the expense of their own industries—thus harming their own economies. Of all of the points outlined in his tentative plan, Dawes saw this one as the most problematic.[24]

Up to this point, the relations among the various committee members had been especially harmonious, but Dawes was under no illusions. "I have had enough experience in inter-Allied conferences to know that men do not throw away preconceived ideas," Dawes observed in his diary. He knew that France was going to make certain demands, and he wanted to know them up front before the serious negotiations on his outline began. "We will steer our ship more safely if we know where and what the rocks are now."[25]

The committee returned to Paris to begin the hard work of ironing out differences and preparing its final report. Dawes hoped they could finish their work by mid-March. As he correctly suspected, there were rocks that needed to be uncovered and removed from the waters. He negotiated with each of the delegates, working diligently with the Frenchmen Parmentier and Allix to obtain their support for giving Germany more autonomy over its own decisions.

France was not easily convinced that it could abandon the Ruhr simply on German assurances of payment. The best way to get France on board was to create a financial incentive. Dawes and Young met with officials at J. P. Morgan, who extended the Bank of France a six-month credit of $100 million. The loan immediately halted the fall of the franc and gained France's cooperation.[26]

Owen Young was an indispensable ally and an even match for Charley's forthrightness. Germany was not invited to the deliberations, so Young took responsibility for negotiating with German industrialists as the committee prepared its final report. When the Germans balked at the proposed taxation plan, Young explained that they had two choices—to accept an economic solution, or to have a military one imposed. Young elaborated that without a clear economic plan, France would continue to occupy the Ruhr. Young brought the German industrialists on board.

The committee estimated that $200 million or more was needed to kick-start the moribund German economy and recommended that other nations lend Germany the money. The idea was to fund investment in Germany so that it could produce goods for trade, and to stabilize the currencies of the United Kingdom and France (apart from the $100 million credit the latter nation had received from Morgan) to enable those nations to buy goods from Germany. The end result, according to the reasoning of the Dawes Plan, was that the trade would generate the revenue Germany needed to pay make its reparations payments.

American bankers were skeptical of their success in floating bonds to lend money to Europe. To encourage banker participation, the president of the New York Federal Reserve Bank, Benjamin Strong Jr., lowered his bank's interest rate from 4.5 percent to 3 percent, making it the lowest in the world at the time. The committee proposed that the Americans lend $100 million; the English, $75 million; and the Allied nations on the Continent, $25 million.[27]

The general attitude among the bankers was that they wanted to see what happened in Germany's scheduled election on May 4. This prompted Robinson to recommend that the First Committee postpone submitting its report until after the German elections. Dawes consulted both Young and Parmentier, both of whom disagreed with Robinson's suggestion. "I can conceive of nothing more disastrous than to purposely delay," Dawes noted.[28] The committees of experts had been created to get an opinion on German finances untarnished by political considerations. To postpone the reports because of an election was to allow politics to control the process.

Dawes was motivated by his still-fresh memories of the war as he pushed the committee to finish its work. "If [the question] is not settled now," he recorded in his journal, "when can it be?" He offered a chilling assessment of what might happen to Europe if the reparations plan failed. "It seems to me that Europe and its civilization is facing its last opportunity to avoid a slow, rudderless drifting into a sea of despair and desolation."[29]

The First Committee of Experts submitted its report to the Reparations Commission on April 9. The text of the opening paragraphs acknowledged that the committee members adopted the report unanimously. In keeping with Dawes's commitment to idealism, he wrote: "Deeply impressed by a sense of its responsibility to your Commission and to the universal conscience, the Committee bases its plan upon those principles of justice, fairness and mutual interest, in the supremacy of which not only the creditors of Germany and Germany herself, but the world, have a vital and enduring concern."[30]

The report was historic in another way. The 44,000-word document was the longest single telegraphic transmission ever sent by wire, and it was the first time that a message had been sent from a foreign point of transmission directly to the recipient without a break or relay.[31]

The plan outlined three sources for reparations payments: assigned revenues from collected taxes; the sale of railway bonds; and the issuing of industrial debentures. Opponents attacked the plan because it meant that Germany would lose control of her railways to foreign ownership through the bond sale. Members of the London financial community decried the interconnected nature of the plan. Its success was too dependent on all the pieces falling into place as designed—the international loan, the sale of the railway stocks, and the sale of industrial bonds.[32]

Officials in the United States were jubilant. Secretary of State Hughes cabled Dawes with his congratulations: "I trust that through your unselfish and most able efforts, the way has at last been opened to European Recuperation with all its resulting benefits to the world."[33]

The Coolidge administration publicly expressed optimism about the report. Privately, Coolidge cabled Dawes: "I wanted to put on paper my deep appreciation of the character of your services. . . . I have said that you and your associates represented not the Government, but the American mind. The success of your work now seems assured, but whatever happens in relation to its acceptance, it is of a character that cannot help but be most helpful in composing European differences."[34]

Herbert Hoover, speaking in his formal capacity as U.S. secretary of commerce, applauded the report. "The greatest single barrier to the economic recuperation of the world has been the unsettlement of German reparations. . . . If the commission now secures just and practical settlement the whole world will benefit."[35]

The Reparations Commission unanimously accepted the Dawes report, and the commission called upon Germany to respond by April 17. Germany answered on April 15. It would accept the report.

With the committee's work completed, Charley and Caro left for Belgium on April 10, where they paid a farewell visit to their friend Aloys Van de Vyvere. Much to Charley's surprise, King Albert of Belgium summoned Dawes to his country palace, and he and Caro spent the day with the king.

From Belgium, Charley and Caro traveled to Rome. Reporters and photographers besieged Dawes; he was the man of the hour. The Italian leader Benito Mussolini sent a car to the train station to pick them up, and Dawes met Mussolini. Charley described Il Duce as a combination of Napoleon Bonaparte and William McKinley. "After leaving him, I felt as if I had seen Julius Caesar."[36]

Charley's time in Italy was an opportunity to indulge in his love of history and antiquities. He visited Palatine Hill and the Vatican. He toured the Roman Forum and the Colosseum and was awestruck by their majesty. "Here I was, suddenly placed in the midst of a bewildering number of Roman ruins, of which I had read from childhood, but of whose grandeur no true conception had ever come to me."[37]

From Rome, he traveled to the Dawes's ancestral home in Mount Ephraim, England, where he had the great pleasure of seeing his five-year-old namesake and godson. "He is a beautiful and intelligent child," Charley wrote with pride, "[and] he told me he was an American."[38]

Charley and Caro boarded the SS *Leviathan* on April 23. Young and Robinson had boarded the evening before at Cherbourg. The *Leviathan* was the same ship that had transported Dawes home following his military service. A hero's welcome awaited him—if he would have permitted it. Evanstonians had planned a large event, complete with bands and speeches, but Dawes headed it off. "He relapsed into peculiarly Dawesian silence and the inevitable cloud of pipe smoke," observed the *Chicago Tribune*.[39]

The Dawes Report was the first real breakthrough in negotiations between the European Allies and Germany since the signing of the Versailles Treaty. But there was still much work to be done to put the plan in place. Political considerations now replaced the nonpolitical stance studiously maintained by Dawes and his fellow committee members. The United Kingdom had new leadership, its first Labor government headed by Ramsay MacDonald having replaced that of the Conservative Stanley Baldwin in January 1924. Germany and France were scheduled to hold elections in May.

International observers closely watched Germany's May 4 national elections. None of the four major parties—Nationalists, Socialists, Communists, and Centrists—won a clear majority. Wilhelm Marx, who was committed to the Dawes Plan, built a successful Centrist coalition and was named chancellor. The world community breathed an optimistic sigh of relief.

In France, Prime Minister Raymond Poincaré was defeated in the elections held on May 11, much to the satisfaction of the British. They saw Poincaré as a stumbling block to the successful implementation of the reparations plan. Poincaré was replaced by Édouard Herriot, who was viewed as more conciliatory toward Germany.

The elections gave American bankers more confidence in floating a loan to Germany, but there were a number of details to be ironed out. Dwight Morrow and Thomas Lamont, J. P. Morgan's representatives, wanted to handpick the individual who would serve as the reparations agent responsible for the collection and disbursement of Germany's payments. Morrow was the bank's, and Dawes's, first choice. German Nationalists let it be known that Morrow was too closely aligned with the House of Morgan and that he was not acceptable as a reparations agent.

In preparation for the London Conference, which would begin to iron out the details of the Dawes Plan, German officials held a private meeting with James A. Logan. Logan was an unofficial diplomat who had been an aide to Hoover in the American Relief Administration and an observer at the meetings of the Reparations Commission since its establishment by the Versailles Treaty. Logan had gained the confidence of the French, British, and German governments, and he functioned as a back-channel messenger among the three nations' leadership.

Following a private meeting with German officials, including Chancellor Marx and Reichsbank President Schacht, Logan reported to the French president that Germany had several concerns about moving forward with implementation of the Dawes Plan. France continued to occupy the Ruhr. It held roughly 1,500 political prisoners and had expelled an estimated 140,000 Germans from their homes in the Ruhr for what the German government saw as political reasons. Germany sought France's withdrawal from the Ruhr and the release of the prisoners. German officials told Logan that they would like to see the Allies acknowledge the Dawes Plan as a solution to the reparations issue.

On the American side, Owen Young returned to London to participate in the conference, scheduled for July 1924. Secretary of State Charles Evans Hughes and U.S. ambassador to Great Britain Frank B. Kellogg also attended. Young, Logan, and Hughes all communicated with Dawes during the proceedings. Dawes was particularly concerned about the selection of the reparations agent. From his standpoint, the individual who filled this position was critical to the success of the plan. Without an agent who would be acceptable to all the parties to the plan and agreeable to the Morgan bank, the Dawes Plan would fail.

Dawes asked for Young's personal commitment to serve as reparations agent. Young agreed, with the stipulation that he would only take the post temporarily so that the German loan would be floated. Their agreement was upended when Lamont and Montagu Norman, the governor of the Bank of England, informed Young that they would not participate in the loan unless a permanent agent was named.

Young, unwilling to commit long-term as the agent, wired Dawes for help. He asked Dawes to reach his contacts in Washington and push for the selection of a permanent agent. Dawes begged Young to accept the temporary position. "The consensus of opinion upon this, shared by our Government, by the members of our Expert Committee and by informed Allied officials, in my judgment, is too significant of the necessities of the situation to justify you in declining temporary appointment."[40] Young agreed to stay on the job temporarily, but he requested that Charley send either Rufus Dawes or Henry Robinson to assist him. Rufus, ever gracious, returned to Europe.

The London protocol, implementing the Dawes Plan, was signed on August 30, 1924. Germany made its first payment on September 1. France and Belgium removed the customs barrier on September 9, and on October 22, their control over the German economy in the region ceased.

In mid-September, S. Parker Gilbert, undersecretary of the treasury and Mellon's second in command, was appointed as the reparations agent. Gilbert was a rising star in the financial world. He graduated from Harvard Law School at the age of twenty-two and worked in the Treasury Department as a member of the war loan staff. Gilbert was promoted to assistant secretary of the treasury when his superior resigned, and at the age of twenty-eight, he became an undersecretary. Gilbert's selection was widely accepted and acclaimed.

With a permanent reparations agent now in place, the German External Loan of 1924 was officially floated on October 14, 1924. The collateral was 7 percent non-redeemable gold bonds (except by sinking fund, the fund set aside to repay the monies borrowed through the issue of the bonds), with a loan term of twenty-five years—from October 15, 1924, to October 15, 1949. Unlike the Anglo-French loan, which was undersubscribed, the External Loan was oversubscribed in every country where it was offered.[41]

German industry was soon up and running. France began to receive its reparations payments. International trade expanded. In 1926, the Norwegian Nobel Committee awarded Charley the Nobel Peace Prize for 1925 (the original 1925 nominees were deemed not to have fit the criteria laid out by Alfred Nobel). He shared the 1925 prize with Sir Austen Chamberlain, who received it for his work in facilitating reconciliation between France and Germany. The 1926 winners were France's foreign minister, Aristide Briand, and Germany's foreign minister, Gustav Stresemann. The awards were the world's way of saying "thank you" to four men who had worked hard to bring the days of carnage and hostility on the European continent to an end. Dawes was the only American in the group.

Dawes did not travel to Oslo to receive his prize. It was accepted on his behalf by the American ambassador to Norway, Laurits Selmer Swenson. Swenson read Dawes's telegram to the American Legation in Oslo. Dawes was characteristically modest and gave credit to all of the members of the First Committee of Experts:

> This award, which is in recognition of the work of the First Committee of Experts, Reparation Commission, of which I was chairman, is gratefully acknowledged. The committee was composed of Owen D. Young, Sir Josiah C. Stamp, Sir Robert M. Kindersley, Jean Parmentier, Edgard Allix, Alberto Pirelli, Frederico [sic] Flora, Emile Francqui, Baron Maurice Houtart, and myself. It was the endeavor of the experts to found their plan upon the principles of justice, fairness, and mutual interest, relying for its acceptance thus prepared upon that common good faith which is the enduring hope for the universal safeguarding of peace. That the results achieved under it have merited in your judgment this high recognition is a tribute to the united efforts of the committee.[42]

Dawes did not deliver the customary Nobel lecture. He donated his $15,775 award to the Walter Hines Page School of International Relations at Johns Hopkins University in Baltimore, Maryland, a project of his friend Owen Young, who was in the process of organizing the school.[43]

Upon his return from Europe, Dawes resumed his life in Evanston and his work with Central Trust. He would not have much time to get comfortable. His international success had put him in the limelight, and there was a movement afoot to make him the Republican vice presidential nominee.

CHAPTER 11

X

The Campaigner

Charley's success in Europe earned him valuable political capital at home. The nomination for the Republican vice presidential slot was wide open, and a "Draft Dawes" movement got underway. Supporters printed and mailed placards with the image of Coolidge and Dawes on one side, and a tribute to Dawes on the other. Charley, who always panned politics, dismissed the efforts.

As the Republican National Convention neared, Frank Lowden and Dawes's long-time friend, Albert Beveridge, in addition to Charley, were mentioned as possibilities for Coolidge's running mate. The president's alleged favorite was Idaho Senator William Borah, a strong Progressive and a noted orator. He was also a prominent isolationist, and his power in the Senate was instrumental in preventing the United States from joining the League of Nations.

The other name under consideration was Dawes's friend and former Illinois governor Frank Lowden. Lowden had not been especially active on the national scene, but he still had a strong core of supporters who were holdovers from his failed presidential run in 1920.

The convention was called to order in Cleveland's Public Auditorium on June 10, 1924. The building had been completed in 1922 and was then the largest convention hall in the United States.

The 1924 convention included female delegates for the first time, who represented about 10 percent of the roughly 1,100 assembled Republicans. The convention was also the first to be broadcast on

180

radio, which had been introduced to the public in 1920. The proceedings were carried on nine stations nationwide to a potential audience of approximately three million radio owners.[1]

Two radio listeners were Dawes and President Calvin Coolidge. Coolidge followed the convention from the White House, and Dawes from Marietta, where he and Caro had traveled to attend Marietta College's commencement and alumni reunion.

Coolidge's nomination as the presidential candidate was a foregone conclusion. He had deftly solidified his control of the Republican National Committee when he became president following Harding's sudden death from a heart attack on August 2, 1923. Coolidge's campaign manager, William M. Butler, a Massachusetts native like Coolidge, controlled the convention proceedings starting with the first call to order on June 10.

The party platform reflected Coolidge's views with a promise of continued economy of spending by the government and limited taxation. The comprehensive document covered everything from agriculture to taking better care of veterans and included a call for federal antilynching legislation. The Republicans committed to continuing a protective tariff to benefit American industries. Reflecting the nation's growing internationalism, the party included language that expressed the belief that the United States should prevent war and preserve peace.[2] Many in the party hoped for a stronger anti–Ku Klux Klan plank in the platform and were disappointed that it was not included.

Coolidge's name was placed in nomination at the opening session of the convention on Thursday morning, June 12. In a nod to the remnants of the Progressive wing of the party, Wisconsin put the name of Senator Robert La Follette in nomination as a favorite son. California did likewise with Senator Hiram Johnson.

Coolidge won handily on the first ballot. The only major dissent came from Wisconsin, North Dakota, and South Dakota. Wisconsin's delegates cast twenty-eight of their twenty-nine votes for La Follette (the lone dissenter supported Coolidge), and North Dakota split its support seven to six between Coolidge and La Follette, respectively. South Dakota gave ten of its thirteen votes to Johnson. When a motion was made to nominate Coolidge unanimously, Wisconsin's and South Dakota's delegations refused.[3]

Following the post-nomination speeches by Coolidge's supporters, the convention adjourned for lunch. The vice presidential candidate would be selected in the afternoon.

For several weeks prior to the convention, rumors circulated that Coolidge favored Idaho Senator William E. Borah as his running mate. On June 12, a 2:00 A.M. edition of the *New York Times* reported that Coolidge had summoned his presumed favorite, Senator Borah, to the White House to apprise him of his plans to put Borah's name forward as the vice presidential candidate. Borah disabused the president of this idea, much to Coolidge's surprise. As a result of Borah's refusal to be nominated, according to the *Times*, Coolidge decided to let the convention select its own candidate without input from him.[4]

The *Atlanta Constitution* reported a different story. The paper stated that Coolidge's men, led by Butler, wanted the vice presidential nomination to go to U.S. Representative Theodore E. Burton of Ohio, a Cleveland native and temporary chair of the convention.[5] Butler's team allegedly spent the morning of June 12 building support for Burton, only to find that the convention delegates had other ideas. Neither story accurately depicted what took place among the delegates.

When the afternoon session was gaveled into order, an Arizona delegate nominated Dawes's friend and former Illinois governor and presidential candidate Frank O. Lowden. Judge William S. Kenyon, a former senator from Iowa, was also nominated, as were Senators Charles Curtis of Kansas and George Norris of Nebraska. The names of Burton, several other members of Congress, Dawes, and Harbord were added to the list. With 555 votes required for the nomination, no winner emerged after the first ballot. Lowden led with 222 votes, Kenyon was second with 172, and Dawes came in third with 149 ballots cast in his favor. Burton trailed Dawes with 139 votes.

The second ballot increased Lowden's total to 413, and state delegations began switching their votes to support him. After the changes were made, the official tally for the second ballot gave the nomination to Lowden with 766 votes. Dawes's total was 49 votes, placing him fourth behind Burton with 94 and Kenyon with 68.[6]

That morning, before the proceedings had begun, Lowden's friend, former representative John W. Dwight of New York, handed a letter from Lowden to Frank W. Mondell, the convention's chairman.

Anticipating that he might be nominated for vice president, Lowden's letter explicitly stated that he would not accept the nomination under any circumstances. The Illinois delegation also had a copy of the letter. For reasons that are unclear, Mondell did not read the letter to the convention before the start of vice presidential nominations. The Illinois delegation likewise did not stop Lowden's name from being put forward. It gave thirty of its fifty-two votes to Lowden on the first ballot. (Of the remaining Illinois delegates, twenty voted for Dawes, one for Harbord, and one for chewing gum magnate William Wrigley.)[7]

Mondell's failure to read Lowden's letter was the result of a revolt that had been brewing among the delegates over the three days of the convention. The delegates overwhelmingly supported Coolidge, but they had wanted a say in the platform and other procedural issues. Butler had given them none. Embittered by the dictatorial way in which Butler had managed the proceedings, the delegates saw the selection of their vice presidential candidate as the only opportunity to make their voices heard. The refusal to share Lowden's letter prior to the nominating process was more a slap at Butler's heavy-handed methods than an attempt to force the nomination on Lowden.[8] It was also a case of denial on the part of the delegates. On June 9, the day before the convention officially convened, the *Washington Post* had written that Lowden had taken himself out of the running.[9]

Mondell finally read Lowden's letter to the convention after it had selected Lowden as the vice presidential candidate. The letter caused mass confusion among the delegates. They questioned when Lowden had written it and asked if he might reconsider. It was then 7:30 in the evening. The delegates were tired, and most had expected to be on their way home. The convention recessed until 9:00 P.M. and did not reconvene until nearly 10:00 P.M. that night. During the short recess, Lowden sent a telegram thanking the convention for the nomination and reiterating his refusal to accept it. Butler was busy, too. He told other members of the convention committee, "It must be [Commerce Secretary Herbert] Hoover." Pennsylvania Senator David Reed replied, "It can't be done. It must be Dawes."[10]

According to the *Post*, Dawes drew his support from those who wanted to see Lowden in the number-two spot. "Dawes is the logical man," Illinois delegate Edward Clifford asserted. "The man who stirred Europe will be chosen."[11]

Dawes was nominated handily on the first ballot following the recess. He received 682½ votes, followed by Hoover, who received 254½, with Kenyon a distant third at 75.[12]

Charley learned of his nomination together with his family, who were gathered at the home of his sister, Mary Dawes Beach, to listen to the convention. The *Marietta Daily Times*, in an extra edition printed June 13, recorded Dawes's uncharacteristically mild reaction: "Well, I declare." It is quite likely that he made some other choice, unprintable comments.

The family apparently accepted the news with laughter and applause. "Charley," Henry told him, "it's up to you again."

When asked if he were actually going to run, Dawes replied, "I guess so, now that they've forced it on me." He telegraphed his appreciation to the convention and accepted the nomination.

Beman, when questioned by a reporter as to whether his brother was surprised, answered, "You bet he was."[13]

Dawes's name had been suggested as a possible running mate with Coolidge in various political circles even before Dawes returned from Europe. When asked in April, upon his return from the Continent, if there were any truth to the rumors that he was a candidate for vice president, Dawes gave his standard reply that he was out of politics and going home.[14]

Ever since his failed Senate attempt in 1902, Dawes repeatedly expressed a disdain for electoral politics, preferring to work in the background as a kingmaker. In a letter to Harbord, Dawes mentioned that he had avoided going through Washington on his way home from Florida because he "hesitated to be drawn into the maelstrom of political gossip which generally revolves around nothing."[15] He had turned down Harding's offer of a cabinet post because he did not want to manage a bureaucratic department. So, the question remains why Dawes did not discourage his name from being placed in nomination, following the examples of Lowden and Borah.

Dawes was more man than the vice presidency needed. John Adams had complained in a letter to his wife, Abigail, "My country has in its wisdom contrived for me the most insignificant office that ever the invention of man contrived or his imagination conceived."[16] Like Adams, Dawes would attempt to reform the Senate and be frustrated by its dogged protection of its institutional prerogatives. However, in the days immediately following the nomination, he felt a heady sense of being called to duty. Dawes wrote in his memoir, "Just then it seemed to me the greatest office in the world."[17]

The team of Coolidge and Dawes was an interesting pairing. Coolidge was famously taciturn, whereas Dawes was equally renowned for his ebullience. While both men held a strong commitment to economy in government, Coolidge carried that view to extremes in his personal life. He and his wife, the vivacious and popular Grace, had lived in the Willard Hotel during Coolidge's years as vice president. (They would not own a home until after Coolidge left the presidency in March 1929.) He was extravagant in his expenditures on clothing for himself and for his wife, whom he enjoyed seeing well-dressed, but he kept careful accounts of the money spent on his meals in the White House and berated the staff when they spent more than he thought they should.

Dawes, on the other hand, was overwhelmingly generous and philanthropic. His internationalism stood in stark contrast to what could be considered Coolidge's provincialism. The president had never traveled outside of the United States. Yet, in spite of these glaring differences, Coolidge expressed his satisfaction with the convention's choice of running mate. "It will be a pleasure to be associated with you in the public service," Coolidge cabled Dawes.[18] Privately, Coolidge wrote to the party's elder statesman Elihu Root, "I am very much pleased with the Convention result, and think we are going into the campaign under as favorable conditions as could possibly be expected."[19]

Europeans, especially the French and Germans, declared delight at the convention's choice of Dawes. In the United States, Republican newspapers dredged up Dawes's appearance before Congress in 1921 and let readers know that "Hell and Maria" Dawes was back in the limelight. The banking and business communities overwhelmingly favored having Dawes on the ticket.

Not everyone was pleased. Raymond Robins, a party reformer who had become a close friend of Borah's, referred to Coolidge and Dawes as "The Morgan Golddust Twins." The Gold Dust Twins were two African

American children pictured doing household chores together in adver-
tisements for Gold Dust Washing Powder, and the reference accused
Coolidge and Dawes of working together to promote the House of Morgan. Borah was reportedly demoralized by the selection of Dawes.[20] The
Democratic *Dallas Morning News* described Dawes as "a misfit, a door-
knob in the egg cup, the pile driver in the china cabinet, a capitalist
yodeler at a proletariat wake." In anticipation of his performance on
the stump, the paper predicted, accurately, "His reputation of saying
things without ruffles, pleats, or embroidery will give the management
of the summer's engagement many an anxious hour. . . . The question is
whether a man who has made his name for the sulfurous halo through
which he is supposed to bark orders hither and yon can alter his tone
and suit his temper to the wheedling of votes from a fickle and free-
voting public."[21]

Coolidge and Dawes had gotten to know each other during Dawes's
year as Harding's budget director. When *A Journal of the Great War* was
published, Dawes sent both volumes to Coolidge. In his thank-you
letter, Coolidge wrote, "There is even greater value in having it [the
journal] because of the great attachment I have for you and the great
confidence I feel in your judgment and ability."[22] In response to the letter of condolence that Dawes mailed to Coolidge after Harding's death,
Coolidge wrote, "When you are in Washington, of course you will come
to see us, in order that we may continue our pleasant relationship, and
that I may have the benefit of your counsel and advice."[23]

Their ancestors were not strangers, either. Coolidge and Dawes were
distantly related by marriage. The Worcester, Massachusetts, grocery
store of "Dawes and Coolidge" was established around 1777. Dawes was
the patriot William Dawes, who rode with Paul Revere. Dawes moved
his family from Boston to Worcester during the siege of Boston and
started the grocery there with John Coolidge. Coolidge was William
Dawes's brother-in-law, who had married Dawes's sister Lydia on January 5, 1772. After the siege ended, the Daweses returned to Boston, and
William operated a grocery there. The formal partnership between the
two men presumably dissolved.[24]

Although Coolidge was the incumbent president, his election to a term
in his own right could not be taken for granted. Coolidge had remained

untainted by the Teapot Dome scandal that had erupted shortly after Harding's death, but the corruption uncovered by the ensuing investigation made for easy campaign attacks by Republican opponents. The Progressives remained a political force to be reckoned with, and there was the danger that they could once again split the popular vote and deny a clear Electoral College victory to any candidate, forcing the 1924 election to be decided in the House of Representatives.

Butler, as campaign chair, left nothing to chance. He hired the advertising and sloganeering genius Bruce Barton, who came up with the phrase "Keep Cool with Coolidge." It was a subtle message suggesting that the turbulent first years of the decade were past and that the nation would continue on its present upward trajectory if it elected Coolidge to a full four-year term. The campaign message conveyed optimism and the promise of continued prosperity.

Coolidge stayed "cool" by operating a low-key, McKinleyesque "front porch" campaign, staying in the White House rather than traveling the campaign trail. He addressed committees and delegations visiting Washington, sticking to discussions of policy matters. Dawes went out on the hustings. The Republican strategists mapped out an extensive travel schedule that had Dawes crisscross the nation through the summer and early autumn leading up to the election. By the end of the campaign, he had logged fifteen thousand miles by special train and delivered one hundred and eight speeches.[25]

Butler wanted Dawes to focus on the economy. That was the central plank of the Republican platform and the one on which the Republican National Committee pinned its hopes for victory. Dawes had his own opinions. He considered La Follette's potential third-party candidacy, and a constitutional amendment La Follette advocated, to be the most important issues of the campaign. La Follette's proposed amendment prohibited the lower federal courts from invalidating any congressional statute and authorized Congress to reenact any legislation overturned by the Supreme Court.[26] Were it to become law, the amendment would tip the balance of federal power toward Congress and water down the judicial review functions of the nation's highest court.

Dawes delivered his unofficial acceptance speech from the front porch of his Evanston home to a crowd estimated at fifty thousand people who gathered on his lawn and stretched to the shores of

Lake Michigan. The candidate took direct aim at La Follette. Dawes declared, "In the campaign which is before me, and as a duty which I owe not simply to a party, but to the citizens of the United States, I pledge myself to adhere to the truth and to common sense conclusions to be drawn therefrom. As to the demagogue on the stump [La Follette], whatever may be his party, I want it distinctly understood that in the coming campaign I ask no quarter and will give none."[27]

Dawes's concerns about La Follette's proposed amendment were not wholly unfounded, although many considered them overblown. The country had ratified the Eighteenth and Nineteenth Amendments to the Constitution within twenty months of each other. Proponents of Prohibition had adopted the suffragists' agenda as a way to promote their own. Savvy organizers had sent supportive representatives and senators to Congress and organized the election of state legislators who passed, and subsequently ratified, the two amendments. La Follette's supporters could use the same tactics to enact their agenda. There were enough disgruntled factions among labor, immigrant groups, "wets" (opponents of Prohibition), and socialists that coalitions could be formed at the state level sufficient to make La Follette's proposal a reality.

Dawes's acceptance speech named La Follette's proposed amendment as the "dominant" issue in the campaign. Butler wanted the speech changed, but Dawes was an old hand at presidential campaign management. He sent his text to Coolidge for approval. Coolidge accepted Dawes's message as written with one small edit: He crossed out "dominant" and replaced it with "important."[28]

The Democratic National Convention opened at New York City's Madison Square Garden on June 24. Republicans may have revolted against Butler's peremptory tactics, but the free-for-all that characterized the Democrats' gathering may have made the GOP appreciate Butler's firm hand. The Democrats in 1924 were less a political party than an amalgamation of factions under a common name. Southern Democrats, who controlled the states that had made up the former Confederacy, were Protestant, pro-Prohibition, pro–Jim Crow (segregation), and fiscally conservative. Democrats from the northern and western states were primarily Catholic or Jewish, and recent immigrants or first-generation Americans born to immigrant parents. These Democrats had fought

Prohibition and believed that government had a role to play in improving people's lives. With such a huge disparity in membership, it is little wonder that the convention ground on for sixteen contentious days, until July 9. It remains the longest political convention in American history.[29]

The Ku Klux Klan made its presence known during the convention. Twenty thousand of its members gathered at Long Branch, New Jersey, on July 4 to protest the potential selection of New York's Governor Alfred Smith, a Catholic who was a leader in the balloting for the Democratic presidential nomination. Smith had deadlocked with Californian William G. McAdoo, who had served as secretary of the treasury to his father-in-law, Woodrow Wilson. McAdoo appealed to the party's southern faction, and Smith, naturally, attracted delegates from the Northeast and from states with large Catholic and immigrant populations. Recognizing the deadlock, Smith dropped out on the ninety-ninth ballot, but his supporters refused to give their votes to McAdoo. Former West Virginia representative and former U.S. ambassador to the United Kingdom John W. Davis was selected as the compromise candidate on the 103rd ballot. His running mate was Nebraska Governor Charles W. Bryan, the brother of William Jennings Bryan.

While the Democrats publicly hashed out their differences and sought to reach consensus around a presidential candidate, the Conference for Progressive Political Action, the organizational arm of the Progressive Party, met in Cleveland's Auditorium on July 4 and 5. Their convention selected La Follette and a Montana senator, Democrat Burton K. Wheeler, to run as president and vice president, respectively, on a Progressive Party ticket. The Progressive platform called for an end to private monopolies; enforcement of guarantees of freedom of speech, the press, and assembly; public ownership and conservation of power supplies and natural resources; tax and financial markets reform; and protection for collective bargaining.[30]

Before the Progressives formally convened, they began their attacks on Dawes. J. A. H. Hopkins, the chairman of the Committee of Forty-Eight, the group that organized the convention of the Conference for Progressive Political Action, called the Dawes Plan to solve the reparations crisis "sinister." Hopkins charged that the plan was designed to funnel wealth to private investors, notably America's major banking houses and particularly the Morgan syndicate working through National City Bank, Chase Bank, Merchants Trust Bank of Chicago, and in conjunction with the Bank of England. The intent of the plan, Hopkins maintained, was to enrich bankers and impoverish Germany's citizens: "That is the essence of the Dawes report; it is also the essence of the Dawes vice presidential candidacy, of the Coolidge platform, and of the Republican reactionary campaign," Hopkins charged. He closed by asserting that the Coolidge-Dawes ticket could not "expect to receive a single vote from labor, farmers or progressives."[31]

The political attacks and the Democratic National Convention were suspended on July 7, when the president's teenage son, Calvin Coolidge Jr., died. Calvin Junior developed a blister on his foot after playing tennis. The blister quickly became infected, and blood poisoning set in. Without antibiotics, which were yet to be discovered, doctors could do little for the young man except make him comfortable. In reflecting on his son's death, Coolidge wrote, "He was a boy of much promise, proficient in his studies, with a scholarly mind, who had just turned sixteen. He had a remarkable insight into things. When he went the power and the glory of the Presidency went with him."[32]

Dawes was all too familiar with the grief of losing a son. He sent a message of condolence to the Coolidges, but he did not attend the funeral, which was held in Plymouth Notch, Vermont, the president's birthplace, on July 9. Unlike Dawes, who reached outward to handle the loss of Rufus Fearing, Coolidge withdrew inward. Although the two men had a shared grief, it did not draw them together in friendship.

The respite from mudslinging was short-lived. In its July 9 issue, the *New Republic* challenged Dawes on his speech calling La Follette a demagogue, suggesting that Dawes needed to clean his own house first. Giving a lengthy recounting of the Lorimer bank scandal, the magazine reported the final decision, rendered by the Illinois State Supreme Court on April 24, 1924, which held Central Trust Company, and Dawes as its president at the time of the transaction, liable for the actions of its cashier in providing the $1.25 million cash loan to the La Salle Street National Bank. The *New Republic* noted Dawes's reference to "the curse of demagoguery in political discussions in this country" and his call to citizens to "unite in demanding from those who represent us in political debates that they present our differences honestly and from the standpoint of truth, not from the standpoint of passion and prejudice."

"Certainly Mr. Dawes cannot complain if the facts regarding his connection with the failure of Lorimer's state bank are presented," wrote *New Republic* writer Donald R. Richberg, "if this is done without any characterizations which might amount to appeals to passion and prejudice. In this case the facts may well be considered without any interpretation other than that which has been furnished by the highest court of the State of Illinois."[33] There was no immediate public response to the article, likely because it appeared as the nation shared the Coolidges' grief, but the Lorimer issue resurfaced later in the campaign.

The same week that the *New Republic* printed the article regarding the Lorimer bank case, the *Literary Digest* wrote about a lawsuit filed by Coolidge's recently named attorney general, Harlan Fiske Stone. As the revelations unfolded related to the Teapot Dome scandal, Coolidge had finally demanded Harry Daugherty's resignation. The appointment of Stone, the dean of Columbia Law School and regarded as having a high degree of integrity, reinstated public confidence in the attorney general's office.

Stone took office on April 1, 1924. In early July, he filed an antitrust lawsuit against the Standard Oil Co., as the primary defendant, and other oil companies as secondary defendants, alleging that the companies pooled their patents to restrict the refining trade. While a number of newspapers across the nation applauded Stone's decision, a few took aim at his singling out Standard Oil when other companies were also involved in the conspiracy. One New England paper observed: "General Charles G. Dawes is understood to have a property interest in [Pure Oil], and his bank in Chicago, the Central Trust Company, is its western financial agent."[34]

Charley had more than a property interest in the Pure Oil Company. In 1914, Beman had begun to develop a new and highly productive oil field known as Cabin Creek, in what would eventually become Dawes, West Virginia, in the Kanawha Valley. In 1917, he purchased the Pure Oil Company, an independent oil firm based in New Jersey. The acquisition gave the Dawes oil interests a ready-made distribution and pipeline network across the United States.

The board of the Ohio Cities Gas Company voted to adopt the name Pure Oil Company in 1920, and the reorganization combined Ohio Cities, the former Pure Oil properties, and the Oklahoma Producing and Refining Corporation. Charley was, of course, a major shareholder.

The *New Republic*, likewise, revealed the connection between Dawes and Pure Oil, but neither Dawes's political enemies nor the major newspapers picked up on the connection and sought to make it a campaign issue.

The date when candidates received official notification of their nomination marked the formal kickoff of the presidential campaign season. Coolidge had initially selected July 24 as his notification date, and Dawes would receive his notification the following week. With the death of Coolidge's son, the date for the president's notification was moved to August 14, and Dawes's to August 19.[35] Dawes did not wait until then to hit the campaign trail. His first assault was on the Ku Klux Klan.

Today's incarnation of the Ku Klux Klan can be traced back to William Joseph Simmons, an Alabama native and graduate of Johns Hopkins University. Simmons held the first Klan meeting at Stone Mountain, Georgia, in 1915. The organization promoted nativism with a strong anti-Catholic and antisemitic message. With the U.S. entry into World War I, the Klan's growth leveled out, although its message of patriotism had widespread national appeal. However, once the war ended, the ensuing economic depression made conditions ripe for expanding Klan membership. Simmons hired two professional marketers, Edward Young Clarke and Elizabeth Tyler, owners of the Southern Publicity Association. Simmons gave the pair wide leeway in promoting the Klan nationwide. Even though the economy had started to improve by 1922, the Klan gained in power and influence in Oklahoma, Texas, Oregon, Indiana, Maine, and New Jersey, in large part thanks to Clarke's and Tyler's efforts.[36]

By 1922, Klan political support had influenced elections across the country, and openly Klan-backed members had been elected to offices in local government, state legislatures, and Congress. Klan dissatisfaction with an elected official could spell the end of the person's tenure in office, as had been the case with Oklahoma Governor Jack C. Walton, a Democrat, who had cracked down on the Klan following the 1921

Tulsa race riot. Walton declared martial law in two Oklahoma counties, Okmulgee and Tulsa, and he suspended the writ of habeas corpus. The latter act violated the state's Constitution, and the Oklahoma Legislature instituted impeachment proceedings.

Walton called the legislature into special session with the intent of avoiding impeachment and of addressing the lawlessness of the Klan, but the organization was more powerful than the governor. The legislature's leaders refused to comply with Walton's request, and he was ousted on November 19, 1923, after only ten months and ten days in office.

On August 22, 1924, Democratic presidential nominee John W. Davis spoke out against the Klan at a rally in Sea Girt, New Jersey, in Monmouth County, the same county where the Klan had held its July 4 rally. Davis reiterated the message of racial and religious tolerance that had been a part of his official acceptance speech. Then, addressing those whom he suggested might not have understood his words the first time, Davis said, "If any organization, no matter what it chooses to be called, whether Ku Klux or by any other name, raises the standard of racial or religious prejudice or attempts to make racial origin or religious belief a test of fitness for public office, it does violence to the spirit of American institutions and must be condemned by all those who believe, as I do, in American ideals." Davis challenged Coolidge to make a similar statement and to remove the Klan issue from the campaign.[37]

Dawes went to Augusta, Maine, the next day, August 23, to speak on behalf of the Republican gubernatorial candidate, Ralph O. Brewster. Brewster had won the Republican gubernatorial primary with Klan backing against Frank G. Farrington, the choice of the Republican state organization. The Klan was strong in Maine, where its membership numbered 20,000 in a total population of 768,014.[38]

That morning, the Portland newspaper carried a challenge from Maine's Democratic candidate for governor, William Robinson Pattangall, for Dawes to denounce the Klan. "If the general were an ordinary, every day politician he would pussyfoot around the Klan issue," Pattangall declared.[39]

Pussyfooting around the issue was exactly what Butler and the Republican National Committee wanted Dawes to do. As Dawes wrote in his memoir, when the state committee learned that he was to mention the "dread words 'Ku Klux,'" it fell into a "state of extreme apprehension which it took no pains to conceal." The committee had forbade any of its Republican candidates from speaking about the Klan.[40]

Asked by reporters if he would lay off the question of the Klan, Dawes replied: "Lay off? Huh! Wait and hear what I have to say." Later that day, when pressed again, he added, "I have been challenged to declare myself on the Klan question, and I am not a man, in politics or otherwise, to refuse a challenge."[41]

Dawes opened his speech by declaring his intent to address the Klan issue. In his pedantic and professorial style, Dawes gave an historical analysis of the creation of the Klan, its appeal to disenfranchised youths, and the efforts the Klan had made to enforce the rule of law where there was little or no enforcement, particularly in areas of anti-Prohibition sentiment. Dawes's recounting was notably silent on the Tulsa race riot, lynchings, and the secretiveness of the Klan. However, once he completed his selective review of the organization's activities, Dawes went on to strongly denounce the organization: "Appeals to racial, religious, or class prejudice by minority organizations are opposed to the welfare of all peaceful and civilized communities. Our Constitution stands for religious tolerance and freedom. . . . To inject religious and racial issues into politics is contrary to the welfare of all the people and to the letter and spirit of the Constitution of the United States."[42]

The estimated audience of six thousand responded with a stunned silence. State Republican leaders were livid. They were convinced that Dawes had lost them the governorship and given the state to the Democrats in the presidential election. At the time, the presidential race was so close that newspapers published a variety of scenarios suggesting that the House of Representatives would pick the next chief executive.

Reaction to Dawes's comments was predictably mixed. Democrats said that Dawes had straddled the issue. Supporters of Dawes applauded his courage. Republicans maintained a numbed silence. The *Atlanta Constitution* called Dawes's speech both a "scorching denunciation of the klan" and "an adroit bid for klan votes." In an editorial, the *New York Times* said that a statement from Coolidge was more important than ever.[43] The African American press adopted a wait-and-see attitude, but it eventually came out in support of Dawes's remarks: "Charles G. Dawes's outspoken condemnation of the Ku Klux Klan . . . [has] done a great deal to warm the cockles of the Colored voters' hearts."[44]

Dawes was equally anxious to make labor a campaign issue. Prior to Harding's death, Dawes had encouraged the president to make labor radicalism a central focus of the 1924 campaign. However, Harding did not agree with Dawes's strident antilabor views. Coolidge, likewise, had no interest in attacking labor.

Dawes was a strong proponent of the open shop, or "American Plan," as the National Association of Manufacturers, an advocacy group representing manufacturing companies, called it. The open shop held that workers should not be required to join a union as a condition of employment. In 1923, Dawes organized a group in Chicago that he called the Minute Men of the Constitution. The Minute Men were a quasi-military body composed of young men, including a large number of veterans, organized into companies and outfitted in uniforms that included a black-and-white cockade. Dawes promoted the Minute Men as a patriotic group intent on protecting America from radicalism. During 1923, Dawes directed the Minute Men to carry out a campaign to support the reelection of Judges Dennis E. Sullivan, a Democrat, and Jesse Holden, a Republican, who had issued injunctions to halt strikes in the Chicago area.

Dawes referred to the city's labor leaders as "gun men and criminals." Although both the head of the Illinois Federation of Labor, Victor Olander, and the head of the American Federation of Labor, Samuel Gompers, were basically conservative-minded men who sought a partnership between business owners and labor, Dawes referred to Olander as a "labor demagogue" and accused Gompers of inciting workers to violence.[45] Labor leaders likened Dawes's Minute Men to Mussolini's Blackshirts, the armed squads of Italian Fascists. Naturally, Charley relished their opposition. It helped to bring about what he called "a square issue between those who believe in law enforcement and those who at heart are against it."[46]

While campaigning in Maine, Dawes attacked the nation's labor leaders with the same rhetoric he had used the previous year in Chicago. He referred to labor leaders as "radicals" and attacked Olander and Gompers.

Not all Republicans shared Dawes's views. Butler did not want to alienate the labor vote. He wrote Dawes, "An attack on labor leaders, good or bad, always consolidates union members and their sympathizers. . . . [Your] speech will solidify labor against our candidates." Dawes's initial reaction to Butler's letter was to insist he would stand firm on his principles.[47]

Dawes had been scheduled to return to Evanston the evening of his Maine Ku Klux Klan speech. Instead, Coolidge phoned Dawes and summoned him to Plymouth Notch, where the president and Mrs. Coolidge were vacationing. Although famous for his lack of words, the president was also noted for his icy anger. The press was poised to report Coolidge's rebuke to his running mate.

The president's father, Colonel John Calvin Coolidge, shared lunch and heard the conversation between Coolidge and Dawes. Afterward, the party adjourned to the sitting room, where the elder Coolidge joined them for a while and then stepped outside. He was immediately assailed by waiting reporters anxious for word about what had been discussed. Through the window, the president and Mrs. Coolidge observed the elder Coolidge talking to the reporters. "I asked him to say nothing," Coolidge said, clearly irritated, when he saw his father with them. Grace Coolidge replied, "I don't think you need to worry."

Once his business with the Coolidges was concluded, Dawes stepped outside and faced the same reporters. "I asked them what they had said to the Colonel," Dawes recorded in his memoir.

"We asked him what you and the President were talking about, of course," the reporters replied.

"What did he say?" I asked.

"My hearing ain't as good as it used to be" had been the Colonel's reply.[48]

Dawes backed off his attacks on the Klan, but he did not completely abandon the labor issue. He did not speak against the Klan when he campaigned in Indiana in the early fall. The group had a strong following in the Hoosier state. The Republican candidate for governor, Edward L. Jackson, was a member of the Klan and was strongly backed by that organization. Instead, Dawes talked about labor issues, where, once again, he used his views as part of an attack on La Follette, who had the support of the Socialist Party, which had been founded by Terre Haute native Eugene V. Debs.[49]

Dawes's internationalism and the Klan's nativism should have made them natural enemies. Nearly two-thirds of Dawes's formal acceptance speech for the vice presidential candidacy addressed the role of the United States in world affairs. He reviewed the history of United States participation in the Reparations Commission. He spoke out against U.S. involvement in the League of Nations but encouraged American engagement in the fledgling Permanent Court of International Justice, also called the World Court. Nevertheless, the Klan appeared to support Coolidge over Davis, and at the local level, especially in northern and western states, it openly supported more Republican candidates than it did Democratic ones.

Throughout the campaign, Dawes kept up his attack on La Follette. He spoke at the Minnesota State Fair in September, a state where the Progressives had strong support. The *New York Times* humorously referred to Dawes's presence at the fair as an "invasion," but it also criticized Dawes's description of La Follette's proposed constitutional changes as mundane and a little loose with the facts. The *Times* added that Dawes "has taught us to expect from him something more spicy and pungent than his speech on LaFollette's native heath."[50]

Republican Iowa Senator Smith W. Brookhart wrote a letter to Butler on September 30 demanding that Dawes resign from the ticket. "Charles G. Dawes has wrecked the Republican campaign, and especially in the Northwest," Brookhart charged. The vice presidential candidate was an "agent of international banking powers, . . . who started out like a bold-faced plutogog but his discourtesy and ungentlemanly language quickly reduced him, in his own vocabulary, to a peewit plutogog."[51] It's not clear what Brookhart meant by "plutogog," a word he apparently coined, but it may have been a combination of "plutocrat" and "demagogue." In his letter, Brookhart demanded that Dawes be replaced with someone who would be acceptable to western farmers and recommended Nebraska Senator George W. Norris.[52] Brookhart, who had a reputation as a renegade when it came to party loyalty, publicly endorsed the Progressive ticket of La Follette and Wheeler. Nevertheless, his critical letter and his endorsement of La Follette revealed fissures in the Republican camp.

Dawes's visibility made him, rather than Coolidge, the lightning rod for attacks, and, in the final month of the campaign, Charley's opponents stepped up the assault. A special committee appointed by the state convention of the Illinois Federation of Labor (IFL) submitted a report to the American Federation of Labor (AFL) reporting on its investigation of Dawes's record with regard to labor. It reviewed the Minute Men's support for Judges Sullivan and Holden in the 1923 election—judges whom Gompers had instructed labor to vote against—and added that Holden "had been very kind to the Dawes' interests" with regard to the Lorimer bank case.[53]

The IFL noted Dawes's frequent use of the term "demagogue" in his attacks against La Follette. Turning that word against Dawes, the IFL report observed, "We cannot refrain from expressing the opinion that as a demagogue Charles G. Dawes has no peer in American politics." The report repeated the history of the Lorimer case and charged that although Dawes spoke about the importance of abiding by the laws of the land, he failed to abide by the laws of the state of Illinois. The IFL committee concluded with an endorsement of La Follette and Wheeler.[54]

In late October, *Baltimore Sun* columnist Frank R. Kent called Dawes "a flop" as a campaigner. The "over-advertised banker . . . with his record of public profanity and his reputation as a fire-eating devil-may-care fellow" had become fixated on one thing and one thing only: the socialism of Robert La Follette and the imperative that he be defeated.[55]

By the end of the campaign, Dawes was tired of being muzzled by Butler and his managers. In Newark, New Jersey, Dawes spoke before a crowd of two thousand. "I blush for my sex when I think of some of the advice that I have received from members of the National Republican Committee of my own sex. They said, 'Don't say this here; don't say that there. Talk about the Ku Klux Klan here and irrigation there. You'll never get votes if you say that.' Not so with the women. They recognize the call to the colors. They understand the menace."[56]

In the days before intensive polling, Wall Street oddsmakers were the bellwether for election outcomes. By mid-October, they began to predict that the Coolidge-Dawes ticket would win a landslide victory. Coolidge-Dawes was the nine to one favorite. La Follette's odds were twenty to one, and Davis's, seven or eight to one.[57]

As Wall Street had determined, the Republicans won a resounding victory on November 4. They received 54 percent of the popular vote and 382 electoral votes. The Democratic ticket of Davis-Bryan received nearly 29 percent of the popular vote and 136 electoral votes. La Follette and Wheeler came in a distant third, with just under 17 percent of the popular vote and 13 electoral votes from Wisconsin, La Follette's home state, the only one he carried.[58]

Congratulations poured in to Dawes from well-wishers and supporters. Evanston was understandably proud of its adopted native son. Dawes took the victory in stride. Ever practical, he began to look at putting his personal affairs in order. In response to those who wondered how he would adjust to his new role, Dawes replied, "I guess I'll manage. I once was a lieutenant-colonel of a regiment." He emphasized the word "lieutenant."[59]

The *Baltimore Sun* perceptively observed: "Some of those who have been associated with him in his vigorous life declared today they could 'hardly conceive of Charley presiding calmly over the Senate.'"[60]

He would prove them right on inauguration day.

CHAPTER 12

X

Vice President

In the annals of American history, Charles G. Dawes ranks with Theodore Roosevelt as two of the nation's most colorful vice presidents. Roosevelt has become a larger-than-life figure in American history, especially in recent years, whereas Dawes and his accomplishments have faded into the background. But in terms of outspokenness, strong convictions, and the personality to outshine the presidents they served, Charley and Teddy were much alike.

Sometimes, however, the tendency to outshine was not intentional.

Such was the case just two weeks after the election when Dawes had emergency surgery on November 16 to repair a hernia. He noticed the bulge after he completed his morning exercise routine. Although the condition was not life-threatening, his physician, W. R. Parks, decided that a repair would be best because of Dawes's active lifestyle.

The operation was big news in the postelection lull, and the surgery was reported nationwide on the front page of the papers, including the New York Times. Dawes always made good copy— even when he was not quoted directly. Speaking to reporters, Parks told them his patient would be on a light diet for a few days, but by the end of the week Dawes would be "digging into ham and eggs and smoking his famous pipe with the same gusto as before his illness."[1]

The papers used the surgery to perpetuate what they perceived as a hint of coolness that had seeped into the Dawes-Coolidge relationship:

the president reportedly failed to send a get-well message to his future vice president.

That coolness got a little chillier when it was made public that Dawes had preempted an invitation from Coolidge to sit in on cabinet meetings by informing the president that he would not do so. Dawes believed that his attendance at the cabinet meetings would lead to what he called "the encouragement of misapprehensions [regarding the relationship between a president and vice president] which are easy to create."[2] When the news was made public, senators expressed their disappointment, as they had hoped that Dawes's presence in the Cabinet Room would serve as a link between Congress and the White House. Political prognosticators believed that Dawes's refusal stemmed from his interest in running for the presidency in 1928.

Dawes's name dominated the news throughout December and January as Europe continued to iron out the details of the Dawes Plan to solve the reparations problem. Germany's currency stabilized, and the nation seemed on its way to economic recovery. It remained an occupied nation. France had occupied the Rhineland in 1920, and French and Belgians had been stationed in the Ruhr Valley since 1923. Charges and countercharges rebounded about the long-term viability of the Dawes Plan, as Germany chafed under the continued presence of foreign soldiers on its soil.

Owen Young lauded Charley's role in crafting the reparations plan at a speech delivered on December 11 at a public dinner organized in Young's honor by the board of the General Electric Company. "I remember . . . during the first two weeks in Paris . . . when things did not look very hopeful, the general said, 'Well, let them call it the Dawes Committee, someone has to stand up and take the garbage or the garlands.' Let me say that at the time when the name 'Dawes' became attached to the committee, it looked as if the bouquets would all be of the back door variety [i.e., would be garbage]."[3]

Things were changing with Charley's brothers, too. Henry resigned as U.S. comptroller of the currency at the beginning of December and assumed the presidency of Pure Oil—another news item that kept the Dawes name in the papers. Beman moved over to the position of chairman of the board. The Teapot Dome investigations continued to be front-page news, but Pure Oil had yet to be identified as being involved, and the public had lost its initial interest in Harlan Stone's lawsuit against Standard Oil and the other oil companies.

At the end of January, Dawes asked E. Ross Bartley, a thirty-two-year-old White House correspondent for the Associated Press, to serve as his press secretary. Bartley had begun his tenure in Washington covering the last year of the Wilson administration. The two men had known each other since Dawes's year as budget director. Bartley had accompanied Harding on his trip to Alaska and was the first reporter to break the story of the president's death.

Dawes and Bartley had carried on an irregularly regular correspondence. Bartley often checked up on people to whom Dawes had provided financial assistance and reported back on their situation. He also shared inside gossip on White House goings-on. Following the 1924 election, Bartley told Dawes the field was wide open for Dawes to take a shot at the presidency—although there were rumors that Herbert Hoover was interested.[4]

For Bartley, Dawes's invitation "came out of the blue." Dawes offered the reporter a higher salary than he was earning and the promise that Dawes would continue to employ him after the end of the vice presidential years. Bartley reflected on the offer for a few days and then accepted.[5]

In the months between the election and the move to Washington, Charley returned to overseeing activities at his bank. He was reelected as chairman of the board of the Central Trust Company at the end of January and resigned a month later in preparation for his inauguration as vice president. On March 1, he and Caro, along with Dana and Virginia, and Francis Kilkenny and Rena Decker, the family's nurse, left Chicago for Washington by train. They arrived in Washington the following day and took a suite of rooms at the Willard Hotel.

Dawes spent the day before inauguration day visiting with Secretary of State Charles Evans Hughes, who was leaving his cabinet post, as well as Secretary of War Weeks, Secretary of the Treasury Mellon, and Director of the Budget Lord, all who were continuing to serve. Later in the day, Dawes joined his brothers and sisters and their children and spouses, who had traveled to Washington for the inauguration.

A sunny March 4, 1925, marked Dawes's fourth inauguration. This time he was a participant, not simply a spectator. Dawes spent the early morning entertaining friends and well-wishers in his rooms. He seemed oblivious to the time, and Caro would periodically remind him that he needed to get ready for the inauguration. Charley good-naturedly shooed her out and continued the conversation with his visitors. Despite his seeming nonchalance, he and Caro made it to the White House as scheduled for the customary ride to the Capitol with President Coolidge.

When Dawes arrived, he was ushered into the chamber where he was to take the oath of office, after which he would swear in the new senators. Dawes shook hands with several old friends, including Iowa Senator Albert B. Cummins, who had been an early supporter of McKinley's in the 1890s. Dawes's good-natured greetings and handclasps gave no hint of the scolding that awaited the senators.

Once he took the oath of office, Charley launched into a critique of the way the Senate conducted its business. It was not so much what he said, but how he said it, with finger wagging, desk pounding, and customary shouting[6]—and the fact that Dawes used as his venue a ceremony that was viewed as little more than a tiny footnote in a day of pageantry celebrating the president, not his understudy.

Dawes first reminded the senators that the Constitution, not they, chose him to preside over their body. Therefore, he considered himself apart from party politics. Dawes's next point was to acknowledge that the senators treated one another with courtesy and fairness, and that their rules preserved this atmosphere. But Dawes objected to Senate Rule XXII, often referred to as the cloture rule, designed to limit debate. Under the cloture rule, sixteen senators filed a motion to close debate. If two-thirds of the senators voted in the affirmative, then each senator would be permitted to speak for only one additional hour before the Senate had to vote on the measure under consideration.

Dawes argued that the Rule XXII was undemocratic and wasteful because it required a two-thirds vote, instead of a simple majority, to close debate, thus giving power to a small group of individuals who could manipulate the rule to prevent a final vote on a bill. "That rule, which at times enables senators to consume in oratory those last precious minutes of a session needed for momentous decisions, places in the hands of one or of a minority of senators greater power than the veto power exercised under the constitution by the president of the United States."

Rule XXII, he continued, had required the president to call Congress into special session to have critical legislation, such as appropriations bills, passed. "As it is the duty on the part of the presiding officer of the Senate to call attention to defective methods in the conduct of business by the body over which he presides, so under their constitutional power, it is the duty of the members of this body to correct them," he concluded.[7]

Senators were shocked that Dawes would use the occasion of their swearing in to attack Senate rules. Spectators applauded. Chief Justice William Howard Taft, himself once president of the United States, wrote his son that Dawes had "made a monkey of himself."[8] Comments predictably broke down along party lines, although some Republicans thought the new vice president had picked the wrong time and the wrong place to badger the Senate about its rules. Some senators were sympathetic. Michigan Senator Woodbridge Ferris, a Democrat who, at age seventy-two, was serving his first term in the Senate, observed: "I think the vice president has the lesson of his life coming to him. He has my profoundest sympathies. The rules of the Senate are hopeless; improvement will have to be deferred to the next world."[9]

Then Dawes proceeded to break more protocol. The custom for swearing in new senators was to have them called up in groups, but Dawes, clearly impatient with the process, ordered that all the senators be called up at one time. His final faux pas was to fail to appear in the Senate Chamber to preside over its adjournment.

On March 5, the day after the inauguration, the *Chicago Tribune* proclaimed, "Dawes Dazes Hoary Senate: Shouts Demand for Reform in Mossy Methods," in large type across its front page. To his hometown audience, Charley was the "supreme sensation of inaugural day and night."[10]

A subdued Dawes presided over the Senate on March 5, where he impassively listened to attacks on his judgment and on his failure to have the newly sworn-in senators sign the register. There was, however, an acknowledgment that Dawes had a point. Oscar Underwood, a Democrat from Alabama and a former Senate minority leader, proposed a modification to the cloture rule, and it was assigned to committee. If Dawes was upset at the attacks aimed at him, or felt some sense of vindication at Underwood's move, he concealed his emotions well.

The era of good feeling lasted less than one week.

On March 10, the Senate debated the nomination of Charles B. Warren, a Michigan attorney and Coolidge's nominee for attorney general to replace Harlan Stone, whom Coolidge had appointed to the Supreme Court. Warren had a distinguished résumé. In 1896, at the age of twenty-six, he was appointed associate counsel for the United States before the Joint High Commission that adjudicated claims between the United States and the United Kingdom in the Bering Sea. In 1909, President Theodore Roosevelt and Secretary of State Elihu Root named Warren as a counsel in negotiations with the United Kingdom over North American fishing rights. He argued the United States case before the Permanent Court of Arbitration at The Hague in the Netherlands. Warren served in the Army Reserves during World War I and helped write the Selective Service Act of 1917. These qualifications should have been sufficient to secure his approval by the Senate.

However, Warren was also identified with the sugar trust, having served as an attorney to H. O. Havemeyer, president of the American Sugar Refining Company. Leading the charge against Warren's confirmation was Montana Democrat Thomas J. Walsh, who had monopolized debate against Warren at a Saturday session when the nomination was under discussion.

Walsh resumed his attacks on Warren on March 10. He charged that Warren had been instrumental in fixing sugar prices and had secretly acquired stock in a Michigan sugar beet company with Havemeyer's knowledge and encouragement. Missouri Senator James A. Reed, also a Democrat, who had referred to Dawes as a "jackass" in reaction to the inauguration speech, jumped into the debate. Reed argued that Havemeyer was to the nation's sugar interests what John D. Rockefeller was to the oil interests. In other words, Havemeyer was determined to control the entire sugar market and destroy his competition. Reed likened approving Warren as attorney general to naming Albert Fall as the prosecution counsel for the Teapot Dome hearings.[11]

Debate ended, and the senators voted on Warren. It was a tie: Forty in favor of confirmation; forty opposed.

Dawes was napping at his suite at the Willard while the Senate debate raged. A frantic call went to his hotel room. He needed to get over to the Senate Chamber and break the tie. It was the height of irony. Dawes had lectured the senators on his constitutional responsibilities in his inaugural speech, and he was missing his moment.

A taxicab carrying Dawes sped to the Capitol. Aides met him at the entrance and practically carried him up the steps in frantic haste. He rushed into the Senate Chamber, but it was too late. North Carolina Democrat Lee Overman, who had originally voted to confirm Warren, declared that he did not think the Senate truly wanted Warren to be attorney general, and he changed his vote. The final tally was forty-one against and thirty-nine for. Dawes arrived too late, and Warren's nomination was defeated.[12]

The newspapers had a field day with Dawes. "The General Takes a Nap," read the headline to the *Chicago Tribune*'s editorial. After accusing the Senate of trying to score points off Dawes for scolding them about how they conducted business, the paper then declared that Dawes might never dare take another nap. "He was asleep at the switch when the administration was going off the rails, and he may be advised hereafter to take coffee in the morning, even if it keeps him awake all day."[13]

In his *Notes as Vice President*, Dawes wrote that "this regrettable incident . . . resulted from my inexperience with the explosive nature of that body [the Senate]." As he recalled it, the day had nearly ended, and six more senators were scheduled to speak before the vote on Warren's nomination. After Dawes left for his hotel, all but one of the speakers dropped out, and so the vote was called much sooner than expected.

The missed vote became a perennial topic at dinners and events throughout Dawes's four years as vice president. "The Gridiron Club has never had a dinner since that time without reminding me of this event, at one time bringing in an alarm clock four feet high for my benefit. However, I was in no danger of forgetting it."[14]

Coolidge (who, incidentally, was also well-known for taking a regular nap) was understandably angry—at his Senate floor leaders, who had botched the vote, and at his vice president, who was rapidly demonstrating that he was not Coolidge's vice president but very much his own man. Coolidge threatened to use his recess appointment authority and name Warren attorney general after the Senate adjourned. He resubmitted Warren's name, and the second vote was even more decisive than the first—forty-six against to thirty-nine for. Coolidge finally nominated a fellow Vermonter, John Garibaldi Sargent, who was confirmed and served all four years of Coolidge's elected presidential term.

The Senate adjourned on March 21, and Charley and Caro left for Evanston.

A month later, Dawes headed to Massachusetts to reenact the one hundred fiftieth anniversary of the ride of Paul Revere and William Dawes. Pershing accompanied him. Dawes, a great-great-grandson of William, shared the dais with Paul Revere's great-granddaughter Pauline Revere Thayer at the Old North Church. "The greatest question before the American people today is, 'What of our character?'" he asked the crowd. He encouraged those in attendance to cultivate self-denial, clean minds, and the subordination of their individual will to the greater good.[15]

Dawes was still, however, on his campaign to get public support for a change in the Senate's rules. Earlier in the day, he renewed his attack by repeating much of his inaugural speech at a luncheon hosted by Boston's Chamber of Commerce. He noted that it was not what he had said at his inauguration that had caused the trouble, but the way he had said it. He then quoted George Bernard Shaw: "No offensive truth is properly presented unless it causes irritation."[16]

From Boston, Dawes took his campaign against the Senate's rules on the road. At the annual Associated Press luncheon, held on April 21, Dawes asked the one thousand two hundred editors present to take his case to the American people through their editorials and their reporting. Senators respond to public sentiment, he said, but senators must be told what that sentiment is. Dawes urged the editors to encourage people to write their senators regarding the need for changes in the rules.[17]

By his estimate, Dawes spoke to audiences ranging in size from six thousand to twelve thousand people. He appeared in auditoriums in Indianapolis, Cincinnati, Denver, Seattle, and Birmingham, Alabama, as well as Chicago and Boston. Senator Underwood often appeared with him and offered strong support, but Dawes soon learned that, although an individual senator might appear on the platform with him in the senator's home state, Senate support for rules change was tepid, at best.

Dawes's attacks on the Senate's rules were in much the same vein as his attacks on La Follette during the presidential campaign. They were sidenotes to larger and more important issues, but Dawes wanted to move his preferred issues to the forefront. Notes and letters of support egged him on, and it was not in his character to back down. By May 1, Dawes had received 927 letters, the majority of which overwhelmingly favored his speech.[18]

Dawes labored in vain to change the filibuster and cloture rule, and the Senate played directly into Dawes's hands on January 20, 1926. The senators were scheduled to vote on the treaty that would have made the United States a part of the World Court. Senator James Reed, a Missouri Democrat, read into the record "some long document forty-odd years old which could not, by any stretch of the imagination, be deemed to have pertinence or be of practical bearing on the topic at hand."[19]

That night, Dawes delivered a scheduled radio talk. He told his audience that he would abandon his prepared text and give them a detailed account of the Senate proceedings for the day. He then proceeded to repeat Reed's recitation of the historic document during the debate. "He [Dawes] reeled it off in entertaining style, vigorously enforcing the day's experience as a glaring illustration of the Senate's stupid squandering of time and money," a Montana newspaper editor wrote.[20]

Commenting on the radio address, a letter writer told Dawes it was interesting that Reed complained of lacking a way to respond to Dawes's speech. "Considering the advantage that critical senators have over you in this respect in the Senate, it would seem that Senator Reed ought to be a better sport than to complain of his inability to reply."[21]

But not everyone supported the vice president. "I heard on Tuesday night your radio speech. . . . After I had listened, I went to bed uttering this prayer: 'Oh, that Calvin Coolidge may be spared to serve his full term!'"[22]

The handicapping for the 1928 presidential race started in early 1927. Dawes's name topped the list as a choice for the Republican nomination. He categorically denied interest in being a candidate, immediately throwing his support behind Frank Lowden, who had renewed his desire for the job and who was favored among Republicans as the western candidate. That did not keep reporters from broaching the subject at every opportunity—and finding reasons to ignore Dawes's emphatic denials.

By 1927, Dawes's rocky start with the senators had given way to a respectful and fruitful relationship. His finely honed negotiating skills had been instrumental in securing the passage of several key pieces of legislation, sometimes against Coolidge's wishes.

Major differences existed between the president and vice president when it came to agricultural policy. While the nation's financial and industrial sectors had recovered and thrived since the postwar recession, America's farmers still lived in dire poverty.

American agriculture had responded to the need for increased food production during and immediately following World War I. However, once the Armistice was signed and Europe no longer used its fields as battlegrounds, it cut orders for American foodstuffs and began to rehabilitate its own agricultural sector. Hoover, when he took on the work of the American Relief Administration, had done his best to insist that Europeans continue to order American farm commodities, but they ignored his requests. With an oversupply of crops, prices dropped and farmers barely eked out a living.

Dawes had hoped to discuss agriculture policy with Coolidge when he met with him in Vermont during the presidential campaign, but that conversation was overshadowed by Dawes's anti–Ku Klux Klan and antilabor speeches in Maine. Although Coolidge had been raised on a small Vermont farm, he lacked understanding of the economics and dynamics of midwestern agriculture. Dawes, on the other hand, having lived in Nebraska and Illinois, and having once owned a packinghouse, had a better appreciation than Coolidge did of the needs of the farmers who fed Americans and the world. The president maintained his conservative attitudes toward helping farmers, whereas Dawes shared the view of the Progressives and backed governmental assistance.

The Progressive wing of the Republican Party, made up heavily of western senators, supported the McNary-Haugen Farm Relief Bill. Among its strongest proponents was Dawes's former nemesis Smith Brookhart. Also known as the Agricultural Surplus Control Bill, McNary-Haugen would have established a national farm policy that would help raise farmers' standard of living. Under the bill, the federal government would purchase surplus farm commodities and sell them overseas. Dawes built a coalition with Brookhart and other supportive western senators, and even secured backing from some reluctant eastern senators, to ensure passage of McNary-Haugen in the face of Coolidge's veto threat. As promised, Coolidge vetoed the bill, because he believed it would foster overproduction. Congress failed to override Coolidge's veto, and the bill never became law. Coolidge never offered an alternative to McNary-Haugen, and the nation's farmers continued to struggle throughout his presidency and well into the succeeding Hoover years.

As he had with McNary-Haugen, Dawes built a coalition to secure passage of the McFadden Act, also debated in 1927. This bill renewed the charter of the Federal Reserve System and introduced major changes in the nation's banking structure. Eastern senators strongly favored the bill, whereas western senators believed the act would allow banks to grow too big and squeeze out small community banks.

The McFadden Act allowed national banks operating in states that permitted branch banking to open branches. This was a change from the original Federal Reserve charter, which did not permit a bank to have multiple locations. Dawes's support marked a change in his view about branch banking. The act also enabled banks to open subsidiary corporations to reduce their risk exposure.

Another major change in the act was to level the playing field between banks that were members of the Federal Reserve System and those that were not. Member banks faced stricter requirements than nonmembers. Member banks were required to maintain higher demand deposit levels and could not engage in certain types of businesses that nonmember banks had found profitable. The McFadden Act modified regulations so that member banks would be more competitive with nonmember banks.[23] Coolidge supported the bill and signed it into law.

The newspapers now characterized the vice president as popular, resourceful, and influential. Senators strolled by his desk to exchange pleasantries or to discuss legislation.[24] The Senate, sometimes called "the most exclusive club in the world," had discovered that underneath Charley's blustery exterior beat a heart of gold.

Charley, Caro, and Virginia traveled to Panama and Cuba following Congress's adjournment at the beginning of March 1927. Although the trip was officially billed as a vacation, Dawes met with the leaders of both countries and was hailed by crowds of well-wishers as a popular and respected leader.

In Central America, Dawes pursued his twin passions of fishing and archaeology. He enjoyed several days of successful fishing and visited Panama's National Museum, where he studied Mayan pottery and talked with museum curators. He was struck by what he saw as Asian influence in the Mayan pottery.

Some of the pieces he shipped home from the trip broke in transit, and he took them to the repairer at Chicago's Field Museum of Natural History. A curator confirmed Dawes's observations that the Mayan pottery showed signs of Chinese inspiration.[25] Dawes's conclusions anticipated the late-twentieth-century scholarship of the author Charles C. Mann, who has made a compelling case for the Chinese arrival in the Americas well in advance of the Europeans.

On April 16, 1927, Caro underwent surgery for an unnamed reason at Chicago's Michael Reese Hospital. She had specifically selected this hospital for her treatment.[26] The hospital was a leader in medical research and patient care, and it had the philosophy that everyone would be treated, regardless of background or ability to pay. One of the hospital's doctors, Julius Hess, pioneered the use of incubators for premature and high-risk infants and invented the "Hess Incubator," which controlled the humidity, temperature, and oxygen for the newborn.[27] Caro's work with orphaned infants and her work with the Cradle Society, an organization that she helped found shortly after the move to Evanston to care for and find homes for orphaned children, had made her well-acquainted with the quality of care at Michael Reese.

The official press release announced simply that she was operated on "for a minor surgical affliction." Dawes's telegram to Beman was similarly cryptic: "Caro underwent an operation at Michael Reese hospital Chicago this morning. She is doing very well and there is no cause for worry."[28] The surgery was not so minor that Caro could be released in a few days. Dawes moved into the hospital suite, and he remained with Caro for the length of her stay.

On August 7, 1927, Dawes represented the United States at the ribbon cutting of the Peace Bridge, a 3,580-foot span that linked Buffalo, New York, with Fort Erie, Ontario. The Prince of Wales and British prime minister Stanley Baldwin represented the United Kingdom, and Canadian Prime Minister William Mackenzie King joined the other high-level dignitaries at the dedication, along with other officials from all three countries. Both the Prince of Wales and Baldwin highlighted the friendship between the United States and Canada in their remarks.

Given the recent failure of the Geneva talks on naval disarmament, these were not simply ceremonial words. The failure of the two nations to arrive at an agreement regarding the size and composition of their respective navies had cast gloom over the hopes for world peace.

Dawes did not rise to the occasion and offer similar conciliatory words. Instead, he criticized the impasse between the United States and the United Kingdom. Participants in the conference maintained that one reason for the failure of the talks had been a lack of adequate preparation on both sides to engage in the negotiations. Dawes echoed this observation. Each nation had focused on its own needs, he continued, to the exclusion of understanding the needs of the other side. The delegates feared domestic repercussions if each country announced a marked change in its naval preparedness programs. However, he said that the talks represented an important step toward eliminating "competitive war preparation."[29]

The newspapers reported that his remarks were undiplomatic, which they were, given the tensions between the two nations. "Dawes Hits Geneva Failure—British Prince and Premier Hear Attack," blared the front-page headline of the *Chicago Daily Tribune*.[30] The *New York Times* headline read: "Dawes Criticizes Failure of Geneva Naval Parley in Peace Bridge Speech—Address Causes Stir."[31] As usual, Dawes dismissed the criticism: "Common sense is never undiplomatic."[32]

In early January 1928, Dawes's name resurfaced as a potential candidate for the Republican presidential nomination. He was mentioned as a serious contender alongside Herbert Hoover, who was rapidly emerging as the front-runner, and Frank Lowden. By the end of February, the newspapers commented on Dawes's failure to act like a serious candidate, but that did not stop anti-Hoover Republicans from putting Dawes on their primary ballots or voting for him in their local conventions.

When Ohio Senator Frank B. Willis, who was running as a favorite-son candidate, died unexpectedly at the end of March, his delegates committed to vote for Dawes. Hoover won the majority of votes in the Ohio primary, but Dawes was awarded twenty delegates. Hoover faced a more formidable pro-Dawes favorite son in James Watson, a senator from Indiana. Watson defeated Hoover in the primary, but Dawes won thirty-three delegates. Watson promised his own delegates to Dawes at the June Republican convention. New York delegates also heavily favored Dawes, although the state's chairman, who was a member of the Republican National Committee, supported Hoover.

Dawes did what he could behind the scenes on behalf of Lowden, but there was widespread belief throughout the winter and early spring of 1928 that Dawes truly wanted the presidency himself. When Lowden testified before a Senate committee on his campaign finances, he insisted that he would not throw his delegate support to Dawes at the convention as part of a secret deal.

By the time the Republican National Convention met in Kansas City, Missouri, on June 12, Hoover had pretty much sewn up the nomination. He had first explored the possibility of a presidential run in 1920 and began to develop a serious organization following Coolidge's inauguration in 1925, when it was rumored that the president would not run for a second full term. One of the big issues that divided Republicans in 1928 was the failure of the McNary-Haugen Farm Relief Bill. Even though Hoover was an Iowa native, he had long been associated with his adopted home state of California. Hoover's support came from urban areas. Men like Lowden and Watson—and Dawes—drew their support from the nation's agricultural midsection.

The Republican Party chose Hoover as its official standard-bearer on the first ballot. Discussion then turned toward the vice presidential nominee, and Dawes's name surfaced as a candidate. Newspapers reported that both Borah and Mellon backed Dawes for the position. But when nominations were made for the vice presidential slot, the delegates selected Charles Curtis of Kansas with only token opposition.

A month later, Hoover and his wife, Lou Henry Hoover, stopped in Evanston for a visit with the Daweses. Dawes saw in Hoover a candidate who "will not make concessions on the prohibition issue; will make a sincere and conciliatory presentation of the agricultural question, and emphasize the desirability of sound governmental administration."[33] Dawes pledged his support for Hoover and offered to make speeches on the candidate's behalf.

Dawes stayed away from Washington for most of the summer and into the early fall of 1928 as his vice presidential term drew to a close. In

August, he traveled to Colorado with his family, where he still had the stamina, at age sixty-three, to embark on a five-mile ride on horseback. As always, Dawes enjoyed fishing; he caught, by his count, ninety-six trout in eight days.[34] Later that summer, the family went to Ontario to spend time with Beman and his family at their summer home.

September 1, 1928, marked the fifth and final year of the settlement under the Dawes Plan, after which Germany was required to meet its annual reparations payments of 2,000,500,000 marks, beginning in 1929.[35]

Discussions were already underway at the start of the year regarding the future of German reparations. After surviving the depression of 1925–1926, Germany's economy showed a remarkable recovery in 1927 and early 1928. Production flourished, Germany had access to credit for business expansion, and the Reichsbank took steps in mid-1927 to curb speculation on the rising German stock market.[36] The nation had met its reparations payments during the four years 1925 to 1928. However, the funds to make those payments had come from floating loans of foreign funds, and Germany contended that, unless its access to foreign credit continued, it could not meet the stepped-up reparations payment schedule.

The Europeans requested the Americans to form another panel of experts, modeled after Dawes's First Committee of Experts appointed in 1923. S. Parker Gilbert, who was still serving as the reparations agent, was asked to serve on the new committee. Gilbert told Dawes he would take the position if Dawes would replace him after his term as vice president had ended. Dawes, however, had made a commitment to the president of the Dominican Republic to travel to that country to create a budget and taxation system. He recommended Owen Young, since Young had been closely associated with the work of the original committee.

Parker advocated that future reparations be calculated as an annual amount, to be paid over a specified number of years—much as an installment loan is repaid. This approach differed from the original discussions under the Dawes Plan, which had called for the establishment of a fixed total sum for which Germany would be responsible. Under Gilbert's proposal, the annual payment due would be tied to Germany's ability to pay. Gilbert also recommended that part of the funding for the reparations come from selling bonds. Dawes kept in close communication with Secretary of State Frank B. Kellogg on the progress of the negotiations. Dawes knew that an agreement was essential to maintaining peace. "A failure to agree now, involving all Europe in acrimonious political struggle, should be avoided," he commented in his *Notes*.[37]

The gist of Gilbert's plan was adopted in 1929 and named the Young Plan after Owen D. Young. The Young Plan reduced the total amount of the reparations due to 121 billion marks, fixed the payment term to fifty-eight years, and called for a floating loan to provide capital for the payments. The Young Plan also ended oversight of Germany's finances and called for the last of the occupying troops to leave German soil. The Bank for International Settlements was created to replace the position of reparations agent and to serve as the collections and disbursement entity for the payments.[38]

The Young Plan was conceived when the world's economies were thriving. In the United States, reduction in taxation and loose business policies had increased corporate wealth, permitted an overall increase in wages, and contributed to a bull stock market. Credit policies were lax, and money flowed freely.

In observing the economic scene at the start of the 1928 election season, Dawes expressed concerns about the future of the economy. He saw that the lax credit policies would reach a point where more credit would be extended than there was cash to cover, and he expected to see a contraction of available credit in the not-too-distant future. He made an eerily accurate prediction:

> Will [the contraction in credits], when reached, make nervous the depositing class, as used to happen in the days prior to the establishment of the Federal Reserve System with its large credit-creating potentiality? Will the American people, as they sometimes do during the closing period of prosperity, while it still persists, suddenly turn over in bed—that is, wake up some morning changed from an optimistic to a pessimistic view of the future as occurred in 1892, culminating in the panic of 1893?[39]

It was a cogent analysis borne of four decades of observing, and being affected by, business cycles; and time would prove Dawes right.

A trip to New York in mid-September brought both sadness and poignant memories. Between his work as director of the budget, followed by his reparations work, and then the vice presidency, Dawes had been absent from Chicago for the better part of seven years. Many of his friends and colleagues had died, and he had few connections to the new generation of Chicago businessmen. He still had friends in New York City, among them Harbord, now president of RCA, and George B. Cortelyou, from the McKinley days. Dawes's friend and business partner from his Lincoln years, Gus Hanna, was his traveling companion.

Dawes also visited with a Marietta College classmate, Ward A. Holden. "I thought of the changes in our lives in the forty-four years during which I have seen Holden only twice," Dawes reminisced. "He is one of New York's successful medical specialists, and I a public official. We used to go together to, and occupy the cheapest seats at, the infrequent plays at the old Marietta City Hall nearly a half-century ago. Here in New York, Mr. [Samuel] Rothafel [owner of the Capitol Theater in New York City] not only gave us our seats for nothing, but a fine luncheon after the performance as well."[40] The trip was a humbling reminder of how far he had traveled, both literally and professionally, since his early years in Marietta.

Dawes maintained his interest in the Rufus and Mary Dawes Hotels throughout his vice presidential years and visited them from time to time when he was in Chicago. Henry regularly furnished copies of the income statements to his brother, and Charley kept track of the hotels' financial performance. They were established to pay for themselves, but the men's hotels generally ran a deficit, in part because they had competition from other shelters and typically were not full.

The women's hotels, however, were generally completely occupied and would occasionally show a profit. This was partially because the Mary Dawes Hotels became a permanent residence for many elderly women over time—a situation for which Dawes credits his mother. The original intent of the hotel was to furnish a bed and a meal for working-women who could not afford a place to live. On the day that the first Mary Dawes Hotel opened, elderly women asked for rooms but were turned away. The women "pleaded their case with Mother, and she, with tears in her eyes, interceded for them with me. Of course, this settled it on the spot."[41]

Charley, Caro, and their nephew, Beman's son Henry, visited the two hotels in Chicago in early October. A man walked up to Dawes, who did not immediately recognize him, and identified himself: "I am Joe." Dawes's eyes lit up in pleasant surprise. Joe had at one time been the leader of a gang of twelve-year-old boys who disrupted the opening night activities at the Rufus Dawes Hotel in January 1914. As someone prepared to call the police, Dawes intervened and invited Joe and his compatriots into the hotel. Caro and Rena Decker washed the boys' hands and faces. Then, they all sat down to dinner, with Dawes at one end and his mother at the other. Dawes had kept contact with Joe and a few of the other boys over the years but had eventually lost touch with Joe. Now, the well-dressed young man told his former benefactor that he was a chauffeur. Dawes described Joe as "honest, well-behaved, and successful."

"Why don't we realize more the enormous returns which come from little kindnesses?" Dawes mused. "On bitter cold winter nights the streets of every great city are a Gethsemane for many of the homeless and half-clad poor—some of them brought to their condition through no fault of their own, but all of them with a right to help if the religion of Christ means anything. On such nights the Rufus Dawes Hotel is filled to overflowing and then is when it does the most good."[42]

Dawes attended the annual postelection Gridiron dinner on December 8, 1928. He sat next to the vice president elect, Charles Curtis, senator from Kansas, also known as Charlie (but spelled differently). In the good-natured hilarity of the evening, Dawes shared a little friendly advice to his successor on what it took to be vice president.

Dubbed the "Dawes Decalogue, or the Letter of a Self-Made Has-Been to His Successor," the letter read:

> Just between us, Charlie, you are getting away to a flying start. "Helen Maria" was my line, but "Too damn dumb" will get you just as far. Out of the depths of my experience, I commend you these Ten Commandments:
>
> Don't steal the first page on inauguration day, and you may be invited to sit in the cabinet.
>
> Don't be afraid to criticize the Senate. You know how much it needs it. The public likes it and the Senate thrives on it.

Don't commit yourself to another fellow's candidacy for president. He may hold you to it.

Don't pretend you understand the equalization fee. Al Smith
found there wasn't a vote in it—so did I.

Don't try to change the Senate rules.

Don't buck the president if you want to stay more than four years.

Don't do your sleeping in the day time.[43]

The final months of Dawes's tenure as vice president were a flurry
of activity as the Coolidge administration sought to finish as much of
its agenda as possible. Congress also wanted to pass legislation under a
president with whom it felt familiar.

The United States had signed the Kellogg-Briand Pact, named for
U.S. Secretary of State Frank B. Kellogg and French Prime Minister
Aristide Briand, on August 27, 1928. The pact, which outlawed war,
grew out of international reaction to the loss and horror of World War
I. A total of fifteen nations signed the pact.

The Senate had the constitutional responsibility to ratify the treaty,
and, following its failure to ratify the Versailles Treaty, the Coolidge
administration could not take Senate approval for granted.

Dawes arrived at his Senate office on January 8 to find a group of
senators, led by Borah and Missouri Democrat James Reed, discussing
modifications to the treaty. Borah, chair of the Senate Committee on
Foreign Relations, had prepared a report on the committee's understanding of the impact of the treaty on the United States. The committee
had voted unanimously for the report. Borah wanted to present the
report to the Senate during its debate on the treaty and sought a ruling
from Dawes on points of order should any senator raise an objection
to the report from the floor. After consulting with the Senate parlia-
mentarian, Dawes informed Borah that he would not sustain points of
order. Dawes used the discussion to impress upon Borah the importance
of ratifying the pact: The main benefit to "humanity was the cause of
peace . . . simple views which I felt had not been stressed enough from
the floor, and which justify the policy of this able statesman in making
some concessions to ensure its ratification."[44]

A week later, Coolidge called Dawes and asked him to talk with a
few senators who were not supportive of the treaty. Dawes committed

to "steam up" during the next day's Senate debate. As he did with most of the Senate's proceedings, Dawes found the debate on the treaty tiresome. He referred to it as "interminable and ponderous." He was forced to listen to "long, drawn-out arguments—some of which by the considerate might be dignified by the term 'legal,' but most of them even more confusing than a legal argument." As usual, the debates irritated him, and he waited, in vain, for a "short, common sense discussion."[45]

The Senate ratified the treaty in an eighty-five to one vote on January 15, 1929. Coolidge signed the treaty in a momentous ceremony in the White House East Room. Dawes attended the ceremony. The ratification was the result of a now-experienced vice president who had deftly used the Senate rules to bring the matter to a vote and secure the treaty's acceptance by a majority of senators, led by the isolationist William Borah.

January 24, 1929, marked the Daweses' fortieth wedding anniversary. Dawes bought flowers for Caro, "which pleased her all the more because, I regret to say, I generally forget the anniversary until she reminds me of it. But this time I did not."[46]

On January 26, Dawes watched as the Senate, by unanimous consent, passed a joint resolution giving official recognition to the Century of Progress International Exhibition, also called the Chicago World's Fair. Rufus had organized the fair, scheduled for 1933, and was president of the organization. As Dawes observed, there was a growing sense that such expositions and fairs had become outdated. The Senate's approval gave him an immense sense of satisfaction that there was still support for international expositions.

The senators presented Dawes with a silver tray in honor of his service as vice president on March 3, his last day as their presiding officer. He was recognized for his impartiality in his rulings, and it was noted that not one of his decisions had ever been appealed. "Fairness and promptness have marked your conduct," Senator Joseph Robinson told him.

Overcome with emotion, Dawes replied, "My friends . . . you have done me a great honor, and I thank you from the bottom of my heart."[47]

Dawes turned over the vice president's gavel to Charles Curtis on a rainy March 4. Charley could not refrain from taking one last shot at the Senate's rules. After assuring those assembled that he held no acrimony toward anyone, he went on to say that he could not be true to himself if he did not address the subject of the defect in the Senate's procedural rules that permitted the filibuster. "I take back nothing," he told his audience.[48]

Curtis, who had been a senator since 1907, told his former colleagues: "The vice president is not one of the makers of the law, nor is he consulted about the rules adopted to govern your actions. His obligations to you senators . . . are to call for a fair and impartial construction of the rules which you, yourselves, have adopted and which you alone may change."[49]

In his *Notes*, Dawes mused about his four years as presiding officer of the U.S. Senate: "For the senators individually I cherish a high regard, but collectively as agents of the government in an organization for business—well! That is something else again." One of the senators, after telling Dawes how much he thought of him, said, "But the Senate got very tired of you at the beginning of your service." Dawes reported his reply: "'I should hate to think that the Senate was as tired of me at the beginning of my service as I am of the Senate at its end.' This, of course, was a joke, but I had unlimited and irrelevant debate in mind."[50]

Charley, Caro, and Virginia arrived in Chicago on March 6. Charley would barely have time to check in with things at the bank and get comfortable in his library in his Evanston home. He was headed to the Dominican Republic, at the request of that nation's president, to help straighten out its finances. It was a short-term assignment, and Dawes planned to make it as short as he could. Herbert Hoover had asked Dawes to become the ambassador to the United Kingdom, and Dawes had accepted the offer.

CHAPTER 13

X

Ambassador to the
Court of St James's

While the page-one headlines of the newspapers reported on Herbert Hoover's inauguration, a small item in the back pages of the *New York Times* announced that Dawes was heading up a mission to reorganize the finances of the Dominican Republic at the invitation of its president, Horacio Vásquez.[1]

The United States had occupied the Dominican Republic since 1916, and, by the time Harding assumed office in 1921, the American public began to tire of its military presence in that nation. In a closely supervised election, Vásquez won the presidency in 1924, and American troops left the Dominican Republic in July. Vásquez had agreed to vacate his office after a four-year term, but he remained in office in 1929, presumably having agreed to stay for an extra two years to stabilize the nation's shaky and corrupt government. The Dawes mission showed that the "United States themselves [*sic*] seem to have been those primarily responsible in revindicating us before the consideration of the rest of the world," Vásquez announced to his countrymen.[2]

In his memorandum of understanding with the Dominican government, Dawes agreed to create a budget system, make recommendations for reorganization of the executive branch of the government with special attention to the Treasury Department and revenue collection and expenditures, review the tariff system, and look at the nation's banking system.[3]

Vásquez had contacted Dawes in mid-February about the Dominican assignment, and Charley's initial plan was to travel to the Caribbean nation in June. Only a few days after Dawes made the commitment, Hoover offered him the ambassadorship to the United Kingdom. In a letter to Owen Young, Dawes referred to the offer as "an unexpected suggestion from the president-elect."[4]

Dawes quickly regrouped, scheduled the trip to the Dominican Republic for late March, and assembled a team of fifteen men for the work. Without divulging his reasons for the precipitous change in plans, Dawes explained to his Dominican contact, Angel Morales, that the large team would help him complete the work more quickly.[5]

Members of the commission included several men who had worked with Dawes on prior projects: Francis Kilkenny, J. C. Roop, Henry Smither, John Sewell, and Henry Robinson. Ross Bartley was still a member of Dawes's team, and George B. Cortelyou Jr., the son of Theodore Roosevelt's personal secretary, traveled as secretary to the group.[6] Dawes also wrangled Harbord's membership on the committee after a series of communications with Owen Young, who also wanted Harbord to assist with the reparations work in Europe. Dawes finally admitted his upcoming ambassadorial appointment to Young in a confidential telegram and expressed his decision to keep his promise to the Dominican government.[7]

Dawes and his team made quick work of their mission, benefiting from a series of memorandums written by U.S. Foreign Service diplomat Sumner Welles that outlined in great detail the existing conditions of the Dominican Republic's government and budget structure. Dawes also secured financial statements and documents related to bond issues that United States banks had handled for the Caribbean nation. On April 23, 1929, the committee submitted its work to Vásquez. The report represented the expertise and insight of America's top financial and governmental experts of the time. Unfortunately, it proved insufficient to secure a democratic Dominican government. Rafael Trujillo overthrew the Vásquez government in February 1930 and instituted a ruthless dictatorship that controlled the country for over thirty years until he was assassinated in 1961.

The news of Dawes's appointment as the next ambassador to the Court of St James's broke on April 9. If modern diplomacy required an ambassador suitable to the days of Queen Elizabeth I, the *New York Times* editorialized, London would not accept Dawes. With his "underslung pipe, his picturesque speech, and his blunt manner," he was certain to become the best example to the British of an "American original."[8]

Humorist Will Rogers proclaimed that Dawes would put the king of England on a budget, and the United Press news agency dubbed the new ambassador "Uncle Sam's Prize Handy Man."[9]

Reports surfaced that Dawes's appointment had been decided at the Republican National Convention, where Hoover presumably turned down Dawes as his vice presidential candidate but promised him an ambassadorial post in exchange for Dawes's releasing his own and Lowden's delegates. Dawes's correspondence does not support that rumor.

Dawes was widely respected in Europe, a plus in the influential and highly visible role of ambassador. The *Baltimore Sun* also pointed out that Dawes, whose net worth was estimated at $5 million, could afford to serve as ambassador to England—a position that paid an annual salary of only $18,000 and had nearly impoverished some of Dawes's predecessors, including the 1924 Democratic presidential candidate, John W. Davis.[10]

United States relations with the United Kingdom still suffered from the failure of the 1927 Geneva Disarmament Conference, and U.S. acceptance of the Kellogg-Briand Pact had done little to ameliorate the tension. In late March 1928, the *New York American* revealed secret documents that disclosed discussions between the United Kingdom's Sir Austen Chamberlain and France's Aristide Briand. In private negotiations, France agreed to the United Kingdom's position that the size of each country's naval fleet should be restricted based on its types of ships and numbers of guns. This differed from the United Kingdom's public position at Geneva, where it had insisted that ships be restricted on the basis of tonnage. In exchange for France's acquiescence, the United Kingdom agreed not to include French reservists in the total count of troop strength.

The difference between how the United States and how the United Kingdom wanted to constitute their respective navies had been a major reason for the failure at Geneva. The United Kingdom favored lighter ships; Americans wanted heavier ones. Under the Anglo-French arrangement, the United Kingdom was free to build as many lightweight ships as it wished, while the United States would still be restricted in the total size of its fleet.

The story on the Anglo-French agreement broke at about the time the U.S. House of Representatives was considering the "cruiser bill," a naval appropriations bill that called for the building of fifteen cruisers. The House quickly approved the bill, but it stalled in the Senate through the summer and into the fall of 1928. Coolidge used the tenth anniversary of the Armistice to encourage the Senate to pass the legislation. The senators finally passed the bill a month before the end of the Coolidge administration on a sixty-eight to twelve vote.[11] Coolidge signed the cruiser bill into law.

When Hoover took office, he faced the challenge of renewing the stalled disarmament talks in the face of the United States embarking on an aggressive shipbuilding program. Given Hoover's Quaker background, the pursuit of peace was in the president's DNA. Since his return from the war, Dawes, too, had become a strong proponent, if not necessarily a strident one, of seeking peaceful solutions to world problems. Both men were anxious for the disarmament talks to resume and to result in a treaty.

Politics abroad gave Hoover and Dawes a boost. On May 30, the United Kingdom's Conservative Party lost its majority in the general election. Although the vote was nearly even between the Conservative and Labor Parties, the makeup of Parliament gave Labor five more seats. Labor leader Ramsay MacDonald, who had pledged during the campaign to restart the negotiations, replaced Stanley Baldwin, who had held office during the Geneva talks.

MacDonald became prime minister on June 5, just as Dawes arrived in Washington to meet with Hoover and Secretary of State Henry L. Stimson to receive his instructions. The Geneva parleys, as they were termed, topped the list. According to Dawes, Hoover wanted to set aside public opinion, which continued to be largely anti-British and strongly favored a naval buildup, and restart the talks. To this point, specifically, Dawes was set to deliver a speech in which he would outline the American proposal—to find a way to reach a "naval yardstick," as he put it, on which all sides could agree.[12]

Dawes, Caro, Virginia, and Beman's son Henry, who would serve as his uncle's personal secretary, departed from New York on the SS *Olympic* on June 7. (Charley and Caro's son Dana was in boarding school at Lawrenceville Academy, near Trenton, New Jersey.) Expectations on both sides of the ocean were that Dawes carried with him official overtures to the new British government regarding a resumption of the talks. En route, Dawes learned that MacDonald would soon leave London for his Scottish estate, Lossiemouth. Dawes cabled the American embassy's *chargé d'affaires*, Ray Atherton, to make sure that a meeting with MacDonald could take place before Dawes's planned speech. Dawes was set to travel to Scotland the Sunday after his arrival to meet the prime minister.

The *Olympic* docked in Southampton, England, on June 14, and Dawes and his family traveled directly to London. When he presented his credentials to King George V the day after his arrival, Dawes was reminded of the first time he had seen the monarch: it was August 1917, when Dawes was a member of the first American troops to set foot on British soil.[13]

Speculation abounded about the nature of Dawes's upcoming meeting with MacDonald. Headlines in British and American papers declared that Dawes's primary purpose was to issue an invitation to the prime minister to meet with Hoover in Washington, where the two leaders could work out a disarmament deal privately. Dawes gave nothing away when he spoke to the press. At the same time, Stimson fielded inquiries in Washington from concerned members of Congress and the diplomatic community. He, too, deflected any suggestion that high-level talks were in the works.[14]

In his meeting with Dawes, MacDonald broached the subject of visiting Washington. Dawes expressed concerns that a visit in advance of some progress in disarmament talks could be construed as securing concessions from Hoover—a perception that would torpedo public and senatorial support for a treaty agreement. MacDonald seemed disappointed but expressed his hope that a visit could eventually be arranged.[15]

On Tuesday, June 18, Dawes delivered his long-awaited address to the Pilgrims of Great Britain, a British-American society that promoted goodwill between the two countries. It traditionally held a dinner to welcome each new U.S. ambassador to the Court of St James's. Hoover,

Stimson, and MacDonald had vetted Dawes's speech. In it, the new ambassador laid out the Hoover administration's approach to the naval disarmament talks. Drawing on the experiences of the Reparations Commission, Dawes observed how economists and statesmen could not come to agreement as long as economics and politics were combined in the decision-making. He noted that a similar problem had resulted from the failed 1927 disarmament parleys.

Quoting the eighteenth-century political thinker Edmund Burke, Dawes told his audience: "Politics ought to be adjusted not to human reasonings, but to human nature, of which the reason is but a part, and by no means the greatest part." To adjust to human nature, Dawes proposed that each nation's naval experts agree to their respective definition of a yardstick by which to measure naval power and then submit these definitions to the statesmen, who would draw up the final agreement.[16]

Dawes spoke to a crowd of over five hundred, composed of many of the United Kingdom's leaders, including Sir Austen Chamberlain but not MacDonald, who was delivering a speech elsewhere that same evening, as well as a number of influential Americans.

The new ambassador was strictly business. Dawes launched directly into his speech without introductory remarks or jokes. Some of the audience were surprised that Dawes was learned, erudite, and articulate. They had expected a more commonplace address studded with oaths.[17]

Public reaction to Dawes's speech was overwhelmingly supportive. Newspapers hailed the speech, and MacDonald's public agreement with Dawes's proposals, as the dawn of a new day in disarmament talks. Work to restart the parleys began immediately.

On June 24, Dawes met with Hugh S. Gibson, the U.S. ambassador to Belgium and one of the key negotiators in the disarmament talks. The two men discussed the best way to bring together the experts who would determine the measures of naval power. Following their private discussions, the two ambassadors met with MacDonald. MacDonald, Gibson, and Dawes then conferred with Japanese ambassador Matsudaira Tsuneo, who would serve throughout the forthcoming negotiations as a go-between for the United States and the United Kingdom.

Negotiations establishing the framework for a new parley got up to full steam by the end of June. Dawes plunged into the thick of the diplomatic talks. Naval experts worked on the definitions to be used when formal discussions were finally underway. Gibson wrote Dawes: "The more I ponder the subject, the more I am convinced that the most effective approach is for us to make haste slowly and take one careful step at a time."[18]

By the end of July, Dawes saw the fruit of his efforts. In a speech before the House of Commons, MacDonald announced that he would travel to Washington in October to meet with Hoover for the purpose of discussing naval disarmament. Following that meeting, the United States and the United Kingdom would issue invitations to other nations to join them in a peace conference. As a goodwill gesture, Mac-Donald ordered that construction be suspended on two cruisers, two submarines, and one submarine depot ship (called a submarine tender by Americans), and he directed the slowdown of dockyard work related to other naval construction.[19] Dawes sat in the visitors' gallery and watched as MacDonald delivered his speech. Hoover responded by delaying work on three American cruisers.[20]

Many inside Parliament disagreed with MacDonald's decision. David Lloyd George warned that the United Kingdom and America might go too far. First Lord of the Admiralty A. V. Alexander observed that the United Kingdom's naval building program was intended to protect it from its enemies and that it made no sense to enter a disarmament agreement with its long-time ally, the United States. Winston S. Churchill, a member of the Conservative Party, took a stand against a naval limitation agreement.[21]

In the United States, Senator William E. Borah strongly supported Hoover's policies. As chair of the Senate Foreign Relations Committee, Borah's backing was critical to Senate ratification of any agreement that would eventually emerge from the multinational talks. Borah had a long history as a leader in disarmament. He had insisted that the United States negotiate with its two principal competitors, the United Kingdom and Japan, at the Washington Disarmament Conference in 1921 and 1922. He defended Hoover's decision to suspend construction of the three ships under provisions contained in the cruiser bill.[22]

At the heart of the discussions was the need to find a point of agreement between the United States and the United Kingdom on achieving parity in fighting strength. But the real, underlying issue, according to those watching diplomats on both sides of the Atlantic, was how each country defined the doctrine of "freedom of the seas."

In peacetime, "freedom of the seas" is usually interpreted to mean that oceangoing vessels, regardless of flag, have the freedom to transport goods without interference from other nations, assuming that the ship did not enter the declared territorial waters of another nation.

However, the interpretation of "freedom of the seas" changes in wartime. The doctrine then assumes that belligerents have the right to stop, board, and seize or sink ships on the high seas. No vessel is guaranteed freedom of passage—not even merchant vessels or, as Hoover desired, food-relief vessels, because the goal of a belligerent nation is to prevent needed supplies and contraband from reaching its enemy through a neutral party.

The United States, having maintained neutrality in World War I for nearly three years before it entered the conflict, assumed that in a future war, it would once again be neutral at the start of hostilities. On the other side, the United Kingdom, having been engaged in the war from its outset—and having suffered severe shipping losses throughout much of the war—anticipated similar circumstances at the start of the next war. The United Kingdom's experience had taught it that blockades of neutral ships were a critical defensive tool. So, in wartime, the British believed that the doctrine of "freedom of the seas" did not apply. The United States disagreed.

The issue of freedom of the seas was high on the list of topics that Hoover wanted to discuss with MacDonald. The political impact of the issue was strong enough to blow up any chance of preliminary agreements that would lead to formal talks. MacDonald rephrased the topic and called it "Rights and Immunities at Sea in Times of War." When the two men met in October, they agreed that naval jurists representing the world's naval powers should study the entire matter of maritime rights. After a thorough study, the jurists would report their findings and recommendations to their respective governments.[23] In other words, the two leaders decided that the best course of action was to form a committee of experts.

Dawes worked on issues with the Young Plan for settling Germany's reparations debts while building bridges with MacDonald and the British government on disarmament talks. Discussions on ratification of the Young Plan took place at The Hague during the summer of 1929. The United States sent observers to the proceedings because it received payments from the Allies for the war loans.

Chancellor of the Exchequer Philip Snowden attacked the Young Plan as unfair to the United Kingdom on August 6 in a speech before The Hague delegates. The United Kingdom was willing to cancel all reparations payments, he told the assembly, if the United States would cancel the debts owed to it. The United States refused to do so.

Both J. P. Morgan and Thomas Lamont called Dawes to discuss the impasse at The Hague. Lamont remained in England and had not traveled to The Hague to observe the talks. In his view, the situation had turned political and needed to be settled by the British prime minister. Morgan feared that no agreement would be reached and that the Young Plan would fail. Dawes believed that a political settlement was possible and counseled his fellow bankers to give the process time to work. It was sound advice. On August 28, the conferees announced that they had reached an agreement on allocations of the reparations payments. Snowden was pleased with the final figures promised to the United Kingdom, and the terms of debt repayment were likewise satisfactory. Germany was expected to agree to the revisions. Following concurrence of all the nations involved, the last step was to establish an international bank, the Bank for International Settlements, to process the payments.

As he always had, Dawes stayed hands-on with his business interests back home. As the family's "business elder statesman," he mentored his nephews. In addition to providing work and experience for his nephew Henry, Dawes provided financial underwriting for Rufus's son Charles Cutler Dawes. He agreed to guarantee a renewal on a note for $233,000 in October with a promise that it would be paid in January.[24] The previous month, Charley wrote his namesake: "I have your letter of August 24th. I congratulate you on getting your business into better shape. You have displayed the recklessness of youth in incurring large obligations without proper consideration of the means with which to liquidate them, but by unusual activity and ability you seem to have succeeded in doing so." In an echo of the letters he had once received from his own uncle, Charley went on, "If I may be permitted to say so, as a friend, you do not yet realize the danger of rushing into debt."[25]

Henry proved an excellent choice as a private secretary. "Henry is doing splendidly," Charley wrote to Beman, "and I have found in him just what I wanted in his place. He is a natural friend-maker, not a self-advertiser, entirely sincere, and very wise in all his contacts with the people who come into the office. He is also exemplary in conduct, spending many evenings at home with us."[26]

Charley and his brother Henry kept up a steady correspondence regarding business conditions, much as they had during the war. "I wish you would write me a letter of advice along financial lines," Henry wrote his brother on August 15. "To reassure you as to my situation . . . I owe very little money myself at the moment." Henry was troubled, however, by the inflation in the securities market. Calling it "simply inconceivable," Henry then added that he thought that "the banks have lost all control over it."[27]

In reply, Charley referred to his brother's analysis as one of "common sense." He went on, "My judgment as to when the general contraction of credits will come in the United States is of little value, but in general it can be said that it will come whenever the depositing class commences to withdraw deposits." This marked the beginning of deflation. "Some things have happened," he told Henry, "that have made me think that the time is not far off, and I fear if any very large failure should occur in the United States it might be the signal of starting of the inevitable readjustment between cash and the too-extended outstanding credit."[28]

In a letter dated September 17, Dawes references his decision to turn down a purchase offer for the public utility companies the brothers owned. "I shall not think of . . . exchanging them into dormant assets until they will produce enough of the latter to satisfy me in regard to income return." Dawes added that he had a number of factors to consider before he would begin to break up the family syndicate. One key factor was that he continued to feel responsible for paying the salaries of those who had assisted in building the business. Nevertheless, Dawes acknowledged that he expected to live about ten more years (he was sixty-four at the time), and he had already begun to take steps to change the structure of his business.[29]

In addition to his work as ambassador, and continuing to maintain oversight of the holdings of Dawes Brothers, Inc., Charley had agreed to help Rufus raise funds for the Chicago World's Fair. He left London for Chicago on October 9 to pick up where he had left off in his fund-raising efforts. Shortly before his departure for England, Dawes had single-handedly assumed responsibility for raising the necessary subscriptions to make the fair a reality. The chair of the finance committee had become ill during Dawes's time in the Dominican Republic, and when no one else stepped in to take over fund-raising, Dawes undertook the task. He fought indifference, and sometimes outright hostility, among the fair's board members.

Dawes called together Chicago's civic leaders who had helped him out in the past. These were men he had always counted on in a pinch. He challenged them to guarantee the $10 million necessary to financially underwrite the fair. His colleagues responded with their support. On June 5, the day before he left for Washington, Dawes closed the agreement on their backing and offered his own personal guarantee to cover the underwriting.

Now, back at home in early October, Dawes learned that no one had been selling bond subscriptions. He got to work immediately, going straight from the train to his office. Within two weeks, he had raised $6,125,000, which was $1,125,000 more than the $5 million needed for Hoover to issue invitations to other nations to participate in the fair. Julius Rosenwald, founder of Sears, Roebuck and Co., and Dawes's longtime friend Samuel Insull had been particularly helpful to Dawes with the fund-raising.[30]

Dawes's arrival coincided with the formation of an investment trust corporation, Central-Illinois Securities Corporation, created by the board of Central Trust Bank. His return fueled speculation that Central Trust was about to merge with another bank. Henry had noted the "merger mania" in a letter to his brother with an accompanying clipping from the *Wall Street Journal*. By July 1, bank mergers totaling $2.5 billion had taken place, with $1.727 billion of that total representing banks that had left the Federal Reserve System. Henry expressed his concern that, at the current rate of consolidations, the United States would have as much a concentration of banks as England did. "While the arguments are made in the name of efficiency," Henry wrote, sounding much like Charley, "the two chief reasons why this is going on are, first, that it affords a medium for speculation in the stocks of banks, and, second, control over the country banks makes them available instruments for the distribution of securities."[31]

Central Trust's president, Joseph E. Otis, asked Henry to serve as chairman of the board of the new securities company. In a telegram to Charley, Henry said he did not think the new investment company was in the bank's interest and preferred not to accept. As he always did, Henry deferred to his brother's wishes, but added that he hoped that Charley did not think Henry should take the position.[32] Charley supported Henry's decision.

While Dawes was still in the United States, the market contraction that he believed was on its way hit investors with a vengeance. "Unexpected Torrent of Liquidation Again Hits Market," read part of one headline in the *New York Times*.[33] In the *Chicago Tribune*, one of several articles reporting on the day's stock market performance said: "Echoes of Day's New Avalanche in Stock Market."[34]

October 29, Black Tuesday as it would come to be known in the history books, was not the first day when stocks had precipitously lost value. Much as an earthquake sends out warning tremors, there had been shaking in the stock market in the previous week. The *New York Times* referred to the crash as a "second hurricane of liquidation."[35]

Dawes was philosophical as he listened to the gloomy news reports on the radio aboard ship as he returned to England. He had warned his friends to get out of the stock market. The Panic of 1893 had been a good teacher. "I learned . . . that a ninety-day note becomes due. Before that time I had regarded them as renewable forever. At the time that panic broke I owed in the neighborhood of two hundred thousand dollars." Dawes counseled young men to always have a plan to get out of debt, and he says he cannot think of one who followed his recommendations. He clearly had forgotten how much his uncle and his brother had urged him not to borrow so much money at one time.[36]

In the United Kingdom, Dawes once again turned his attention to high-level diplomacy. MacDonald's visit to Washington moved the disarmament talks to a new level, and Dawes now functioned in a supportive, rather than in a lead, role. On November 24, he delivered a speech to the Chartered Institute of Journalists, a professional association of British journalists, that he considered the successor address to his Pilgrims speech. The United States, France, and the United Kingdom had already agreed that no naval experts would be members of their respective negotiating teams but would serve as technical experts. The upcoming talks, Dawes told his audience, were taking place under the aegis of the Kellogg-Briand Pact, and the purpose of the conference was to foster world peace.[37]

The United States, France, the United Kingdom, Italy, and Japan were parties to the talks. London was chosen as the site for the negotiations. Secretary of State Henry L. Stimson led the U.S. delegation. Senator David A. Reed of Pennsylvania, Senator Joseph T. Robinson of Arkansas, Secretary of the Navy Charles Francis Adams, Ambassador to Mexico Dwight Morrow, Ambassador to Belgium Hugh Gibson, and Dawes made up the U.S. team.[38] Gibson's and Dawes's names were added at the last minute, but it had long been expected that they would be a part of the delegation. The *New York Times* credited Dawes with ironing out the differences between the United States and the United Kingdom on cruiser strength. Gibson was recognized for his experience at the 1927 Geneva talks and for his regular communication with Dawes during the latter's talks with MacDonald.[39]

Over the years, Dawes had won over people by his sheer audacity. During the war, he attended a dinner given by Nancy Leeds—the widow of William B. Leeds, the man known as the tinplate king—who was living in the Ritz. Dawes sat next to Lady Sarah Wilson, aunt of the duke of Marlborough and a white-haired grande dame. Dawes did not drink alcohol, so when the waiter began to fill Dawes's glass with champagne, Dawes stopped him and asked for a big cup of coffee with some cream.

Lady Sarah looked at Dawes and said, "Colonel Dawes, if you are dining as a lady's guest and want something different, don't give the order to the waiter, but ask your hostess."

Dawes, in his typically blunt fashion, replied that as a "plain American," he did not understand European customs, and that he preferred a cup of coffee with his dinner. Then he asked his companion's name.

"Lady Sarah Wilson," she replied.

"Lady Sarah Wilson? I can never get these titles over here straight. I'll give you a choice. I'll call you either Mrs. Wilson or just plain Sarah."

"Of the two, I think I prefer to have you call me Sarah."

"Then you call me Charley," Dawes told her, and the two proceeded to have a delightful conversation throughout the remainder
of the evening.[40]

Dawes was also a man who had a tremendous sense of humor and
enjoyed a good joke. His humor, much like his straightforward speeches,
sometimes stretched the boundaries of what was acceptable. At a diplomatic dinner for Prime Minister MacDonald, Dawes, with Caro secretly
but reluctantly cooperating, arranged for his friend, the comedian Leon
Errol, to act as a drunken waiter. The ruse was a notorious breach of diplomatic protocol, and an especially pointed jab at the intensely formal
British. To his credit, Dawes had selected his guests carefully. "Friends
who enjoyed a joke, and would not spoil it by telling their wives of
my reprehensible plans for their discomfiture and subsequent resuscita-
tion." The only other woman, besides Caro, who knew the plan Dawes
had concocted was the Infanta of Spain, the daughter of the king.[41]

As a waiter, Errol was expected to serve the guests and remove plates
without disrupting the flow of dinner table conversation. Instead, he
dropped silverware, served from the wrong side, and clanged plates.
When the Infanta, playing her role beautifully, asked Errol for a glass of
sherry, the comedian drunkenly replied, "We don't keep it in the house,
ma'am, but maybe I can get you some outside."[42] (The Daweses had
chosen to observe Prohibition in the embassy in London.)

Just as the main course was served, Errol slipped into an empty seat
at the table. The strongest reaction came from the American-born Lady
Astor, who was a member of Parliament, and with whom Charley and
Caro had become good friends. Not knowing of the ruse, she rose to
confront Dawes about allowing a servant, and a drunken one at that, to
join them for dinner. At that point, Dawes laughingly identified Errol
to his appalled guests. "The dinner we gave last Friday at the embassy
will live long in the memory of our guests and ourselves," Dawes noted
of the evening.[43]

On January 1, 1930, Charley and Caro celebrated the New Year by
listening to radio broadcasts from the different nations across Europe.
Dawes was intrigued by how radio could communicate across the time

differences, with a ringing bell broadcast from each respective nation in the British Commonwealth as it officially welcomed in the year in its time zone. Radio communication fascinated Dawes. After delivering an address in support of Hoover's presidential candidacy in Madison Square Garden, Dawes had marveled at the number of people he encountered immediately afterward on the streets on New York City who mentioned hearing his speech.

A letter from his cousin William R. Dawes, who had managed the Lincoln properties for years and was now a vice president at Central Trust, may have warmed Charley's heart as much as the New Year's broadcasts. "The expected dividend on Union Gas and Metropolitan added not a little to my own comfort and pleasure [of celebrating Christmas]. It must be a source of great satisfaction to yourself to see so successful an outcome of your companies. Those of us who have retained our original holdings are certainly very grateful."[44] The dividend was paid out while shareholders in other companies watched their wealth disappear.

Dawes did not plan to hold on to either Union Gas or Metropolitan much longer. He had begun a strategy to liquidate the extensive holdings of Dawes Brothers, Inc. In response to a request from Beman for a loan, Charley instructed his brother on how to value his shares of Dawes Brothers stock to provide it as collateral. However, he told Beman, the collateral should not include any manufacturing stock. "My plans for liquidation of Union and Metropolitan companies now in progress and my tentative plan for creating an investment trust in connection with Dawes Brothers makes it impracticable for them to take the parent manufacturing company loan you mention."[45]

To Henry, Charley wrote:

> You might exercise your ingenuity in considering with me jointly the matter of the eventual form of Dawes Brothers, Inc.—as a matter for mental exercise if nothing else. . . . I do not permanently want to keep Dawes Brothers in the form of a corporation, thus bequeathing the management of large assets to those unacquainted by experience with the difficulties of their accumulation. Nor do I want to leave these large assets exposed to the machinations of those who become hard up, who will find many avenues of access

through a corporation which would be closed in case an investment trust is formed, under strict banking supervision.[46]

The oil business was still soft at the end of the year, but Pure Oil
had gained the rights to 80 percent of the oil production in the eastern
Van Zandt County oil field, near Grand Saline, Texas. Henry estimated
production at a minimum of 5,000 barrels from the smallest well up to
20,000 barrels from the largest. As he explained to Charlie: "We have
to keep our guesses as to the size of these wells confidential or our whole
unit arrangement will 'blow up,' which would be a catastrophe."[47]

Henry, in a Christmas letter to his namesake uncle, wrote to thank
him for his Christmas gift. Likely aware of the correspondence between
his two uncles, the younger Henry added: "The financial troubles of the
United States seem so far away that I cannot possibly realize the full
extent of them. I rather feel that I am missing an educational experience as well as the hard times."[48]

On January 21, Dawes sent a congratulatory telegram to Owen
Young on the signing of the plan that bore his name. As had been
the case with the Dawes Plan, last-minute objections threatened the
Young Plan's ratification. Forty-eight hours of nearly nonstop negotiations eventually ironed out the last of the challenges to the plan, most
of which came from the United Kingdom's Snowden, who still was
unhappy with his nation's repayment schedule to the United States.
The ratification of the Young Plan added to the air of optimism growing
over the international community that peace would be fully established.

Dawes's telegram to Young coincided with the opening of the London Naval Conference. All eyes now turned to the delegates from the
five nations participating in the talks. Churches had declared Sunday, January 19, "Disarmament Sunday" and offered prayers for the
conference's success. In his farewell remarks to the American delegation, Hoover stressed the importance of the conference and his hopes
for a good outcome. He instructed the negotiators to strive for actual
reductions in naval building programs, not simply limitations on what
could be built. He urged the men to be conciliatory to the other delegations. The progress of world peace, he said, "rests in great measure
on the shoulders" of the men he selected to represent the United
States.[49]

It was clear from the outset that the conference would not proceed smoothly. Germany expressed anger that it had not been invited to participate in the talks—an omission that was keenly felt, particularly in the wake of the successful conclusion of the negotiations over the Young Plan. Japan was expected to hold fast for some level of parity in fleet size and strength, as was Italy. France, once again, appeared to be the potential wild card.

The leaders of the United Kingdom and the United States had held high-level talks in advance of the parleys. Japan had mediated between those two countries in the years between the failed Geneva talks and the Hoover-MacDonald rapprochement. Italy benchmarked its own fleet size with the size of the French navy. France was essentially isolated at the talks.[50]

As expected, the talks stalled by early March. France interjected a demand for a security pact into the negotiating terms, and the United Kingdom refused to honor the French request. The British argued that the French pact would take steps to prevent a war, thereby rendering military measures unnecessary.

Speaking on behalf of the U.S. position, Stimson said that the United States would not enter into a security pact because it did not want to put itself in a position of having to come to the aid of a nation should that nation be attacked.[51]

On April 18, the United States, the United Kingdom, and Japan agreed to a three-power treaty. The first agreement was on tonnage, with consensus on a ratio of ten to seven—if the United States had ten light cruisers and destroyers, Japan would have seven. A ten to six ratio was the initial agreement for heavy cruisers, but the United States suspended its cruiser building program to allow Japan to catch up, and the eventual ratio became ten to seven.

The three nations also agreed to a maximum tonnage for light cruisers. The United States held firm on an upper limit of ten thousand tons, and the United Kingdom and Japan conceded, though both would have preferred a lighter weight of seven thousand tons.

Finally, the agreement allowed for tonnage on light auxiliary ships, using Japan's desired ratio of ten to ten to seven. Maximum tonnage for this class of ships was 339,000 tons for British ships, 323,500 for American ships, and 208,850 tons for Japanese ships.[52]

Although essentially an observer, Dawes had attended the sessions regularly and assumed the role of host for the delegation. It was his first opportunity to get to know Charles Francis Adams III, the great-great-grandson of John Adams and great-grandson of John Quincy Adams. The twentieth-century Adams had made a fortune as a wills and trusts attorney and served on a number of corporate boards. Like Dawes, he was an understated man of wealth and philanthropy, and the two had a great deal in common. Dawes also renewed his friendship with Dwight Morrow, a fellow financier who had been a good friend of Calvin Coolidge and who was the father-in-law of Charles Lindbergh.

Dawes hoped that the signing of the disarmament agreement would make it possible for him to resign as ambassador. He felt the pull of his responsibilities for fund-raising for the Century of Progress International Exhibition, the name given to the upcoming Chicago World's Fair. "For the ungrateful task of raising the money there are no volunteers and no 'draft' law which can be invoked." He was also becoming bored with the job of ambassador. "Except for the naval work which has now occupied ten months and in which there was a specific objective, there has been little work of importance in this position, and under normal circumstances the life of an ambassador here seems largely a round of social events, public speaking on non-controversial subjects, and idle enjoyments."[53] It was not the kind of life for a decisive and active man like Charles Dawes.

On April 23, Joseph P. Cotton, the acting secretary of state, cabled Dawes that Hoover might want him to travel to the United States to help guide the disarmament treaty through the Senate. Dawes was unhappy at the news. His close friends Tiffany Blake and John T. McCutcheon and their families, and Dan Wing and his wife, were due for a visit. The plans had been in the making for over a year. Dawes was beginning to feel his age, and maintaining his contacts with friends had become increasingly important to him. "We will not pass this way again," he noted in his journal.[54]

A few days later, he received another communication from Washington that Hoover had adopted a wait-and-see attitude. The trip to Washington turned out to be unnecessary, and Dawes enjoyed immensely the visits with his friends.

Most of 1930 was a year more typical for an ambassador. Dawes and his family participated in a variety of social events. Caro presented Carolyn to the king and queen at court during Carolyn's visit in late May. In June, Dawes and his nephew Henry traveled to the United States, where they attended Dana's graduation from Lawrenceville. After visiting with Dwight Morrow, who was running for the U.S. Senate, Dawes and Henry proceeded to Chicago.

The brothers' uncle W. W. Mills died in mid-March 1931. He had visited Charley and his family in London less than a year earlier. All the Dawes brothers felt his loss keenly. In a letter to Henry, Charley acknowledged the debt he owed to Mills: "It was because of him that I weathered the 1893 panic." In closing, he told Henry, "We have all lost our best friend."[55]

Henry kept Charley carefully apprised of conditions in the oil industry. Prices were low, due, in part, to overproduction in the oil fields relative to the demand. The state of Oklahoma had intervened to put a cap on production there after Harry Sinclair, the founder of Sinclair Oil, had entered into an agreement with small producers. Standard Oil of Indiana had reduced the price of its crude, and Henry expected the impact to be felt across all oil companies. Henry thought the price from their Van Zandt County wells would barely enable the company to make its bond payments. "It is very foolish to pretend that the situation is not a very serious and critical one for everyone in the business," Henry reported to Charley. "Our statement this year will be very bad."[56] In a letter written a few weeks later, Henry penned as a postscript: "Business generally is in a deplorable condition." Henry wrote his brother, "Phil Clarke [head of Central Trust] is a Godsend at the bank."[57]

On May 9, 1931, the *Chicago Tribune* broke the news that Dana Dawes had eloped to Honolulu and married Eleanor Dillingham on April 11. The two had met the previous summer aboard ship traveling from the United Kingdom back to the United States. Dana had just completed his freshman year at Williams College in Williamstown, and Eleanor her sophomore year at Mount Holyoke College in South Hadley, both in Massachusetts. Charley and Caro issued a tersely worded press statement: "Mrs. Dawes and I knew that the young people were interested in each other. When my son wrote us of his marriage we sent him and his wife our love and best wishes. We welcome the young lady into the family."[58] Charley cabled Dana that he would increase his daily allowance.

At the end of May, Dawes traveled to the United States on the SS *Bremen* to continue his work on a bond issue for the fair. Aboard ship, he was asked to visit the stateroom of Franklin Delano Roosevelt, who was also on the *Bremen* after visiting his mother in Europe. Dawes did not recall meeting FDR during the latter's tenure as assistant secretary of the navy during the Wilson years, but Roosevelt told Dawes they had met at Bordeaux, France, during the war.

Roosevelt invited Dawes to dinner, and Dawes described it as "a regular Rooseveltian evening—both delightful and strenuous." The men talked for over four hours, and Dawes thoroughly enjoyed his evening with the man who would become Hoover's presidential opponent in the coming year.[59]

Dawes spent some time at the New Jersey home of Dwight and Elizabeth Morrow, and he met Charles and Anne Morrow Lindbergh during his stay. The young couple impressed Charley. He was less enamored with some of the Morrows' other guests, whom he called "parlor socialists." It was "my first experience with these curious, well-meaning, but inexperienced children, who defend vigorously the retention of their own inherited wealth but are full of plans entailing self-sacrifice or slavery upon the part of others."[60] Dawes makes no mention of engaging the Morrows' guests in a debate, although it is difficult to imagine him not challenging their thinking.

In Chicago, Dawes worked to raise a half million dollars worth of bond sales for the World's Fair in the face of a rapidly declining economy. Ever the optimist, he observed: "It is a good deal like working in a morgue, but occasionally one comes across financial life where he expected death."[61]

While he was home, the "merger mania" that Henry had commented on two years earlier reached Central Trust. The bank had merged with the National Bank of the Republic on June 8, 1931. Chicago's depressed business community had driven the consolidation, and the two banks hoped the merger would allow them to successfully weather the ongoing financial storm.

The new bank was the Central Republic Bank and Trust Company. Philip Clarke, who had been president of Central Trust, kept his position in the new bank. Joseph E. Otis, who was chairman of the board of Central Trust, now served as a cochairman of the board with his counterpart from Republic, David R. Forgan. Dawes retained the title of honorary chairman of the board. The merger appeared to put the two banks in a strong cash position, with a reported capital surplus of $28 million and combined capital and surplus in the investment affiliate of $5 million. But there were loans and investments on the books that threatened the bank's solvency.[62]

Economic conditions continued to deteriorate in the United States. The number of unemployed had doubled between 1930 and 1931, jumping from four million to eight million. Nearly 16 percent of the U.S. labor force was out of work.[63] Gross national product had dropped from $68.9 billion in 1930 to $54.5 billion in 1931, a 21 percent decline. Business inventories had been revalued at a loss of $2.8 billion.[64]

Europe's economic situation was equally dismal. The Bank of Austria teetered on the brink of failure, and there was a run on gold in the Bank of England. In an effort to protect the world economic markets and stabilize gold reserves, Hoover proposed a postponement of debt reparations. France, predictably, complained about the loss of payments that it would receive and requested that the unconditional portion of the reparations payments continue. Hoover, in a deft political move, reminded the French that, under the Young Plan, it was required to make a security payment to the Bank for International Settlements if Germany placed a moratorium on its payments. If France accepted Hoover's proposal, this security payment would not be required. France acquiesced, and Hoover's proposal of postponement was accepted.[65]

By the fall of 1931, the United States economy had worsened. Hoover had struggled through most of the year to get a recalcitrant Congress to pass the legislation he recommended to bring relief to the unemployed, the failing banks, and the faltering industries. The Democratic majority had little or no interest in working with a Republican president, and Hoover, who had never established a warm relationship with the press, found it difficult to get public opinion behind his initiatives.

The bankers, however, supported Hoover's efforts to establish an emergency credit corporation. Writing to Henry, Charley observed that the president's plan appeared well thought out, and Charley added that he believed the initiative had the potential to protect sound banks against reasonable contingencies regarding withdrawals and to help restore confidence.[66]

In addition to business activity being severely depressed, the city of Chicago was bankrupt and not paying its debt obligations. In November, Henry wrote Charley that Philip Clarke wanted to absorb the investment house that Central Trust had opened two years earlier and place it in the bank's bond department. Clarke would have happily sold the entity for the right cash price, but the timing was "not ripe."[67]

As employment conditions worsened, Dawes received an increasing number of letters from friends, acquaintances, and purported distant relatives asking for employment. In many cases, Dawes had little to offer them, and in other situations, he did what he could. Charley forwarded a letter from one James B. Dawes of West Virginia to Henry with the request that Henry see if he could find employment for James at one of Pure Oil's service stations. In the early 1930s, both Charley and Henry often offered employment at a gas station to those who asked for a job.[68]

The brothers also agreed to open the doors of the Rufus Dawes Hotels in both Chicago and Boston to provide beds for the overflow from the city's shelters. The only stipulation was that the hotels' regular clients were to be served first, and the overflow from city shelters could not arrive at the hotels before 9:00 P.M. Henry instructed the manager of the Chicago hotel to drop the rate from twenty-five cents to twenty cents. "I am sure that you will agree with this," Henry wrote Charley, "and if you would like to reduce the charges to fifteen cents or even ten cents, I would be glad if you would cable me. . . . You would make less money at ten cents, of course, but I am inclined to think you might break even as evidently the need for lodging is increasing."[69] Charley agreed to the reduction.

On November 5, reports reached the United States that the Chinese had declared war on the Japanese in Manchuria. Skirmishes erupted along the border with Russia, near the Eastern Chinese Railway, of which China and Russia each owned a 50 percent interest. The Sino-Japanese conflict threatened to grow quickly, dragging Russia into a war to protect its interests in the railway, which formed part of the

Trans-Siberian Railway connecting the port of Vladivostok with the rest of the Soviet Union.

The League of Nations called a meeting in Paris to discuss a truce, and Hoover sent Dawes as an observer. Several of the nations discussed an embargo against Japan as a punishment for its aggressive behavior with China. In a conversation with Dawes, Stimson explained that Hoover believed an embargo would lead to further war. Hoover's instructions were to avoid saying or doing anything that could be construed as wanting war with Japan.[70]

Dawes met privately with the Japanese ambassador, Matsudaira, with whom he had developed a strong relationship during the naval disarmament talks. Dawes also conferred with the new British foreign secretary, John Simon. Through his behind-the-scenes diplomacy, Dawes helped to arrange a decision by the official league members that called for the withdrawal of Japanese troops and the establishment of a commission of inquiry. Four weeks after he had departed London for Paris, the league's members passed the resolution. "The President and I are highly gratified by the manner in which you handled a most difficult job while in Paris," Stimson cabled Dawes. "Your success in cooperating with the League materially assisted in obtaining a successful conclusion to the negotiations and your ability in the situation in upholding American prestige was skillful."[71]

In the wake of his success in Paris, Dawes now began to confer with Stimson regarding the planned disarmament conference to begin in February in Geneva. Hoover wanted Dawes to chair the United States committee. Dawes responded that he lacked the technical competence to hold such a position and recommended Hugh Gibson. Hoover, however, wanted Dawes.

A few days later, the president changed his mind. Hoover asked Dawes to return to the United States to chair the newly formed Reconstruction Finance Corporation, the name given to the emergency credit corporation that Dawes believed held promise for American banks. His new job would start February 2, 1932.

At the end of November, Henry had written Charley:

> I am following your work in the papers with even greater enthusiasm than I have ever had, and I think I am doing so with more

pride than ever in connection with any of your accomplishments. It may be that you will be responsible for stopping a great war, but how ever this may be, your approach to this problem will establish precedents in the handling of these matters which I think will mark an epoch. . . . It seems to me that what you are developing is neither shirt-sleeve diplomacy with its ignorance, nor Wilsonian vagueness, but real statesmanship.[72]

The brothers had no way of knowing that some of Charley's hardest work still lay ahead.

CHAPTER 14

X

A Banker Once Again

The announcement of Dawes's resignation as ambassador to the United Kingdom was met with speculation in some sectors as a tacit acknowledgment of his plan to run against Hoover for the Republican presidential nomination in 1932. So, when it was finally learned that the reason he left his diplomatic post was to become president of the newly created Reconstruction Finance Corporation (RFC), there was general applause from the financial sector.

The home team of Chicago bankers cheered. "I cannot approve too heartily the wisdom of President Hoover in selecting General Dawes for the post and the patriotism of the Chicagoan in accepting it," George M. Reynolds, chairman of the executive committee of the Continental Illinois Bank and Trust Company, said approvingly.[1]

"Mr. Dawes is well qualified to head such a corporation for he has not only had experience as a banker, but in addition has been a statesman and international financier," the business reporter for the *Pittsburgh Courier* editorialized.[2]

Eugene Meyer, governor of the Federal Reserve System, had urged President Herbert Hoover to submit the legislation creating the RFC to Congress and recommended it be modeled after the War Finance Corporation that Meyer had led during World War I, a government corporation that had given financial support to industries considered essential for the war. The bill received widespread bipartisan support in Congress and passed quickly.[3] Hoover signed the

Reconstruction Finance Corporation Act into law on January 22, 1932.

The act authorized the RFC to provide funds as an acceptable form of exchange among financial institutions. Secondly, to help the hard-hit rural economy, the RFC enabled the secretary of agriculture, or one of his agencies, to make loans. There was a provision for making loans directly to railroads, and, finally, the RFC was authorized to make loans directly to banks or financial institutions. In the case of direct lending to banks, the loan period was three years, although an extension to five years was possible.[4]

Between February 2 and April 19, the RFC authorized loans to 1,520 banks in the amount of $243,248,769, of which $10,047,158 had already been repaid.[5] A list of banks receiving RFC funds during Dawes's four-month tenure shows that the corporation lent money to institutions in a broad spectrum of locales from major cities to small rural towns across the nation. Unlike other new endeavors that he headed, Dawes's contributions to the fledgling RFC were negligible. Eugene Meyer, the Federal Reserve governor who had lobbied for the agency's creation, dominated the work of the corporation.

Nevertheless, Dawes was still answerable to Congress for the RFC's decisions. He addressed charges that large banks had been favored over small ones in the granting of loans. "That is beside the point," Dawes told the House Ways and Means Committee in what was, for him, a calm tone. "The number of depositors to be saved by sustaining a given bank is where the real interest of the public lies. . . . The important thing which the Reconstruction Finance Corporation endeavors to keep in mind is that the banks, large or small, as the trustees of the depositors of the public, shall be treated alike in the interest of the public without discrimination and without fear or favor."[6]

Those words would come back to haunt Dawes within a matter of months.

In June 1931, Chicago experienced a depositor run, primarily on banks that were not members of the Federal Reserve System.[7] City National Bank absorbed the chain of banks known as the Foreman banks, at about the same time as the National Bank of the Republic and Central Trust had merged. Bank stocks continued to fall throughout the summer of 1931, and, by mid-September, they had hit new lows. First National had lost nineteen points in the week prior to September 20. Continental Illinois sold at a new low of two hundred forty-five points below its previous price. Central Republic was doing well by comparison, off by only twenty-eight points from its price the previous week.[8] There was one key reason for the bank run: Samuel Insull's empire was imploding.

The use of electric power had grown exponentially since the 1890s, when Insull arrived in Chicago and took charge of Chicago Edison. Electric power supplied the energy for lights, cookstoves, refrigeration, industrial plants, and the new technology of radio. Insull's holdings had expanded throughout the cities and suburbs of the Midwest. Insull's company, Middle West Utilities Company, had lines extending into thirty-two states and serviced five thousand communities.[9]

Both Insull and Dawes operated their holding companies conservatively. Stocks were closely held, and debt was managed carefully. In Dawes's case, he retained tight control over the decision-making regarding stock purchases and sales. Henry, who acted with his brother's power of attorney, shared Charley's cautious approach.

Samuel Insull's situation was different. His brother Martin Insull oversaw Middle West Utilities, and he lacked Sam's circumspection. In 1928, Martin led Middle West in the acquisition of two holding companies serving fourteen eastern states. Although the companies were financially sound, they were heavily leveraged. It was not the kind of deal Samuel Insull favored. He commented that it would take "ten years to tear down this pyramid and make this a reasonable investment." Despite his misgivings, he signed the papers for the sale, little realizing that he had just placed himself squarely inside a lion's den.[10]

For most of the early decades of the twentieth century, bankers had paid little attention to utilities as a form of investment, a fact that both Insull and Dawes had used to their advantage to build their personal wealth. By the mid-1920s, bankers were looking for new securities, and utilities, nearly a $1 billion-a-year market, became highly attractive equities. One of those bankers who took an interest in utilities was J. P. Morgan. He organized a group of major utility companies in 1929 to form the United Corporation. The new concern controlled 38 percent of the electric power produced in twelve eastern states and 20 percent of the nation's total supply. The only power producer bigger than Morgan was Insull, and Insull had just acquired two companies that bordered Morgan's service area.[11]

For years, Insull had refused to defer to Morgan. Unsurprisingly, there was no love lost between the two tycoons. In the summer of 1928, shortly after Insull had closed the deal on the eastern utilities, Cyrus Eaton, a Cleveland investor with his own small utility empire, began to purchase large blocks of shares of Middle West Utilities. Recognizing the threat to his own empire, Insull reorganized his holdings and formed Insull Utility Investments. He exchanged his and his family's holdings in Commonwealth Edison, Peoples Gas Light & Coke Co., Public Service Company of Northern Illinois, and Middle West Utilities for shares in the new holding company.[12] Once again, he made decisions counter to his own business philosophies, but, in the face of the rapidly rising stock market, he set aside his concerns.

Middle West Utilities did extremely well when trading first started on January 17, 1929. Insull had settled on an initial share price of $12. Shares of Insull Utility opened at $25 and closed at $30. In the summer, they jumped to $150. In the fifty days ending August 23, Insull Utilities appreciated at a rate of $7,000 a minute with a total rise in value of $500 million.[13]

Insull was not happy with the skyrocketing stock price. It made it difficult for him to purchase shares and keep control of his company. To remedy this situation, Insull created another holding company, Corporation Securities Company of Chicago, known as Corp. Corp was designed to operate as a voting trust to protect against an outside raid on the company. Corp's assets were the Insull family's holdings in Insull Utilities. Corp started trading on October 5, 1929.

Simultaneously, Insull took advantage of the rapidly rising stock market and launched a major refinancing of Middle West Utilities. He sought as many shareholders as possible, and, to achieve this, he declared a ten-to-one stock split. He retired all outstanding notes and floating debt, called in the outstanding 8 percent shares of preferred stock, and issued 5 percent preferred shares in their place. He also changed the dividend policy on common stock from cash to a stock dividend. The result was that Middle West had no debt and hardly any fixed charges.[14]

Insull weathered the October 29 crash with an impressive resiliency. He covered the margin calls of his employees who had purchased Insull stocks. He helped Chicago avoid another round of bankruptcy and rescued the city's still-floundering transportation system. He continued to subscribe to bonds for the upcoming Century of Progress. But developments behind the scenes laid the groundwork for the denouement of a powerful and successful businessman.

Once again, Martin Insull's poor financial judgment hurt his brother's financial wizardry. While Samuel traveled in Europe in 1930, Martin took advantage of low loan rates to increase Insull companies' funded debt by about 10 percent. Insull Utilities issued $60 million in debentures, and Corp issued $30 million in notes to complete the Insull company stock purchases.[15]

Insull commented that he "had never owed so much money in all my life put together," and he counted on his collateral to see him through a decline in stock prices. He did not count on the value of that collateral, which consisted of his real property holdings and equipment, steadily depreciating and reducing his borrowing power.

Unaware of the financial storm brewing around Insull's empire, Rufus wrote to Charley (who was in London) in February 1931: "On February 28 at the Palmer House a dinner will be tendered to Samuel Insull, in celebration of his entering into the electrical business in the United States fifty years ago. Mr. Martin Insull . . . very much desires that a telegram from you should be received in time to be read at that meeting, and I have assured him that nothing would be more agreeable to you than to send such a message."[16] Charley responded with a message praising his business colleague and friend.

By September 1931, Insull Utility Investments was trading at a low of 13¾, down by 1⅞ from its previous low.[17] Insull carried on as if nothing was happening with his business. "We are actively engaged in getting the various electric light companies into line for the exhibit of the operating companies at the Century of Progress," Insull wrote Charley in early October. "I am hoping to be able to announce to your brother, Rufus, that the arrangements have been completed [by the end of October]."[18]

One month later, the court appointed a receiver for Insull's Middle West Utilities Company. The Insull empire began to unravel in public, and its future would have a direct impact on Central Trust. The Insull companies had $11 million in outstanding loans with Central

Trust, representing 40 percent of the bank's position, collateralized by Insull companies' stock.[19] It was the kind of exposure that Charley had avoided during his entire banking career, but he was no longer in charge of what had long been known as the "Dawes bank."

With the devaluation of Insull stock, the Central Trust loans became worthless. The Insull debacle triggered a shock wave across all the Loop banks. The banks, which had heavily invested in real estate through mortgage lending, had been in a precarious position since the real estate market softened. Unable to meet the cash needs of a company as large as Insull's, the Loop banks deferred to the New York banks, and at the head of those banks was Insull's enemy J. P. Morgan.[20]

The superior attitude of New York banks toward banks in other regions of the country revealed itself when the New York banks began to call in Insull's loans. When he could not make the payments, the accounting firm Arthur Andersen conducted an investigation under court order. By February 1932, Andersen's thorough inquiry into the finances of Insull's companies uncovered a number of irregularities. On June 6, while Dawes was submitting his resignation as president of the RFC to return to save his bank, Insull was forced to resign from every one of his sixty companies. He fled to Europe.[21] Charley, disgusted by his longtime friend's cowardice in the face of his failures, broke all personal ties with Insull.

Dawes returned to Chicago as the old lion in a business community led by younger cubs. The men whom he had known and alongside whom he built his bank were gone. Julius Rosenwald had died in January, Lyman Gage had died in 1927, James Forgan in 1924, and, of course, Insull had fled the country and was now persona non grata. The only men in Chicago who had the depth and breadth of Dawes's experience were his brothers, Rufus and Henry; his cousin W. R. Dawes, who remained an officer in the bank; and Joseph Otis, who had served faithfully and ably for many years as head of Central Trust. Dawes may have been an old man and out of active banking for over a decade, but he was recognized for his leadership skills and his political connections, and the Loop's bank leaders turned to him to save Chicago's financial sector.

Central Republic's board wasted no time returning Dawes to the position of chairman of the board in an unprecedented Sunday meeting on June 26. In the week prior to retaking his leadership position, Dawes watched a run on his bank's deposits in the amount of $13,474,000.[22]

Dawes led his board in an extraordinary meeting on that Sunday evening. In addition to his board members, the meeting included leaders of Chicago's major banks and Jesse H. Jones, vice chairman of the RFC, who was in town for the Democratic National Convention.

After examining Central Republic's financial condition, Dawes announced to a shocked room that he would not open the bank on Monday. Although the bank was solvent, he had watched the run on the clearinghouse. Five Chicago area banks had closed in the previous week. The *New York Herald Tribune* reported that there was an "epidemic of bank closings" in Chicago that had tied up millions of dollars and left depositors without access to cash for everyday expenses. Depositors in the larger Loop banks had begun withdrawing cash to make sure they had money on hand.[23] In the wake of the panic in the region, Dawes was unwilling to allow fearful depositors to draw down the bank's assets while friendly and trusting depositors who kept their money in the bank might lose their funds should the bank be forced to liquidate.[24]

The Chicago bankers representing the other major Loop banks of National City Bank and Continental Illinois National Bank and Trust Company feared that if Central Republic failed, their institutions would also go under. They asked Jesse Jones to call Hoover and request his intervention to secure an RFC loan on behalf of Dawes's bank. What followed was an eighteen-hour marathon session on Sunday of interconnected telephone calls among the boards of the Chicago banks, the New York correspondent banks, RFC officers in Washington, and Hoover, who was spending the weekend at his retreat, Camp Rapidan in Virginia. Hoover wanted as much participation in the loan from the Chicago banks as possible. By 2:00 A.M., they committed to $5 million, secured by Central Republic's foreign securities. It was less than Hoover requested, but as much as the Chicago banks felt comfortable lending.[25]

In spite of pressure from Jones, Treasury Secretary Ogden Mills, and New York Federal Reserve President George Harrison, the New York banks refused to participate in the loan. The refusal was a slap at Dawes, who had put his reputation on the line on Morgan's behalf seventeen years earlier to help underwrite the Anglo-French loan and had worked hand-in-hand with Morgan officials to arrange loans to the French and the Germans through the Dawes Plan.

The RFC gave Central Republic a secured loan of $90 million, collateralized by the $33 million of remaining assets and the shareholders' liability, should the bank liquidate. The terms called for repayment in six months at an interest rate of 5.5 percent. Charley had expressed optimism that an economic turnaround was imminent, but the prevailing conditions gave no hint that such optimism was realistic. Even if a dramatic recovery occurred, it would take more than six months for deposits and revenues to be restored to precrash levels. The alternative was to let the bank fail, which, in Jones's opinion, is what would have happened without the loan.[26]

With the loan terms in place, Dawes issued the following public statement: "The demands on the Central Republic Bank and Trust company made necessary recourse to borrowing to meet them. These loans have been completed and place the bank in an impregnable cash position. The loans negotiated are for current requirements and to pay depositors and not for purposes of liquidation."[27]

Chicago businesses and banks breathed a sigh of relief. The Dawes bank had been saved, bank closures in the region slowed, and a major financial catastrophe had apparently been averted.

Dawes's old friend and law school classmate Clayton W. Delamatre wrote him a congratulatory letter and referenced another of their classmates, Atlee Pomerene, who had succeeded Dawes as head of the RFC. In a letter to Delamatre, Pomerene said of Dawes: "I, too, have every confidence in the honor and integrity of Charles Dawes. There is more religion in one of his 'damns' than there is in a good many people's prayers."[28]

In reply, Charley wrote his friend, "I thought I was a retired businessman and would be free in the future from all business cares. I find myself more thoroughly immersed in them, and perplexing ones at that. What I have done, however, was from a sense of duty."[29]

Two and a half weeks after the RFC approved the Dawes loan, the Senate approved a resolution, introduced by Senator James Couzens, a Republican from Michigan, to investigate loans made by the RFC. Senators supporting the resolution cited the recent loan to the Dawes bank as the motivation for the investigation.[30]

On October 7, 1932, the Chicago papers announced to Central Republic's customers:

EFFECTIVE TODAY

Effective today the Commercial, Savings, and Checking Savings Departments of this bank have been transferred to the City National Bank and Trust Company of Chicago.

The announcement assured customers that they would continue to receive the same high level of service from City National that they had received from Central Republic, and that City National would honor checks drawn on Central Republic.[31]

City National absorbed the commercial-savings and checking-savings business of Central Republic Bank and Trust and opened with deposits of $72,330,629. Dawes was chairman of the reorganized bank and a major shareholder. He purchased, together with other members of Central Trust's board, 11,000 shares of City National at a value of $1,375,000. This represented a little over 98 percent of the $1.4 million valuation of City National stock. In its press release, the board of directors explained that the reorganization was to reduce the banks' operating costs and to help both entities operate more efficiently.[32] Central Republic Bank and Trust served as the liquidating shell company for the bank's liabilities.

The establishment of City National was the result of Dawes's usual financial creativity combined with the goodwill of business partners and friends. Dawes's return to the helm of Central Trust and the RFC loan had not stemmed the withdrawals of deposits. He determined that the creation of a new bank would allow him to recapitalize the loan and Central Trust's assets, and the announcement of a new bank would be a great psychological boost to the troubled financial community.

Creation of a new bank required approval of the RFC, so Dawes called his old friend and colleague Owen D. Young to Evanston. Dawes outlined his idea to Young and asked him to present it to the members of the RFC. The new bank would be a national bank, opening with a capitalization of $3 million. The proceeds of the RFC loan would go to the new bank, thereby covering all liabilities. Central Trust would pledge $3 million in collateral as security on the loan. Dawes negotiated a reduced rent on the bank premises, representing additional reductions in operating costs. Shares in the new bank would replace shares in Central Trust at a ratio of 1 to 1½.

In general, the RFC approved Dawes's plan, but the RFC required a capitalization of $5 million. Dawes, who was still trying to raise funds for the Century of Progress, which was to open in less than a year, was not happy about having to find an additional $2 million for the bank. Young and Bernard Baruch helped, and Dawes and his associates invested $1,375,000 of their own funds.[33]

Dawes acknowledged Young's help in the bank reorganization in a letter to Harbord: "I shall never forget the self-sacrificing, arduous, and successful assistance Young gave me in connection with the bank situation. All through my difficulties, he had only 'the steadfast heart.'"

Dawes was hopeful that 1933 would see a turnaround in the economic situation—a hope that he had expressed through most of 1932, and which had not come to pass. "Relative to the prophecy of better times ahead," he concluded to Harbord, "perhaps it would be better if I followed the example of Alexander Legge [president of International Harvester] who, when asked when times were going to be better, replied: 'There is one kind of business from which I have permanently retired and that is prognostication.'"[34]

Dawes received a number of congratulatory letters from friends and business associates on the creation of City National. "May I take a minute out of your busy day to let you know how delighted I am with the new set-up," wrote one Chicago business owner. "My relations with you as client and banker began more than a quarter of a century ago, and the prosperity of my company is due largely to that relationship. Please accept my heartiest congratulations in which you have met and overcome a most difficult situation."[35]

"Permit me to be one of the number to congratulate you on the good work you have done in saving—as I believe you did—the old institution," wrote another Chicago businessman.[36]

Amid the letters of congratulations from businesses and other banks, Dawes received a neatly handwritten letter from Dorothy D. Carothers, the daughter of an investor:

> Dear Mr. Dawes:
>
> As administratrix of the Estate of my father—John B. Caroth-ers, I am extremely interested in the information that has come to me recently concerning the Central Republic Bank and Trust Company, its affiliates, and the new bank.
>
> Knowing the high regard father had for your various enterprises—and the interest with which he followed them as a friend and investor, I wonder if you could possibly advise me as to what course I should pursue with some of these investments? . . .
>
> The Estate is not large and naturally none of us like to face the possibility of undue shrinkage—especially at this time.[37]

She followed up with another letter explaining that her work sched-ule would make it easier for her to meet with Dawes on a Saturday or a Monday, since she would have to travel from Cincinnati, where she lived, to Chicago. In the midst of all that consumed him, Dawes made time to assist Dorothy Carothers. He replied: "You will of course bring with you a list of the securities which your father held. It will be conve-nient for me to see you any Saturday or Monday."[38]

Dawes also dealt personally with those who complained about changes in the new bank. The checking-savings accounts had been an unprofitable business for Central Republic, and City National phased out this service a few weeks after its formation. An unhappy customer wrote:

> You are accustomed to handling problems so vast that they sometimes affect whole nations, and what one small and unprof-itable customer in your new bank may think probably doesn't concern you very much—if any. But when such a customer is mul-tiplied by thousands, maybe it is of interest.
>
> I'm talking about the letter to your Checking-Savings custom-ers. I can well remember when there was an entirely different attitude, for I secured several such accounts for the bank.[39]

Chapter 14

The letter he received in return was warm and friendly.

> Dear Mr. Cole:
> During these trying times you have probably had to face many
> new and difficult problems. Most of us have. The same thing has
> been true of business houses. In the banking field the burden has
> been particularly heavy, as I'm sure you realize.

After explaining how unprofitable the checking-savings business had
been for the bank, Dawes reminded him that his checks would still be
honored through January 1, and that Cole would still have the benefit
of a passbook savings account where he would receive "the full prevailing savings interest on your entire balance," and he would be able to
make withdrawals as he had previously.

> Should you feel that your banking needs require checking
> facilities, you are most cordially invited to confer with any of our
> officers (before January 1, please) with respect to a regular check-
> ing account in our Commercial Department. . . .
> You are an old friend, and we want to do everything we can to
> keep and strengthen your friendship, which we value most highly.[40]

A personal secretary may have drafted the letter, but it was hand signed
by Dawes.
　The political fallout from the RFC loan was huge. Hoover, in his last
major campaign speech, delivered in St. Louis on November 5, justified the loan. Without initially naming the bank in question, Hoover
referred to a "major bank in a major city" and told the crowd:

> The failure of this bank to continue business would have added
> to the panic which threatened to swoop down on other banks in
> that city and spread in turn to other cities and involve many trust
> and insurance companies. The immediate problem was to provide
> before Monday morning a sufficient sum of money to quiet unrea-
> soning fear and give absolute assurance that funds were available
> to pay every depositor in full without question.[41]

Hoover continued by giving a detailed analysis of the type and number of accounts held at the "major bank": 122,000 depositors, of whom 105,000 were savings depositors with an average account balance of $140; 17,000 commercial depositors, many of whom were small businesses, but which also included 755 country banks in communities with populations of five thousand or fewer people.[42] Summing up the details, Hoover said to the audience: "This is the story of the Dawes bank in Chicago. You know the use our political opponents have made of this incident."

Hoover concluded by explaining that Dawes had not wanted to ask for funds from the RFC, fearing the political backlash, but, as Hoover told it, Democratic members of the RFC and the Federal Reserve Board urged Dawes to make the request.[43] Jones's later recounting of the events that led to the loan corroborate Hoover's speech.

Dawes received congratulatory messages from many of his friends, but the speech did not stem the electoral tide that had turned inexorably toward Franklin Delano Roosevelt. Hoover was defeated in a landslide. Roosevelt, who won 57.4 percent of the popular vote, carried the electoral vote in all but six states. Not even Hoover's native state of Iowa, nor his adopted state of California, gave him a majority.[44]

"You have fought and won a great fight for your country during three years of unparalleled economic crisis," Dawes cabled Hoover the day after the election. "Through it all you fought the hardest when surrounding difficulties were the greatest, just as you did in the campaign."[45]

As always, Charley gave attention to family matters. Dana's wife, Eleanor, gave birth to a little girl at the beginning of December, whom the couple named Elizabeth Dillingham Dawes. She was born in Newark, Ohio, where Dana was working in sales for Pure Oil. The Newark Hospital mailed Charley a statement for the hospital charges of $63.40, on which was written: "At the request of your son we are mailing you this statement."[46]

Dawes wrote to Dana: "Your mother has handed me your letter of Thursday, December 8th. I am glad to know everything goes well with your wife and daughter, and that you are feeling all right yourself. I note that you are paying the trained nurse $49 per week. I do not know how many weeks to calculate the payments, but send you herewith a check for $100, and if more is needed on this account, let me know."[47]

With Hoover's defeat, Dawes received letters from well-wishers who wanted to see him run for president, and he also heard from people seeking employment. Charley acknowledged many of these letters personally, thanking those who sent him encouraging notes and doing his best to boost the spirits of those for whom he could not provide employment. He also received a number of speaking requests, the overwhelming majority of which he graciously declined, citing the press of business matters.

Dawes had remained confident through 1932 that an economic upturn was right around the corner, but he did not feel sufficiently optimistic to engage in new ventures. The oilman I. B. Humphreys asked Dawes to give some time to one of Humphrey's associates with regard to a new investment opportunity. Dawes replied: "Am not looking for outside investments, but will be glad to see any friend of yours."[48]

Ignoring his own advice to abandon prognostication in his previous letter to Harbord, Dawes wrote his friend at the end of the year:

> I regard 1933 as the fourth year of a five year depression. Looking back, not only upon my own experience in the depression of 1893–1898, but remembering the general trend of things in 1897, I notice this fact which will be common to the two periods; that the fourth year is the year when the mass of the people regain their nerve and the intelligentsia lose it. . . . I expect, therefore, that during the year unless some egregious and improbable mistakes occur in the national administration such as a demonstration of an unwillingness or admitted inability to balance the budget in a reasonable time, we will experience the beginning of a business revival.[49]

As history has shown, the Depression moved into a fifth year.

Beman wrote to invite Charley to Florida to enjoy some fishing with Pershing. Hoover had recently visited and caught three sailfish. "We are completely off by ourselves and yet near plenty of excitement at Palm Beach," Beman told his brother. "You owe it to yourself as well as to all the rest of us to take a little rest."[50] Charley had turned down several previous invitations that Beman and his wife, Bertie, had extended since his return to Chicago to join them for some rest and recreation. There is no indication that Charley accepted this invitation either. He was immersed in his work at the bank.

The political fallout from the RFC loan did not wait until FDR's inauguration on March 4, 1933. Dawes received a letter from the RFC dated February 20, 1933, that contained a list of all institutions that had received a loan from the RFC from its inception on February 2, 1932, through January 31, 1933. In conjunction with Senator James Couzens's resolution to investigate the RFC that the Senate had passed the previous summer, Dawes was asked to report whether he had been an officer or a board member of any of the names on that list, or whether he had a substantial interest as a stockholder or in some other capacity.[51]

While Dawes was not being singled out—all past and present members of the RFC board received the same letter—the timing of the request was suspiciously political. The request originated from Senator John James Blaine, a Wisconsin Republican and a strong Progressive, who chaired the Senate Subcommittee on Financial Institutions that was looking into loans made by the RFC. Blaine had been one of the few senators to vote against Dawes's nomination as president of the RFC and had referenced the Lorimer bank scandal during Dawes's confirmation hearings.

In his response, Dawes informed the RFC that his only stock interest was in the Central Republic Bank and Trust Company of Chicago, "in which I owned fifty-two shares directly and had an indirect interest amounting to about 1,008 shares additional." He continued that he held the title of honorary chairman of the board from January 22, 1932, until June 27, 1932, "but was not an actual officer or director until this later date." He concluded the letter by stating that he was elected chairman of the board on June 27, 1932 [sic], and "resigned as such October 5, 1932."[52] The October 5 date was the date of the reorganization of Central Republic into City National Bank, but that bank was not the entity that had received the RFC loan.

Not surprisingly, Central Republic could not fully repay the RFC loan according to the terms agreed to in June. As of February 4, 1933,

Central Republic had paid back $23,576,238. It still showed $70,405,000 in unliquidated loans on its books. This was an improvement over its position on September 30, immediately prior to the creation of City National, which showed loans and discounts of $91,807,000.[53]

In November 1933, the RFC issued its first demand for repayment of the loan in full, under the terms of the loan agreement. It reissued the demand in July. On November 19, 1934, the RFC filed legal action against Central Trust. By that time, the bank had repaid $32,893,000 to the RFC and $3,768,000 to the other Loop banks that had participated in the loan.[54]

The case dragged through the courts for nearly three years. Dawes Brothers, Inc. was the major shareholder of Central Trust stock. The number of shareholders in Dawes Brothers had grown from the small group of family and close acquaintances to an estimated eight hundred to nine hundred shareholders, which included corporations and individuals, in addition to Henry, Rufus, Charley, and their cousin William.[55] The attorney for Dawes Brothers, Inc., in an attempt to protect the smallest shareholders, argued in court that the holding company could not be owners of the stock. Under the corporate laws of the state of Illinois, it was an indefensible legal argument. The hearing also revealed that Charley had paid his personal assessment on the RFC loan of $6,800, unbeknownst to Dawes Brothers' attorney, which indicated acceptance of his liability. The case was further complicated because several groups of stockholders, believing they were not well represented by the firm's attorney, secured their own counsels. The independently organized shareholder groups fought among one another and filed cross-suits.[56]

Dawes's life was as busy as ever. The Century of Progress International Exhibition opened on May 27, 1933, with a first-day attendance of more than one hundred fifty thousand people. The fair was hailed as a display of humanity's triumphs in science and industry.[57] The exposition was so popular that it continued into 1934 and reported total profits of more than half a million dollars. It was a triumph for Charley's fund-raising prowess and Rufus's organizational acumen.[58]

The court finally ruled on Central Republic's RFC case in July 1936. In accordance with Illinois corporate law, the bank's shareholders were responsible for payment of the total value of their stock, which amounted to $10,500,000.[59] The decision was appealed to the Supreme Court of the United States, which declined to review the case in October 1939, letting stand the lower court ruling.

Charley, Rufus, and Henry dissolved Dawes Brothers, Inc. in 1938, the year before the Supreme Court decision and seven years after Charley first mentioned his plans to Henry to liquidate the holding company. The public reasons given for the dissolution were the uncertainty of the investment business and the cost of operations. The *Chicago Daily Tribune* published the holdings of Dawes Brothers, Inc. The majority of the stock was divided between the banks and Pure Oil: 32,768 shares in Central Republic; 29,000 common shares in Central-Illinois Securities Corporation; 32,500 preferred shares in Central-Illinois Securities; 6,310 shares in City National; and 28,363 common shares in Pure Oil. Other holdings included Scott Paper Company, Willys-Overland Motor Company, Central Public Utility Corporation, and a newspaper, the *Chicago Journal of Commerce*.[60] The dissolution of the holding company did not release the shareholders of Central Trust stock from their liability, and two-thirds of those shareholders are reported to have paid their assessment.

Dawes's persistent optimism in an economic recovery had finally paid off. The company had held onto its stocks and began to see a marked appreciation in value when the stock market began to recover in 1936. By 1938, many of the values of Dawes Brothers' holdings had been sufficiently restored to merit the liquidation Charley had long intended.

The liquidation of Dawes Brothers, Inc. did not affect Central Trust's repayment of the RFC loan. The RFC's August 31, 1944, report showed that the old bank had paid back the loan in full. The total amount of the repayment was $99,506,533. The difference between the original $90 million loan and the total amount paid represented an interest rate of 2.2 percent.[61] In the Dawes archives can be found his handwritten record as each portion of the loan was paid off. The debt remained a burden to him until it was fully discharged.

With the persistence of the Depression, Dawes continued to promote at every opportunity his beliefs in low taxation and balanced budgets as a solution to the faltering economy. In a letter to the president of the Chicago Association of Commerce and Industry, written in May 1939,

Dawes criticized the capital gains tax as making it "improbable, if not impossible, the return of normal prosperity to the United States, and in the interest of all citizens, rich and poor, [the tax] should be repealed or drastically reduced."[62]

A year later, in May 1940, Dawes was back in Washington to address a capacity crowd of the United States Chamber of Commerce and to advocate for a balanced budget. It was an approach completely opposite the policies of the Roosevelt administration, which had adopted the recommendations of the British economist John Maynard Keynes, whom Dawes had met during his ambassadorial years. Keynes promoted deficit spending as a stimulus to economic recovery, with the government functioning as a primary purchaser of goods and services to inject money into the economy. Congress and Roosevelt had adopted Keynes's philosophies in an effort to restart the nation's moribund finances.

Dawes, however, continued to believe that a balanced budget was essential to a healthy economy. "General Dawes picked up this theme with all of the old-time fire for which he was noted while vice president during the Coolidge administration. He assailed the record of the present administration and warned that the next president must be made of 'sterner stuff.'" Dawes blamed the Roosevelt administration for "continuance of the depression and the presence of 'insidious dangers' within the nation." He pointed out "the need of internal strength in a period of world disorder and conflict."[63] Economists have long argued about how best to avoid prolonged depressions, and they have yet to find one approach that guarantees sustained and steady growth without cyclical downturns. Dawes, having seen the success of balanced budgets and reduced taxes during the Coolidge years, remained convinced that it was the soundest economic and fiscal policy.

Charley watched as the world he had once helped to build changed into one in which he no longer played a role, but that did not keep him from trying to exert influence. Just as the federal government abandoned a balanced budget as a matter of policy, so, too, changes took place internationally. Dawes watched as his hard work of reparations, disarmament, and peace negotiations unraveled across Europe.

His book *A Journal of Reparations* was published in fall 1939. By then, Adolf Hitler was completing his sixth year as Germany's chancellor.

All reparations payments had long since ceased. Hitler had begun his march across Europe with invasions into Austria, Czechoslovakia, and Poland. The United Kingdom and France had declared war on Germany in September 1939.

Reviewers of Dawes's book considered his observations during his work on the Reparations Commission in the light of current events. "General Dawes's *Journal* shows the difference of outlook in 1924," wrote one reviewer. It was a reminder that "Hitler was not the first German leader 'to get away with' a breach of the legal basis of a sound European order."[64]

The reviewer for the *Mississippi Valley Historical Review*, a scholarly publication for which Dawes had been one of the guarantors for many years, also considered the book in the context of events in Europe. Commenting on Dawes's ability to get the British to help secure France's reluctant support for the Dawes Plan, the reviewer noted French Premier Georges Clemenceau's pessimism about the future and his "grave doubts that 'Germany would ever show good faith in its acceptance or carrying-out of the plan presented in our report.'"

The review continued, "But Dawes remained the invincible optimist, and he assured his friends that the nations of the world were 'facing away from the chaos left by the war . . . with sincere determination to found an enduring and Christian peace based upon common good faith.'" It would be interesting, the reviewer mused, to see Dawes's marginal notes on that passage in light of the conflict in Europe.[65]

Dawes's "marginal notes" would show that he fully anticipated that the United States would ultimately enter the war. He urged the federal government to adopt the practices he had established and advocated during and immediately following World War I. "If the government does not set up immediately an effective system of internal coordination as it enters upon an additional and gigantic effort for war preparedness, it will fail, wasting not only enormous resources, but, what is more important, incalculable time," he told the midyear convention of the National Retail Dry Goods Association in an address that was broadcast on Chicago's WGN radio. "Committee management was fatal in 1917" to proper military preparedness, and it was already proving fatal in the United Kingdom's and France's efforts to stop Hitler. "A cabinet is only a committee," he told his audience.[66]

While he urged war preparedness, Dawes was no longer a man of war. He told old friends and colleagues at the 17th Engineers Club that he believed U.S. entry into the war would prolong the conflict by thirty years.[67]

The following year, in May 1941, Herbert Hoover solicited Dawes's help in keeping the United States out of the war in Europe. "It is vital that the United States stay out [of Europe]," the former president wrote his friend. "The voices, such as mine . . . and those of others, together with the more extreme groups, are pretty well worn out. . . . But I believe there are two voices in the United States that have not yet been sounded which could turn the whole question: they are those of General Pershing and yourself."[68]

One month prior to the Japanese attack on Pearl Harbor, Hoover wrote Dawes: "The idea of a nation like this going into a war with no determined objective except certain platitudes of crushing Hitler is one of the most appalling phrases of the times."[69]

Events, however, ended all talk of neutrality. The Japanese bombed Pearl Harbor on December 7, 1941, and the United States entered the war in Europe in 1943. Hitler had marched across the Continent. England was the last bastion of democracy in Europe. Every one of Dawes's contributions to establish a lasting world peace had come undone.

CHAPTER 15

X

The Last Lion

August 27, 1950, marked Charles G. Dawes's eighty-fifth birthday. He still went to his office at City National daily, and he continued to eschew birthdays. "This reporter, as he has done on previous occasions," wrote Philip Hampson, who had been covering Chicago business—and Charles G. Dawes—for the *Chicago Daily Tribune* for over six years, "went to the general's office on La Salle Street to try to get a birthday interview. And, as in the past, the interview attempt was a flat failure, in most respects. The general does not care to discuss the topics of the day for publication."

Hampson did leave with some of Dawes's favorite reminiscences about his late friend John T. McCutcheon and with an autographed book and a box of Havana cigars. "The reporter departed wondering whose birthday was being celebrated."[1]

The previous year, the U.S. Senate honored Dawes on his eighty-fourth birthday with a unanimous resolution that read, in part:

> Resolved that the Senate of the United States extends most cordial greetings and felicitations to the Honorable Charles Gates Dawes, on the occasion of his eighty-fourth birthday, August 27, 1949, for during a long and distinguished career he has served his country in a most conspicuous and devoted manner as a financial expert, as a soldier, as a diplomat, and as vice president of the United States and president of this august body.[2]

The annual birthday publicity started about the time Dawes turned eighty and seemed like something of a death vigil, as if that particular year would mark his last birthday celebration.

Dawes had outlived most of his colleagues and contemporaries. His friend Walter Delamatre had been killed in an automobile accident in 1937, at the age of seventy-seven. Dawes's son-in-law, Melvin Ericson, died in November 1939, from what an obituary described as a lengthy illness. George B. Cortelyou passed away in 1940, Harbord died in 1947, and Pershing died the following year, 1948.

Charley's brother Rufus died suddenly of a heart attack in January 1940, and Rufus's widow, Helen, succumbed to a stroke in July 1941. Henry, Beman, and their wives were still alive to help Dawes celebrate his eighty-fifth birthday.

There had been family changes, too. Dana's wife, Eleanor, divorced him in October 1939. The couple had two children, Elizabeth and Charles Gates Dawes II. Dana remarried in April 1942. He and his second wife, Alice "Susie" Seward, had two more children.

Virginia had married Richard Cragg in September 1936. On June 16, 1945, Dawes walked his granddaughter Caroline Ericson down the aisle for her wedding to Albert Stoneman Long Jr.

Family records indicate that Caro and Charley's decision to adopt had a strong influence on their children. Each of their children themselves adopted a child.

Herbert Hoover, nine years Dawes's junior, remained a regular correspondent in the last decade of Dawes's life. In 1942, Hoover authored a book with Hugh S. Gibson, the former Belgian ambassador and member of the 1930 U.S. team at the disarmament talks. In the book, titled *The Problems of a Lasting Peace*, they studied the factors that make for a permanent end to war. Hoover sent Dawes a draft copy of the book with a series of questions related to its content and the advisability of having the book sent for publication while the United States was engaged in the war.

In response to whether the book should be published in the current war environment, Dawes wrote to Hoover:

> It is quite probable that from the outcome of the present battle between Russia and Germany the final result of the world war itself

may be plainly forecast. If Russia wins, then the general nature of
the European post-war settlement will be chiefly dictated by Russia. Russia already has an engagement with England and probably
with ourselves that her post-war boundaries will include Estonia,
Latvia, Lithuania, a part of Poland and Bessarabia [portions of
Moldova, Romania, and Ukraine].

Dawes had little hope for a reasonable peace settlement if the Western
powers had to negotiate with the Soviet leader Joseph Stalin, and he
believed that if Germany should prevail in its battle with Russia, there
could be no hope of peace whatsoever.[3]

Throughout the war, Hoover and Dawes continued to discuss ways
in which peace could be achieved. As a follow-up to the book Hoover
and Gibson published in 1942, the two men worked on another publication to promote ways to establish a lasting peace with the hope of
having their work form the basis of a peace plank for the 1944 Republican National Convention. "We proposed wholly new approaches to
the machinery for the making of a lasting peace so as to avoid another
debacle like Versailles," Hoover wrote to Dawes. "And we proposed
new approaches to the long-view peace settlements." Once again, the
former president asked for Dawes's comments.[4]

"There is no one in the party better qualified than yourself to write
the plank on this subject for the Republican platform," Dawes replied.
"If a platform could be prepared, setting out and advocating the new
approaches to the machinery for peace making, suggested in your book,
it would be much better than a plank outlining a peace plan. I think
that when the time has arrived to formulate the Republican platform,
there will be a common desire to have you draw the peace plank."[5]

Dawes continued through the 1940s to raise money on behalf
of youth groups. He collected funds in support of the Boys' Clubs of
America, an organization that provided after-school programs for
young people and was strongly supported by Hoover, who served as its
chairman of the board. "I cannot let the opportunity pass of telling you
how happy [your efforts in Chicago] made me and to send you a word
of personal appreciation," Hoover wrote Dawes in 1945.[6] Dawes
agreed to chair the Chicago-area appeal for the Boys' Clubs and served as a
national associate until his death.

Dawes's views regarding the importance of a federal budget had changed little since his years as Harding's budget director. Frank Pace Jr., President Harry S. Truman's choice to head the Budget Bureau, interviewed all his living predecessors, including Dawes. In Dawes's mind, the director of the budget had more power and influence than the vice president. "Young man," Dawes told Pace, "you should always keep in mind that these cabinet officers are the executive vice presidents in charge of spending and as such the natural enemies of the President." With that, Dawes dismissed Pace with a curt, "Good day, young man."[7]

During his twelve years in office, FDR had pointedly excluded the Republican men who had led the nation through most of the first three decades of the twentieth century. He had not sought their advice, and he did not invite them back to Washington. That attitude changed with the Truman administration.

In 1949, Dawes joined a commission, organized by President Truman and chaired by Hoover, to look at the reorganization of the federal government. Following completion of the commission's work and its submission to Congress for consideration, Dawes wrote Hoover a detailed plan outlining the importance of getting public opinion on board so that Congress would feel public pressure to accept the plan. Dawes told Hoover: "This contest for the adoption of the Hoover Plan is one of the most important we have ever had in the history of our country. We are in a crisis."[8] After a lengthy fight, Congress adopted a number of the plan's recommendations, including the unification of the armed services, a reorganization of the State Department, and the creation of the General Services Administration, in early 1950.

The two men shared an August birthday. Hoover's was August 10, and the two exchanged best wishes on each other's birthdays. In 1949, Dawes wired Hoover: "When I remember that you are nine years younger than I am, I can understand better your indefatigable work and youthful buoyancy."[9]

Dawes's heart gave out on Monday night, April 23, 1951, as he sat in the library of his Evanston home talking to Caro. He remained active until the very last, having recently accepted an appointment as honorary chair of the committee to greet General Douglas MacArthur on his upcoming visit to Chicago. Dawes had, as was his custom, visited his bank on Saturday and lunched with friends.[10]

In an editorial eulogy, the *Chicago Tribune* wrote:

His talents were as varied as they were great. He was in turn lawyer, businessman, banker, soldier, statesman, and diplomat. He
made his mark in every field but the law, in which his training
guided all his other efforts to success. He might also have been
called a politician, except that the rambunctious Dawes personality was better calculated to serve the public than to win him the
allegiance of politicians. . . . Among his other blessings, General
Dawes counted a long and happy marriage. To Mrs. Caro Blymyer
Dawes, to whom he was married in 1889, and their children, Chicago extends its condolences.[11]

AUTHOR'S NOTE

*I*t is impossible to spend time with Charley Dawes and not fall in love with him. He was both brilliant and irascible, a fascinating amalgam of financial and organizational genius with an utter disregard for decorum and formality. It is ironic to think that he spent at least one-third of his career as a diplomat, when some of his most remembered moments were those when he threw tact to the wind.

Charley belongs to an era that produced some truly gifted political and business leaders. These were fiscally conservative men with compassionate hearts, whose ideas for improving people's lives came from encouraging individual effort and keeping government as small as possible. That formula appeared to fail during the years of the Great Depression and the unprecedented twelve years of Franklin Roosevelt in the White House. So, Dawes's story and the stories of men like him have gathered dust in libraries and archives around the country. We would do well to go back and look at the contributions they made to the fabric of our national life.

I want to thank Jennifer Pritzker and the Tawani Foundation for their generosity in funding the research and writing of this book, thus making it possible for me to learn about Charley Dawes. Likewise, my thanks go to Eden Juron Pearlman, director of the Evanston History Center, for asking me to write Dawes's biography. Members of the staff at the center were especially helpful. My thanks to Lori Osborne for her assistance in selecting the photographs that appear in the book. I am especially appreciative for Kris Hartzell's careful reading of the initial manuscript and her correction of factual errors about Dawes's personal life. Thanks, also, to Jenny Thompson for her encouragement.

This book was not a solo effort. It could not have taken shape in the year's time I had to write Charley's story were it not for the tremendous assistance of Sigrid Pohl Perry, a special collections assistant at the Charles Deering McCormick Library of Special Collections at Northwestern University in Evanston, Illinois. Sigrid made the organizing and cataloging of the massive Dawes archive a special project, and her knowledge of the archive and assistance in locating material were essential to the completion of this book. Special thanks, also, to Scott Krafft, curator of Special Collections, and Kevin Leonard, Northwestern University archivist, for their work to provide me with a digital copy of the Dawes biography written by John Pixton. Many thanks to the other staff in Special Collections and for the research work done by the efficient Nora Epstein and Grace Schwartzenberger.

Major Rory McGovern, currently an instructor at the United States Military Academy, gave me a crash course in the realities of our lack of preparedness in World War I. I am very thankful for his time and his insights into this era of American history. Also, thanks to Jesse Stiller, historian at the U.S. Office of the Comptroller of the Currency, who answered my questions regarding some of Dawes's decisions while U.S. comptroller.

I like to take every opportunity to compliment the interlibrary loan staff of my award-winning home public library system, Cumberland County (N.C.) Public Library & Information Center, and also to thank the University of North Carolina–Chapel Hill (UNC) for on-campus access to its physical and online collections. Thanks to Stewart Varner at the UNC University Libraries for helping me find additional resource material on Dawes in a pinch. Special thanks, also, to the incomparable staff at the Hoover Presidential Library and Museum in West Branch, Iowa, for assistance in providing details about the 1930 disarmament talks.

In addition to the Tawani Foundation and the Evanston History Center, I owe the opportunity to write about Dawes to Jane Frances Bunker, director of Northwestern University Press, who remembers me from my first faltering days as a biographer and recommended me to the director of the Evanston History Center.

My husband, Bill, graciously allowed me to spend my nights and weekends with another man for the better part of two years. With Bill's encouragement—and great cooking—I completed this book.

NOTES

Abbreviations

CGD—Charles Gates Dawes
RCD—Rufus Cutler Dawes
CDBD—Caro Dana Blymyer Dawes
HMD—Henry May Dawes
BGD—Beman Gates Dawes
DP-EHC—Dawes Papers, Evanston History Center, Evanston, Illinois
DP-NU—Dawes Papers, Northwestern University, Evanston, Illinois

Chapter 1

1. Carolyn Dawes Ericson, "Mary Beman Gates," vol. 1, unpublished manuscript, n.d., Dawes Family Collection, Evanston (Illinois) History Center, 62–63.

2. William Richard Cutter, *New England Families, Genealogical and Memorial*, vol. 2 (New York: Lewis Historical Publishing, 1913), 493, https://play.google.com/books/reader2?id=ofcsAAAAYAAJ.

3. *Marietta Intelligencer* (Marietta, Ohio), August 29, 1839, 1, quoted in Gerald S. Greenberg, "Beman Gates and the *Marietta Intelligencer* 1839–1854," *Publishing History* 38 (1995): 59, doi:http://hdl.handle.net/1811/47389.

4. Cutter, *New England Families*, 495.

5. Henry Ware Holland, *William Dawes and His Ride with Paul Revere: An Essay Read before the New England Genealogical Society on June 7, A.D. 1876* (Boston: John Wilson and Son, 1878), vii, http://books.google.com/books/reader?id=WD2477M66jAC.

6. Rufus R. Dawes to CGD, June 2, 1882, DP-EHC.

7. Robert H. Ferrell, ed., "Young Charley Dawes Goes to the Garfield Inauguration: A Diary," *Ohio History Journal* 70, 4 (October 1961): 334, http://www.ohiohistory.org/ohstemplate.cfm.

8. Charles Gates Dawes, Scrapbook, n.d., n.p., DP-NU.

9. Ibid.

10. Jacob D. Cox to Charles F. Manderson, April 6, 1887, Dawes Scrapbook, DP-NU.

Chapter 2

1. CGD to Clayton Delamatre, August 23, 1887, Dawes Scrapbook, DP-NU.

2. *Columbus Journal* (Columbus, Neb.), November 23, 1887, in *Chronicling America: Historic American Newspapers*, Library of Congress, http://chronicling america.loc.gov/lccn/sn95073194/1887–11–23/ed-1/seq-2/.

3. William Leese to CGD, November 19, 1887, Dawes Scrapbook—DP-NU.

4. *Omaha Daily Bee* (Omaha, Neb.), December 29, 1887, in *Chronicling America: Historic American Newspapers*, Library of Congress, http://chronicling america.loc.gov/lccn/sn99021999/1887–12–29/ed-1/seq-5/.

5. *Omaha Daily Bee* (Omaha, Neb.), February 27, 1888, in *Chronicling America: Historic American Newspapers*, Library of Congress, http://chronicling america.loc.gov/lccn/sn99021999/1888–02–27/ed-1/seq-5/.

6. *Omaha Daily Bee* (Omaha, Neb.), April 27, 1888, in *Chronicling America: Historic American Newspapers*, Library of Congress, http://chroniclingamerica .loc.gov/lccn/sn99021999/1888–04–27/ed-1/seq-4/.

7. Rufus R. Dawes to CGD, [April 30?], 1888, Dawes Scrapbook—DP-NU.

8. Jacob D. Cox to CGD, May 7, 1888, Dawes Scrapbook—DP-NU.

9. Francis Beidler to J. A. Buckstaff, April 6, 1891, DP-NU.

10. Louis W. Koenig, *Bryan: A Political Biography of William Jennings Bryan* (New York: G. P. Putnam's Sons, 1971), 56.

11. Edward A. Goedeken, "The Dawes-Pershing Relationship during World War I," *Nebraska History* 65 (1984): 108–29, http://www.nebraskahistory.org/ publish/publicat/history/full-text/1984-1-Dawes_Pershing.pdf, 109.

12. "Leap Year Catches," *Nebraska State Journal* (Lincoln, Neb.), January 1, 1888, Dawes Scrapbook, DP-NU.

13. Sigrid Pohl Perry, "Charles Gates Dawes: From Private Face to Public Place," in *At Home in Evanston: The Charles Gates Dawes House*, ed. Elizabeth A. Myers (Evanston, Ill.: Evanston Historical Society, 2000), 51.

14. Dana Dawes, transcript of oral history tapes, p. 81, quoted in "Service from the Hearth: The Lives of Caro Blymyer Dawes and Helen Palmer Dawes," lecture given by Sigrid Pohl Perry to the Evanston History Society Guild, November 8, 1995.

15. Charles Gates Dawes, *Notes as Vice President, 1928–1929* (Boston: Little, Brown, 1935), 253, digitized version by HathiTrust Digital Library, http:// catalog.hathitrust.org/Record/000576188.

16. "New Companies Incorporated," Dawes Scrapbook [January 1891?] n.p., DP-NU.

17. William W. Mills to CGD, April 23, 1891, DP-NU.

18. *Saturday Morning Courier* (Lincoln, Neb.), January 13, 1894, in *Chronicling America: Historic American Newspapers*, Library of Congress, http://chronicling america.loc.gov/lccn/2010270512/1894–01–13/ed-1/seq-1/.

19. William W. Mills to CGD, December 16, 1893, DP-NU.

20. William W. Mills to CGD, December 28, 1892, DP-NU.

21. RCD to CGD, April 1, 1893, DP-NU.

22. William W. Mills to CGD, May 19, 1893, DP-NU.

23. Charles G. Dawes, *A Journal of the McKinley Years, 1893–1913*, ed. Bascom N. Timmons (Chicago: Lakeside Press, 1950), 47.

24. William W. Mills to CGD, October 13, 1893, DP-NU.

25. CGD to BGD, April 3, 1919, DP-NU.

26. RCD to CGD, October 16, 1893, DP-NU.

27. Ibid.

28. RCD to CGD, December 15, 1893, DP-NU.

29. United States Senate, "Charles G. Dawes, 30th Vice President (1925–1929)," *Senate History*, http://www.senate.gov/artandhistory/history/common/generic/VP_Charles_Dawes.htm.

Chapter 3

1. Dawes, *A Journal of the McKinley Years*, 49.

2. Heritage Research Center, "What Is Manufactured Gas?" 3, http://www.heri tageresearch.com/documents/More%20About%20Manufactured%20Gas .pdf.

3. Dawes, *A Journal of the McKinley Years*, 59.

4. Ibid., 46–47.

5. Harold L. Platt, "Samuel Insull and the Electric City," in *A Wild Kind of Boldness: The Chicago History Reader*, ed. Rosemary K. Adams (Chicago: Chicago Historical Society; Grand Rapids, Mich.: William B. Eerdmans, 1998), 215–16.

6. Federal Reserve Bank of Philadelphia, "The Fed Today: History of Money and Banking in the U.S.," 3, http://www.philadelphiafed.org.

7. Charles G. Dawes, *The Banking System of the United States and Its Relationship to the Money and Business of the Country* (Chicago: Rand McNally, 1894), 7, Google e-book edition, //books.google.com/books/reader?id=ZO9HAAAAI AAJ.

8. Ibid., 59.

9. Ibid., 65–66.

10. RCD to CGD, November 24, 1894, DP-NU.

11. WWM to CGD, November 20, 1894, DP-NU.

12. *The Herald* (Los Angeles), in *Chronicling America: Historic American Newspapers*, December 23, 1894, Library of Congress, http://chroniclingamerica.loc.gov/lccn/sn85042461/1894-12-23/ed-1/seq-9/.

13. William McKinley to CGD, December 13, 1894, DP-NU.

14. WWM to CGD, November 20, 1894, DP-NU.

15. Dawes, *A Journal of the McKinley Years*, 12.

16. Granacki Historic Consultants, "Architectural Resources in the Lakeshore Historic District Evanston, Illinois: A Summary and Inventory" (2012), 7–8, https://cityofevanston.org/assets/Evanston%20Lakeshore%20Final%20Report%20File%201%20%28report%20and%20cover%29.pdf.

17. Marcus A. Hanna to CGD, December 11, 1894, DP-NU.

18. David Kenney and Robert E. Hartley, *An Uncertain Tradition: U.S. Senators from Illinois, 1818–2003* (Carbondale: Southern Illinois University Press, 2003), 79–84.

19. Marcus A. Hanna to CGD, February 24, 1896, DP-NU.

20. Ibid.

21. Rufus C. Dawes Diary, unpublished, February 12, 1896, DP-NU.

22. William McKinley to CGD, April 30, 1896, quoted in Charles G. Dawes, *A Journal of the McKinley Years*, 81.

23. CGD to CDBD, March 14, 1896, DP-EHC.

24. Charles G. Dawes to William McKinley, March 18, 1896, William McKinley Papers, Library of Congress, Washington, D.C.

25. John McNulta to William McKinley, April 9, 1896, William McKinley Papers, Library of Congress, Washington, D.C.

26. "To Work from Chicago," *Chicago Daily Tribune*, July 16, 1896, ProQuest Historical Newspapers: Chicago Tribune (1849–1990).

27. Charles G. Dawes to Marcus A. Hanna, July 30, 1896, William McKinley Papers, Library of Congress, Washington, D.C.; Charles G. Dawes to William McKinley, August 1, 1896, William McKinley Papers, Library of Congress, Washington, D.C.

28. W. G. Edens to CGD, September 8, 1896, DP-NU.

29. Dawes, *A Journal of the McKinley Years*, 102, 106.

30. David Leip, "1896 Presidential General Election Results," *David Leip's Atlas of U.S. Presidential Elections*, http://uselectionatlas.org/RESULTS/national.php?year=1896.

31. William McKinley to CGD, November 9, 1896, DP-NU.

32. Dawes, *A Journal of the McKinley Years*, 105.

33. Marcus A. Hanna to CGD, November 27, 1896, DP-NU.

34. HMD to CGD, December 5, 1896, DP-NU.

35. Dawes, *A Journal of the McKinley Years*, 108.

36. Ibid., 112.

37. United States Comptroller of the Currency, *Office of the Comptroller of the Currency: A Short History* (Washington, D.C.: Government Printing Office, 2011), 13, http://www.occ.gov/about/what-we-do/history/OCC%20history%20final.pdf.

38. *Morning Times* (Washington, D.C.), February 1, 1897, in *Chronicling America: Historic American Newspapers*, Library of Congress, http://chroniclingamerica.loc.gov/lccn/sn84024442/1897-02-01/ed-1/seq-4/.

39. J. D. Cox to CGD, September 23, 1896, DP-NU.

Chapter 4

1. *Morning Times* (Washington, D.C.), March 5, 1897, in *Chronicling America: Historic American Newspapers*, Library of Congress, http://chroniclingamerica.loc.gov/lccn/sn84024442/1897-03-05/ed-1/seq-1/.

2. Dawes, *A Journal of the McKinley Years*, 115.

3. Luther Allen to CGD, September 22, 1897, DP-NU.

4. Edwin F. Brown to CGD, September 16, 1897, DP-NU.

5. William R. Dawes to CGD, September 15, 1897, DP-NU.

6. RCD to CGD, September 16, 1897, DP-NU.

7. RRD to CGD, September 30, 1897, DP-NU.

8. Dawes, *A Journal of the McKinley Years*, 133.

9. Ibid., 138.

10. Charles G. Dawes, "Annual Report of the Comptroller of the Currency," *Bankers Magazine* 57, no. 6 (December 1898): 776.

11. Dawes, *A Journal of the McKinley Years*, 138.

12. Ibid., 141; "Chestnut Street Bank," *New York Times*, March 29, 1898, ProQuest Historical Newspapers, New York Times (1857–1922).

13. Email correspondence between author and Jesse Stiller, Historian, Office of the Comptroller of the Currency, U.S. Department of the Treasury, November 4, 2015.

14. Studebaker v. Perry, 184 U.S. 258 (1902), in Justia, "US Supreme Court," https://supreme.justia.com/cases/federal/us/184/258/case.html.

15. Dawes, *A Journal of the McKinley Years*, 143.

16. Ibid., 147.

17. Ibid., 163.

18. Ibid., 158.

19. Ibid., 158–59.

20. Charles G. Dawes, "Annual Report of the Comptroller of the Currency," *Bankers Magazine* 57, no. 6 (December 1898): 963.

21. Charles G. Dawes, "Annual Report of the Comptroller of the Currency," *Bankers Magazine* 59, no. 6 (December 1899): 920C.

22. Dawes, *A Journal of the McKinley Years*, 206.

23. Ibid., 211.

24. Ibid., 218.

25. Ibid., 197.

26. "Peoria Contest Grows Warmer," *Chicago Daily Tribune*, May 8, 1900, 1, ProQuest Historical Newspapers, Chicago Daily Tribune (1872–1922).

27. Ibid.

28. Dawes, *A Journal of the McKinley Years*, 228.

29. Ibid., 232–33.

30. Ibid., 232.

31. Ibid., 259.

32. Woodrow Wilson, "When a Man Comes to Himself," *Century Magazine* 62 (June 1901): 272, http://www.unz.org/Pub/Century-1901jun-00268.

33. Ibid., 271.

34. Dawes, *A Journal of the McKinley Years*, 271.

35. Ibid., 241–42.

36. Ibid., 275.

37. H. H. Kohlsaat, "From McKinley to Harding: Personal Recollections of Our Presidents," *Saturday Evening Post* 195, no. 4 (July 22, 1922): 19, https://books.google.com/books?id=eCskAQAAMAAJ.

38. Dawes, *A Journal of the McKinley Years*, 284.

39. Ibid., 286.

Chapter 5

1. Dawes, *Journal of the McKinley Years*, 275.

2. Ibid., 288.

3. "Indorsement of Hopkins Passed by Convention," *Chicago Daily Tribune*, May 9, 1902, 1, ProQuest Historical Newspapers, Chicago Daily Tribune (1872–1922).

4. Dawes, *Journal of the McKinley Years*, 310.

5. Ibid., 362.

6. Ibid., 372.

7. Ibid., 311.

8. Ibid.

9. Ibid., 341.

10. "Chicago and Vicinity," *Bankers' Magazine* 84, no. 5 (May 1912): 733, http://search.proquest.com/docview/124404426?accountid=12861.

11. Charles G. Dawes, "Corporation Reform," reprinted in *Essays and Speeches* (New York: Houghton Mifflin, 1915), 80–81.

12. "A Poor Illustration," *The Commoner* (Lincoln, Neb.), November 3, 1905, 1, in *Chronicling America: Historic American Newspapers*, Library of Congress, http://chroniclingamerica.loc.gov/lccn/46032385/1905–11–03/ed-1/seq-1.

13. Dawes, *A Journal of the McKinley Years*, 421–22.

14. "Defends Aldrich Bill," *Washington Post* (Washington, D.C.), April 15, 1908, 4, ProQuest Historical Newspapers, Washington Post (1877–1922).

15. Federal Reserve Bank of Kansas City, "Federal Reserve Act Signed by President Wilson," *Federal Reserve History*, http://www.federalreservehistory.org/Events/DetailView/10.

16. "Business, Commercial and Financial Section," *Chicago Daily Tribune*, December 27, 1913, 11, ProQuest Historical Newspapers, Chicago Daily Tribune (1872–1922).

17. *Rock Island Argus* (Rock Island, Ill.), December 18, 1905, 1, in *Chronicling America: Historic American Newspapers*, Library of Congress, http://chroniclingamerica.loc.gov/lccn/sn92053934/1905–12–18/ed-1/seq-1/.

18. Dawes, *Journal of the McKinley Years*, 293.

19. Joel A. Tarr, "J. R. Walsh of Chicago: A Case Study in Banking and Politics, 1881–1905," *Business History Review* 40, no. 4 (Winter 1966): 451, http://www.jstor.org/stable/3112123.

20. Ibid., 464; Dawes, *Journal of the McKinley Years*, 408–9.

21. *Rock Island Argus* (Rock Island, Ill.), January 15, 1908, in *Chronicling America: Historic American Newspapers*, Library of Congress, 1, http://chroniclingamerica.loc.gov/lccn/sn92053934/1908–01–15/ed-1/seq-1/; *Rock Island Argus* (Rock Island, Ill.), February 13, 1908, 1, in *Chronicling America: Historic American Newspapers*, Library of Congress, 1, http://chroniclingamerica.loc.gov/lccn/sn92053934/1908–02–13/ed-1/seq-1/; *Rock Island Argus* (Rock Island, Ill.), March 13, 1908, 1, in *Chronicling America: Historic American Newspapers*, Library of Congress, http://chroniclingamerica.loc.gov/lccn/sn92053934/1908–03–13/ed-1/seq-1/.

22. John R. Walsh to CGD, August 27, 1907, DP-NU.

23. Dawes, *A Journal of the McKinley Years*, 372.

24. Enclosure to letter from BGD to CGD, January 13, 1902, DP-NU.

25. C. H. Bosworth to CGD, March 19 [1896?], DP-NU.

26. History Channel, "Oil Industry—Facts & Summary," http://www.history.com/topics/oil-industry.

27. HMD to CGD, February 2, 1901, DP-NU.

28. HMD to CGD, April 24, 1901, DP-NU.

29. West Virginia, *Governor's Message Submitted to Legislature of 1903, with the Accompanying Reports and Documents Covering the Two Fiscal Years October 1, 1900 to September 30, 1902*, n.p., 1903: 143, https://books.google.com/books?id=FdcaAQAAIAAJ.

30. CGD to Samuel M. Felton, October 26, 1908, DP-NU.

31. Unpublished statement of CGD relative to formation of Dawes Brothers, Inc. [1907?], n.p., DP-NU.

32. "1907 Dollars in 2015 Dollars," http://www.in2013dollars.com/1907-dollars-in-2015?amount=400000.

33. RCD to CGD, August 19, 1892, DP-NU.

34. "Ohio Cities Gas," *Poor's Manual of Public Utilities, 1915* (New York: Poor, 1915), 1326, https://books.google.com/books?id=DWk3AQAAMAAJ.

35. RCD to CGD, December 16, 1914, DP-NU.

36. Carolyn Hughes Crowley, "Meet Me at the Automat," *Smithsonian Magazine*, August 2001, http://www.smithsonianmag.com/history/meet-me-at-the-automat-47804151/?no-ist.

37. George P. Earle Jr. to CGD, September 3, 1915, DP-NU.

38. Richard Guy Wilson, "The Chateau on Lake Michigan," in *At Home in Evanston: The Charles Gates Dawes House* (Evanston, Ill.: Evanston History Center, 2000), 21.

Chapter 6

1. United States Senate, "The Election Case of William Lorimer of Illinois (1910; 1912)," *Senate History*, http://www.senate.gov/artandhistory/history/common/contested_elections/095William_Lorimer.htm.

2. Ibid.

3. Ibid.

4. Ibid. Note: The Lorimer trial took place while the states were debating ratification of the Seventeenth Amendment to the Constitution calling for direct election of senators. Some historians maintain that the Lorimer case pushed a majority of states to ratify the amendment.

5. Lawrence Y. Sherman to CGD, January 20, 1913, DP-NU.

6. "Lorimer's Banks Will Open Soon," *Chicago Daily Tribune*, April 13, 1910, 3, ProQuest Historical Newspapers, Chicago Daily Tribune (1872–1922).

7. "The Dawes Bank Charges," *Literary Digest* 83, no. 4 (October 25, 1924): 8–9, http://unz.org/Pub/LiteraryDigest-1924oct25-00005?View=PDF.

8. "Charles G. Dawes' Son Is Drowned: Death Race Lost," *Chicago Daily Tribune*, September 6, 1912, 1, ProQuest Historical Newspapers, Chicago Daily Tribune (1872–1922).

9. Ibid.

10. Dawes, *Journal of the McKinley Years, 1893–1913*, 443.

11. Ibid., 445.

12. *Helen Palmer Dawes Journal*, entry for February 4, 1906, n.p., DP-NU.

13. Dawes, *Journal of the McKinley Years, 1893–1913*, 445.

14. Lawrence Y. Sherman to CGD, October 4, 1909, DP-NU.

15. Lawrence Y. Sherman to CGD, March 21, 1914, DP-NU.

16. *Helen Palmer Dawes Journal*, entry for December 12, 1912, n.p., DP-NU.

17. *Helen Palmer Dawes Journal*, entry for November 26, 1914, n.p., DP-NU.

18. Charles G. Dawes, *Journal of the McKinley Years*, 348.

19. "Starts Big Hotel for Needy Men," *Chicago Daily Tribune*, August 20, 1913, 3, ProQuest Historical Newspapers, Chicago Daily Tribune (1872–1922).

20. "Homeless Fill Rufus F. Dawes Memorial Hotel," *Chicago Daily Tribune*, Jan 2, 1914, 2, ProQuest Historical Newspapers, Chicago Daily Tribune (1872–1922).

21. Lawrence Y. Sherman to CGD, January 3, 1914, DP-NU.

22. Sigrid Pohl Perry, "Service from the Hearth: The Lives of Caro Blymyer Dawes and Helen Palmer Dawes," lecture delivered to Evanston Historical Society, November 8, 1995.

23. Molly Kettler, "Tribute to Caro Blymyer Dawes," *TimeLines*, Evanston History Center, Spring 2013, 7.

24. Council for Library and Museum Extension, *Educational Opportunities in Chicago* (Chicago: Council for Library and Museum Extension, 1912), 80, https://books.google.com/books?id=65MnAAAAMAAJ.

25. James Langland, ed., *Chicago Daily News Almanac and Yearbook for 1922* (Chicago: Chicago Daily News, 1921), 899–900, https://books.google.com/books?id=JQ8fAQAAMAAJ.

26. Charles G. Dawes, *A Journal of the McKinley Years, 1893–1913*, 410.

27. "Melody in A Major" went on to have a career of its own. It became a hit pop tune, known as "It's All in the Game," which was released shortly after Dawes's death in 1951 and became the number-one pop hit in 1958 for singer Tommy Edwards. The Four Tops and Van Morrison also eventually recorded the song. Source: Sigrid Pohl Perry, "Charles Gates Dawes: From Private Face to Public Place," 55.

28. George B. Cortelyou to CGD, December 29, 1914, DP-NU.

29. Sigrid Pohl Perry, "Service from the Hearth."

30. Email correspondence with Kris Hartzell, Director of Facilities, Visitor Services and Collections, Evanston History Center, September 2015. Note: Decker's obituary referred to her as "family nurse" to Charles Dawes.

31. Madame X, "Comment by Mme. X," *Chicago Daily Tribune*, April 25, 1915, D2, ProQuest Historical Newspapers, Chicago Daily Tribune (1872–1922).

32. Mary Beman Dawes to CGD, April 30, 1915, DP-NU.

33. Mary Beman Dawes to CGD, September 9, 1915, DP-NU.

34. Mary Beman Dawes to CGD, September 16, 1915, DP-NU.

35. *Bankers Magazine* 83 (January–June 1914): 638, http://babel.hathitrust.org/cgi/pt?id=uc1.b2875465;view=1up;seq=11.

36. "Dawes-Lorimer Story to Come in Civil Suit," *Day Book* (Chicago), September 29, 1915, 1.

37. Richard Garrett Sherman, "Charles Gates Dawes: An Entrepreneurial Biography, 1865–1951," Ph.D. diss.: University of Iowa, Iowa City, 1960, 97.

38. *Day Book* (Chicago), February 11, 1916, 4, in *Chronicling America: Historic American Newspapers*, Library of Congress, http://chroniclingamerica.loc.gov/lccn/sn83045487/1916–02–11/ed-1/seq-4/.

39. *Day Book* (Chicago), July 8, 1916, 1, in *Chronicling America: Historic American Newspapers*, Library of Congress, http://chroniclingamerica.loc.gov/lccn/sn83045487/1916–07–08/ed-1/seq-1/.

40. Sherman, "Charles Gates Dawes: An Entrepreneurial Biography," 97–98.

41. J. P. Morgan & Co. to CGD, September 30, 1915, DP-NU.

42. Ibid.

43. Thomas W. Lamont to CGD, September 29, 1915, DP-NU.

44. CGD to *Chicago Tribune*, September 30, 1915, DP-NU.

45. "Death Threats Sent to Dawes; Guard at Home," *Chicago Daily Tribune*, October 1, 1915, 3, ProQuest Historical Newspapers, Chicago Daily Tribune (1872–1922).

46. E. S. Taylor to CGD, October 13, 1915, DP-NU.

47. J. C. Rudolph to A. J. Earling, October 1, 1915, DP-NU.

48. "Sell $320,000,000 of Allies' Bonds," *New York Times*, December 12, 1915, ProQuest Historical Newspapers, New York Times (1857–1922).

49. Anonymous letter to CGD, December 14, 1915, DP-NU.

50. Anonymous letter to CGD, March 2, 1916, DP-NU.

51. "Foreign Financing after the European War," *Bonds and Mortgages* 63, no. 4 (April 1916): 4, https://books.google.com/books?id=xkJJAQAAMAAJ.

Chapter 7

1. Woodrow Wilson, *War Messages*, 65th Cong., 1st Sess., Senate Doc. no. 5, Serial no. 7264, Washington, D.C., April 2, 1917, 3–8, http://wwi.lib.byu.edu/index.php/Wilson%27s_War_Message_to_Congress.

2. Address of the President of the United States to the Senate, January 22, 1917, http://wwi.lib.byu.edu/index.php/Address_of_the_President_of_the_United_States_to_the_Senate.

3. Office of the Historian, United States Department of State, "American Entry into World War I, 1917," https://history.state.gov/milestones/1914–1920/wwi.

4. John S. D. Eisenhower, *Yanks: The Epic Story of the American Army in World War I* (New York: Free Press, 2001) 31.

5. John J. Pershing, *My Experiences in the World War*, vol. 1 (New York: Frederick A. Stokes, 1931), 24.

6. CGD to CDBD, June 1, 1917, DP-EHC.

7. Frank O. Lowden to CGD, May 21, 1917, DP-NU.

8. Frank O. Lowden to CGD (telegram), May 22, 1917, DP-NU.

9. Herbert Hoover to CGD (telegram), June 13, 1917, DP-NU.

10. Charles G. Dawes, *Journal of the Great War*, vol. 1 (Boston: Houghton Mifflin, 1921), 5.

11. CGD to CDBD, June 1, 1917, DP-EHC.

12. CGD to CDBD, July 27, 1917, DP-EHC.

13. CGD to CDBD, August n.d., 1917, DP-EHC.

14. Carolyn Dawes Ericson, *Mary Beman Gates*, 195.

15. CGD TO CDBD, August n.d., 1917, DP-EHC.

16. Dawes, *A Journal of the Great War*, vol. 1, 9.

17. Ibid., 10.

18. Ron Chernow, *The House of Morgan* (New York: Grove Press, 1990), 186–87.

19. Dawes, *A Journal of the Great War*, vol. 1, 12.

20. Ibid., 17.

21. Pershing, *My Experiences in the World War*, vol. 1, 27–28.

22. Ibid., 78.

23. Johnson Hagood, *The Services of Supply: A Memoir of the Great War* (Boston: Houghton Mifflin, 1927), 25, http://hdl.handle.net/2027/mdp.39015063013919.

24. Pershing, *My Experiences in the World War*, vol. 1, 64.

25. Martin Gilbert, *The First World War: A Complete History* (New York: Henry Holt, 1994), 358.

26. Pershing, *My Experiences in the World War*, vol. 1, 147.

27. Center of Military History, United States Army, *United States Army in the World War, 1917–1919*, vol. 16, *Reports of the Commander-in-Chief, Staff Sections, and Services* (Washington, D.C.: Government Printing Office, 1991), 76, http://www.314th.org/center-of-military-history/CMH-Pub-23–22-General-Orders-GHQ-AEF-Volume-16.pdf.

28. CGD to CDBD, August 30, 1917, DP-EHC.

29. Dawes, *A Journal of the Great War*, vol. 1, 21.

30. Christian Gauss, "The Education of General Harbord," *Saturday Evening Post* 205, no. 5 (July 30, 1932): 28–63, Academic Search Alumni Edition, EBSCOhost, http://search.ebscohost.com/login.aspx?direct=true&Authtype=cookie,url,ip,uid&db=a2h&AN=18053250.

31. James G. Harbord, *Leaves from a War Diary* (New York: Dodd, Mead, 1925), 141.

32. Ibid.

33. Historical Plans, War Branch Division General Staff, United States War Department, *Organization of the Services of Supply* (Washington D.C.: Government Printing Office, 1921), 36, https://play.google.com/books/reader?printsec=frontcover&output=reader&id=9rpBAAAAIAAJ.

34. Dawes, *A Journal of the Great War*, vol. 1, 22.

35. Ibid., 22–23.

36. State Historical Society of Missouri, "John J. Pershing (1860–1948)," in *Historic Missourians*, http://shs.umsystem.edu/historicmissourians/name/p/pershing/#section6.

37. Dawes, *A Journal of the Great War*, vol. 1, 23.

38. CGD to HMD, October 12, 1917, DP-NU.

39. CGD to Mary Beman Dawes, October 23, 1917, quoted in Dawes, *A Journal of the Great War*, vol. 1, 47–48.

40. S. L. A. Marshall, *World War I* (Boston: Houghton Mifflin, 1992), 281–82.

41. Gilbert, *The First World War*, 339.

42. Dawes, *A Journal of the Great War*, vol. 1, 28.

43. Pershing, *My Experiences*, vol. 1, 48.

44. Dawes, *A Journal of the Great War*, vol. 1, 31.

45. Lloyd C. Griscom, *Diplomatically Speaking* (Boston: Little, Brown, 1940), 412.

46. Pershing, *My Experiences*, vol. 1, 145.

47. Jeremy Wormell, *The Management of the National Debt of the United Kingdom, 1900–1932* (London: Routledge, 2000), 176.

48. Dawes, *A Journal of the Great War*, vol. 1, 42–43.

49. Ibid., 62–63.

50. Hagood, *The Services of Supply*, 41.

51. Dawes, *A Journal of the Great War*, vol. 1, 64.

52. Harbord, *Leaves from a War Diary*, 200.

53. Dawes, *A Journal of the Great War*, vol. 1, 61.

54. Ibid., 64.

55. CGD to CDBD, December 12, 1917, DP-EHC.

56. CGD to CDBD, December 23, 1917, DP-EHC.

57. RCD to CGD, February 5, 1918, DP-NU.

58. CGD to CDBD, December 22, 1917, DP-EHC.

59. CGD to CDBD, November 15, 1917, DP-EHC.

60. CGD to CDBD, December 23, 1917, DP-EHC.

61. CGD to HMD, February 9, 1918, DP-NU.

62. CGD to CDBD, December 22, 1917, DP-EHC.

63. Dawes, *A Journal of the Great War*, vol. 1, 69.

64. Ibid., 72.

65. CGD to RCD, March 9, 1918, DP-NU.

66. Dawes, *A Journal of the Great War*, vol. 2, 70–71.

67. Hagood, *The Services of Supply*, 149–50; Eisenhower, *Yanks*, 64.

68. Hagood, *The Services of Supply*, 150–51.

69. Dawes, *A Journal of the Great War*, vol. 1, 99.

70. Ibid.

71. Ibid.

72. Ibid., 86.

73. Ibid., 96.

74. Harbord, *Leaves from a War Diary*, 353–54.

75. Dawes, *A Journal of the Great War*, vol. 1, 121.

76. Ibid., 123.

77. Hagood, *The Services of Supply*, 198.

78. Report of Colonel (later Major General) Hanson E. Ely on the operation against Cantigny, May 28, 1918, National Archives, Record Group 120, quoted in Eisenhower, *Yanks*, 132.

79. Harbord, *Leaves from a War Diary*, 309.

80. Dawes, *A Journal of the Great War*, vol. 1, 137–38.

81. Ibid., 143, 145.

82. Ibid., 151–52.

83. Ibid., 172.

84. Hagood, *The Services of Supply*, 316–17.

85. Dawes, *A Journal of the Great War*, vol. 1, 176–77.

86. Ibid., 178.

87. Ibid., 189.

88. Harbord, *Leaves from a War Diary*, 356.

89. Pershing, *My Experiences in the World War*, vol. 2, 342.

90. Dawes, *A Journal of the Great War*, vol. 1, 187.

91. Ibid., 200.

92. Ibid., 202.

93. CGD to Mary B. Dawes, November 14, 1918, DP-NU.

94. Harbord, *Leaves from a War Diary*, 398.

95. Charles G. Dawes to Mary B. Dawes, November 14, 1918, DP-NU.

Chapter 8

1. Dawes, *A Journal of the Great War*, vol. 1, 210.

2. Frank Macy Surface and Raymond L. Bland, *American Food in the World War and Reconstruction Period* (Palo Alto, Calif.: Stanford University Press, 1931), 52.

3. CGD to CDBD, November 24, 1918, DP-EHC.

4. Dawes, *A Journal of the Great War*, vol. 1, 230.

5. Carol R. Byerly, "The U.S. Military and the Influenza Pandemic of 1918–1919," *Public Health Reports* 125, supplement 3 (2010): 82.

6. Dawes, *A Journal of the Great War*, vol. 1, 236.

7. Lawrence Y. Sherman to CGD, December 10, 1918, DP-NU.

8. CGD to Lawrence Y. Sherman, January 15, 1919, DP-NU.

9. Dawes, *A Journal of the Great War*, vol. 1, 220.

10. James G. Harbord to CGD, January 31, 1919, DP-NU.

11. Dawes, *A Journal of the Great War*, vol. 1, 233.

12. John J. Pershing to CGD, March 28, 1919.

13. CDBD to CGD, February 2, 1919, DP-EHC.

14. Arthur Robert Burns, "Surplus Government Property and Foreign Policy," *Foreign Affairs* 23, no. 3 (April 1945): 485–95, http://www.jstor.org/stable/20029912.

15. Edwin B. Parker, *Final Report of United States Liquidation Commission* (Washington, D.C.: War Department, 1920), 11–12.

16. Ibid.

17. "Equipment Abroad to Be 'Liquidated,'" *Automobile Topics* 53, no. 2 (February 15, 1919): 1.

18. Surface and Bland, *American Food in the World War and Reconstruction Period*, 53; "Sold War Stocks for $822,923,225," *New York Times*, June 7, 1920, 19, ProQuest Historical Newspapers, New York Times (1851–2010).

19. Dawes, *A Journal of the Great War*, vol. 1, 250.

20. Dawes, *A Journal of the Great War*, vol. 1, 260.

21. Ibid., 271.

22. James G. Harbord to CGD, August 8, 1919, DP-NU.

23. CGD to James G. Harbord, October 14, 1920, DP-NU.

24. European Relief Council, *Interim Report of European Relief Council, Including Statement of Contributions by States, and Auditors' Preliminary Report on Accounts* (New York: M. B. Brown, 1921), 4, http://libcudl.colorado.edu/wwi/pdf/i73698155.pdf.

25. Ibid., 14.

26. "House Probers Scan Acts of $1 a Year Men," *New York Tribune*, June 25, 1919, 11, in *Chronicling America: Historic American Newspapers*, Library of Congress, http://chroniclingamerica.loc.gov/lccn/sn83030214/1919–06–25/ ed-1/seq-11/.

27. Ibid.

28. CGD to John J. Pershing, October 14, 1919, DP-NU.

29. Senate Committee on Military Affairs, United States Congress, *Reorganization of the Army, Hearings before the Subcommittee of the Committee on Military Affairs*, vol. 2 (Washington, D.C.: Government Printing Office, 1920), 249, http://books.google.com/books/reader?id=32hKAAAAYAAJ.

30. Alan Brinkley, *American History: A Survey*, 11th ed., vol. 2 (New York: McGraw Hill, 2003), 640–41.

31. CGD to John J. Pershing, October 14, 1919, DP-NU.

32. "Pershing and His Men Share Final Tribute," *Chicago Daily Tribune*, December 22, 1919, 1, ProQuest Historical Newspapers, Chicago Tribune (1849–1990).

33. "Pershing Aloof from Politicians," *Chicago Daily Tribune*, December 22, 1919, 1, ProQuest Historical Newspapers, Chicago Tribune (1849–1990).

34. CGD to James G. Harbord, December 27, 1919.

35. J. G. Quekemeyer to CGD, January 17, 1920, DP-NU.

36. John J. Pershing to CGD, June 2, 1920, DP-NU.

37. John J. Pershing to CGD, June 6, 1920, DP-NU.

38. CGD to James G. Harbord, June 15, 1920, DP-NU.

39. Charles G. Dawes, "The Next President of the United States and the High Cost of Living," *Saturday Evening Post* 193, no. 14 (October 2, 1920): 7.

40. Ibid., 182.

41. "Harding Talks U.S. Economy with C. G. Dawes," *Chicago Daily Tribune*, December 21, 1920, 7, ProQuest Historical Newspapers, Chicago Tribune (1849–1990).

42. United States House of Representatives, *War Expenditures: Hearings before Subcommittee No. 3 (Foreign Expenditures) of the Select Committee on Expenditures in the War Department*, vol. 4, parts 75–78 (Washington, D.C.: Government Printing Office, 1921), 4501, https://books.google.com/books?id =335HAQAAMAAJ.

43. "Victory Bigger than Red Tape, Dawes' Retort," *Washington Herald* (Washington, D.C.), February 3, 1921, 1, in *Chronicling America: Historic American Newspapers*, Library of Congress, http://chroniclingamerica.loc.gov/lccn/sn830 45433/1921–02–03/ed-1/seq-1/.

44. *Washington Times* (Washington, D.C.), February 3, 1921, 1, in *Chronicling America: Historic American Newspapers*, Library of Congress, http://chronicling america.loc.gov/lccn/sn84026749/1921–02–03/ed-1/seq-1/.

45. John J. Pershing to CGD, February 5, 1921, DP-NU.

46. CGD to Lawrence Y. Sherman, May 27, 1920, DP-NU.

Chapter 9

1. United States Department of Veterans Affairs, *VA History in Brief* (Washington, D.C.: Government Printing Office, 1977), 7–8.

2. "The Dawes Report," *The Independent* (London), April 23, 1921, 429, http://www.unz.org/Pub/Independent-1921apr23:15.

3. National Archives, "Records of the Bureau of the Budget," *Guide to Federal Records: Records of the Office of Management and Budget*, 8, http://www.archives.gov/research/guide-fed-records/groups/051.html#51.

4. "Needs a Tonic," *Washington Herald Weekly Review* (Washington, D.C.), June 26, 1921, 9, in *Chronicling America: Historic American Newspapers*, Library of Congress, http://chroniclingamerica.loc.gov/lccn/sn83045433/1921–06–26/ed-1/seq-44.pdf.

5. George Rothwell Brown, "Dawes Budget Chief," *Washington Post* (Washington, D.C.), June 22, 1921, 1, ProQuest Historical Newspapers, Washington Post (1877–1997).

6. William Howard Taft, "Harding's Choice of Dawes Is Fortunate, Says Taft," *Washington Post* (Washington, D.C.), June 27, 1921, 6. http://pqasb.pq archiver.com/washingtonpost/.

7. Shirley Anne Warshaw, *Guide to the White House Staff* (Los Angeles: Sage Reference, CQ Press, 2013), 46.

8. Ibid., 48.

9. Ibid., 49.

10. Federal Reserve Bank of St. Louis, *Message of the President of the United States Transmitting to the Two Houses of Congress the Budget for the Fiscal Year Ending June 30, 1923 and the Report of the Director of the Bureau of the Budget* (Washington, D.C.: Government Printing Office, 1921), 55, https://books.google.com/books?id=h9sgAQAAMAAJ.

11. Miller Center of Public Affairs, University of Virginia, "Warren G. Harding," *American President: A Reference Resource*, http://millercenter.org/president/harding/essays/biography/4.

12. Ibid.

13. Laton McCartney, *The Teapot Dome Scandal* (New York: Random House, 2008), 45–46.

14. Miller Center of Public Affairs, University of Virginia, "Warren G. Harding."

15. Charles G. Dawes, *The First Year of the Budget of the United States* (New York: Harper and Brothers, 1923), 6.

16. Ibid., 8.

17. "Dawes Puts Whole Government Back of Economy Drive," *New York Times*, June 30, 1921, ProQuest Historical Newspapers, New York Times (1851–2010).

18. Robert P. Murphy, "The Depression You've Never Heard Of: 1920–1921," *The Freeman* 59, no. 10 (2009), Foundation for Economic Education (FEE), http://www.fee.org/the_freeman/detail/the-depression-youve-never-heard -of-1920–1921; Thomas E. Woods Jr., "The Forgotten Depression of 1920," Ludwig von Mises Institute, Auburn, Ala., November 27, 2009, http://mises .org/daily/3788.

19. Dawes, *The First Year of the Budget of the United States*, 21.

20. "Dawes Takes Office; Berates Congress," *New York Times*, June 24, 1921, 1, ProQuest Historical Newspapers, New York Times (1851–2010).

21. Dawes, *The First Year of the Budget of the United States*, 22.

22. Ibid., 23.

23. Ibid.

24. Ibid., 24.

25. Ibid., 68.

26. Ibid., 93.

27. Ibid.

28. Silas Bent, "Next in Power to Harding," *New York Times*, September 4, 1921, 29, ProQuest Historical Newspapers, New York Times (1851–2010).

29. "Dawes Tells How He Will Cut Budget," *New York Tribune*, September 15, 1921, 1, in *Chronicling America: Historic American Newspapers*, Library of Congress, http://chroniclingamerica.loc.gov/lccn/sn83030214/1921–09–15/ed -1/seq-1.pdf.

30. Dawes, *The First Year of the Budget of the United States*, 80.

31. "Big Cut Ordered in Every Branch of Army Service," *New York Tribune*, September 15, 1921, 19, in *Chronicling America: Historic American Newspapers*, Library of Congress, http://chroniclingamerica.loc.gov/lccn/sn83030214/ 1921–09–15/ed-1/seq-19.pdf.

32. "The Aldrich-Dawes Gospel," *New York Tribune*, September 16, 1921, 12, in *Chronicling America: Historic American Newspapers*, Library of Congress, http://chroniclingamerica.loc.gov/lccn/sn83030214/1921–09–16/ed-1/seq -12.pdf.

33. "Unemployment Figures," *New York Tribune*, September 16, 1921, 12, in *Chronicling America: Historic American Newspapers*, Library of Congress, http://chroniclingamerica.loc.gov/lccn/sn83030214/1921–09–16/ed-1/seq-12.pdf.

34. "Economy Now Popular," *New York Times*, September 16, 1921, 13, ProQuest Historical Newspapers, New York Times (1851–2010).

35. Dawes, *The First Year of the Budget of the United States*, 23.

36. Warren G. Harding to CGD, November 28, 1921, quoted in Dawes, *The First Budget of the United States*, 94.

37. CGD to Warren G. Harding, November 29, 1921, quoted in Dawes, *The First Budget of the United States*, 94–95.

38. William D. Hassett, "Keep within Appropriations Limit or Be Jailed, Bureau Chiefs Told," *Washington Post* (Washington, D.C.), November 27, 1921, 2, http://pqasb.pqarchiver.com/washingtonpost/.

39. Dawes, *The First Year of the Budget of the United States*, 138.

40. "The Budget before Congress," *The Outlook*, December 14, 1921, 591, http://www.unz.org/Pub/Outlook-1921dec14–00591.

41. Dawes, *The First Year of the Budget of the United States*, 96.

42. "Dawes Waves Brooms in Wrath; Shows Lack of Unity in Economy," *Washington Post* (Washington, D.C.), February 4, 1922, 1, http://pqasb.pqarchiver.com/washingtonpost/.

43. Ibid.

44. Ibid.

45. "President Praises Budget System as Dawes Rakes Chiefs," *New York Times*, February 4, 1922, 1, ProQuest Historical Newspapers, New York Times (1851–2010).

46. "Raid in House on Budget Plan Vexes Harding," *New York Tribune*, March 29, 1922, 3.

47. "Editorial Package," *The Nation* 114, no. 2964 (April 26, 1922): 482, http://www.unz.org/Pub/Nation-1922apr26.

48. White House Office of Management and Budget, "Table 1.1—Summary of Receipts, Outlays, and Surpluses or Deficits: 1789–2020," *Historical Tables*, http://www.whitehouse.gov/omb/budget/Historicals.

49. Charles G. Dawes, *Notes as Vice President*, 65.

50. "Gen. Lord to Succeed Dawes as Budget Chief," *New York Times*, June 24, 1922, 6, ProQuest Historical Newspapers, New York Times (1851–2010).

51. Webster K. Nolan, "Capital Loses as Gen. Dawes Says Good-Bye," *Washington Times* (Washington, D.C.), June 28, 1922, in *Chronicling America: Historic American Newspapers*, Library of Congress, http://chroniclingamerica.loc.gov/lccn/sn84026749/1922–06–28/ed-1/seq-7.pdf.

52. CGD to George Horace Lorimer, October 8, 1920, DP-NU.

Chapter 10

1. Bernard M. Baruch, *The Making of the Reparation and Economic Sections of the Treaty* (New York: Harper and Brothers, 1920), 27, 35.

2. Ibid., 6.

3. Federal Reserve Bank of St. Louis, Minutes No. 294, Reparations Commission, Meeting of June 6 and 7, 1922, n.p. https://fraser.stlouisfed.org/docs/historical/frbny/strong/strong_1600_01_reparation_commission_1921–1924.pdf.

4. Ibid.

5. *Washington Herald* (Washington, D.C.), December 30, 1922, in *Chronicling America: Historic American Newspapers*, Library of Congress, http://chroniclingamerica.loc.gov/lccn/sn83045433/1922–12–30/ed-1/seq-1/.

6. Nicholas Roosevelt, "The Ruhr Occupation," *Foreign Affairs* 4, no. 1 (October 1925): 112–22, http://www.foreignaffairs.com/articles/68633/nicholas-roosevelt/the-ruhr-occupation.

7. Max Sering, *Germany under the Dawes Plan: Origin, Legal Foundations, and Economic Effects of the Reparation Payments*, trans. S. Milton Hart (London: P. S. King and Sons, 1929), 52.

8. Rufus C. Dawes, *The Dawes Plan in the Making* (Indianapolis: Bobbs-Merrill, 1925), 18.

9. Ibid., 20–21.

10. Frank Costigliola, "The United States and the Reconstruction of Germany in the 1920s," *Business History Review* 50, no. 4 (Winter 1976): 486.

11. "General Dawes Off to 'Assay' Germany," *New York Times*, December 30, 1923, 4, ProQuest Historical Newspapers, New York Times (1851–2010).

12. Ibid.

13. Dawes, *A Journal of Reparations* (London: Macmillan, 1939), 20.

14. Ibid., 42.

15. Ibid., 51.

16. Dawes, *The Making of the Dawes Plan*, 107–8.

17. Ibid., 115.

18. *Literary Digest* 112, no. 4 (January 27, 1932), quoted in Charles G. Dawes, *A Journal of Reparations*, 78.

19. Dawes, *A Journal of Reparations*, 63.

20. Ibid., 12–13.

21. Dawes, *The Making of the Dawes Plan*, 88.

22. Ibid., 58–61.

23. Dawes, *A Journal of Reparations*, 89–90.

24. Ibid., 98–99.

25. Ibid., 106.

26. Costigliola, "The United States and the Reconstruction of Germany in the 1920s," 489.

27. Ibid., 490.

28. Ibid., 178.

29. Ibid., 112–13.

30. Ibid., 214.

31. "Establish Records on Dawes Report," *New York Times*, April 9, 1924, ProQuest Historical Newspapers, New York Times (1851–2010).

32. "An Expert View of the Dawes Plan," *Literary Digest* 81, no. 7 (May 17, 1924): 21. http://unz.org/Pub/LiteraryDigest-1924may17:1.

33. Dawes, *A Journal of Reparations*, 228.

34. Telegram from Calvin Coolidge to CGD, April 21, 1924, quoted in Dawes, *A Journal of Reparations*, 247.

35. Special to the *New York Times*, "Unanimous Report Cheers Washington," *New York Times*, April 10, 1924, 14, ProQuest Historical Newspapers, New York Times (1923–Current File).

36. Dawes, *A Journal of Reparations*, 226.

37. Ibid., 225.

38. Ibid., 230.

39. "Dawes Back; Is Mum on Europe; Out of Politics," *Chicago Daily Tribune*, May 2, 1924, ProQuest Historical Newspapers, Chicago Tribune (1849–1990).

40. Telegram from CGD to Owen D. Young, August 17, 1924, quoted in Dawes, *A Journal of Reparations*, 262–63.

41. "Ten Months under the Dawes Plan," *Editorial Research Reports 1925* 1 (February 28, 1925): 80, Washington, D.C.: CQ Press, http://library.cqpress .com/cqresearcher/cqresrre1925022800.

42. Nobelprize.org, "Acceptance Speech: Acceptance by Charles Gates Dawes," official website of the Nobel Prize, http://www.nobelprize.org/nobel _prizes/peace/laureates/1925/.

43. Genevieve Forbes Herrick, "Dawes Donates Nobel Prize to Study of Peace," *Chicago Daily Tribune*, January 16, 1927, 5, ProQuest Historical Newspapers, Chicago Tribune (1849–1999).

Chapter 11

1. John J. Grabowski, ed., "Republican National Convention of 1924," *Encyclopedia of Cleveland History* (Cleveland, Ohio: Case Western Reserve University, 1987), http://ech.case.edu/cgi/article.pl?id=RNCO1.

2. John T. Woolley and Gerhard Peters, "Republican Party Platform of 1924," in *American Presidency Project: Political Party Platforms* (Santa Barbara:

University of California, Santa Barbara, 1999–2016), http://www.presidency
.ucsb.edu/ws/?pid=29636.

3. Official Proceedings Republican National Convention 1924, 182–86,
quoted in Edward Ranson, *The American Presidential Election of 1924: A Political Study of Calvin Coolidge*, Book 1 (Lewiston, N.Y.: Edwin Mellen Press,
2008), 440.

4. Richard V. Oulahan, "Borah Agreed as Vice Presidential Nominee in
Midnight Conference of Convention Leaders," *New York Times*, June 12 1924,
http://partners.nytimes.com/library/politics/camp/240612convention-gop-ra
.html.

5. "Calvin Coolidge and Charles G. Dawes Named by G.O.P. Convention
to Lead Ticket of 1924," *Atlanta Constitution*, June 13, 1924, ProQuest Historical Newspapers, Atlanta Constitution (1868–1945).

6. Official Proceedings Republican National Convention 1924, 182–86,
quoted in Ranson, *The American Presidential Election of 1924*, Book 1, 453.

7. "Calvin Coolidge and Charles G. Dawes Named by G.O.P. Convention
to Lead Ticket of 1924," *Atlanta Constitution*.

8. Ibid.; Richard V. Oulahan, "Revolt Puts Dawes Over," *New York Times*,
June 13, 1924, ProQuest Historical Newspapers, New York Times (1851–
2010).

9. "Boosters of Dawes for Vice-Presidency Renew Efforts," *Washington Post*
(Washington, D.C.), June 9, 1924.

10. "Calvin Coolidge and Charles G. Dawes Named by G.O.P. Convention
to Lead Ticket of 1924," *Atlanta Constitution*.

11. "Boosters of Dawes for Vice-Presidency Renew Efforts," *Washington Post*, 1.

12. Official Proceedings Republican National Convention 1924, 190–
94, quoted in Ranson, *The American Presidential Election of 1924*, Book 1,
453–54.

13. "News Causes Only Flurry," *Marietta Daily Times* (Marietta, Ohio), June 13,
2014, http://extras.mariettatimes.com/history/pdfs/dawesEXTRA.pdf; "Dawes
Promptly Accepts Nomination," *New York Times*, June 13, 2014, ProQuest
Historical Newspapers, New York Times (1851–2010).

14. "Dawes in N.Y.; Not Entry for Vice President," *Chicago Daily Tribune*,
April 29, 1924, ProQuest Historical Newspapers, Chicago Tribune (1849–
1990).

15. CGD to James G. Harbord, January 16, 1920, DP-NU.

16. White House, "John Adams," http://www.whitehouse.gov/about/presi
dents/johnadams.

17. Dawes, *Notes as Vice President*, 18.

18. Calvin Coolidge to CGD, June 13, 1924, DP-NU.

19. Calvin Coolidge to Elihu Root, June 14, 1924, Calvin Coolidge Papers, Northampton, Mass., PPF 253, quoted in Ranson, *The American Presidential Election of 1924*, Book 1, 463.

20. Robert James Maddox, *William E. Borah and American Foreign Policy* (Baton Rouge: Louisiana State University Press, 1969), 163.

21. "What Dawes Brings to the Republican Ticket," *Literary Digest* 81, no. 13 (June 28, 1924): 7–8, http://www.unz.org/Pub/LiteraryDigest-1924jun 28-00005:1.

22. Calvin Coolidge to CGD, June 29, 1922, DP-NU.

23. Calvin Coolidge to CGD, August 23, 1923, DP-NU.

24. "'Dawes and Coolidge' Old Colonial Firm," *New York Times*, June 17, 1924, ProQuest Historical Newspapers, New York Times (1851–2010).

25. Dawes, *Notes as Vice President*, 19.

26. Federal Judicial Center, "History of the Federal Judiciary," http://www .fjc.gov/history/home.nsf/page/talking_ji_tp.html.

27. "Dawes Will Wage War on Demagogue, He Tells Friends," *Washington Post* (Washington, D.C.), June 18, 1924, 1.

28. Dawes, *Notes as Vice President*, 19.

29. Library of Congress, "Democratic National Political Conventions, 1832–2008," http://www.loc.gov/rr/main/democratic_conventions.pdf, 14.

30. Ranson, *The American Presidential Election of 1924*, Book 2, 650.

31. "Dawes Attacked by the Third Party," *New York Times*, June 15, 1924, 1, ProQuest Historical Newspapers, New York Times (1851–2010).

32. Coolidge, *The Autobiography of Calvin Coolidge*, 189–90.

33. Donald R. Richberg, "De-Bunking Mr. Dawes," *New Republic* 39 (July 9, 1924): 180–83.

34. "After Standard Oil Again," *Literary Digest* 82, no. 2 (July 12, 1924), 13.

35. "President Decides on August 14 as Notification Date," *Washington Post* (Washington, D.C.), July 15, 1924, 1.

36. John Augustus Davis, "The Ku Klux Klan in Indiana, 1920–1930: An Historical Study," Ph.D. diss., Northwestern University, Evanston, Ill., 1966, 11–12; Infoplease.com, "Ku Klux Klan: The Second Ku Klux Klan," http://www.info please.com/encyclopedia/history/ku-klux-klan-the-second-ku-klux-klan.html.

37. "35,000 Hear Jersey Speech," *New York Times*, August 23, 1924, 1, Pro-Quest Historical Newspapers, New York Times (1851–2000).

38. Maine Historical Society, "The Nativist Klan," *Maine History Online*, https://www.mainememory.net/sitebuilder/site/783/slideshow/427/display ?format=list&prev_object_id=1192&prev_object=page&slide_num=1; "US Population by State from 1900," http://www.demographia.com/db-state 1900.htm.

39. Philip Kinsley, "Dawes Stamps Un-American Brand on Klan," *Chicago Daily Tribune*, August 24, 1924, 1, ProQuest Historical Newspapers, Chicago Tribune (1849–1990).

40. Dawes, *Notes as Vice President*, 23.

41. "General 'Opposed to' Klan," *New York Times*, August 24, 1924, 1, ProQuest Historical Newspapers: New York Times (1851–2000).

42. Ibid.

43. "Dawes on the Klan," *Atlanta Constitution*, August 25, 1924, 1, ProQuest Historical Newspapers, Atlanta Constitution (1845–1945); "A Challenge," *New York Times*, August 24, 1924, 1, ProQuest Historical Newspapers, New York Times (1851–2000).

44. Cleveland G. Allen, "William H. Allen Making Big Mistake, Declares Noted Writer," *Chicago Defender* (National Edition), October 4, 1924, 3, ProQuest Historical Newspapers, Chicago Defender (1910–1975).

45. Robert H. Zieger, *Republicans and Labor: 1919–1929* (Lexington: University of Kentucky Press, 1969), 76.

46. Ibid., 77.

47. William Butler to Charles G. Dawes, ca. August 9, 1924, quoted in Zieger, *Republicans and Labor*, 185.

48. Dawes, *Notes as Vice President*, 24.

49. "Dawes in Indiana Attacks LaFollette," *New York Times*, October 4, 1924, 1, ProQuest Historical Newspapers, New York Times (1851–2000).

50. "Dawes in Wisconsin," *New York Times*, September 12, 1924, ProQuest Historical Newspapers, New York Times (1851–2010).

51. George William McDaniel, *Smith Wildman Brookhart: Iowa's Renegade Republican* (Ames: Iowa State University Press, 1995), 162.

52. "Brookhart Demands Dawes Quit Ticket; Wants Norris Named," *New York Times*, October 1, 1924, 1, ProQuest Historical Newspapers, New York Times (1851–2000).

53. "Labor Committee Condemns Dawes," *New York Times*, October 4, 1924, ProQuest Historical Newspapers, New York Times (1851–2000).

54. Ibid.

55. Frank R. Kent, "Dawes Called Virtual 'Flop' as Campaigner," *Baltimore Sun*, October 28, 1924, ProQuest Historical Newspapers, Baltimore Sun (1837–1988).

56. "Gen. Dawes Assails His Party's Leaders," *New York Times*, October 25, 1924, ProQuest Historical Newspapers, New York Times (1851–2000).

57. "9 to 1 on Coolidge; 9 to 5 on Gov. Smith," *New York Times*, November 1, 1924, ProQuest Historical Newspapers, New York Times (1851–2000).

58. David Leip, "1924 Presidential General Election Results," *David Leip's Atlas of U.S. Presidential Elections*, http://uselectionatlas.org/RESULTS/national.php?year=1924.

59. "Dawes Preparing Quietly for 'Job,'" *Baltimore Sun*, November 6, 1924, ProQuest Historical Newspapers, Baltimore Sun (1837–1988).

60. Ibid.

Chapter 12

1. "Dawes Cracks Jokes in Hospital Bed; May Eat Thanksgiving Dinner at Home," *New York Times*, November 18, 1924, 1, ProQuest Historical Newspapers, New York Times (1851–2010).

2. Charles G. Dawes, *Notes as Vice President*, 33–34.

3. "Full Text of Owen D. Young's Speech at Dinner," *New York Times*, December 12, 1924, 12, ProQuest Historical Newspapers, New York Times (1851–2010).

4. E. Ross Bartley to CGD, January 20, 1925, DP-NU.

5. E. Ross Bartley to CGD, January 27, 1925, DP-NU.

6. "Vice President Causes Stir," *New York Times*, March 5, 1925, 1, ProQuest Historical Newspapers, New York Times (1851–2010).

7. Ibid.

8. William H. Taft to Charles P. Taft II, March 8, 1925, Taft Papers, Box 575, quoted in "Calvin Coolidge: A Study in Presidential Inaction," by Guy Fair Goodfellow, Ph.D. diss., University of Maryland, College Park, 1969, 346.

9. "Senators Comment Bitterly on Dawes," *New York Times*, March 5, 1925, 1, ProQuest Historical Newspapers, New York Times (1851–2010).

10. James O'Donnell Bennett, "Dawes Dazes Hoary Senate: Shouts Demand for Reform in Mossy Methods," *Chicago Daily Tribune*, March 5, 1925, 1, ProQuest Historical Newspapers, Chicago Tribune (1849–1999).

11. James O'Donnell Bennett, "Dawes Fails to Save Warren: Senate in Tie, Vice President Taking a Nap," *Chicago Daily Tribune*, March 11, 1925, 1, ProQuest Historical Newspapers, Chicago Tribune (1849–1999).

12. Ibid.

13. "General Dawes Takes a Nap," *Chicago Daily Tribune*, March 12, 1925, 8, ProQuest Historical Newspapers, Chicago Tribune (1849–1999).

14. Dawes, *Notes as Vice President*, 184.

15. James O'Donnell Bennett, "Paul Revere's Lamps Gleam Again as of Old," *Chicago Daily Tribune*, April 19, 1925, 1, ProQuest Historical Newspapers, Chicago Tribune (1849–1999).

16. Ibid.

17. James O'Donnell Bennett, "Fighting Dawes Whales Senate before Editors," *Chicago Daily Tribune*, April 22, 1925, 3, ProQuest Historical Newspapers, Chicago Tribune (1849–1999).

18. "Statement by States Showing the Number of Letters Received by the Vice President Commending Him upon His Inaugural Address," May 1, 1925, DP-NU.

19. "The Difference," unidentified newspaper clipping, n.p., January 21, 1926, DP-NU.

20. Ibid.

21. Edward D. Howell to CGD, January 21, 1926, DP-NU.

22. George Gilbert to CGD, January 21, 1926, DP-NU.

23. United States Federal Reserve System, "McFadden Act of 1927," *100 Years Federal Reserve System*, http://www.federalreservehistory.org/Events/DetailView/11.

24. Arthur Sears Henning, "Capital Fails to Thaw Out Dawes on Presidency," *Chicago Daily Tribune*, December 1, 1927, 5, ProQuest Historical Newspapers, Chicago Tribune (1849–1990).

25. Dawes, *Notes as Vice President*, 101–2.

26. Herman Smith, M.D., to CGD, April 15, 1927, DP-NU.

27. Michael Reese Health Trust, "Michael Reese Hospital History," http://www.healthtrust.net/content/about-us/michael-reese-hospital-history.

28. CGD to BGD, April 16, 1927, DP-NU.

29. Dawes, *Notes as Vice President*, 103–4.

30. "Dawes Hits Geneva Failure—British Prince and Premier Hear Attack," *Chicago Daily Tribune*, August 8, 1927, 1, ProQuest Historical Newspapers, Chicago Tribune (1849–1990).

31. "Dawes Criticizes Failure of Geneva Naval Parley in Peace Bridge Speech—Address Causes Stir," *New York Times*, August 8, 1927, 1, ProQuest Historical Newspapers, New York Times (1851–2010).

32. Dawes, *Notes as Vice President*, 104.

33. Ibid., 52.

34. Ibid., 91.

35. Dawes, *Notes as Vice President*, 75.

36. Carl T. Schmidt, *German Business Cycles, 1924–1933* (Washington, D.C.: National Bureau of Economic Research, 1934), 45, http://www.nber.org/chapters/c4934.pdf.

37. Dawes, *Notes as Vice President*, 77.

38. U.S. Department of State, Office of the Historian, "The Dawes Plan, the Young Plan, German Reparations, and Inter-Allied War Debts," *Milestones: 1921–1936*, https://history.state.gov/milestones/1921–1936/dawes.

39. Dawes, *Notes as Vice President*, 34–35.

40. Dawes, *Notes as Vice President*, 115.

41. Ibid., 126.

42. Ibid., 127–28.

43. Ibid., 183.

44. Ibid., 216.

45. Ibid., 229–30.

46. Ibid., 254.

47. Ibid., 309.

48. "Dawes and Curtis Clash over Rules," *Daily Boston Globe*, March 5, 1929, 29, ProQuest Historical Newspapers, Boston Globe (1872–1982).

49. Ibid.

50. Dawes, *Notes as Vice President*, 255.

Chapter 13

1. Special to the *New York Times*, "Dawes Makes Plain San Domingo Task," *New York Times*, March 4, 1929, ProQuest Historical Newspapers, New York Times (1923–Current File).

2. Horacio Vásquez, "Dawes, Economy, and Finances," transcription and translation of speech delivered on Listín Diario, Santo Domingo, Dominican Republic, March 7, 1929, n.p., DP-NU.

3. Memorandum of Understanding between Government of the Dominican Republic and Charles G. Dawes, February 20, 1929, n.p., DP-NU.

4. CGD to Owen D. Young, February 28, 1929, DP-NU.

5. CGD to Sumner Welles, March 19, 1929, DP-NU.

6. List of participants in mission to Dominican Republic, n.d., n.p., DP-NU.

7. CGD to Owen D. Young, March 7, 1929, DP-NU.

8. "Ambassador Dawes," *New York Times*, April 10, 1929, 22, ProQuest Historical Newspapers, New York Times (1851–2010).

9. Will Rogers, "Will Rogers Discusses Heflin and Dawes as an Ambassador," *New York Times*, April 10, 1929, 24, ProQuest Historical Newspapers, New York Times (1851–2010); "Dawes Tackles Great Britain," *Literary Digest* 101, no. 3 (April 20, 1929): 12, http://www.unz.org/Pub/LiteraryDigest-1929apr20?View=PDF.

10. J. F. Essary, "Dawes Chosen U.S. Envoy to Great Britain," *Baltimore Sun*, April 10, 1929, 1, ProQuest Historical Newspapers, Baltimore Sun (1837–1988).

11. Charles G. Dawes, *Notes as Vice President*, 269.

12. Charles G. Dawes, *Journal as Ambassador to Great Britain* (New York: Macmillan, 1939), 11.

13. Ibid., 13.

14. George Vincent Fagan, "Anglo-American Naval Relations, 1927–1937," Ph.D. diss., University of Pennsylvania, Philadelphia, 1954, 98–99.

15. Charles G. Dawes, *Journal as Ambassador to Great Britain*, 14–15.

16. Ibid., 18–22.

17. *Foreign Affairs*, London, XI (July 1929), 153, quoted in Fagan, "Anglo-American Naval Relations, 1927–1937," 112.

18. Charles G. Dawes, *Journal as Ambassador to Great Britain*, 27.

19. Fagan, "Anglo-American Naval Relations," 143.

20. Edwin L. James, "Premier Acts on Navies: Halts British Building to Press Negotiations with America," *New York Times*, July 25, 1929, 1, ProQuest Historical Newspapers, New York Times (1851–2010).

21. Edwin L. James, "Navy Halt Elates Britain; Hoover's Move Applauded; Paris Weighs Her Position," *New York Times*, July 26, 1926, 1, ProQuest Historical Newspapers, New York Times (1851–2010).

22. Charles G. Dawes, *Journal as Ambassador to Great Britain*, 44.

23. "Washington Hails Naval Parity Move," *New York Times*, July 26, 1929, 1, ProQuest Historical Newspapers, New York Times (1851–2010).

24. Central Hanover Bank and Trust Company (New York) to CGD, December 7, 1929, DP-NU.

25. CGD to Charles Cutler Dawes, September 5, 1929, DP-NU.

26. CGD to BDG, July 16, 1929, DP-NU.

27. HMD to CGD, August 15, 1929, DP-NU.

28. CGD to HMD, August 31, 1929, DP-NU.

29. CGD to HMD, September 17, 1929, DP-NU.

30. Dawes, *Journal as Ambassador to Great Britain*, 94.

31. HMD to CGD, July 1, 1929, DP-NU.

32. HMD to CGD, October 1, 1929, DP-NU.

33. "Premier Issues Hit Hard: Unexpected Torrent of Liquidation Again Hits Market," *New York Times*, October 29, 1929, 1, ProQuest Historical Newspapers, New York Times (1851–2010).

34. "Echoes of Day's New Avalanche in Stock Market," *Chicago Tribune*, October 29, 1929, 31, ProQuest Historical Newspapers, Chicago Tribune (1849–1990).

35. "Premier Issues Hit Hard," *New York Times*.

36. Dawes, *Journal as Ambassador to Great Britain*, 98–99.

37. Ibid., 102.

38. Ibid., 44.

39. "Morrow and Adams Join Naval Parley," *New York Times*, November 21, 1929, 1, ProQuest Historical Newspapers, New York Times (1851–2010).

40. Griscom, *Diplomatically Speaking*, 417.

41. Robert H. Ferrell, "A Dawes Diplomatic Dinner," *Journal of the Illinois State Historical Society (1908–1984)* 55, no. 3 (Autumn 1962): 252, http://www.jstor.org/stable/40190337.

42. Ibid., 254.

43. Ibid., 251.

44. William R. Dawes to CGD, December 28, 1929, DP-NU.

45. CGD to BGD, December 28, 1929, DP-NU.

46. CGD to HMD, December 30, 1929, DP-NU.

47. HMD to CGD, December 11, 1929, DP-NU.

48. Henry Dawes to HMD, January 8, 1930, DP-NU.

49. "Hoover Says Advance of World Peace Rests on Navy Conference at London," *New York Times,* January 8, 1930, 1, ProQuest Historical Newspapers, New York Times (1851–2010).

50. "4 Main Obstacles Face Naval Parley," *New York Times,* January 6, 1930, 9, ProQuest Historical Newspapers, New York Times (1851–2010).

51. Dawes, *Journal as Ambassador to Great Britain,* 171.

52. Office of the Historian, U.S. Department of State, "The London Naval Conference, 1930," *Milestones: 1921–1936,* https://history.state.gov/milestones/1921–1936/london-naval-conf.

53. Dawes, *Journal as Ambassador to Great Britain,* 193.

54. Ibid.

55. CGD to HMD, March 25, 1931, DP-NU.

56. HMD to CGD, March 6, 1931, DP-NU.

57. HMD to CGD, April 15, 1931, DP-NU.

58. Statement by CGD, May 9, 1931, DP-NU.

59. Dawes, *Journal as Ambassador to Great Britain,* 196.

60. Ibid., 348.

61. Ibid.

62. "Dawes Remains Honorary Head in Bank Merger," *Chicago Tribune,* June 13, 1931, 5, ProQuest Historical Newspapers, Chicago Tribune (1849–1990).

63. Stanley Lebergott, "Annual Estimates of Unemployment in the United States, 1900–1954," in *The Measurement and Behavior of Unemployment, A Conference of the Universities-National Bureau of Economic Research* (Princeton, N.J.: Princeton University Press, 1957), 213–38, http://www.nber.org/chapters/c2644.pdf.

64. United States Department of Commerce, Bureau of Foreign and Domestic Commerce, *Survey of Current Business,* vol. 22 (Washington, D.C.: Government Printing Office, 1942), 12.

65. Dawes, *Journal as Ambassador to Great Britain,* 355–56.

66. CGD to HMD, October 8, 1931, DP-NU.

67. HMD to CGD, November 17, 1931, DP-NU.

68. CGD to HMD, November 9, 1931, DP-NU.

69. HMD to CGD, December 4, 1930, DP-NU.

70. Richard A. Current, *Secretary Stimson: A Study in Statecraft* (New Brunswick, N.J.: Rutgers University Press, 1954), 83, Internet Archive, http://archive.org/stream/seretarystimsona006740mbp/seretarystimsona006740mbp_djvu.txt.

71. Dawes, *Journal as Ambassador to Great Britain*, 430.

72. HMD to CGD, November 17, 1931, DP-NU.

Chapter 14

1. "Chicago Bankers Pleased with Dawes as Fund Director," *Chicago Daily Tribune*, January 20, 1932, 6, ProQuest Historical Newspapers, Chicago Tribune (1849–1990).

2. William Occomy, "Business Review," *Pittsburgh Courier*, January 30, 1932, 10, ProQuest Historical Newspapers, Pittsburgh Courier (1911–2002).

3. Michael Gou, Gary Richardson, Alejandro Komai, and Daniel Park, "Banking Acts of 1932," *100 Years Federal Reserve System*, http://www.federalreserve history.org/Events/DetailView/12.

4. J. Franklin Ebersole, "One Year of the Reconstruction Finance Corporation," *Quarterly Journal of Economics* 47, no. 3 (May 1933): 473, http://www.jstor.org/stable/1883981.

5. "Dawes's Statement on Reconstruction," *New York Times*, April 22, 1932, 2, ProQuest Historical Newspapers, New York Times (1851–2010).

6. Ibid.

7. Gary Richardson, "Banking Panics of 1930 and 1931," *100 Years Federal Reserve System*, http://www.federalreservehistory.org/Events/DetailView/20.

8. "Bank Issues Here Sag during Week," *Chicago Daily Tribune*, September 20, 1931, A7, ProQuest Historical Newspapers, Chicago Tribune (1849–1990).

9. Maury Klein, *The Power Makers: Steam, Electricity, and the Men Who Invented America* (New York: Bloomberg Press, 2008), 435.

10. Ibid.

11. Ibid.

12. Ibid., 436.

13. Ibid., 436–37.

14. Ibid., 437.

15. Ibid., 438.

16. RCD to CGD, February 3, 1931, DP-NU.

17. "Short Covering Unable to Cover Decline on Curb," *Chicago Daily Tribune*, September 20, 1931, A7, ProQuest Historical Newspapers, Chicago Tribune (1849–1990).

18. Samuel Insull to CGD, October 2, 1931, DP-NU.

19. Sherman, "Charles Gates Dawes: An Entrepreneurial Biography," 120.

20. Klein, *The Power Makers*, 440.

21. Ibid.

22. Sherman, "Charles Gates Dawes: An Entrepreneurial Biography," 125.

23. "The Chicago Bank Failures," *Literary Digest* 114, no. 2 (July 9, 1932): 37, http://unz.org/Pub/LiteraryDigest-1932jul09:37.

24. Jesse H. Jones, "The Dramatic Story of the $90 Million Loan," *Finance*, August 25, 1945, 30.

25. Sherman, "Charles Gates Dawes: An Entrepreneurial Biography," 128–29.

26. Jones, "The Dramatic Story of the $90 Million Loan," 30.

27. Howard Wood, "Dawes Makes Statement on Cent. Republic," *Chicago Daily Tribune*, June 28, 1932, 23, ProQuest Historical Newspapers, Chicago Tribune (1849–1990).

28. C. W. Delamatre to CGD, August 9, 1932, DP-NU.

29. CGD to C. W. Delamatre, August 12, 1932, DP-NU.

30. "Senate Votes to Investigate Loans by RFC," *Chicago Daily Tribune*, July 12, 1932, 4, ProQuest Historical Newspapers, Chicago Daily Tribune (1923–1963).

31. Display Ad 30, *Chicago Tribune*, October 7, 1932, 31, ProQuest Historical Newspapers, Chicago Tribune (1849–1990).

32. Thomas Furlong, "Cent. Republic Owners Ratify Bank Transfer," *Chicago Daily Tribune*, November 20, 1932, A7, ProQuest Historical Newspapers, Chicago Tribune (1849–1990).

33. Sherman, "Charles Gates Dawes: An Entrepreneurial Biography," 132–33.

34. CGD to James G. Harbord, December 14, 1932, DP-NU.

35. F. E. Compton to CGD, October 7, 1932, DP-NU.

36. W. E. Clow to CGD, October 6, 1932, DP-NU.

37. Dorothy D. Carothers to CGD, October 16, 1932, DP-NU.

38. CGD to Dorothy D. Carothers, October 28, 1932, DP-NU.

39. R. G. Cole to CGD, December 5, 1932, DP-NU.

40. CGD to R.G. Cole, n.d., DP-NU.

41. "Complete Text of Hoover's Address at St. Louis," *Atlanta Constitution*, November 5, 1932, 2, ProQuest Historical Newspapers, Atlanta Constitution (1881–1945).

42. Ibid.

43. Ibid.

44. John Woolley and Gerhard Peters, "Election of 1932," in *American Presidency Project: Presidential Elections* (Santa Barbara: University of California, Santa Barbara, 1999–2016), http://www.presidency.ucsb.edu/showelection.php ?year=1932.

45. CGD to Herbert Hoover, November 9, 1932, DP-NU.

46. Newark Hospital Association Invoice, December 14, 1932, DP-NU.

47. CGD to Dana McCutcheon Dawes, December 14, 1932, DP-NU.

48. CGD to I. B. Humphreys, November 10, 1932, DP-NU.

49. CGD to James G. Harbord, December 29, 1932, DP-NU.

50. BGD to CGD, December 31, 1932, DP-NU.

51. G. R. Cooksey, Secretary of the Reconstruction Finance Corporation, to CGD, February 20, 1933.

52. CGD to G. R. Cooksey, March 3, 1933.

53. Howard Wood, "Cent. Republic Reduces R.F.C. [Reconstruction Finance Corporation] Debt 23 Million," *Chicago Daily Tribune*, February 4, 1933, 23, ProQuest Historical Newspapers, Chicago Daily Tribune (1923–1963).

54. Sherman, "Charles Gates Dawes: An Entrepreneurial Biography," 135.

55. "Old Dawes Bank Owners Lose 14 Million in Fight," *Chicago Daily Tribune*, October 10, 1939, 23, ProQuest Historical Newspapers, Chicago Daily Tribune (1923–1963).

56. Ibid., 137.

57. "Opening Day's Crowd Cheers Fair Officials," *Chicago Daily Tribune*, May 28, 1933, 2, ProQuest Historical Newspapers, Chicago Daily Tribune (1923–1963).

58. Earl Mullin, "Fair Shows Half Million Profit; Receipts Gaining," *Chicago Daily Tribune*, July 22, 1934, 7, ProQuest Historical Newspapers, Chicago Daily Tribune (1923–1963).

59. "Dawes Bank," *Time* 28, no. 20 (November 16, 1936): 121, Academic Search Complete, http://search.ebscohost.com.turing.library.northwestern.edu /login.aspx?direct=true&db=a9h&AN=54810818&site=ehost-live.

60. "Dawes Family Investment Co. to Be Dissolved," *Chicago Daily Tribune*, April 30, 1938, 23, ProQuest Historical Newspapers, Chicago Daily Tribune (1923–1963).

61. Philip Hampson, "Old RFC Dawes Bank Loan Paid with Interest," *Chicago Daily Tribune*, September 15, 1944, 29, ProQuest Historical Newspapers, Chicago Daily Tribune (1923–1963).

62. "Capital Gains Tax Is Assailed by Gen. Dawes," *Chicago Daily Tribune*, May 19, 1939, 31, ProQuest Historical Newspapers, Chicago Daily Tribune (1923–1963).

63. John Fisher, "Dawes Advises How to Balance Federal Budget," *Chicago Daily Tribune*, May 1, 1940, 33, ProQuest Historical Newspapers, Chicago Daily Tribune (1923–1963).

64. E. L. Woodward, "Reparations," *Economic History Review* 13, no. 1–2 (1943): 128, http://www.jstor.org/stable/2590529.

65. Charles Callan Tansill, "Book Reviews: A *Journal of Reparations*," *Mississippi Valley Historical Review* 27, no. 2 (September 1940): 312, http://www.jstor.org/stable/1896849.

66. "Let One Leader Push Rearming, Dawes Pleads," *Chicago Daily Tribune*, June 20, 1940, 29, ProQuest Historical Newspapers, Chicago Daily Tribune (1923–1963).

67. "Gen. Dawes Hits Drive to Force Nation into War," *Chicago Daily Tribune*, November 9, 1940, 3, ProQuest Historical Newspapers, Chicago Daily Tribune (1923–1963).

68. Herbert Hoover to CGD, May 1, 1941, DP-NU.

69. Herbert Hoover to CGD, November 3, 1941, DP-NU.

Chapter 15

1. Philip Hampson, "Gen. Charles Dawes Peers into Past: 85 Years of It," *Chicago Daily Tribune*, August 27, 1950, 1, ProQuest Historical Newspapers, Chicago Daily Tribune (1923–1963).

2. "Senate Hails Gen. Dawes, 84 Saturday," *Chicago Daily Tribune*, August 26, 1949, 1, ProQuest Historical Newspapers, Chicago Daily Tribune (1923–1963).

3. CGD to Herbert Hoover, April 17, 1942, DP-NU.

4. Herbert Hoover to CGD, April 6, 1943, DP-NU.

5. CGD to Herbert Hoover, April 19, 1943, DP-NU.

6. Herbert Hoover to CGD, February 12, 1945, DP-NU.

7. Jerry N. Hess, "Frank Pace, Jr.: Oral History Interview," Harry S. Truman Library and Museum, Independence, Mo., January 22, 1972, http://www.truman library.org/oralhist/pacefj2.htm.

8. CGD to Herbert Hoover, May 26, 1949, DP-NU.

9. Herbert Hoover to CGD, August 29, 1949, DP-NU.

10. "Charles G. Dawes, Ex-Vice President Dies," *Chicago Daily Tribune*, April 24, 1951, 1, ProQuest Historical Newspapers, Chicago Daily Tribune (1923–1963).

11. "Charles Gates Dawes," *Chicago Daily Tribune*, April 25, 1951, 16, ProQuest Historical Newspapers, Chicago Daily Tribune (1923–1963).

BIBLIOGRAPHY

Books

Adams, Rosemary K., ed. *A Wild Kind of Boldness: The Chicago History Reader.* Chicago: Chicago Historical Society; Grand Rapids, Mich., William B. Eerdmans, 1998.

Andrews, Martin R., ed. *History of Marietta and Washington County, and Representative Citizens.* Chicago: Biographical Publishing Co., 1902. https://play .google.com/books/reader2?id=1d4yAQAAMAAJ.

Baruch, Bernard M. *The Making of the Reparation and Economic Sections of the Treaty.* New York: Harper and Brothers, 1920.

Brinkley, Alan. *American History: A Survey.* 11th ed. vol. 2. New York: McGraw Hill, 2003.

Bryan, William Jennings, and Mary Baird Bryan. *The Memoirs of William Jennings Bryan.* Philadelphia: United Publishers of America, 1925.

Cannadine, David. *Mellon: An American Life.* New York: Alfred A. Knopf, 2006.

Chernow, Ron. *The House of Morgan.* New York: Grove Press, 1990.

Clements, Kendrick A. *The Life of Herbert Hoover: Imperfect Visionary, 1918–1928.* New York: Palgrave Macmillan, 2010.

Cooke, James J. *Pershing and His Generals: Command and Staff in the AEF* [American Expeditionary Forces]. Westport, Conn.: Praeger, 1997.

Coolidge, Calvin. *The Autobiography of Calvin Coolidge.* New York: Cosmopolitan Book Corporation, 1929. Reprint of the 1929 New York edition, Universal Digital Library, 2004. http://www.archive.org/details/autobiographyofc 011710mbp.

Council for Library and Museum Extension. *Educational Opportunities in Chicago.* Chicago: Council for Library and Museum Extension, 1912. https:// books.google.com/books?id=65MnAAAAMAAJ.

Current, Richard A. *Secretary Stimson: A Study in Statecraft.* New Brunswick, N.J.: Rutgers University Press, 1954. Internet Archive. http://archive.org/ stream/seretarystimsona006740mbp/seretarystimsona006740mbp_djvu.txt.

Cutter, William Richard. *New England Families, Genealogical and Memorial,* vol. 2. New York: Lewis Historical Publishing, 1913. http://play.google.com/ books/reader2?id=ofcsAAAAYAAJ.

Dawes, Charles G. *The Banking System of the United States and Its Relationship to the Money and Business of the Country.* Chicago: Rand McNally, 1894. Google e-book edition. http://books.google.com/booksreader?id=ZO9HAA AAIAAJ.

———. *Essays and Speeches.* Boston: Houghton Mifflin, 1915.

———. *The First Year of the Budget of the United States.* New York: Harper and Brothers, 1923.

———. *Journal as Ambassador to Great Britain.* New York: Macmillan, 1939.

———. *A Journal of Reparations.* London: Macmillan, 1939.

———. *A Journal of the Great War.* 2 vols. Boston: Houghton Mifflin, 1921.

———. *A Journal of the McKinley Years, 1893–1913.* Edited by Bascom N. Timmons. Chicago: Lakeside Press, 1950.

———. *Notes as Vice President, 1928–1929.* Boston: Little, Brown, 1935. Digitized version of the 1935 Boston edition by HathiTrust Digital Library. http://babel.hathitrust.org/cgi/pt?id=mdp.39015018008246;view=1up;seq=36.

Dawes, Mary Beman Gates. *A History of the Establishment of Diplomatic Relations with Persia.* Marietta, Ohio: E. R. Alderman and Sons, 1887. https://archive.org/stream/ahistoryestabli00dawegoog#page/n55/mode/2up.

Dawes, Rufus C. *The Dawes Plan in the Making.* Indianapolis: Bobbs-Merrill, 1925.

Dawes, Rufus R. *Service with the Sixth Wisconsin Volunteers.* Marietta, Ohio: E. R. Alderman and Sons, 1890. http://books.google.com/books/reader?id=JRxCA AAAIAAJ.

Eisenhower, John S. D. *Yanks: The Epic Story of the American Army in World War I.* New York: Free Press, 2001.

Federal Reserve Bank of St. Louis. *Message of the President of the United States Transmitting the Budget for the Service of the Fiscal Year Ending June 30, 1923.* Washington, D.C.: Government Printing Office, 1921. http://fraser.stlouis fed.org/docs/publications/usbudget/usbudget_1923.pdf.

Ferris, Mary Walton. *Dawes-Gates Ancestral Lines: A Memorial Volume.* 2 vols. Milwaukee: Wisconsin Cuneo Press [private printing], 1943.

Gilbert, Clinton Wallace. *"You Take Your Choice."* New York: G. P. Putnam Sons, 1924.

Gilbert, Martin. *The First World War: A Complete History.* New York: Henry Holt, 1994.

Gomes, Leonard. *German Reparations, 1919–1932: A Historical Survey.* London: Palgrave Macmillan, 2010.

Griscom, Lloyd C. *Diplomatically Speaking.* Boston: Little, Brown, 1940.

Gustaitis, Joseph. *Chicago's Greatest Year, 1893.* Carbondale: Southern Illinois University Press, 2013.

Hagood, Johnson. *The Services of Supply: A Memoir of the Great War.* Boston: Houghton Mifflin, 1927. http://hdl.handle.net/2027/mdp.39015063013919.

Harbord, James G. *Leaves from a War Diary.* New York: Dodd, Mead, 1925.

Hayes, A.B., and Sam D. Cox. *History of the City of Lincoln, Nebraska.* Lincoln, Neb.: State Journal Company, 1889. http://www.archive.org/details/historycityoflin00haye.

Holland, Henry Ware. *William Dawes and His Ride with Paul Revere: An Essay Read before the New England Genealogical Society on June 7, A.D. 1876.* Boston: John Wilson and Son, 1878. http://books.google.com/books/reader?id=WD2477M66jAC.

Kenney, David. *An Uncertain Tradition: U.S. Senators from Illinois, 1818–2003.* Carbondale: Southern Illinois University Press, 2003.

Klein, Maury. *The Power Makers: Steam, Electricity, and the Men Who Invented America.* New York: Bloomberg Press, 2008.

Koenig, Louis W. *Bryan: A Political Biography of William Jennings Bryan.* New York: G. P. Putnam's Sons, 1971.

Lamont, Thomas W. *Henry P. Davison: The Record of a Useful Life.* New York: Harper and Brothers, 1933. https://archive.org/stream/henrypdavison the017785.

Langland, James, ed. *Chicago Daily News Almanac and Yearbook for 1922.* Chicago: Chicago Daily News, 1921. https://books.google.com/books?id=JQ8fA QAAMAAJ.

Lawrence, William. *Decisions of the First Comptroller in the Department of the United States Treasury, Vol. I,* 2nd ed. Washington, D.C.: Government Printing Office, 1881. http://books.google.com/books?id=zx0rAAAAYAAJ.

Lebergott, Stanley. "Annual Estimates of Unemployment in the United States, 1900–1954." In *The Measurement and Behavior of Unemployment, A Conference of the Universities-National Bureau of Economic Research,* 213–38. Princeton, N.J.: Princeton University Press, 1957. http://www.nber.org/chapters /c2644.pdf.

Livesey, Anthony. *The Historical Atlas of World War I.* New York: Henry Holt, 1994.

Maddox, Robert James. *William E. Borah and American Foreign Policy.* Baton Rouge: Louisiana State University Press, 1969.

Marshall, S. L. A. *World War I.* Boston: Houghton Mifflin, 1992.

McCarthy, Kathleen D. *Noblesse Oblige: Charity and Cultural Philanthropy in Chicago, 1849–1929.* Chicago: University of Chicago Press, 1982.

McCartney, Laton. *The Teapot Dome Scandal: How Big Oil Bought the Harding White House and Tried to Steal the Country.* New York: Random House, 2008.

McDaniel, George William. *Smith Wildman Brookhart: Iowa's Renegade Republican.* Ames: Iowa State University Press, 1995.

Parker, Edwin B. *Final Report of United States Liquidation Commission.* Washington, D.C.: War Department, 1920.

Perry, Sigrid Pohl. "Charles Gates Dawes: From Private Face to Public Place." In *At Home in Evanston: The Charles Gates Dawes House,* edited by Elizabeth A. Myers, 51–70. Evanston, Ill.: Evanston Historical Society, 2000.

Pershing, John J. *General Pershing's Official Story of the American Expeditionary Forces in France.* New York: Sun Sales, 1919. http://hdl.handle.net/2027/loc.ark:/13960/t40s0g00m.

———. *My Experiences in the World War.* New York: Frederick A. Stokes, 1931. http://hdl.handle.net/2027/mdp.39015014559135.

Platt, Harold L. *The Electric City: Energy and the Growth of the Chicago Area, 1880–1930.* Chicago: University of Chicago Press, 1991.

Poole, William Frederick. *The Ordinance of 1787, and Dr. Manasseh Cutler as an Agent of Its Formation.* Cambridge, Mass: Welch, Bigelow, 1876. https://books.google.com/books?id=x4d2AAAAMAAJ.

Poor's Manual of Public Utilities, 1915. New York: Poor, 1915. https://books.google.com/books?id=DWk3AQAAMAAJ.

Pope, George S. "Caddo Oil and Gas Field." *Bulletin—United States Geological Survey.* Bulletin 428. Washington, D.C.: Government Printing Office, 1910. https://books.google.com/books?id=ww4lAQAAIAAJ.

Proceedings before the Committee on Privileges and Elections and a Subcommittee Thereof of the United States Senate in the Matter of the Investigation of Certain Charges against William Lorimer, a Senator from the State of Illinois. 3rd Sess., 61st Cong., Report No. 942, Part 2. December 21, 1910. Retrieved from Google Books. https://books.google.com/books?id=E2YDAAAAYAAJ.

Ranson, Edward. *The American Presidential Election of 1924: A Political Study of Calvin Coolidge.* 2 vols. Lewiston, N.Y.: Edwin Mellen, 2008.

Schacht, Hjalmar. *The End of Reparations.* Translated by Lewis Gannett. New York: Jonathan Cape and Harrison Smith, 1931.

Schmidt, Carl T. *German Business Cycles, 1924–1933.* Washington, D.C.: National Bureau of Economic Research, 1934. http://www.nber.org/chapters/c4934.pdf.

Schmiel, Eugene D. *Citizen-General: Jacob Dolson Cox and the Civil War Era.* Athens: Ohio University Press, 2014.

Senate Committee on Military Affairs, United States Congress. *Reorganization of the Army, Hearings before the Subcommittee of the Committee on Military Affairs.* Vol. 2. Washington, D.C.: Government Printing Office, 1920. http://books.google.com/books/reader?id=32hKAAAAYAAJ.

Sering, Max. *Germany under the Dawes Plan: Origin, Legal Foundations, and Economic Effects of the Reparation Payments*. Translated by S. Milton Hart. London: P. S. King and Sons, 1929.

Starling, Edmund W. *Starling of the White House: The Story of the Man Whose Secret Service Detail Guarded Five Presidents from Woodrow Wilson to Franklin D. Roosevelt, as Told to Thomas Sugrue*. New York: Simon and Schuster, 1946.

Surface, Frank Macy, and Raymond L. Bland. *American Food in the World War and Reconstruction Period*. Palo Alto, Calif.: Stanford University Press, 1931.

Tooze, Adam. *The Deluge: The Great War, America, and the Remaking of the Global World Order, 1916–1931*. New York: Viking, 2014.

United States Department of Veterans Affairs. *VA History in Brief*. Washington, D.C.: Government Printing Office, 1977.

Vinson, John Chalmers. *William E. Borah and the Outlawry of War*. Athens: University of Georgia Press, 1957.

Warshaw, Shirley Anne. *Guide to the White House Staff*. Los Angeles: Sage Reference, CQ Press, 2013.

Wormell, Jeremy. *Management of the National Debt of the United Kingdom, 1900–1932*. London: Routledge, 2000.

Zieger, Robert H. *Republicans and Labor: 1919–1929*. Lexington: University of Kentucky Press, 1969.

Zwetsch, H. C. *A Brief History of the Natural Gas Industry*. New York: Zwetsch, Heinzelmann, 1927. http://babel.hathitrust.org/cgi/pt?id=mdp.39015021303642;view=1up;seq=1.

Archival Material

George B. Cortelyou Papers. Library of Congress. Washington, D.C.

Caro D. B. Dawes Correspondence. Dawes Family Papers. Evanston (Ill.) History Center.

Charles G. Dawes Papers. Northwestern University Library Special Collections, Evanston, Ill.

Dawes, Charles G. *1st Scrapbook of Charles G. Dawes 1882–1891*. Northwestern University Library Special Collections, Evanston, Ill.

Dawes, Dana McCutcheon. Oral History. 1988. Dawes Family Papers. Evanston (Ill.) History Center.

Dawes, Helen Palmer. *Journal*. Northwestern University Library Special Collections, Evanston, Ill.

Ericson, Carolyn Dawes. "Family History," 2 vols. Unpublished manuscript. n.d. Dawes Family Papers. Evanston (Ill.) History Center.

Ferris, Mary Walton. *Dawes-Gates Ancestral Lines: A Memorial Volume Containing the American Ancestry of Rufus R. Dawes*. Privately printed, 1943. Northwestern University Library Special Collections, Evanston, Ill.

Warren G. Harding Papers. Library of Congress. Washington, D.C.

William McKinley Papers. Library of Congress. Washington, D.C.

John Callan O'Laughlin Papers. Library of Congress. Washington, D.C.

Perry, Sigrid Pohl. "Service of the Hearth: The Lives of Caro Blymyer Dawes and Helen Palmer Dawes." Lecture delivered to Evanston History Society, Evanston, Ill., November 8, 1995.

William Howard Taft Papers. Library of Congress. Washington, D.C.

Periodicals

"An Expert View of the Dawes Plan." *Literary Digest* 81, no. 7 (May 17, 1924): 20–21. http://unz.org/Pub/LiteraryDigest-1924may17:1.

Bagby, Wesley M. "The 'Smoke Filled Room' and the Nomination of Warren G. Harding." *Mississippi Valley Historical Review* 41, no. 4 (March 1955): 657–74. http://www.jstor.org/stable/1889182.

Bankers Magazine 83 (January–June 1914). New York: Bankers Publishing Company, 1914. http://babel.hathitrust.org/cgi/pt?id=uc1.b2875465;view=1 up;seq=11.

Beth, Richard S., and Valerie Heitshusen. "Filibusters and Cloture in the Senate." *Congressional Research Service.* May 31, 2013. http://www.senate.gov/CRSReports/crs-publish.cfm?pid=%270E%2C*PLW%3D%22P%20%20%0A.

Blount, James H. "The Lorimer Case." *North American Review* 193, no. 667 (June 1911): 871–78. http://www.jstor.org/stable/25106952.

Burns, Arthur Robert. "Surplus Government Property and Foreign Policy." *Foreign Affairs* 3, no. 3 (April 1945): 485–95. http://www.jstor.org/stable/20029912.

Byerly, Carol R. "The U.S. Military and the Influenza Pandemic of 1918–1919." *Public Health Reports* 125, supplement 3 (2010): 82–91.

"Chicago and Vicinity," *Bankers' Magazine* 84, no. 5 (May 1912): 733. ProQuest Historical Newspapers.

Costigliola, Frank. "The United States and the Reconstruction of Germany in the 1920s." *Business History Review* 50, no. 4 (Winter 1976): 477–502. http://www.jstor.org/stable/3113137.

Crowley, Carolyn Hughes, "Meet Me at the Automat." *Smithsonian Magazine.* August 2001. http://www.smithsonianmag.com/history/meet-me-at-the-automat-47804151/?no-ist.

"Dawes Bank." *Time* 28, no. 20 (November 16, 1936): 121. Academic Search Complete. http://search.ebscohost.com.turing.library.northwestern.edu/log in.aspx?direct=true&db=a9h&AN=54810818&site=ehost-live.

"The Dawes Bank Charges." *Literary Digest* 83, no. 4 (October 25, 1924): 8–9. http://www.unz.org/Pub/LiteraryDigest-1924oct25–00008.

Dawes, Charles G. "Annual Report of the Comptroller of the Currency." *Bankers Magazine* 57, no. 6 (December 1898). American Periodicals.

———. "Annual Report of the Comptroller of the Currency." *Bankers Magazine* 59, no. 6 (December 1899). American Periodicals.

———. "The Next President of the United States and the High Cost of Living." *Saturday Evening Post* 193, no. 14 (October 2, 1920): 7, 182–86.

Dunlap, Annette B. "William McKinley and the Making of the Gold Standard." *White House History* no. 39 (Spring 2016).

Ebersole, J. Franklin. "One Year of the Reconstruction Finance Corporation." *Quarterly Journal of Economics* 47, no. 3 (May 1933): 454–92. http://www.jstor.org/stable/1883981.

Esposito, David M. "Woodrow Wilson and the Origins of the AEF [American Expeditionary Forces]." *Presidential Studies Quarterly* 19, no. 1, Part 1: American Foreign Policy for the 1990s, and Part 2: T. R., Wilson and the Progressive Era, 1901–1919 (Winter 1989): 127–40. http://www.jstor.org/stable/40574570.

European Relief Council. Interim Report of European Relief Council Including Statement of Contributions by States and Auditors' Preliminary Report on Accounts. New York: M. B. Brown, 1921. 4. http://libcudl.colorado.edu/wwi/pdf/i73698155.pdf.

Ferrell, Robert H. "A Dawes Diplomatic Dinner." *Journal of the Illinois State Historical Society* 55, no. 3 (Autumn 1962): 250–54. http://www.jstor.org/stable/40190337.

Ferrell, Robert H., ed. "Young Charley Dawes Goes to the Garfield Inauguration: A Diary." *Ohio History* 70, 4 (October 1961): 332–42. http://www.ohiohistory.org/ohstemplate.cfm.

"Foreign Financing after the European War." *Bonds and Mortgages* 63, no. 4 (April 1916): 4. https://books.google.com/books?id=xkJJAQAAMAAJ.

Gauss, Christian. "The Education of General Harbord." *Saturday Evening Post* 205, no. 5 (July 30, 1932): 28–63. Academic Search Alumni Edition, EBSCOhost. http://search.ebscohost.com/login.aspx?direct=true&Authtype=cookie,url,ip,uid&db=a2h&AN=18053250.

Ghent, Jocelyn Maynard and Frederic Cople Jaher. "The Chicago Business Elite: 1830–1930, a Collective Biography." *Business History Review* 50, no. 3 (Fall 1976): 288, Periodicals Archive Online.

"Glimpses of Banking in Chicago." *Bankers' Magazine* 78, no. 4 (April 1909). American Periodicals.

Goedeken, Edward A. "A Banker at War: The World War I Experiences of Charles Gates Dawes." *Illinois Historical Journal* 78, no. 3 (Autumn 1985): 195–206. http://www.jstor.org/stable/40191858.

———. "The Dawes-Pershing Relationship during World War I." *Nebraska History* 65 (1984): 108–29. http://www.nebraskahistory.org/publish/publicat/history/full-text/1984-1-Dawes_Pershing.pdf.

Greenberg, Gerald S. "Beman Gates and the *Marietta Intelligencer* 1839–1854." *Publishing History* 38 (1995): 55–75. doi:http://hdl.handle.net/1811/47389.

Grey of Fallodon, Viscount (Edward Grey). "Freedom of the Seas." *Foreign Affairs.* April 1930. http://www.foreignaffairs.com/articles/69053/viscount-grey-of-fallodon/freedom-of-the-seas.

Horn, Martin. "A Private Bank at War: J. P. Morgan & Co. and France, 1914–1918." *Business History Review* 74, no. 1 (Spring 2000): 85–112. http://www.jstor.org/stable/3116353.

Jones, Jesse H. "The Dramatic Story of the $90 Million Loan." *Finance.* August 25, 1945. 29–30, 52.

Kettler, Molly. "Tribute to Caro Blymyer Dawes." *TimeLines.* Evanston (Ill.) History Center. Spring 2013. 3–8.

Kohlsaat, H. H. "From McKinley to Harding: Personal Recollections of Our Presidents." *Saturday Evening Post* 195, no. 4 (July 22, 1922): 18–19. https://books.google.com/books?id=eCskAQAAMAAJ.

Koszewski, Andrew. "Career Differentiation: The Legal Community in Lincoln, Nebraska 1880–1891." *Great Plains Research: A Journal of Natural and Social Sciences.* Paper 76. 1992. http://digitalcommons.unl.edu/greatplainsresearch/76.

Link, Arthur S. "What Happened to the Progressive Movement in the 1920s?" *American Historical Review* 64, no. 4 (July 1959): 833–51. http://www.jstor.org/stable/1905118.

Lord, H. M. "War Department Finances." *Banking: Journal of the American Banking Association* 12, no. 11 (November 1919). http://books.google.com/books?id=brBLAQAAIAAJ.

"The Lorimer Case." *The Outlook* 97, no. 1 (January 7, 1911): 13. http://www.unz.org/Pub/Outlook-1911jan07-00013.

Mahoney, Timothy R. "The Great Sheedy Murder Trial and the Booster Ethos of the Gilded Age in Lincoln." *Nebraska History* 82 (2001): 163–79. http://www.nebraskahistory.org/publish/publicat/history/full-text/2001-Sheedy_Trial.pdf.

Millett, Lt. Col. John D. "The Direction of Supply Activities in the War Department: An Administrative Survey, I." *American Political Science Review* 38, no. 2 (April 1944): 249–65. http://www.jstor.org/stable/1950165.

"Natural Gas News." *Gas Record* 17, no. 9 (May 12, 1920). http://books.google .com/books?id=v1BCAQAAMAAJ.

Plehn, Carl C. "War Profits and Excess Profits Tax." *American Economic Review* 10, no. 2 (June 1920): 283–98. http://www.jstor.org/stable/1804867.

Richberg, Donald R. "De-Bunking Mr. Dawes." *New Republic* 39 (July 9, 1924): 180–83.

Roosevelt, Nicholas. "The Ruhr Occupation." *Foreign Affairs* 4, no. 1 (October 1925): 112–22. http://www.foreignaffairs.com/articles/68633/nicholas -roosevelt/the-ruhr-occupation.

Tansill, Charles Callan. "Book Reviews: *A Journal of Reparations.*" *Mississippi Valley Historical Review* 27, no. 2 (September 1940): 311–12. http://www.jstor .org/stable/1896849.

Tarr, Joel A. "J. R. Walsh of Chicago: A Case Study in Banking and Politics: 1881–1905." *Business History Review* 40, no. 4 (Winter 1966): 451–66. http:// www.jstor.org/stable/3112123.

United States Department of Commerce. *Survey of Current Business* 22 (May 1942).

Wilson, Woodrow. "When a Man Comes to Himself." *Century Magazine* 62 (June 1901): 268–72. http://www.unz.org/Pub/Century-1901jun-00268.

"'Wined' and Dined." *Gas Record* 17 (March 24, 1920). http://books.google .com/books?id=v1BCAQAAMAAJ.

Woodward, E. L. "Reparations." *Economic History Review* 13, no. 1–2 (1943): 127–29. http://www.jstor.org/stable/2590529.

Internet Resources

Abraham Lincoln Presidential Library and Museum. "Pure Oil Company Research Materials (1924–1964)." *Chronicling Illinois.* http://alplm-cdi.com/ chroniclingillinois/items/show/521.

AFL-CIO. "Labor History Timeline." *AFL-CIO: America's Unions.* http://www .aflcio.org/About/Our-History/Labor-History-Timeline.

Allen, Bernard L., and David Matchen. "Natural Gas and Petroleum." *The West Virginia Encyclopedia.* May 10, 2012. http://www.wvencyclopedia.org/ articles/1600.

Ancestry.com. "Bio: Francis Kilkenny." http://boards.ancestry.com/localities .britisles.ireland.let.general/4491/mb.ashx.

"Banker Dawes a Soldier." *Chicago Eagle.* September 1, 1917. In *Chronicling America: Historic American Newspapers.* Library of Congress. http://chronicling america.loc.gov/lccn/sn84025828/1917-09-01/ed-1/seq-1.pdf.

Brigham Young University Library. *The World War I Document Archive.* http:// wwi.lib.byu.edu/index.php/1917_Documents.

Brophy, L. A. "Charles Dawes Retires after Stormy Career." *Reading Eagle* (Reading, Pa.), March 4, 1929. http://news.google.com/newspapers?nid=1955& dat=19290302&id=GMEhAAAAIBAJ&sjid=A50FAAAAIBAJ&pg= 3058,688751.

Budget and Accounting Act of 1921. S. 1084. 67th Cong. (1921). https://bulk .resource.org/gao.gov/67–13/00001A37.pdf.

Business Historical Society, Harvard University. "Daniel G. Wing." *Bulletin of the Business Historical Society* (now *Business History Review*) 10, no. 1 (February 1936): 17–18. Published online July 24, 2012. doi:http://dx.doi.org/10 .1017/S0007680500007820.

Caddohistory.com. "Oil and Natural Gas." http://www.caddohistory.com/oil_ gas.html.

"Charles Beecher Warren." *Bay-Journal* (Bay City, Mich.). http://bjmi.us/ bay/1he/writings/warren-charles-b.html.

"Chicago Growth: 1850–1990." http://tigger.uic.edu/depts/ahaa/imagebase/ chimaps/mcclendon.html.

Chicago History Museum, Newberry Library, and Northwestern University. "Classical Music." In *Encyclopedia of Chicago*. Edited by Janice L. Reiff, Ann Durkin Keating, and James R. Grossman. http://www.encyclopedia.chicago history.org/pages/295.html.

City of Marietta, Ohio. "City of Marietta, Ohio." http://www.mariettaoh.net/ government/mayor/history.

Demographia. "US Population by State from 1900." http://www.demographia .com/db-state1900.htm.

Dunlap, Annette B. "William McKinley." In *Chronology of the U.S. Presidency, Vol. 3*. 739–72. Edited by Mathew Manweller. Santa Barbara, Calif.: ABC-CLIO, 2012. http://public.eblib.com/choice/publicfullrecord.aspx?p= 877598.

Evanston Women's History Project. "Helen Virginia Dawes (Palmer)." http:// www.epl.org/ewhp/display.php?bioid=101.

Executive Committee of the Indianapolis Monetary Convention. *Report of the Monetary Commission to the Executive Committee of the Indianapolis Monetary Convention*. n.p. 1897.

Federal Judicial Center. "History of the Federal Judiciary." http://www.fjc.gov/ history/home.nsf/page/talking_ji_tp.html.

Federal Reserve Bank of Philadelphia. "The Fed Today: History of Money and Banking in the U.S." http://www.philadelphiafed.org.

Federal Reserve Bank of Richmond. "Federal Reserve Act Signed by President Wilson." *Federal Reserve History*. http://www.federalreservehistory.org/ Events/DetailView/10.

―――. *One Hundred Years Federal Reserve System*. http://www.federalreserve history.org.

Federal Reserve Bank of St. Louis. Minutes No. 294, Reparations Commission. Meeting of June 6 and 7, 1922. n.p. https://fraser.stlouisfed.org/docs/historical /frbny/strong/strong_1600_01_reparation_commission_1921–1924.pdf.

Fox News Channel. "Republican National Convention Firsts." http://www .foxnews.com/projects/pdf/Republican_National_Convention_Firsts.pdf.

Georgen, Cynde. "John B. Kendrick: Cowboy, Cattle King, Governor, and US Senator." wyohistory.org, a project of the Wyoming State Historical Society. http://www.wyohistory.org/encyclopedia/john-kendrick.

Grabowski, John J., ed. *The Encyclopedia of Cleveland History*. Cleveland, Ohio: Case Western Reserve University, 1987. https://ech.case.edu.

Granacki Historic Consultants. "Architectural Resources in the Lakeshore Historic District Evanston, Illinois: A Summary and Inventory." Chicago: Granacki Historic Consultants, 2012. https://cityofevanston.org/assets/Evanston%20Lakeshore%20Final%20Report%20File%201%20%28report%20 and%20cover%29.pdf.

Heritage Research Center, "What Is Manufactured Gas?" http://www.heritage research.com/documents/More%20About%20Manufactured%20Gas.pdf.

Hess, Jerry N. "Frank Pace, Jr.: Oral History Interview." Harry S. Truman Library and Museum. Independence, Mo. January 22, 1972. http://www.trumanlibrary .org/oralhist/pacefj2.htm.

IIT (Illinois Institute of Technology) Chicago-Kent College of Law. "McGrain v. Daugherty." *Oyez Scholars*. http://www.oyez.org/cases/1901–1939/1924/1924_28.

Indiana Journalism Hall of Fame. "E. Ross Bartley 1971." http://indianajournal ismhof.org/1971/01/e-ross-bartley/.

Infoplease.com. "Cabinet Members under Harding." http://www.infoplease.com /ipa/A0101244.html.

―――. "Ku Klux Klan: The Second Ku Klux Klan." http://www.infoplease .com/encyclopedia/history/ku-klux-klan-the-second-ku-klux-klan.html.

Justia. "US Supreme Court." https://supreme.justia.com/cases/federal/us/184 /258/case.html.

Kendrick, M. Slade. "A Century and a Half of Federal Expenditures." National Bureau of Economic Research (1955). http://www.nber.org/books/kend55–1.

Kurz, Daniel B. "In Our Own Backyard: Klan Activity in the Garden State during the 1920's." http://sites.bergen.org/ourstory/Resources/NJ_Klan/Invisible %20Empire%201920s%20Maps/back.pdf.

Leip, David. "1896 Presidential General Election Results." *David Leip's Atlas of U.S. Presidential Elections*. http://uselectionatlas.org/RESULTS/national.php ?year=1896.

———. "1924 Presidential General Election Results," http://uselectionatlas .org/RESULTS/national.php?year=1924.

Library of Congress. "Democratic National Political Conventions 1832–2008." http://www.loc.gov/rr/main/democratic_conventions.pdf.

———. "Republican National Political Conventions 1856–2008." http://www .loc.gov/rr/main/republican_conventions.pdf.

Maine Historical Society. "The Nativist Klan." *Maine History Online.* https://www.mainememory.net/sitebuilder/site/783/slideshow/427/ display?format=list&prev_object_id=1192&prev_object=page&slide_ num=1.

McElwee, Neil. "Pure Oil Company." *Oil 150: Essays, Pennsylvania Oil Companies.* Posted February 23, 2009. http://www.oil150.com/essays/article?article _id=167.

Michael Reese Health Trust. "Michael Reese Hospital History." http://www .healthtrust.net/content/about-us/michael-reese-hospital-history.

Miller Center of Public Affairs, University of Virginia. *American President: A Reference Resource.* http://millercenter.org.

Murphy, Robert P. "The Depression You've Never Heard Of: 1920–1921." *The Freeman* 59, no. 10 (2009). Foundation for Economic Education (FEE). November 18, 2009. http://www.fee.org/the_freeman/detail/the-depression -youve-never-heard-of-1920-1921.

NebraskaStudies.org. "William Jennings Bryan." *Roots of Progressivism.* http:// www.nebraskastudies.org/0600/frameset_reset.html?http://www.nebraska studies.org/0600/stories/0601_0304.html.

Nobelprize.org. "Acceptance Speech: Acceptance by Charles Gates Dawes." Official website of the Nobel Prize. http://www.nobelprize.org/nobel_prizes/ peace/laureates/1925/dawes-acceptance.html.

Ohio Civil War Central. "Camp McClellan (Marietta, Ohio)." http://www .ohiocivilwarcentral.com/entry.php?rec=346.

Oulahan, Richard V. "Borah Agreed as Vice-Presidential Nominee in Midnight Conference of Convention Leaders." *New York Times,* June 12, 1924. http:// partners.nytimes.com/library/politics/camp/240612convention-gop-ra.html.

Plains Humanities Alliance, University of Nebraska–Lincoln. "Gilded Age Plains City." http://gildedage.unl.edu/.

Rebhahn, Peter. "And Aren't We Glad They Did." *Juneau County* (Wisconsin) *Star Times.* May 24, 2014. http://www.wiscnews.com/news/local/article _4a6ab45c-d39c-5cff-9aca-2d963f812ff7.html.

Restaurant Ware Collectors Network. "T. R. Marshall—Cafe at the Sea— Losekam—Washington, D.C." http://www.restaurantwarecollectors.com/ forums/showthread.php?t=18558&p=115937&viewfull=1.

"The Security for Allied Loans." London: Eyre and Spottiswoode, 1915–1918. http://libcudl.colorado.edu/wwi/pdf/i73753695.pdf.

State Historical Society of Missouri. "John J. Pershing (1860–1948)." *Historic Missourians*. http://shs.umsystem.edu/historicmissourians/name/p/pershing/#section6.

"Ten Months under the Dawes Plan." In *Editorial Research Reports 1925*, 1 (February 28, 1925): 80. Washington, D.C.: CQ Press, 1925. http://library.cqpress.com/cqresearcher/cqresrre1925022800.

United States Army. *United States Army in the World War 1917–1919, Reports of the Commander-in-Chief, Staff Sections, and Services*. Vol. 16. Washington, D.C.: Center of Military History, 1991. http://www.314th.org/center-of-military-history/CMH-Pub-23-22-General-Orders-GHQ-AEF-Volume-16.pdf.

United States Comptroller of the Currency. *Office of the Comptroller of the Currency: A Short History*. Washington, D.C.: Government Printing Office, 2011. http://www.occ.gov/about/what-we-do/history/OCC%20history%20final.pdf.

United States Congress. *Biographical Dictionary of the United States Congress*. http://bioguide.congress.gov.

United States Department of State, Office of the Historian. "The Dawes Plan, the Young Plan, German Reparations, and Inter-Allied War Debts." *Milestones: 1921–1936*. https://history.state.gov/milestones/1921–1936/dawes.

———. "The London Naval Conference, 1930." *Milestones: 1921–1936*. https://history.state.gov/milestones/1921–1936/london-naval-conf.

———. *Milestones: 1914–1920*. https://history.state.gov/milestones/1914–1920.

United States Department of the Interior. Bureau of Land Management. *Mineral Leasing Act of 1920 as Amended*. Retranscribed August 9, 2007. http://www.blm.gov/pgdata/etc/medialib/blm/wo/Communications_Directorate/legislation.Par.23212.File.dat/mla_1920_amendments1.pdf.

United States Department of the Treasury. "Lyman J. Gage (1897–1902)." http://www.treasury.gov/about/history/pages/ljgage.aspx.

United States Government Accountability Office (GAO). "GAO: Working for Good Government since 1921." http://www.gao.gov/about/history/articles/working-for-good-government/01-introduction.html.

United States House of Representatives. *War Expenditures: Hearings before Subcommittee No. 3 (Foreign Expenditures) of the Select Committee on Expenditures in the War Department*. Vol. 4, Serial 4—Parts 75–78. Washington: Government Printing Office, 1921. https://books.google.com/books?id=335HAQAAMAAJ.

United States Senate. "Art and History." https://www.senate.gov/artandhistory/.

————. "April 15, 1922: Senate Investigates the 'Teapot Dome' Scandal." https://www.senate.gov/artandhistory/history/minute/Senate_Investigates_the_Teapot_Dome_Scandal.htm.

United States War Department. War Branch Division General Staff. Historical Plans. *Organization of the Services of Supply*. Washington D.C.: Government Printing Office, 1921. https://play.google.com/books/reader?printsec=frontc over&output=reader&id=9rpBAAAAIAAJ.

United Steel Workers. http://www.usw-608.com/ocaw-history-page.html.

West Virginia. *Governor's Message Submitted to Legislature of 1903, with the Accompanying Reports and Documents Covering the Two Fiscal Years October 1, 1900 to September 30, 1902*. n.p. 1903. https://books.google.com/books ?id=FdcaAQAAIAAJ.

White House. "John Adams." http://www.whitehouse.gov/about/presidents/johnadams.

White House. Office of Management and Budget. "Historical Tables." http://www.whitehouse.gov/omb/budget/Historicals.

————. "Section 15—Basic Budget Laws." http://www.whitehouse.gov/sites/default/files/omb/assets/a11_current_year/s15.pdf.

————. "Table 1.1—Summary of Receipts, Outlays, and Surpluses or Deficits: 1789–2020." *Historical Tables*. http://www.whitehouse.gov/omb/budget/Historicals.

Wilson, Woodrow. War Messages. 65th Cong., 1st Sess. Senate Doc. No. 5, Serial No. 7264, Washington, D.C., 3–8, April 2, 1917. http://wwi.lib.byu.edu/index.php/Wilson%27s_War_Message_to_Congress.

Woods, Thomas E., Jr. "The Forgotten Depression of 1920." Ludwig von Mises Institute. Auburn, Ala. November 27, 2009. http://mises.org/daily/3788.

Woolley, John, and Gerhard Peters. "Election of 1932." In *American Presidency Project: Presidential Elections*. Santa Barbara: University of California, Santa Barbara, 1999–2016. http://www.presidency.ucsb.edu/showelection.php?year=1932.

Woolley, John T., and Gerhard Peters. "Republican Party Platform of 1924." In *American Presidency Project*. Santa Barbara: University of California, Santa Barbara, 1999–2016. http://www.presidency.ucsb.edu/ws/?pid=29636.

Wyoming State Historical Society. "John B. Kendrick: Cowboy, Cattle King, Governor, and US Senator." http://www.wyohistory.org/encyclopedia/john-kendrick.

Dissertations

Davis, John Augustus. "The Ku Klux Klan in Indiana, 1920–1930: An Historical Study." Ph.D. diss., Northwestern University, Evanston, Ill., 1966.

Fagan, George Vincent. "Anglo-American Naval Relations, 1927–1937," Ph.D. diss., University of Pennsylvania, Philadelphia, 1954.

Goedeken, Edward Adolph. "Charles Gates Dawes in War and Peace, 1917–1922." Ph.D. diss., University of Kansas, Lawrence, 1984.

Goodfellow, Guy Fair. "Calvin Coolidge: A Study in Presidential Inaction." Ph.D. diss., University of Maryland, College Park, 1969.

Pixton, John. "American Pilgrim: A Biography of Charles Gates Dawes." Ph.D. diss., Pennsylvania State University, State College, 1970.

Sherman, Richard Garrett. "Charles Gates Dawes: An Entrepreneurial Biography, 1865–1951." Ph.D. diss., University of Iowa, Iowa City, 1960.

Newspapers

Atlanta Constitution

Baltimore Sun

Chicago Day Book

Chicago Defender

Chicago Tribune

Marietta Daily Times (Marietta, Ohio)

New York Times

Pittsburgh Courier

Washington Post (Washington, D.C.)

Library of Congress. *Chronicling America: Historic American Newspapers.* http://chroniclingamerica.loc.gov/.

INDEX

House of Morgan. *See* J. P. Morgan &
Co.; Morgan, J. P.
Houtart, Maurice, 167
Hoyt, Harry, 76
Hughes, Charles Evans, 9, 150, 164, 174,
177, 202
Humphrey, J. B., 258

Illinois Children's Home and Aid
Society, 86–87
Illinois Federation of Labor, 195, 198
Illinois National Bank, 51
Illinois politics: Cook county, 66. *See also*
Republican Party
Illinois state politics. *See* Republican Party
income tax, 141–42
Indianapolis Monetary Convention
(1898), 55
influenza, 130
Insull, Martin, 247, 249
Insull, Samuel, 33, 73, 246–50
Insull Utility Investment, 248, 249
International Workers of the World
(IWW), 138
Interstate Commerce Commission, 40
Irish National League, 21, 23, 40
Italy, 128, 129, 175, 233, 237; food relief,
129; liquidation, 133

Jackson, Edward L., 196
Jackson, Huntington W., 49
Jackson, John Price, 116
Japan, 233, 237, 242–43
Jay, Nelson Dean, 109, 169
Johns Hopkins University, 179
Johnson, Hiram, 139, 181
Johnson, Homer H., 133
Johnson, Royal, 142, 143, 144
Joint Committee on the Conduct of the
War, 136–37
Jones, Jesse, 251, 257
Journal of the Great War, 98
J. P. Morgan & Co., 92–96, 177;
European affiliates, 102–3, 169; World
War I and, 102–3

Kahn, Otto H., 87
Kansas City, Missouri, 213

Kellogg, Frank B., 215, 217–18
Kellogg-Briand Pact, 217–18, 223, 233
Kemmerer, Edwin W., 171, 172
Kenilworth, Illinois, 33
Kent, Frank R., 198
Kenyon, William S., 182
Kerens, R. C., 62
Keynes, John Maynard, 161, 262
Kilkenny, Francis J., 42, 100, 134, 152,
202, 222
Kindersley, Robert, 167, 171
King, John T., 140
King, William Mackenzie, 211–12
Kirkman, Marshall M., 76
Kohlsaat, H. H., 64
Kreisler, Fritz, 88
Kuhn Loeb & Co., 87
Ku Klux Klan, 189, 192–94

labor unrest, 137–38, 195–98; open shop,
195
Lacey, Edward, 73
La Crosse, Wisconsin, 34
La Follette, Robert, 81, 181, 187–88,
189, 196, 198–99, 207
Lamont, Thomas W., 93, 176, 229
LaSalle Street National Bank, 82, 190–
91
LaSalle Street Trust and Savings Bank,
51, 83, 89–91
LaSalle Street Trust Company, 82
Lasker, Albert, 153
League of Nations, 180, 243
Leeds, Nancy, 233
Leeds, William B., 233
Leese, William, 22
Lincoln, Nebraska, 5, 19, 20–31; history
of, 20–21; as railroad hub, 20;
Tenderloin district, 21, 31
Lincoln Board of Trade, 21–22
Lincoln Packing Company, 28–29, 48, 73
Lindbergh, Anne Morrow, 240
Lindbergh, Charles, 240
Literary Digest, 191
Logan, James A., 176–77
Loire River, 103
London Conference (reparations),
176–78

London Naval Conference, 236
Long, Albert Stoneman, 266
Long, John D., 61
Longfellow, Henry Wadsworth, 3
Lord, Herbert Mayhew, 135–36, 137,
   152–53, 162, 202
Lorimer, William, 6, 38, 52, 59, 66, 81–
   83, 89–91, 190–91
Lorimer, William, Jr., 82
Lorimer bank scandal, 52, 82–83, 89–91,
   190–91, 259
Lorimer-Tanner machine (Illinois), 59,
   66
Los Angeles Herald, 37
Lowden, Frank O., 54, 68, 99, 138,
   140, 180, 182, 183, 208, 212,
   213, 223
Ludendorff, Erich (General), 121
Lusitania, 100

MacArthur, Douglas, 268
MacDonald, Ramsay, 224, 226, 232–33
MacMillen, Francis, 87–88
Madden, Martin B., 159
Manchuria, 242
Manderson, Charles F., 19
Manila, Philippines, 53
Mann, Charles C., 211
manufactured gas, 32–34; infrastructure,
   32; rates, 32–33. *See also specific*
   companies
Marietta, Ohio, 4–5, 12–19, 15, 216
Marietta Academy, 17
Marietta and Cincinnati Railroad, 14
Marietta College, 14, 17, 181
Marietta Daily Times, The, 184
Marietta Gas Company, 14
Marietta Gazette, 13
Marietta Intelligencer, 13, 14
Marquette, Turner M., 22
Mary Gates Dawes Hotel, 86, 216
Mason, William, 50
Matsudaira Tsuneo, 226, 243
Maxwell, Samuel, 23
Mayflower yacht, 155
Mayo, Henry T., 111
McAdoo, William G., 189
McCormick, Harold, 87

McCormick, Robert, 92
McCoy, Frank, 134
McCoy, Harbord, 134
McCutcheon, John T., 238, 265
McFadden Act, 210
McKenna, Reginald, 166
McKeon, John C., 49
McKim, Mead, and White, 79
McKinley, Ida, 45, 48, 64
McKinley, William, 5, 9, 16, 24, 37–
   46; assassination, 63–64; campaign,
   37–46; currency reform bill, 56–58;
   expansionism, 53–54; inauguration,
   46–47; oath of office, 47; Spanish-
   American War, 52–53
McKinley Tariff, 37, 54
McNary-Haugen Farm Relief Bill, 209,
   213
McNulta, John (general), 42, 49, 54
Mellon, Andrew, 7, 9, 142, 149, 152,
   156, 202
Mexico, 97
Meyer, Eugene, 245
Middle West Utilities Company, 247,
   248, 249
Military Board of Allied Supply
   (MBAS), 112, 121–27, 128, *gallery*
Mills, Ogden, 251
Mills, William W., 5, 14, 28–29, 34, 36,
   37, 48, 76, 239
Milner, Alfred, 120
Minute Men of the Constitution, 195,
   198
Mississippi Valley Historical Review, 263
Mitchell, John J., 73
Mondell, Frank W., 182–83
Morgan, J. P., 91, 92–96, 102, 173, 176,
   229, 247
Morning Times (Washington), 47
Morris Hunt, Richard, 79
Morrow, Dwight, 120, 176, 233, 238,
   239, 240
Morrow, Elizabeth, 240
Morton, Joy, 62
Mosely, George Van Horn, 152, 154
Mulloney, Dalton, 134
Munday, Charles B., 82–83, 90–91
Mussolini, Benito, 175, 195